John E. H̶[illegible]

+ 2009, FALL - EDS

W9-BNO-798

THE EPISCOPALIANS

THE EPISCOPALIANS

DAVID HEIN
and
GARDINER H. SHATTUCK JR.

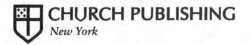 CHURCH PUBLISHING
New York

CONTENTS

Copyright © 2004 by David Hein and Gardiner H. Shattuck Jr.

All rights reserved. No portion of this book may be reproduced, by any process or technique, without the express written consent of the publisher.

Cataloging in Publication data available from The Library of Congress.

Originally published in hardcover by Praeger Publishers an imprint of Greenwood Publishing Group.

Church Publishing Incorporated
445 Fifth Avenue
New York, NY 10016
churchpublishing@cpg.org
www.churchpublishing.org

ISBN 0-89869-497-3

PREFACE

A branch of the worldwide Anglican Communion, the Episcopal Church in the United States possesses a character that may seem somewhat indefinite, especially as that identity has evolved over recent decades. No distinctive confessional statement—like the Augsburg (Lutheran) or the Westminster (Presbyterian)—identifies Anglican and Episcopal beliefs. No familiar phrase—like "inner light" (Quakers) or "strangely warmed" (Methodists)—comes to mind when someone says "Episcopalian." Members of this denomination would have trouble naming their "founder" because, for various reasons, they do not look upon King Henry VIII as the Anglican counterpart to Martin Luther, Joseph Smith, or Mary Baker Eddy.

The name itself—"Episcopal"—does not tell the observer much about what distinguishes this denomination. The word points to a polity (form of church government) that Episcopalians share with the vast majority of the world's Christians, for Roman Catholics and Orthodox Christians also have bishops. In addition, the Episcopal Church possesses a streak of congregationalism in its actual laws and practice. Theologically and liturgically, the denomination is both Catholic and Protestant. And identifying markers that in the past might have proved helpful—the church's establishmentarian cast, for example, or its disinclination to enter into substantial ecumenical agreements—by the 1990s were no longer reliable indicators of this denomination's positions on key issues. Finally, the church's once-distinctive liturgy is now offered in a wide variety of styles (from very traditional to virtually free-form), including a contemporary version that appears familiar to both Lutherans and Roman Catholics.[1] How then to delineate the unique elements of a denomination that, one often hears, is most appropriately characterized in terms of an ethos, a vision, a sensibility?

One approach is by means of a book like this one, in which a distinctive pattern gradually emerges in the fabric of a long and rich history. Here the reader will find an account of a church that evolved into a denomination of the urban establishment, a politically, theologically, and socially moderate religious body that appealed to those seeking a refined liturgy, literate preaching, beautiful music and architecture, and the society of their peers. At the same time, however, the reader will come upon the fascinating stories of those whom the dominant society often denied access to power—African and Hispanic Americans, women, and American Indians—as well as accounts of significant changes that have occurred in this old-line denomination.

This narrative discusses the Anglican establishment in the American colonies, the crisis caused by the American Revolution, the organization of the Episcopal Church and the loss of "market share" to Baptists and Methodists in the early nineteenth century, the recovery with the rise of large industrial centers, the social and intellectual debates that took place between 1865 and 1914, and the church's responses to the challenges posed by two world wars and a severe economic depression. The book goes on to examine the period of revitalization following World War II, an era that the Episcopal historian Robert W. Prichard has referred to as the time of "the Church Triumphant."[2] It reviews the struggles in the 1960s and beyond as the leadership of the Episcopal Church revised its liturgy, incorporated the insights of its women and minorities, and entered into fresh discussions with other Christian churches. This historical survey carries the story to the beginning of the third millennium—when evangelicalism became a formidable alternative to the Protestant mainline, when Episcopalian young people increasingly drifted into secularity or were attracted by New Age spirituality and Asian religions, and when the denomination's liberal-conservative rift deepened and threatened to cause a major schism.

Throughout this narrative, the authors grapple with questions of Episcopal identity, especially as they relate to the sources of authority within this denominational tradition. To cite one important example, the recent controversy over the election of an openly gay bishop involved debates on ecclesiastical identity and authority. In the aftermath of this historic decision, the Episcopal Church entered a new period in which it strived to address, in as irenic a fashion as possible, the implications of its changing stance on sexual morality and the American church's relation to the worldwide Anglican Communion.

The authors of this book also attempt to convey a sense of what this religious body is all about by examining not only the denomination's clerical and lay leadership but also the experience of the ordinary worshiper in an Episcopal parish. They look, for example, not only at official texts and statistics but also at the forms and functions of sacred space. And they regularly discuss the Episcopal Church in its larger ecclesiastical context, focusing especially on ecumenical relations with other Christian communities.

The authors of the present volume examine what occurred within the history of this one denomination without losing sight of the historical context—contemporaneous events in the life of the nation as a whole. Often wielding an influence out of proportion to their relatively small numbers, Episcopalians played significant roles in the political and cultural life of the United States over more than two hundred years. Mindful of the neglect that mainline traditions such as the Episcopal Church have suffered at the hands of historians in recent decades, as scholars have focused instead on religious "outsiders," the authors of this book, Episcopalians themselves, have made a conscious attempt to inquire into the identity of one influential, old-line denomination.[3] In a small way, they intend thereby to help offset an imbalance in the historiography caused by what one historian has referred to as "the [odd] neglect of the Protestant mainstream"— odd because it was, as another historian has noted, "precisely . . . the mainline denominations [that] were, and still are, the ones whose history is bound up most closely with the formation and development of the United States."[4]

In attempting to limn the features of the Episcopal Church, the authors offer not an idealized portrait but what they hope is a fair rendering. The work of insiders, this book aims at balance as well as accessibility. While for the most part this study offers no radically new arguments, it does attempt to bring forward the best interpretations based on a thorough grounding both in primary research and in secondary texts in the thriving field of American religious history.

Addressing the question of Anglican and Episcopal identity, a recent arch-bishop of Canterbury (the spiritual leader of the Anglican Communion) observed that the religious lives of Anglicans are largely shaped by other individuals, by those "whose lives of prayer and scholarship, pastoral zeal, prophetic insight or artistic achievement have been grounded in the scriptures and the liturgy as tradition has handed them down to us."[5] The authors of the present volume, as well as the editor of this series, heartily concur with this statement about the significance of influential persons in the histories of both individuals and institutions. Hence, they affirm the need for biographical treatments that are intermixed with and adjunctive to the main historical narrative.

In its second major section, then, this book offers 100 individual biographical sketches of well-known and of more obscure figures in Episcopal Church history, from Thomas Bradbury Chandler and Samuel Seabury to Pauli Murray and Paul Washington. The reader will find mini-biographies of architects (Ralph Adams Cram), soldiers (Robert E. Lee), preachers (Phillips Brooks), U.S. cabinet members (Frances Perkins), financiers (J. P. Morgan), novelists (Harriet Beecher Stowe), schoolmasters (Henry A. Coit), intellectuals (Alexander Crummell), institution builders (William A. Muhlenberg), intrepid adventurers (Hudson Stuck), and many others. In this history of a church not famous for evangelism or ecumenism, the reader will find biographies of daring missionaries such as Jackson Kemper, of indefatigable evangelists such as George Whitefield, and of enterprising ecumenists such as Robert H. Gardiner III. In these biographies of members of a denomination often seen as elitist, the reader will discover such champions of the underdog as Richard T. Ely and Vida D. Scudder. These sketches are brief but intriguing portraits, providing enough material to introduce their subjects and entice the reader to look for further information. Together, this cast of characters—a variety of church people, all of whom are now deceased—makes the Episcopal story more engaging, the historical fabric more textured.

In conclusion, the authors wish to state how much they are indebted to the series editor, Henry Bowden, for his advice in preparing this volume and particularly for his patience while it was being written. We would also like to express appreciation to Don Armentrout, Mary Sudman Donovan, and Charles Lippy for their advice and assistance in correcting a number of mistakes in the initial version of our manuscript. And we wish to offer special thanks to David L. Holmes for helping inspire this project. Professor Holmes provided us with valuable assistance in reading portions of the manuscript and in drafting the list of biographical sketches. We also relied heavily on his work on Anglicanism and the American Revolution in the preparation of Chapter 3. We are very grateful to Professor Holmes for his personal support, for his thorough knowledge of the field, and for his good counsel all the way through.

NOTES

1. See David Hein, "New Wave Evangelism," *AEH* 71 (2002): 304–9.
2. *HEC,* 229.
3. Martin E. Marty, "American Religious History in the Eighties: A Decade of Achievement," *CH* 62 (1993): 336–37.
4. D. G. Hart, "The Failure of American Religious History," *Journal of the Historical Society* 1 (2000): 17.
5. Robert Runcie, *Christian Thinking: The Anglican Tradition of Thoughtful Holiness* (Tulsa, Okla.: University of Tulsa, 1991), 11.

ABBREVIATIONS FOR STANDARD SOURCES

AAP	*Annals of the American Pulpit,* ed. William B. Sprague, 9 vols. (New York, 1857–69; 1969).
ACAB	*Appleton's Cyclopaedia of American Biography,* ed. James Grant Wilson and John Fiske, 7 vols. (New York, 1898–1900).
AEC	Archives of the Episcopal Church, Austin, Tex.
AEH	*Anglican and Episcopal History*
ANB	*American National Biography,* ed. John A. Garraty and Mark C. Carnes, 24 vols. (New York, 1999).
AR	Peter W. Williams, *America's Religions: From Their Origins to the Twenty-First Century* (Urbana, Ill., 2002).
ATR	*Anglican Theological Review*
BB	Robert W. Prichard, *The Bat and the Bishop* (Harrisburg, Pa.: Morehouse, 1989).
BHEC	David L. Holmes, *A Brief History of the Episcopal Church* (Valley Forge, Pa., 1993).
CH	*Church History*
DAB	*Dictionary of American Biography,* ed. Allen Johnson and Dumas Malone, 20 vols. (New York, 1928–37; eight supplements, 1944–88).
DANB	*Dictionary of American Negro Biography,* ed. Rayford W. Logan and Michael R. Winston (New York, 1982).
DARB	*Dictionary of American Religious Biography,* 2nd ed., ed. Henry Warner Bowden (Westport, Conn., 1993).

DC	Mary Sudman Donovan, *A Different Call: Women's Ministries in the Episcopal Church, 1850–1920* (Wilton, Conn., 1986).
DCA	*Dictionary of Christianity in America,* ed. Daniel G. Reid, Robert D. Linder, Bruce L. Shelley, and Harry S. Stout (Downers Grove, Ill., 1990).
DW	*Documents of Witness: A History of the Episcopal Church, 1782–1985,* [ed.] Don S. Armentrout and Robert Boak Slocum (New York, 1994).
EAAR	*Encyclopedia of African American Religions,* ed. Larry G. Murphy, J. Gordon Melton, and Gary L. Ward (New York, 1993).
EARH	Edward L. Queen II, Stephen R. Prothero, and Gardiner H. Shattuck Jr., *Encyclopedia of American Religious History,* rev. ed. (New York, 2001).
ECUS	James Thayer Addison, *The Episcopal Church in the United States* (New York, 1951).
EDC	*An Episcopal Dictionary of the Church: A User-Friendly Reference for Episcopalians,* ed. Don S. Armentrout and Robert Boak Slocum (New York, [1999]).
ERS	*Encyclopedia of Religion in the South,* ed. Samuel S. Hill (Macon, Ga., 1984).
FD	*Freedom Is a Dream: A Documentary History of Women in the Episcopal Church,* ed. Sheryl A. Kujawa-Holbrook (New York, 2002).
HAEC	William Wilson Manross, *A History of the American Episcopal Church* (New York, 1935).
HEC	Robert W. Prichard, *A History of the Episcopal Church,* rev. ed. (Harrisburg, Pa., 1999).
HMPEC	*Historical Magazine of the Protestant Episcopal Church*
HPEC	Raymond W. Albright, *A History of the Protestant Episcopal Church* (New York, 1964).
MCTA	*Makers of Christian Theology in America,* ed. Mark G. Toulouse and James O. Duke (Nashville, 1997).
MM	E. Clowes Chorley, *Men and Movements in the American Episcopal Church* (New York, 1946).
NAW	*Notable American Women, 1607–1950: A Biographical Dictionary,* ed. Edward T. James et al. (Cambridge, Mass., 1971); vol. 4, *The Modern Period,* ed. Barbara Sicherman et al. (Cambridge, Mass., 1980).

NCAB	*National Cyclopedia of American Biography,* 63 vols. (New York, 1892–1984; current series, vols. A–M, 1930–78).
NCE	*New Catholic Encyclopedia,* 16 vols. (New York, 1967, 1974).
NYT	*New York Times*
RHAP	Sydney E. Ahlstrom, *A Religious History of the American People* (New Haven, 1972).
SBAE	Hermon Griswold Batterson, *A Sketch-Book of the American Episcopate during One Hundred Years, 1783–1883* (Philadelphia, 1884).
SH	*New Schaff-Herzog Encyclopedia of Religious Knowledge,* ed. Samuel M. Jackson et al., 13 vols. (New York, 1908–14).
SPCK	*The SPCK Handbook of Anglican Theologians,* ed. Alistair E. McGrath (London, 1998).
TLC	*The Living Church*
WMQ	*William and Mary Quarterly*
WWWA	*Who Was Who in America,* 9 vols. (Chicago, 1985).

In the biographical section of this book, asterisks indicate subjects treated in their own sketches. And in the bibliographies at the end of each sketch, works listed under "A" refer to writings by the subject of the biographical sketch, and works listed under "B" refer to writings that discuss the subject.

Part One
THE EPISCOPALIANS:
A HISTORY

1
ENGLISH AND AMERICAN BEGINNINGS: 1534–1662

Episcopalians in the United States trace their religious roots back to the sixteenth century, when Anglicanism emerged as a distinct denominational tradition out of the Protestant Reformation in England.[1] Originally a missionary extension of the Church of England in colonial America, the Episcopal Church itself was organized in the aftermath of the American Revolution. Because "Church of England" was no longer suitable as an ecclesiastical designation in the new United States, a convention of Anglican clergy and laity meeting in Chestertown, Maryland, in 1780 chose the name "Protestant Episcopal Church" instead. The term "Protestant" differentiated the denomination from Roman Catholicism, and "Episcopal" signified that the church's polity had retained the ministry and authority of bishops.[2] From the outset, Episcopalians emphasized that their church included Catholic as well as Protestant elements—a heritage both ancient and reformed.

PRE-REFORMATION BRITISH CHRISTIANITY

Although there is no certain date for the planting of Christianity in Britain, it was probably established there by soldiers during the Roman occupation. The earliest archaeological evidence dates from the fourth century, after Christianity had become the official religion of the Roman Empire, and three bishops from England are known to have attended the Council of Arles in 314. The British monk Pelagius, whose views on human free will brought him into conflict with the theologian Augustine of Hippo, had a profound impact on church life in the early fifth century. Whereas Pelagius believed that Christians could rely on their own willpower to live morally perfect lives, Augustine argued that men and women attained salvation by virtue of divine grace alone. Augustine's ideas prevailed, and Pelagianism was eventually condemned as heretical at the Council of Ephesus in 431.

With the sack of Rome in 410 and the general collapse of imperial authority in the West, Saxons and other pagan tribesmen effectively destroyed the structures of government, culture, and religion in England. Although the British churches were cut off from communication with the papacy in Rome, the Celtic monastic tradition in Ireland and in the western and northern regions of Britain remained vibrant over the next two centuries. To restore papal authority over the British isles, Pope Gregory the Great organized a mission under the leadership of the Benedictine monk Augustine in 597. Augustine landed in Kent, where he was well received by the pagan Saxon king. A few months after his arrival, he was consecrated as the first bishop of the English people, and according to one report, he baptized about ten thousand pagan converts in the Canterbury area at the end of the year.[3] Despite Augustine's success in evangelizing the Saxons, inconsistencies between Celtic and Roman Christianity—most notably, disagreement about the dating of Easter day—proved to be troublesome and enduring. Not until the Synod of Whitby in 664 were Celtic liturgical practices and beliefs finally brought into line with those of the church at Rome.

Its official allegiance to the traditions of Roman Catholic Christianity notwithstanding, the church in England, like the church in France, enjoyed a considerable measure of autonomy throughout the medieval period. Moreover, during the fourteenth and fifteenth centuries, western Christendom as a whole was torn by a series of crises that further undercut papal power: first, the removal of the papacy from Rome to Avignon in France (1305–1377); second, the development of the Great Schism (1378–1417), when there were two, and later three, popes; and finally the rise of the conciliar movement (1418–1449), when the reunited papacy contended against a succession of general councils for supremacy within the church. As the prestige of the papacy waned during this era, English bishops increasingly recognized the authority of the king, rather than of the pope, in ecclesiastical matters in their nation. The passage of several secular statutes in the fourteenth century further curtailed the ability of the papacy to exercise control over the church in England—legislative actions that would be used as precedents for severing ties to Rome two centuries later.

Reformer John Wyclif was undoubtedly the most influential religious leader in English Christianity in the late Middle Ages. Wyclif not only attacked priests and bishops who abused their power in the church but also emphasized the importance of the Bible and encouraged its translation from Latin into English. In addition, he expressed strong doubts about papal supremacy, suggesting that the papacy was an institution of the Antichrist and arguing that it was the God-given responsibility of secular rulers to reform a corrupted church. The fact that criticism of Wyclif was relatively muted during his lifetime (he died in 1384) suggests a far broader range of acceptable theological opinion in England than in other Catholic countries in Europe during the fourteenth century. Indeed, a follower of Wyclif put to death in 1401 was the first person to be executed for heresy in England since 1216—a remarkably tolerant record given the nature of religious affairs in those times.[4] Although Wyclif's teachings were not an immediate cause of the English Reformation, his ideas certainly helped foster the intellectual atmosphere in which later church reforms were nurtured.[5]

One of the most heated debates among modern-day scholars concerns the character of religious faith in England immediately preceding the Reformation. On the one hand, widening educational opportunities in the sixteenth century helped create a relatively literate laity within the ranks of leading landowners and merchants. This group became increasingly aware of both the criticisms of conventional piety and the demands for church reform that were then surfacing in the great centers of learning on the European continent. On the other hand, traditional Catholicism still retained a strong hold on the English population as a whole. As historian Eamon Duffy has argued, the beliefs and practices of most English Christians on the eve of the Reformation were remarkably conservative. Despite inroads made by the earliest Protestants, much of the older imagery and forms of reverence in English parishes remained largely unchanged in the early sixteenth century.[6] Because this liturgical and theological conservatism was so strong, the unwarranted *secular* privileges of the church, rather than any defects in traditional Catholic piety, tended to motivate the first ecclesiastical changes that occurred in England.[7]

Although the medieval ideal of a unified Christendom was still officially intact when Henry VIII ascended the English throne in 1509, the long-standing symbiosis of church and society in Europe was about to be destroyed. This unity was irrevocably sundered on December 10, 1520, when Martin Luther publicly burned both the papal bull condemning his teachings and the books of canon law binding Western Christianity to the authority of the pope. Yet despite the religious revolt led by Luther in Germany and by Ulrich Zwingli in Switzerland in the 1520s, English church leaders initially resisted the spread of Protestantism into their country from the Continent. The bishop of London and the archbishop of Canterbury both condemned William Tyndale's groundbreaking translation of the New Testament into English, and Henry himself received the title "Defender of the Faith" from Pope Leo X for his opposition to Luther's teachings on the sacraments. Thomas More also rose in the king's favor at this time and took an active role in suppressing Lutheran ideas in England. Thus, when Henry's break from Rome finally did take place, those who favored the independence of the English church advanced their arguments primarily in political, not theological or liturgical, language.

THE REFORMATION ERA

Although Henry originally had no intention of encouraging the growth of the Reformation in his realm, an unplanned series of events effected a profound revolution within the church in England. The process of ecclesiastical change began during the reign of Henry's father, Henry VII. In an effort to secure a useful diplomatic alliance, Henry VII gave his eldest son, Arthur, into marriage with Catherine of Aragon, daughter of the powerful King Ferdinand and Queen Isabella of Spain. When Arthur died after only a few months of marriage, the English king offered his second son, Henry, to the young widow. Since church canons forbade such a union on the basis of biblical passages in Leviticus (ancient Israelite laws that equated sexual relations between a man and his brother's wife with incest), a special papal dispensation had to be obtained from Pope Julius II.

Julius allowed Henry and Catherine to be married in 1509, but despite receiving the pope's blessing, the English royal couple saw only one child (Mary Tudor, born in 1516) survive from Catherine's numerous pregnancies. By the time Catherine reached age 40 in 1525, Henry believed that his wife would no longer be able to conceive or bear children. Because he needed a male heir to secure the stability of the Tudor reign, and because he may genuinely have believed that he had committed a grave sin by marrying his brother's wife, Henry asked Pope Clement VII to annul his marriage to Catherine. The pope, however, refused. Since he was a virtual prisoner of the most powerful ruler in Europe—Charles V, Holy Roman emperor and Catherine's nephew—Clement was in no position to grant the English king's request.[8]

The pope's understandable rebuff set the stage for Henry to declare the independence of the English church from obedience to Rome. In January 1533, Thomas Cranmer, the newly appointed archbishop of Canterbury, pronounced Henry's marriage to Catherine invalid, and at the same time he officiated at the king's marriage to his mistress Anne Boleyn, then pregnant with the future queen, Elizabeth I. Meanwhile, a series of parliamentary acts culminated in the 1534 declaration that the king was "the only supreme head on earth of the Church of England." At the same time, the English clergy officially affirmed that no foreign bishops, including the pope, had any right to exercise jurisdiction over ecclesiastical affairs in Henry's realm.[9] Although Thomas More, the former lord chancellor, and John Fisher, bishop of Rochester, were later executed for refusing to accept the royal supremacy in church matters, most religious and secular leaders in England acquiesced because they did not think that ecclesiastical independence implied the repudiation of Catholic doctrine. Indeed, Henry's Six Articles act of 1539 upheld such traditional Catholic teachings as transubstantiation (the substance of the communion bread and wine is miraculously transformed into the actual body and blood of Christ), private confession to a priest, and mandatory clerical celibacy.

When Henry died in 1547, he was succeeded by Edward VI, the child of his third wife, Jane Seymour. Since Edward was only a boy when he ascended the throne, his uncle Edward Seymour was appointed lord protector, thereby assuming control over the affairs of state. Since both Seymour and his successor, John Dudley, were avowed Protestants, significant changes began to occur in English church life during Edward's reign. All persecution of Protestants was ended, and a number of leading continental reformers, such as Martin Bucer and Peter Martyr Vermigli, were invited to serve at university posts in England. In addition, laws prohibiting clerical marriage were abandoned, and the use of English (instead of Latin) in worship was strongly encouraged. The scholarly archbishop Thomas

Cranmer proved to be the principal architect of church reform in this period. He was the author of the first *Book of Common Prayer* in 1549, and when some militant reformers criticized his work as too "popish" and conservative, he helped produce a revised, more identifiably "Protestant" prayer book, which was mandated for use in English parishes three years later, in 1552. Cranmer also composed the Forty-Two Articles, a statement of faith that took a mediating position between the theological views of Martin Luther and John Calvin, repudiated papal supremacy and key medieval eucharistic doctrines, and vigorously condemned the radical, antinomian Protestantism espoused by Anabaptists on the Continent.

Despite the significance of the many church reforms introduced during Edward's reign, the young king's early death and the accession of his half-sister Mary in 1553 brought about the temporary restoration of Roman Catholicism in England. Viewed from Mary's perspective, the situation was extraordinarily serious, for the English people had fallen into a state of mortal sin when her father severed the nation's ties with Rome.[10] Thus, in an effort to save souls, she employed her powers as supreme head of the church to forbid further use of the English Prayer Book, to depose any priest who had broken his vow of celibacy, and ultimately to repeal all antipapal legislation.

Although these actions were by no means unacceptable to the majority of the English people, whose hearts and minds were still strongly attached to Catholicism, Mary's religious zeal led her to make two crucial mistakes. First, to bring her country into a closer relationship with continental Catholicism, she married the son of Emperor Charles V, Philip II of Spain, thus identifying her reign with the nation that was England's most bitter rival. Second, against the advice of even Philip and Charles, she revived the application of medieval heresy laws—a policy that occasioned the martyrdom of about three hundred Protestants, including leading figures such as Thomas Cranmer. The threat of martyrdom also forced many other Protestants to flee to the Continent, where in areas controlled by Lutherans, Zwinglians, and Calvinists their theological views were further radicalized. Thus, contrary to Mary's fondest wishes, her actions succeeded only in turning her subjects against the faith in which she believed. Expressed most vividly in John Foxe's *Acts and Monuments* (first published in 1554), a cultural mind-set developed during Mary's reign that for several centuries blended English nationalistic sentiments with a staunch anti-Catholicism. When the queen died in 1558, she had effectively destroyed the possibility that the English church would ever again swear loyalty to the pope.

The next monarch—Elizabeth I—was, like her father Henry, more Catholic than Protestant in her personal religious sympathies. She preferred the use of traditional vestments in worship, thought priests should be celibate, and believed in the corporal presence of Christ in the eucharistic elements. Unlike her half-sister Mary, however, Elizabeth was willing to make her personal liturgical and theological preferences subservient to the greater goal of peace and national unity. As a consequence, she sought to restore political stability by implementing a *via media*—a middle-of-the-road religious policy—that avoided the extremes that had marked the reigns of her two predecessors. In 1559 Parliament passed legislation that both recognized Elizabeth as the church's "supreme governor" (considered to be a more suitable term for a woman than "supreme head") and reintroduced the *Book of Common Prayer,* now shorn of the most extreme Protestant elements introduced in the 1552 book.[11] Although the position Elizabeth assumed pleased neither radical Protestants nor diehard Roman Catholics, she held that, as long as her subjects' outward religious acts conformed with England's laws, she had little interest in probing their inmost spiritual thoughts.[12]

Elizabeth helped formulate a distinctly "Anglican" solution for the various matters of doctrine, church discipline, and worship that had troubled England since Henry's death. The most overt threat to the ecclesiastical settlement she devised came from dissident Roman Catholics. In 1569 there was a Catholic uprising, quickly suppressed, that sought to advance the cause of her cousin Mary Stuart, and in 1570 a papal bull of excommunication formally relieved Elizabeth's Catholic subjects of all oaths of allegiance to her. The queen responded to these threats by having all Jesuits in England condemned as traitors in 1585, and two years later she ordered Mary's execution. However, despite the potential dangers posed by either a foreign invasion or an internal rebellion under the direction of Rome, English Catholicism looked considerably more subversive than it actually was. Although there was certainly a small minority involved in plotting against the queen, most Roman Catholics in England had little difficulty reconciling their religious and political loyalties.[13]

CONFLICT WITH PURITANISM

As the subsequent history of England in the seventeenth century demonstrates, Protestant opposition to the Anglican *via media* presented a far more serious threat to the Elizabeth settlement than Roman Catholicism. This opposition, embodied in the Puritan movement, emerged in the 1560s as a reaction against Elizabeth's anti-Roman but still broadly Catholic approach to church affairs. Many of those who had fled to the Continent during Mary's reign returned to England committed to the Protestant belief that the Bible alone provided the basis for religious, social, and political order. This group wanted to *purify* the English church by effecting a thoroughgoing transformation of its worship and polity. According to the Cambridge Puritan William Perkins, the Bible was meant to be the "rule and square whereby we are to frame and fashion all our actions."[14] Thus, the Puritans strongly opposed the use of traditional Catholic liturgical vestments and ceremonial practices. They also sought to replace the top-down episcopal system of church governance with a more democratic form, organized along either presbyterian or congregational lines, which they believed was more consistent with the norms of the early church.[15]

Divisions within the English church became increasingly pronounced during the late sixteenth and early seventeenth centuries. After Elizabeth's death and with the accession of James I in 1603, the Puritan party pressed even more vigorously for religious and political reform. However, in spite of his staunch Calvinist theological views, the new king was committed to retaining both royal supremacy and the rule of bishops in the church. In James's eyes, monarchy and episcopacy stood together as the twin pillars of authority in English society, and at the Hampton Court conference of January 1604, he rejected Puritan requests for change with the cry, "No bishop, no king."

The situation became even worse for the Puritans after James's son Charles I became king in 1625. Charles and his advisers implemented repressive measures to enforce ecclesiastical conformity. Beyond that, as strong believers in the divine right of kings, they also attempted to rule England without calling the Puritan-dominated Parliament into session. Such despotism helped promote both the large-scale emigration of Puritans to America (a permanent settlement was established at Boston in 1630) and the steady drift toward internecine conflict at home. The English Civil War and the triumph of the parliamentary army under Oliver Cromwell eventually led to the overthrow of episcopacy and monarchy together. As a result of this struggle, England became a Protestant republic for a brief period. Between the execution of Charles I in 1649 and the restoration of the Stuart rulers under Charles II in 1660, episcopacy was abolished, hundreds of Anglican clergy were ejected from their parishes, and the liturgy of the *Book of Common Prayer* was proscribed.

In the midst of these bitter church controversies, English Episcopalians advanced what proved to be a lasting defense of the Anglican *via media* against its detractors on both the Protestant left and the Roman Catholic right. The basis of Anglican identity, they argued, was located as much in the traditions of the first five centuries of Christian history as in the Bible. Despite separating from Rome and overturning the alleged accretions of the medieval period, Anglicans emphasized their continuity with the past, especially with the church in the patristic era. Thus, in rejecting the authority of the papacy, they sought the restoration not of the New Testament church but of the beliefs and practices of the "old Catholic fathers." As John Jewel, the bishop of Salisbury, asserted in 1570, the patristic writers were "witnesses unto the truth, . . . worthy pillars and ornaments in the Church of God," with whom Anglicans wished to remain in theological communion.[16]

The classic expression of Anglican thinking on the nature of the church was advanced by theologian Richard Hooker in his *Laws of Ecclesiastical Polity* first published during Elizabeth's reign in 1593. In contrast to the relatively static positions adopted by Puritans and Catholics—the Puritan insistence on the sufficiency of scripture and the Catholic emphasis on the primacy of the traditions of Rome—Hooker focused on the evolution of church institutions and practices. The church, he believed, was an organic body that was capable of changing its governance according to circumstances. Human reason, moreover, played a critical role in the church's ongoing development. Reason was a divinely implanted instrument that enabled human beings to apprehend the truths continually revealed by God in nature and in scripture. Hooker's affirmation of scripture, tradition, and reason as a "threefold cord not quickly broken" soon became one of the principal hallmarks of Anglican teaching.[17] In fact, during the sixteenth and seventeenth centuries, when other European churches were seeking to narrow the standards of orthodox belief and practice, the official policies of the Church of England, under the influence of Hooker's intellectually expansive teachings, remained remarkably open to diverse understandings and interpretations.[18]

TRANSPLANTING TO AMERICA

While Anglicans and Puritans vied for dominance in the domestic affairs of their church and nation, many explorers, traders, and settlers traveled overseas, carrying English Protestantism with them to other lands. The European discovery of America had begun in the late fifteenth century, a generation before the beginning of the Reformation, and over the next two hundred years Spain, France, England, Portugal, and the Netherlands sought to develop worldwide empires. The leaders of those nations not only wanted raw materials and profits from the New World but also understood their explorations in religious terms. For example, Columbus's first entry in the diary recording his journey to America in 1492 expressed the hope that he would be able to convert the native peoples he encountered to the Catholic faith.[19] A year later, Pope Alexander VI issued a bull dividing the newly discovered western lands between Portugal and Spain, giving each nation permission to occupy its allotted territories and convert the inhabitants of those regions to Christianity.

The initial English claim to North America was established by John Cabot, sailing under the auspices of Henry VII, in 1497. While it is likely that an English priest accompanied Cabot's voyage and celebrated the Latin mass when the explorers reached land, the honor of conducting the first English Protestant service in North America belonged to a clergyman who celebrated communion at Hudson Bay in 1578.[20] During Elizabeth's reign, the Anglican priest Richard Hakluyt became the leading proponent of England's overseas mission. He believed that England had a unique, God-given responsibility to spread its political and religious virtues throughout the world. Concerned that two Catholic countries, Spain and France, had moved ahead of England in settling new territories and disseminating the *wrong* kind of Christianity among the native population of America, Hakluyt called his people to send preachers of the gospel "for the salvation of those poore people which have sitten so longe in darkenes and in the shadowe of deathe."[21]

The literature of colonization that Hakluyt's writings exemplified was intended to inspire English men to travel to North America for the glory of both God and nation. In the early seventeenth century, Virginia became the primary focus of English colonial efforts, and it took very little prodding to convince James I to assume control over the process by which the holdings and interests of the crown were expanded in America. James gave colonization rights in Virginia to two trading companies in April 1606, and 13 months later the Virginia Company established a rude settlement at Jamestown, named in honor of the king. Robert Hunt, an Anglican clergyman who was one of the original petitioners for the Company's charter, celebrated the first communion service in the colony on May 14, 1607. Interpreting the founding of the settlement as evidence of divine hand-iwork, John Smith, the soldier-adventurer who led the colony, observed that Virginia was reminiscent of the biblical Eden, "being a plaine wildernes as God first made it."[22]

A deep religious commitment also motivated many of the early leaders of the Virginia Company, and they placed Anglican spirituality at the heart of the colony's life. After building a fort to protect themselves against attack, the Jamestown settlers constructed a makeshift church building where they held daily worship services using the *Book of Common Prayer.* Company managers screened the clergy who volunteered for missionary service in the New World, and they dispatched only the most qualified to Virginia. As a result, there was a surprisingly strong ministerial presence in the colony during the period it was controlled by the Virginia Company. In fact, between 1607 and 1624, 22 clergymen served under its auspices, and a 1616 document reported that there were four ministers among the 351 inhabitants of the settlement—a ratio of clergy to laity rarely found in England during that period.[23]

After the Virginia Company was reorganized in 1619, a local legislature, called the House of Burgesses, was formed. This assembly decided that a "glebe" (a tract of farmland) and a fixed revenue would be provided for each clergyman in his parish—the first act by which the Church of England was legally established in Virginia. The legislature gradually extended this religious establishment over the next few decades. In 1626, it decreed that the colony ought to observe as closely as possible the church canons then in effect in England, and later it levied church taxes and ordered Virginia settlers to give clergy their best tobacco as payment for their pastoral and sacerdotal services.

The process of church establishment in Virginia culminated in the creation of local parish vestries in 1662. Parish vestries were themselves an evolving institution in England at that time. The term "vestry" had once referred to the regular meetings in which all parish members gathered to provide for the maintenance of church properties. The situation changed a bit in 1598, however, when Parliament passed a law making vestries responsible for the care of the poor in each parish. This decision in turn encouraged the development of "select vestries," a group of leading men elected to provide for the poor between sessions of the larger congregational meeting. And in the seventeenth century, vestries began to assume additional responsibilities, such as the care of roads and the oversight of certain minor judicial matters.[24] The practice of the select vestry was then copied in America. According to the action of the Virginia legislature in 1662, each parish was to elect a vestry of 12 men, including 2 church wardens. These vestrymen served as executive officers responsible for a diverse set of duties within the boundaries of their parish: the collection of taxes; the construction and maintenance of church buildings; the administration of the local welfare system (assistance to widows, orphans, illegitimate children, and the handicapped); the hiring of lay readers to lead worship whenever ordained ministers were not available; and the financial support of clergy.[25]

Despite these legislative decisions and the initial enthusiasm of secular and religious leaders in England, seventeenth-century Virginia proved to be an extraordinarily difficult place in which to organize and govern a church. General social instability and an appalling death rate, caused by disease, malnutrition, and frequent warfare with Indians, marked the first decades of the colony's existence. With some aggressive recruiting, the Virginia Company poured approximately 10,000 English settlers into Jamestown between 1607 and 1622, but only about 20 percent were still alive in 1622. As one critic of the venture remarked, "instead of a plantacion, Virginia will shortly get the name of a slaughterhouse."[26] Clergy suffered at the same rate as the rest of the populace, for about two-thirds of the 67 Anglican clergymen who served in Virginia between 1607 and 1660 died within five years of their arrival.[27]

As the historian Jon Butler has observed, institutional Anglicanism experienced "its own starving time" in the colony throughout the middle decades of the seventeenth century.[28] Many parishes had neither a church building nor a permanent priest, and lay readers often had to officiate at prayer on Sunday mornings. The geographical size of many parishes also proved to be a major obstacle, for it was impossible for a single priest to provide adequate supervision for a parish that stretched over an area 30 to 100 miles long. Furthermore, in contrast to England, where a bishop exercised control over each diocese, Virginia had no bishops, and English ecclesiastical authorities were unable to exercise direct jurisdiction over the colony. Although the royal governor had the theoretical power to carry out some of the administrative functions of a bishop, for instance, the induction of clergymen as rectors of parishes, vestries usually resisted the governor's attempt to exercise this authority. Vestries not only controlled the recruitment and selection of clergy but also refused to present their clergy for induction as rectors. As a result, vestries in Virginia were free to govern their parishes in any manner they chose. Clergy often complained about the chaos that reigned in the colony, and they continually petitioned English leaders for increased material and financial support.

Over time, the pursuit of wealth from the cultivation of tobacco gradually replaced missionary zeal as the principal motivation for settling in Virginia. In conjunction with this shift from a religious to a commercial focus, Dutch traders began to bring enslaved Africans as workers into the colony. While the initial small group of Africans who arrived in 1619 were probably treated about the same as white servants, race-based slavery eventually emerged by the 1660s. The House of Burgesses decreed in 1662 that, in the case of children of African descent, legal status depended not on that of their father (as in English law) but on that of their mother. Thus, since the child of a black slave woman had to be a slave as well, the words "Negro" and "slave" soon became synonymous. Before that period, Christianity and slavery had also been assumed to be incompatible, and slaves who could prove that they had been baptized were often freed. However, as the slave population expanded during the 1660s, the Virginia assembly declared that baptism did not affect the civil status of Africans or Indians who were held in bondage. Although that act was designed to encourage masters to Christianize their slaves, it in fact removed one of the most powerful incentives for a slave to seek baptism.[29]

Although most Anglican clergymen still wished to convert Virginia's so-called "heathen" Indian and African populations to Christianity, their fellow church members proved to be largely indifferent to that task. The threat of Indian attacks motivated whites to place short-term concerns about their physical security over the long-term spiritual (as well as practical) benefits of native evangelism. Relations with Indians significantly worsened as colonial authorities used military force either to kill Indians or to push them westward. And fears about the presence of a free black population ended the custom of granting freedom to any slave who became a Christian. Despite the high hopes of the colony's original leaders, seventeenth-century Virginia did not prove to be a congenial place in which to establish or support English religious institutions. For a time, it seemed that the Church of England might never succeed in gaining control over the sparsely settled, poorly governed wilderness of Virginia.

NOTES

1. "Anglican" derives from the Latin word *Anglicanus* ("English"), and the expression *ecclesia Anglicana* (designating the Catholic church in England) was common in the Middle Ages. The use of that term in the title of John Jewel's defense of the English Reformation, *Apologia Ecclesiae Anglicanae* (1562), established its association with the Church of England, organized after Henry VIII's break from Roman Catholicism in 1534.

2. "Episcopal" derives from the word *episkopos,* which was used in classical Greek to designate inspectors, temple supervisors, or municipal officials. In the New Testament, the term (meaning "overseer" or "bishop") was applied to leaders in the earliest Christian churches—see, for example, 1 Timothy 3:1–7. The word "bishop" is an Anglo-Saxon corruption of *episkopos,* while English usage of the word "episcopal" ("of or pertaining to a bishop") dates from the fifteenth century.

3. Martin Henig, "Religion in Roman Britain," in *A History of Religion in Britain: Practice and Belief from Pre-Roman Times to the Present,* ed. Sheridan Gilley and W.J. Sheils (Oxford: Blackwell, 1994), 28.

4. Norman Tanner, "Piety in the Later Middle Ages," in *History of Religion in Britain,* 74.

5. A.G. Dickens, *The English Reformation,* 2nd ed. (University Park, Pa.: Pennsylvania State University Press, 1989), 58–59.

6. Eamon Duffy, *The Stripping of the Altars: Traditional Religion in England, 1400–1580* (New Haven: Yale University Press, 1992), 1–6.

7. W.J. Sheils, "Reformed Religion in England, 1520–1640," in *History of Religion in Britain,* 151–52.

8. For a detailed analysis of Henry's attempt to obtain an annulment of his marriage, see *BHEC,* 179–97.

9. "The Supremacy Act" (1534), in *The Anglican Tradition: A Handbook of Sources,* ed. G.R. Evans and J. Robert Wright (Minneapolis: Fortress, 1991), 136.

10. Carter Lindberg, "The Late Middle Ages and the Reformations of the Sixteenth Century," in *Christianity: A Social and Cultural History,* ed. Howard Clark Kee et al. (New York: Macmillan, 1991), 389–90.

11. Dickens, *English Reformation,* 350–51, 357–58.

12. Lindberg, "Late Middle Ages," 393.

13. Dickens, *English Reformation,* 366–67.

14. Quoted in William P. Haugaard, "From the Reformation to the Eighteenth Century," in *The Study of Anglicanism,* ed. Stephen Sykes and John Booty (Minneapolis: Fortress, 1988), 11.

15. "Presbyterianism," which derives from the Greek term for "elder" *(presbyteros),* is based on the belief that all Christians share in the leadership of the church. In Presbyterianism, there is a graduated series of governing councils from the local congregation to the national level. "Congregationalism" is based on the belief that authority in the church resides fundamentally within the membership of individual congregations.

16. John Jewel, *A Treatise of the Holy Scriptures* (1570), in *Anglican Tradition,* 154. See also Peter M. Doll, *Revolution, Religion, and National Identity: Imperial Anglicanism in British North America, 1745–1795* (Madison, N.J.: Fairleigh Dickinson University Press, 2000), 14.

17. Quoted in Paul Avis, *Anglicanism and the Christian Church: Theological Resources in Historical Perspective* (Minneapolis: Fortress, 1989), 63–65.

18. Haugaard, "From the Reformation to the Eighteenth Century," 14.

19. Mark A. Noll, *A History of Christianity in the United States and Canada* (Grand Rapids, Mich.: Eerdmans, 1992), 11–12.

20. *HPEC,* 12–13.

21. Richard Hakluyt the Younger, *Discourse of Western Planting* (1584), in *A Documentary History of Religion in America,* vol. 1, ed. Edwin S. Gaustad (Grand Rapids, Mich.: Eerdmans, 1993), 53.

22. Quoted in Edward L. Bond, *Damned Souls in a Tobacco Colony: Religion in Seventeenth-Century Virginia* (Macon, Ga.: Mercer University Press, 2000), 40.

23. Jon Butler, *Awash in a Sea of Faith: Christianizing the American People* (Cambridge: Harvard University Press, 1990), 38–39.

24. *HEC,* 9–10.

25. "Church Establishment," in *Documentary History of Religion in America,* vol. 1, 97–98.

26. Quoted in Alan Taylor, *American Colonies* (New York: Viking, 2001), 130.

27. John Frederick Woolverton, *Colonial Anglicanism in North America* (Detroit: Wayne State University Press, 1984), 38.

28. Butler, *Awash in a Sea of Faith,* 42.

29. Edmund S. Morgan, *American Slavery, American Freedom: The Ordeal of Colonial Virginia* (New York: Norton, 1975), 331–33.

2
ANGLICANISM IN COLONIAL AMERICA: 1662–1763

As several recent histories of colonial North America have emphasized, cities and towns along the eastern seaboard of what is now the United States displayed a distinctly religious character in the eighteenth century. Visitors to those areas could not go very far without spotting a church or meetinghouse, or hearing bells ringing from a church steeple, or watching congregations gather for worship and preaching on a Sunday morning. It was also axiomatic in political thought that social stability and orderly government depended upon the guardianship of public morality by a single state church. In fact, with the exception of Maryland, where toleration was granted to all Christians in 1649, every colony founded in the New World prior to the mid-seventeenth century, whether Spanish, Portuguese, French, Swedish, Dutch, or English, reproduced the European model of an established church.[1] The progress of Anglicans in transplanting the Church of England in America must therefore be understood within this larger social, cultural, and religious context.

THE POSITION OF ANGLICAN CHURCHES IN THE COLONIES

Although the Jamestown colony represented both the first permanent English settlement and the first English religious establishment in America, the position of Anglican ecclesiastical institutions in Virginia initially proved to be quite tenuous, especially in relationship to what was accomplished by the Congregational settlement in Massachusetts and Connecticut. Whereas the Puritan migration from England did not begin in earnest until 1630, the colonies of New England attained a high degree of social and religious cohesion far more quickly than the Virginia colony. Because of momentous political changes that occurred in England, however, the situation in Virginia began to improve significantly after 1660. With the end of Puritan supremacy and with the restoration of the monarchy under Charles

II, Anglican leaders were able to gain much greater control over ecclesiastical affairs in Virginia. Charles took measures to curtail the authority of the colonial government, including the powers exercised by the lay vestries. And in tandem with his secular policies, Charles granted greater authority to the bishop of London for the supervision of the church and clergy in Virginia.

Although the bishop of London had long held nominal jurisdiction over Anglican churches in the New World, most of the men who occupied that post between 1630 and 1675 had viewed the mission in America more as a nuisance than as an opportunity. However, with Charles's appointment of Henry Compton to the see in 1675, the bishop of London began to take an active interest in the spiritual well-being of English settlers overseas. Compton sought to improve both the quantity and the quality of clergy in Virginia. He not only tried to recruit a suitable candidate for each vacant parish position but also restrained colonial governors from inducting clergy until he had first confirmed their moral character and orthodox theological views. In addition, he gained the right to appoint a "commissary" as his personal representative overseeing church affairs in each English colony. The ability of the bishop of London to assign commissaries helped cement his relationship with the colonial churches and was to have a profound effect on the evolution of American Anglicanism over the next one hundred years.[2] *Bishop of London*

In 1689, Compton appointed James Blair of Virginia to serve as the first Anglican commissary in America. Blair had come to Virginia four years before, and he had served in three different parishes in the colony. He immediately brought order to the affairs of the church by instituting a convocation system, by enforcing laws on morality, and by attempting to have the value of tobacco (with which clergy were paid) standardized. He also helped increase the number of clergy in Virginia from 22 in 1696 to 40 in 1707. Blair's most important achievement, however, was the founding of the College of William and Mary in 1693. Having persuaded the House of Burgesses of the need to have a school for the training of new clergy, he obtained in England both a charter and the funding for the project. Although Harvard College, which was founded in 1636, had the distinction of being the first institution of higher learning in America, William and Mary was the second; as such it was the first college established by Anglicans in the colonies.

Blair's success in Virginia convinced Compton of the usefulness of the commissary system, and in 1695 he appointed Thomas Bray to the position in Maryland, where the organization of church life had initially been even more desultory than in Virginia.[3] In the aftermath of the Glorious Revolution of 1688 and with the accession of the Protestant rulers William and Mary to the English throne, however, the Maryland legislative assembly passed three acts establishing the Church of England as the colony's official state church. The assembly also organized 30 parishes with vestries to collect taxes and to manage religious and social affairs throughout the colony. Although Bray actually spent only three months in Maryland, his efforts there were similar to those of Blair in Virginia:

organizing and encouraging the clergy, warning the laity about the dangers of immorality, and attempting to raise funds for the church.

In addition to his responsibilities in America, Bray remained strongly involved in church affairs in England. In 1698, he founded the Society for Promoting Christian Knowledge as a publisher of books designed to instruct other Christians about the unique virtues of Anglicanism, and in 1701 he founded the Society for the Propagation of the Gospel in Foreign Parts (SPG) for the recruitment and training of Anglican missionaries in the colonies. At a time when the Church of England was feeling renewed pressure from nonconformist Protestants at home, Bray was determined to support the missionary efforts of colonial Anglicanism. The societies he founded were characterized by the same notions of reformed catholicity to which he was committed: abhorrence of popery, opposition to Protestant dissent, doctrinal orthodoxy, and emphasis on the necessity of bishops in church governance.[4]

By 1700, the Church of England ranked second to Congregationalism in overall numeric strength in America.[5] Although there were more than one hundred Anglican churches scattered from Massachusetts to South Carolina, 80 percent of those were situated in either Virginia or Maryland. Most of the Virginia parishes were located in settlements and plantations along the colony's rivers. Each parish typically comprised three or four churches or chapels, and the goal was to place a church building not more than six miles from every home in the colony in order to make weekly public worship accessible to every settler. The number of parishes in Virginia had grown steadily from 48 in 1671, to 53 in 1726, to 107 in 1784, and it is likely that there were at least two congregations in every parish. In Maryland steady growth also occurred in the eighteenth century, and by 1767 there were 44 parishes in that colony. Indeed, the Chesapeake region continued to represent the stronghold of Anglicanism throughout the colonial period, and Virginia was the only colony to have a commissary in residence between 1689 and 1776.[6]

The Church of England was established throughout the rest of the southern colonies, but it was strong only in South Carolina. The South Carolina establishment act followed a bitter and complicated transatlantic debate about the civil rights of non-Anglicans. Although the original bill would have disenfranchised Protestant dissenters, a more moderate bill passed in 1706 that allowed non-Anglicans to vote. Whereas the establishment act created 10 parishes, Anglicanism was significant mainly in the area around Charleston—St. Philip's (1722) and St. Michael's (1761) being the two oldest and most prominent churches in that city—and most of the backcountry was left to the Presbyterians and Baptists. The progress of Anglicanism in North Carolina was even slower than in South Carolina. The Church of England was established there in 1715, but in 1765 only 5 of the 32 Anglican parishes had ministers or church buildings. Finally, in Georgia, which was the least prosperous colony, there were never more than five Anglican churches during the colonial period.

In the middle colonies, where Presbyterians, Dutch Reformed, Lutherans, and

Quakers predominated, the Church of England exercised a role far out of proportion to the actual number of its adherents. Anglicanism was the most robust in New York, where it was established in the four lower counties of the colony in 1693.[7] Trinity, New York, was the colony's preeminent parish, and in time it became the richest church in any denomination in the United States. The Church of England in Pennsylvania was small (representing only about 2 percent of the population), but it too became increasingly influential as more and more wealthy Quakers in the Philadelphia area converted to Anglicanism. Christ Church, Philadelphia, the oldest and most prominent parish in the colony, was founded in 1695. By 1775 Pennsylvania had 19 Anglican clergy serving in 22 churches. Delaware, which was part of Pennsylvania until 1704, had 12 more churches. Anglicanism grew slowly in New Jersey in the decades prior to the American Revolution. In 1776 there were 11 clergymen and 20 congregations in the colony, and the center of Anglican influence was located in St. Mary's Church in Burlington (founded in 1703).

In New England—the traditional stronghold of anti-Anglicanism, where Congregationalism was established by law in all colonies except Rhode Island—the Church of England grew steadily as a dissenting intruder, thereby gaining a spiritual resiliency that it lacked in other colonies. The denomination grew rapidly in Connecticut after a group of seven Congregational ministers, all faculty at Yale College, converted to Anglicanism. Thanks to the efforts of SPG missionaries in Connecticut, these men had been reading and discussing works by Anglican authors commending episcopacy as the only proper form of ecclesiastical governance. During the Yale commencement exercises in September 1722, the ministers announced that they no longer considered themselves to be validly ordained. Four of them sailed to England to seek re-ordination by an Anglican bishop, and three later returned to assume prominent positions in the American church: Timothy Cutler, the former president of Yale, became the first rector of Christ Church, Boston, where he served until 1765; James Wetmore, a recent Yale graduate, became rector of Christ's Church, Rye, New York; and Samuel Johnson, who had been a Yale tutor, served from 1754 to 1763 as the first president of King's (now Columbia) College in New York.

During the Great Awakening of the mid-eighteenth century, many New Englanders seeking greater liturgical formality and less religious emotionalism turned to the Church of England. Starting in 1689 with only one clergyman and one church (King's Chapel, Boston), by 1768 Anglicans had about twenty congregations served by a dozen clergy in Massachusetts. Although Anglicanism remained small in New Hampshire (two clergymen and two parishes by 1774) and in the region that is now the state of Maine (five congregations served by one missionary), it had respectable strength in tiny but religiously diverse Rhode Island. Trinity Church, Newport (founded in 1704), for example, was influential enough to have the British philosopher George Berkeley as a frequent preacher in the early 1730s.

THE LAITY

In colonial America, members of parish vestries exercised far more authority and influence than did their counterparts in England. Lacking a resident bishop, Anglican laymen prior to the American Revolution were able to play a major role in church government—a pattern that eventually helped define the relationship between clergy and laity in the Episcopal Church. Anglican rectors in England had life tenure and could be dismissed only by bishops and only if they had committed a grave offense. Vestries in Virginia, on the other hand, tended to keep control over their clergy by offering them only renewable annual contracts. As a result of this arrangement, the financial well-being of the clergy was usually contingent upon maintaining the goodwill of their wealthy employers. Lacking autonomy, clergy were also loath to censure the immoral behavior of leading parishioners.

After 1650, Virginia vestries became closed corporations, in which vacancies were filled by the vote of the members remaining. Control of the parish stayed, then, in the hands of a few interrelated planter families, usually major landowners such as the Carters, the Byrds, and the Randolphs. In one Virginia parish, for instance, only 66 people served on the 12-person vestry between 1690 and 1767.[8] Since this system identified Anglicanism inextricably with the local aristocracy, residents of the colony complained that, whereas the Church of England levied taxes on everyone, its lay leadership was derived from only a few self-selected families. Because the church was supported by taxes rather than by voluntary support, this arrangement ultimately left Anglicanism vulnerable to popular resentments and contributed to the collapse of the established church in Virginia during the America Revolution.

In other colonies the Anglican vestries were more democratic, being elected either by all the freeholders of the parish or by the members of the church itself. In Maryland, vestries were smaller (six vestrymen and two churchwardens) and their responsibilities were not as wide-ranging as those in Virginia. For example, county courts rather than vestries provided for the poor in Maryland. Although the vestries did police moral infractions committed by laity within their boundaries, only the governor was allowed to appoint and remove clergy; hence, vestries could not discipline clerical incumbents. Maryland vestrymen instead tended to vent their frustrations through vicious personal attacks on the clergy, thus giving them a somewhat underserved reputation as gamblers, drunkards, and fornicators.[9]

Vestries in the middle colonies of New York, Pennsylvania, New Jersey, and Delaware lacked the legal status of establishment and were left with the responsibility of raising funds as they chose. They enjoyed the right of selecting their own clergy, however, and had the authority to grant or deny life tenure without interference from the government of their colony. New England vestries were organized in much the same way. Their membership varied in number from six to nine men, and they tended to be self-perpetuating, as in Virginia. They had no civic duties at all, for those responsibilities were carried out by the Congregational establishment. In fact, the New England vestries played a leading role in the eventually successful struggle against mandatory taxation for the support of the Congregational churches.

People from all sorts of social backgrounds worshiped at Anglican churches during the colonial era. The majority of American Anglicans were not gentry, but most churchgoers were small landholders, craftsmen, and agricultural workers. Sacred and secular mixed easily on the Anglican Sabbath as parishioners mingled and caught up on gossip before and after worship. Parishioners and visitors discussed family news, the price of tobacco, and the quality of horseflesh. All were conscious of their position in the social hierarchy. Ladies showed off the latest fashions from London, while gentlemen waited until the service was beginning, then walked in and took their places in the pews in front. As the historian Rhys Isaac observes about the church in colonial Virginia, "the combination of ordered service and animated conversation produced . . . a blend of formality and informality—of convivial engagement and structured relationship" that was typical of most social gatherings of that time.[10]

Churchgoing was mainly but not exclusively an adult activity in colonial America. In rural areas, there were not many young children in attendance because parents were usually reluctant to expose them to the rigors of travel that churchgoing entailed. In towns and cities, however, older boys and girls participated more regularly in parish life. For many of them, Sunday was an important day on the social calendar, and one Philadelphia rector organized a society of young people that met on Sunday evenings to listen to sermons, study the Bible, and sing psalms. Older children also tended to concentrate their attendance in the Lenten period, when clergy provided instruction in the catechism. Although no bishop resided in the colonies and so confirmation could not be held, ministers usually examined young people at about 16 years old and, when satisfied with their preparation, admitted them to communion.[11]

While African Americans, American Indians, and white indentured servants might also occasionally attend church, their participation in worship was for the most part quite restricted. White resistance to the conversion and catechizing of slaves, for example, tended to increase in relation to the number of slaves in a colony. Thus, in Maryland, where the slave population was relatively low (12 to 18 percent in the early eighteenth century), slaves were more likely to be baptized, attend church, and take communion than in Virginia. Although the Great Awakening eventually did encourage some African American evangelism, especially among free people of color in the northern colonies, blacks and Indians were only a marginal presence in the Anglican churches in the early eighteenth century. There were no black or American Indian candidates for the priesthood during that period, and most southern blacks and Indians remained unchurched. White servants, too, were unlikely either to participate in Sunday services or to take religious instruction, especially in rural areas. As Thomas Bray remarked, "Servants & Children, God help them, must remain at Home."[12]

Despite being denied formal institutional roles as clergy or vestry members in colonial Anglicanism, women of the upper and middle classes were still important participants in church life. Women, in fact, usually outnumbered men at Sunday services, and they exercised considerable influence in the religious life of the home by reading the Bible and teaching prayers to their children. Diaries and letters also indicate that the wives of Anglican planters and merchants were sometimes widely read in theology. For example, Frances Tasker Carter of Virginia impressed her family's Princeton-trained tutor with her extensive knowledge of theological matters.[13] In South Carolina, too, devout mothers strove to protect their children from irreligion and dissent. Eliza Lucas Pinckney made certain that her children not only attended church but also memorized the opening prayer and read the scriptural text of the Sunday sermon from their own Bibles. And Mrs. Thomas Broughton, wife of a member of the governor's council, urged her son to remember the vows made for him at baptism, to be mindful of eternity, to study the catechism, and to partake of the Holy Communion.[14]

THE CLERGY

The fact that the Church of England supplied no bishop for the "episcopal" church it established in America was, in the view of noted Episcopal historian Raymond Albright, "a tragedy."[15] A resident American bishop not only would have provided order and direction for the church—improving clerical standards and decreasing the friction between vestries and their clergy—but also might have developed plans for Anglican expansion throughout all the colonies. In addition, the presence of a bishop in America would have eliminated the perils that men and their families faced when they crossed the Atlantic in search of ordination by bishops in England. Transatlantic voyages, in fact, claimed the life of one out of every five ministerial candidates in the eighteenth century.[16]

Efforts to secure a bishop for the colonies began in earnest in 1706, when 14 clergy from New York, New Jersey, and Pennsylvania sent one of their number to England to petition the church authorities. These efforts eventually caught the attention of Queen Anne, and in 1713 she instructed her chief minister to prepare legislation authorizing the consecration of bishops for the colonies. But the queen's death in 1714 prevented any further action from taking place. Similar requests were made in subsequent decades, but the Whig majority in Parliament feared that an expanded Anglican episcopate would only further the political aims of its Tory opponents.[17] Although the Great Awakening sparked some renewed calls for the establishment of a colonial episcopate, lay Anglicans, especially in the South, resisted the proposal because they recognized that it would necessarily curb their control over local parish affairs.[18] During the tense political climate of the 1760s, moreover, non-Anglicans in America were especially opposed to the introduction of the episcopate; to many of them, the imposition of English spiritual rulers on America exemplified the tyranny of British imperial leaders.[19]

While it is true that Anglican worshippers would never have encountered a bishop in a colonial parish, they often would not even have seen a priest. Although the number of Anglican clergy serving in the colonies increased markedly in the decades before the American Revolution, there was always a shortage of trained ministers. Vestries frequently had to employ clerks to read the services and to carry out other ministerial duties that required a priest. In Virginia, clerks played an especially important role. Since a priest could usually lead worship at only one of the congregations in his parish each Sunday, clerks were needed to conduct services at the parish's other churches. Many parishes also recruited their clergy from among these lay readers, and men who followed this path into the ordained ministry rarely had trouble dealing with their vestries or parishioners.[20]

Clergy who served in the southern colonies (from Maryland to Georgia) were financially supported by revenues from taxation. In Maryland, for example, the sheriff collected a tobacco tax and paid it directly to the minister. By 1767 the average annual salary for a rector in that colony was about 275 pounds, which was the highest salary for Anglican clergy in America. In 1696 the Virginia General Assembly adopted a uniform salary for clergy (16,000 pounds of tobacco a year), and this figure remained unchanged over the next 80 years. Since tobacco was an export crop whose value depended upon European market prices, clergy could never be certain what their yearly salary would actually be worth. South Carolina paid its clergy out of a general treasury, and by 1765 the annual stipend for clergy there was 110 pounds.[21]

Many clergy outside the South were aided by the SPG, which proved to be especially helpful to the growth of the church in New England and the middle colonies. The Society supplied countless Bibles, prayer books, catechisms, devotionals, and books of sermons, and it enabled congregations to pay a living wage to their clergy. Parishes in the northern and middle colonies also raised funds for their work through pew rents (making payment a prerequisite for voting in parish elections), subscriptions, and lotteries. Burial and marriage fees added to the ministers' support, as did income they earned through tutoring, operating schools, farming, and even practicing medicine.[22]

The colonial Anglican clergy were, by and large, a conscientious, learned, and devout group of men, but on occasion, a powerful planter wishing to oust his rector would not hesitate to besmirch his parson's good name. After about 1750, Presbyterian and Baptist antagonists in the South also added their voices to the criticism, presenting a picture of a lazy, drunken, and immoral Anglican clergy. Although there were, indeed, cases of clerical alcoholism, insanity, graft, and sexual misconduct, recent research has demonstrated that the image that prevailed for many years of a wholly dissolute Anglican clergy was highly exaggerated. As one southern minister remarked, a single moral slip "seldom misses of being improved into a scandal & prejudice against . . . the church & whole order of the Clergy."[23] As a group the SPG clergy were generally superior to ordinary parochial clergy. The Society carefully selected and supervised its clergy, and the demanding life of a missionary tended to attract only the most idealistic and committed clergy. (For example, John Wesley, the great evangelical leader and founder of Methodism, served in Georgia as an SPG missionary.) In sum, at least 90 percent of the colonial Anglican clergy performed their duties with at least a reasonable degree of competence and integrity.[24]

WORSHIP AND ITS ARCHITECTURAL SETTING

The typical eighteenth-century Anglican church was located either close to the banks of a river or in a cleared area at a crossroads near the geographical center of a parish. The first thing one would have seen when entering the churchyard was the building itself. It was either rectangular or cruciform in shape, often lacking a steeple or belfry. This plain structure was usually built in the Georgian style and made of brick (especially after 1720), and it would have had tall, arched windows with clear panes of glass to let in the light. Services were conducted in an architectural setting that contained four liturgical stations: the baptismal font, the pulpit, the reading desk, and the communion table.[25]

Most churches placed the font in a special baptismal pew just inside the west entrance, symbolizing the belief that Christians enter the church through the sacrament of baptism.

The pulpit was normally of double- or triple-decker design. This impressive structure was, on most Sundays, the center of attention throughout the entire service. Anglican worship in this period focused on the written or spoken word. In rectangular churches, the pulpit was most commonly placed at the midpoint of the north wall, as at Pohick Church in Lorton, Virginia, or in the center of the east wall above the holy table. It could also be located in the center aisle some yards in front of the holy table, as at Trinity Church in Newport, Rhode Island. (After the Great Awakening, when even greater emphasis was placed on the hearing of God's word, large, centrally positioned pulpits became even more commonplace.[26]) In cruciform churches, such as Christ Church in Lancaster County, Virginia, the pulpit was also placed at one of the points where the transepts intersected the main church.

The lowest level of a triple-decker pulpit was reserved for the reading desk, at which the lay clerk led the singing and verbal responses of the service. Above the clerk's desk was the minister's reading desk, where a Bible, a large prayer book, and a metrical psalter were usually placed. Here, the minister read the lessons from Scripture and led prayers. Above this desk was the top deck, 10 feet or more above the floor, where the minister preached his sermon. Sometimes one desk served for both clerk and clergyman, and the middle tier was absent.

The holy table was a wooden table with legs, placed against a flat wall and covered with a "carpet" of silk that normally reached to the floor on all sides. Red and green were the colors typically used for the hangings, though sometimes more somber colors were used during Lent and Advent. When Holy Communion was celebrated, the carpet was covered with a linen tablecloth that reached almost to the floor. No flowers or cross adorned the holy table, but on it sat the prayer book (attractively bound and placed on a cushion), alms basins, plates (called "patens") for the communion bread, and chalices and flagons for the communion wine. Communicants were reminded both of the church's basic teachings and of their religious duties through the use of panels, containing the Lord's Prayer, the Ten Commandments, and the Apostles' Creed, fastened on the wall on either side of the communion table.

Pews (which had come into use in the late Middle Ages) were typically box-shaped, with plank seats, sometimes cushioned, on three or more sides. They had high sides to keep out drafts in an unheated building, and worshipers customarily brought foot-warmers with them on cold days. Occasionally, parishioners furnished the area within their pews with movable chairs or stools. The closer a family sat to the pulpit or holy table, the higher the family's status. Slip pews (pews arranged in straight or slightly rounded lines) and backless benches were placed at the rear of the church, and those areas (as well as specially constructed galleries) were usually reserved for slaves and servants.[27]

On Sundays, most Anglican churches held services both in the morning and in the afternoon. The typical Sunday morning service consisted of Morning Prayer, the Litany, and Ante-Communion (the first part of the service of Holy Communion, ending with the gospel), a sermon, and concluding prayers. This service lasted from 75 to 90 minutes, but when communion was administered, it was usually about two hours long. In warm months, services started at 11 A.M., and in cold months they started at noon—a delay that not only gave worshipers more time to reach the church but also allowed the sun to warm the building. Communion was generally administered four times a year, but it was administered as often as once a month in some churches in northern cities.[28]

In this word-centered service, closer in form to the worship of the New England Puritans than to the worship of the Lutherans or Roman Catholics of colonial America, music was generally limited to the singing of "the Psalms of David in Metre." The service usually began with a metrical psalm such as "Old Hundredth," and in many churches the clerk read out each line before the congregation sang it. In leading the singing, the clerk might also have been assisted by a group of singers either in the rear gallery or in a "singing pew" in the nave. Music was sometimes accompanied by an organ (imported from England in wealthier urban parishes) or by local musicians playing violins, bassoons, or flutes. By the 1780s some churches also had vested choirs that sang music known as "Anglican chant" in addition to the usual psalms.[29]

Those attending a Sunday service would watch for the parish clergyman as he appeared for worship at the appointed hour. He would then walk toward the pulpit, sometimes speaking to his parishioners in their pews as he passed. They would see him robed in the plain dignity of his office, wearing either a black gown with muslin bands or a white, ankle-length vestment with long sleeves (the surplice). Most eighteenth-century Anglican parsons preached for about twenty minutes, but some, especially those influenced by the evangelicalism of the Great Awakening, might preach for as long as an hour. While an evangelical clergyman's preaching was concerned about individual conversion, emphasizing sin, atonement, and salvation, the more typical Anglican sermon was a carefully framed discourse on character, moral obligation, the orderliness and harmony of creation, and the reasonableness of Christianity. It was aimed at convincing men and women, who were assumed already to be virtuous and rational, to curb their passions, thereby maintaining both control over themselves and the stability of their society. The style of preaching in colonial Anglicanism was thus quiet, genteel, and rational—intellectual treatises read from manuscripts, designed to educate the mind rather than to arouse the emotions.[30]

On most Sundays, the sermon was the central event of a service. However, on Sundays when Holy Communion was celebrated, the minister left the high pulpit at the appropriate time and walked over to stand at one end of the holy table. Since this meant that his body was turned sideways toward the congregation, the people could clearly see him breaking the bread and performing other ritual actions. Real bread and hearty red wine were used for communion. Communicants were expected to do more than sip daintily from the chalice, and ministers sometimes figured a quarter of a pint of wine for each person![31]

THE APPEAL OF ANGLICANISM

Visitors to a colonial Anglican church would have noticed an extremely reserved religious demeanor among their fellow worshipers. During the sermon, most people paid respectful attention to the preacher and refrained from any emotional outbursts of "enthusiasm." On the way out of church, parishioners would usually congratulate the minister on a carefully crafted sermon, but speculation on how it might apply to their own spiritual lives was generally reserved for private meditations or discussions within the family.[32] Anglicanism was attractive mainly to those Americans who, according to the historian Henry May, "considered themselves modern, rational, moderate, enlightened—in a word, English."[33] It represented a literate, low-keyed, and hopeful approach to religion. Many Marylanders and Virginians simply took the established church for granted, looking to it in all seasons for comfort and guidance, but it also represented a welcome religious alternative to ordinary working-class New Englanders who felt socially excluded from the established Congregational churches.[34]

Thomas Cradock, rector of St. Thomas' Parish, Garrison Forest (in the northwestern section of Baltimore County, Maryland), personified the temperate brand of Anglicanism that prevailed in America during the late colonial period. The religion he embraced was an enlightened form of Christianity that asserted the compatibility of faith and reason. "Thus are Reason & Faith distinguished," he wrote, "both excellent in their Kinds; nor need we set them at Variance, nor disparage the One by over praising the other. They are distinct but not contrary. Reason . . . is the Gift of God, as well as Faith."[35] Cradock criticized Calvinism for teaching, in its doctrine of predestination, that human beings are not free and rational agents who truly control their own destinies. He also rejected Quaker teaching on the distinctive "inner light" and preferred to stress the light of reason and conscience, implanted by God in all human beings. He harshly condemned religious enthusiasts, inspired by the revivals of the Great Awakening, for wishing to substitute emotion for reason. And he totally rejected Roman Catholicism as being little more than superstition.[36]

Cradock's sermons were composed in a plain, unadorned style. They were full of quotations from Scripture—reason thus supplemented by biblical revelation—and written by a man well versed in history, literature, and philosophy. He spoke with eloquence about the joys of Christian faith and practice, the avoidance of vice, the "errors of popery," the faults of Deism and religious skepticism, and the order and beauty of the world. His sermons indicate that he was a man of deep and sincere conviction who felt strong empathy for the condition of his parishioners. In the estimation of scholars who have analyzed the sermons of this Maryland rector, Cradock personified Christian moderation—the classic Anglican *via media*—"preaching both rationalism and faith, adherence to the established church and toleration of others, enjoyment of the world's pleasures and restraint."[37]

THE CHALLENGE OF EVANGELICALISM *The Great awakening*

Despite the widespread acceptance of Cradock's views among adherents of the Church of England in America, the phenomenal progress of the Great Awakening throughout the colonies in the middle decades of the eighteenth century began to alter the character of Anglicanism in small ways. Evangelical preaching was first heard in Virginia in the 1740s, as "New Light" (revival-oriented) Presbyterian clergy ministered to Scots-Irish settlers then migrating into the backcountry. The few Anglican clergy who embraced the evangelical Awakening were in agreement with the New Light preachers that personal religious experience, not simply rational argument, was needed to bring sinful human beings to salvation. Logical demonstration alone could not lay claim to the human heart. To reach the feelings of the people in their congregations, some Anglican clergy put aside their manuscripts and started preaching extemporaneously, employing dramatic gestures and displaying emotion as they spoke. They began to look for evidence of a fundamental change in the lives of their parishioners—evidence of a new birth, in which the person turned from self to God as the only source of hope and life.[38]

The Anglican priest George Whitefield, who began his first evangelistic tour of the American colonies in 1738, was the most successful exemplar of this new style of preaching. Educated at Cambridge University in England, Whitefield joined a prayer and study group, sometimes called the "Holy Club" or "Methodists" (because of the members' systematic method of pursuing piety), led by John and Charles Wesley. After undergoing a conversion experience in his early twenties, he was ordained to the Anglican priesthood and began to preach about the need for Christians to recognize their sinfulness and focus on spirituality. His evangelical emphases, however, soon brought him into conflict with the Anglican establishment. He prayed extemporaneously, instead of following the fixed forms

Logic could not lay claim to the Human Heart.

of the *Book of Common Prayer;* he rejected the historic episcopate as a necessary prerequisite for a valid ordained ministry; he questioned the salvation of those who had not undergone a conversion experience; he denounced leading prelates, such as the highly respected archbishop John Tillotson; and his Calvinist theological views clashed with the Arminianism then popular in Anglican circles.[39] As a result of the open hostility of many of his fellow Anglican clergy, Whitefield began to preach in Congregational, Baptist, Presbyterian, and Reformed churches as well as occasionally outdoors.

On the whole, the response of colonial Anglicanism to the Great Awakening was negative. The vast majority of clergy rejected conversion-centered, experiential religion and tended to see the Awakening not as a force for renewal but as an effort to destroy the Church of England.[40] In the late 1750s and early 1760s, however, a few of the younger Anglican clergy recognized the value in Whitefield's emphasis on spiritual rebirth and less formal worship. Among the clergy with such evangelical leanings were William McClenachan of St. Paul's Church, Philadelphia (1761); Samuel Peters of the Anglican congregation in Hebron, Connecticut; Samuel Magaw of Dover, Delaware; and Robert McLaurine, Archibald McRoberts, Charles Clay, and Devereux Jarratt, who all actively supported the Awakening in Virginia.[41]

Jarratt was by far the most significant Anglican evangelical of the pre-revolutionary period. He played a leading role in the Great Awakening in the South, itinerating through almost 30 counties in Virginia and North Carolina, and traveling as many as six hundred miles in one trip. A forceful preacher who did not delve into matters of theological or moral complexity, Jarratt implored his congregation to seek refuge in Christ, and having done so, to "hold on your way, rejoicing in the Lord, and in the power of his might. Enter more and more into the Spirit of the gospel, and the depths of holiness."[42] Since the "Methodist societies" were still part of the Church of England at this time, Jarratt became a close friend of Wesleyan leader Francis Asbury and cooperated with Methodist itinerants in Virginia in the early 1770s. However, when the Methodists separated from Anglicanism in 1784, Jarratt reacted bitterly and felt betrayed by his erstwhile associates who placed greater emphasis on spiritual independence than on loyalty to tradition.[43]

Despite Anglicanism's appeal to those who valued such qualities as theological liberality, social deference, and liturgical decorum, this denominational tradition was unattractive to the vast majority of American Christians, who regarded its reputed virtues simply as vices—moral laxity, doctrinal indifference, worldliness, and vain pomp.[44] Ordinary people in Virginia, for instance, started leaving the established church in the 1740s. The Baptists in particular, active and gaining strength from 1765 on, rejected the style and vision of the Anglican planter's world. Disaffected, rebelling against cultured society, they created their own communities, in which an austere appearance and formal modes of address were outward ways of expressing an internal spiritual change. Such communities, made up largely of the poor and unlearned, provided a close, supportive fellowship, a place where emotions could be expressed and voices heard, where someone could call another person "brother" and "sister" and not be concerned about worldly privileges and social rank.[45]

Thousands of people throughout the American colonies responded fervently to the new faith espoused by itinerant preachers. In reaction, the Anglican gentry and their clergy expressed alarm at this challenge to the religious establishment and condemned the evangelical enthusiasm that was disturbing the existing social order. Methodists and Baptists gained the most from the religious revivals and spiritual fervor of the Great Awakening. In 1776 the Congregationalists, Anglicans, and Presbyterians were the three principal Christian denominations in America, but between 1776 and 1850 their numbers decreased markedly in proportion to the rest of the religious population. Although the absolute number of Anglicans/Episcopalians grew during that period, their percentage relative to the total population declined precipitously, slipping from approximately 16 percent in 1776 to less than 4 percent by the mid-nineteenth century.[46]

ANGLICANISM AND SLAVERY

Since rationality, personal discipline, and the maintenance of social order were three of the major hallmarks of the Church of England in the colonies, it is not surprising that Anglicanism had a significant impact on the early development of the slaveholding ethic in the South. Many Anglicans, including quite a few clergy, owned slaves and benefited from their labor but evinced no pangs of conscience concerning the prevailing norms of their society. As Jonathan Boucher, a priest who served in Virginia and Maryland, coldly observed, enslaved Africans in the American colonies were "as well-clad, as well-fed, and in every respect as well off as nine out of ten of the poor in every kingdom of Europe."[47]

Despite Boucher's unsympathetic views on the physical condition of African Americans, he and other clergy were actively involved in the evangelization and baptism of the slaves in their parishes. According to William Fleetwood, a bishop engaged in the earliest missionary efforts of the SPG, English settlers in America had a duty as Christians to preach the gospel to the rapidly increasing African slave population in the colonies. Unlike many English slaveholders, Fleetwood believed in the full humanity of Africans. As he said in a sermon in 1711, enslaved Africans were "equally the Workmanship of God . . . endued with the same Faculty, and intellectual powers; Bodies of the same Flesh and Blood, and Souls as certainly immortal" as English men and women. They were, therefore, worthy of being spiritually nurtured in the Christian faith.[48]

As Fleetwood knew, however, Anglican clergy who wished to minister to enslaved Africans faced considerable opposition from English slaveholders. Some whites simply resisted being in the presence of Africans and declared that they would not come to services in which Africans participated. An even more troubling objection concerned fears about the economic implications of converting slaves to Christianity. Many slaveholders wondered whether the Christian faith might enhance the slaves' feelings of self-worth, thus making them less compliant to their masters' directives. When one SPG missionary in South Carolina declared that all festivals of the church year would be observed in his parish, planters boycotted worship services because his policy meant that slaves would not have to work on those religious holidays.[49] Responding to this problem, Anglican proponents of African evangelization emphasized the irrelevance of baptism to a slave's civil status. Following a line of reasoning used by such notable theologians as the Apostle Paul, Augustine of Hippo, and Martin Luther, they differentiated between "Christian liberty," which was spiritual, and ordinary forms of freedom, which were not applicable to enslaved Africans.[50]

The activities of Francis Le Jau, an Anglican priest and SPG missionary in South Carolina between 1706 and 1717, illustrate how religious ideas about freedom and bondage functioned in the everyday lives of planters and slaves in colonial America. Despite the resistance of the planter elite, Le Jau was committed to promoting the conversion of Africans in his parish. He was determined, however, that converts to Christianity would subscribe to the complete Anglican gospel and not transfer their own spiritual presuppositions into the faith they adopted. Thus, to deal with the apprehensiveness of slaveholders about the potentially liberating effects of evangelism, Le Jau instituted a ritual for the baptism of slaves. Before he baptized enslaved Africans, he required them to stand in front of their masters and repeat an oath that he had taught them for the occasion. They swore that they did not seek baptism out of any desire to free themselves from duties owed to their master but simply "to partake of the Graces and Blessings promised to the Members of the Church of Jesus Christ." In addition, each man agreed to give up African sexual customs by having only one wife rather than a "plurality of Wives."[51] Although it is not certain how the enslaved Africans interpreted either this ritual or baptism itself, the meaning of Le Jau's rite was clear at least to the English slaveholders: Christianity could be a valuable means of cultural indoctrination and social control.[52]

Although Anglicans such as Fleetwood and Le Jau were instrumental in creating the paternalistic ethic that characterized the religious thought of American slaveholders a century later, this ideology never had much appeal to the Anglican gentry who dominated the planter class in the eighteenth-century South. Despite the determined efforts of their clerical leaders, most Anglican laity who owned slaves continued to assume that any promise of liberty, whether material or spiritual, would inevitably undermine their economic interests. In the 1750s and 1760s, moreover, planters saw their fears realized in the preaching of upstart evangelicals, many of whom denounced the harsh treatment of slaves and even the morality of slavery itself. The popularity of Anglican revivalist George Whitefield among enslaved Africans especially gained the attention of his fellow church members. The informal setting of Whitefield's public services allowed slaves to have easy access to his preaching, and many of them responded enthusiastically to the spiritually liberating message he proclaimed.[53] In reaction against the social threat posed by evangelicalism, the Virginia House of Burgesses passed legislation in 1772 that stipulated severe penalties for any preacher who condemned slavery as unchristian or who taught slaves to disobey their masters. Although Protestant evangelicalism in the South drifted away from its roots and became progressively more proslavery in the decades following the American Revolution, colonial Anglicanism played a critical role in the early formation of religious attitudes about the moral legitimacy of slaveholding.[54]

NOTES

1. Patricia U. Bonomi, *Under the Cope of Heaven: Religion, Society, and Politics in Colonial America* (New York: Oxford University Press, 1986), 13–15; and Nancy L. Rhoden, *Revolutionary Anglicanism: The Colonial Church of England Clergy during the American Revolution* (New York: New York University Press, 1999), 10–11.

2. Edward L. Bond, *Damned Souls in a Tobacco Colony: Religion in Seventeenth-Century Virginia* (Macon, Ga.: Mercer University Press, 2000), 215–21.

3. Jon Butler, *Awash in a Sea of Faith: Christianizing the American People* (Cambridge: Harvard University Press, 1990), 102.

4. Peter M. Doll, *Revolution, Religion, and National Identity: Imperial Anglicanism in British North America, 1745–1795* (Madison, N.J.: Fairleigh Dickinson University Press, 2000), 67–68.

5. Despite the fact that the Act of Union of 1707 legally established the Church of England in all British territories except Scotland, thereby making Anglicanism theoretically inseparable from British rule in North America, imperial authorities continued to tolerate the establishment of Congregationalism in the New England colonies (Doll, *Revolution, Religion, and National Identity,* 86).

6. John K. Nelson, *A Blessed Company: Parishes, Parsons, and Parishioners in Anglican Virginia, 1690–1776* (Chapel Hill: University of North Carolina Press, 2001), 29, 124.

7. For a discussion of the minimal degree to which Anglicanism was "established" in the four lower counties of New York, see Bonomi, *Under the Cope of Heaven,* 51–53.

8. Nelson, *Blessed Company,* 36–37.

9. Charles G. Steffen, *From Gentlemen to Townsmen: The Gentry of Baltimore County, Maryland, 1660–1776* (Lexington: University Press of Kentucky, 1993), 117.

10. Rhys Isaac, *The Transformation of Virginia, 1740–1790* (Chapel Hill: University of North Carolina Press, 1982), 60.

11. Bonomi, *Under the Cope of Heaven,* 115–16.

12. Harold T. Lewis, *Yet with a Steady Beat: The African American Struggle for Recognition in the Episcopal Church* (Valley Forge, Pa.: Trinity Press International, 1996), 21–24; and Bonomi, *Under the Cope of Heaven,* 119–23 (Bray quotation on 122).

13. *The Journal and Letters of Philip Vickers Fithian, 1773–1774: A Plantation Tutor of the Old Dominion,* ed. Hunter D. Farish (Williamsburg, Va.: Colonial Williamsburg, 1945), 61. See also Joan R. Gundersen, "The Non-Institutional Church: The Religious Role of Women in Eighteenth-Century Virginia," *HMPEC* 51 (1982): 347–57.

14. S. Charles Bolton, *Southern Anglicanism: The Church of England in South Carolina* (Westport, Conn.: Greenwood, 1982), 122. See also Joanna Bowen Gillespie, *The Life and*

Times of Martha Laurens Ramsay, 1759–1811 (Columbia: University of South Carolina Press, 2001).

15. *HPEC*, 95.

16. Doll, *Revolution, Religion, and National Identity*, 172.

17. *HEC*, 29.

18. Bolton, *Southern Anglicanism*, 7; and Nelson, *Blessed Company*, 58.

19. Butler, *Awash in a Sea of Faith*, 197–99.

20. Frederick V. Mills Sr., *Bishops by Ballot: An Eighteenth-Century Ecclesiastical Revolution* (New York: Oxford University Press, 1978), 7–8.

21. The average annual stipend for a rector in England at this time was about 125 pounds.

22. Nelson, *Blessed Company*, 48–49; and Mills, *Bishops by Ballot*, 9–11.

23. Quoted in Bonomi, *Under the Cope of Heaven*, 45.

24. Bonomi, *Under the Cope of Heaven*, 44–49.

25. Peter W. Williams, *Houses of God: Region, Religion, and Architecture in the United States* (Urbana: University of Illinois Press, 1997), 104.

26. *HEC*, 64.

27. Marion J. Hatchett, "A Sunday Service in 1776 or Thereabouts," *HMPEC* 45 (1976): 369–72; John Frederick Woolverton, *Colonial Anglicanism in North America* (Detroit: Wayne State University Press, 1984), 33–35; *BHEC*, 96–99; and Williams, *Houses of God*, 104–5.

28. *BHEC*, 99.

29. David L. Holmes, "The Anglican Tradition in Colonial Virginia," in *Perspectives on American Religion and Culture*, ed. Peter W. Williams (Malden, Mass.: Blackwell, 1999), 67; *BHEC*, 100; and Hatchett, "Sunday Service in 1776," 372.

30. Carol Lee van Voorst, "The Anglican Clergy in Maryland, 1692–1776" (Ph.D. diss., Princeton University, 1978), 280; *BHEC*, 99–100; Nelson, *Blessed Company*, 205–6; and Bonomi, *Under the Cope of Heaven*, 98.

31. *Eerdmans' Handbook to Christianity in America*, ed. Mark A. Noll et al. (Grand Rapids, Mich.: Eerdmans, 1983), 80; and *BHEC*, 100–101.

32. Paul Elmen, "Anglican Reserve: Historical Reflections," *Sewanee Theological Review* 38 (1995): 158; and Bonomi, *Under the Cope of Heaven*, 101–2.

33. Henry F. May, *The Enlightenment in America* (New York: Oxford University Press, 1976), 66.

34. Woolverton, *Colonial Anglicanism*, 34, 201.

35. Quoted in Steffen, *From Gentlemen to Townsmen*, 122.

36. Nelson Waite Rightmyer, *Maryland's Established Church* (Baltimore: Church Historical Society, 1956), 177; David Curtis Skaggs, "Thomas Cradock and the Chesapeake Golden Age," *WMQ*, 3d ser., 30 (1973): 93–117; Donald K. Enholm et al., "Origins of the Southern Mind: The Parochial Sermons of Thomas Cradock of Maryland, 1744–1770," *Quarterly Journal of Speech* 73 (1987): 202; and Steffen, *From Gentlemen to Townsmen*, 121–23.

37. David C. Skaggs and Gerald E. Hartdagen, "Sinners and Saints: Anglican Clerical Conduct in Colonial Maryland," *HMPEC* 47 (1978): 192–93; David Curtis Skaggs, "The Chain of Being in Eighteenth Century Maryland: The Paradox of Thomas Cradock," *HMPEC* 45 (1976): 155–64; David Curtis Skaggs, "Thomas Cradock's Sermon on the

Governance of Maryland's Established Church," *WMQ,* 3d ser., 27 (1970): 630–53; Skaggs, "Thomas Cradock and the Chesapeake Golden Age," 99–104; and Enholm et al., "Origins of the Southern Mind," 202 (source of quotation).

38. *HEC,* 46–47, 59–60.

39. In his theological writings, Protestant reformer John Calvin emphasized the absolute sovereignty of God, the total depravity of sinful humanity, and God's predestination both of the elect to salvation and of the reprobate to eternal damnation. Although the Dutch Reformed theologian Jacobus Arminius was a committed Calvinist, he also believed that Calvin had underestimated the role of the human will in the salvation process. As a result, he and his followers rejected Calvin's idea that divine grace was irresistible, and they stressed instead the importance of human moral effort in seeking to love and obey God. Although "Arminianism" was formally rejected at the Synod of Dort in the Netherlands in 1610, it remained a highly influential theological position within the Church of England in the seventeenth century and beyond.

40. Gerald J. Goodwin, "The Anglican Reaction to the Great Awakening," *HMPEC* 35 (1966): 343–71.

41. Robert C. Monk, "Unity and Diversity among Eighteenth Century Colonial Anglicans and Methodists," *HMPEC* 38 (1969): 51–69; and *HEC,* 55–59.

42. Quoted in *Readings from the History of the Episcopal Church,* ed. Robert W. Prichard (Wilton, Conn.: Morehouse-Barlow, 1986), 44–53.

43. Devereux Jarratt, *The Life of the Reverend Devereux Jarratt* (Cleveland: Pilgrim, 1995); Harry G. Rabe, "The Reverend Devereux Jarratt and the Virginia Social Order," *HMPEC* 33 (1964): 299–336; David L. Holmes, "Devereux Jarratt: A Letter and a Reevaluation," *HMPEC* 47 (1978): 37–49; and Douglass Adair, "The Autobiography of Devereux Jarratt, 1732–1763," *WMQ,* 3d ser., 9 (1952): 346–93. By 1780, there were approximately 12,000 members in the Methodist societies, located mainly in the colonies south of Maryland. In September 1784 John Wesley and Thomas Coke ordained two lay preachers for service as the first Methodist ministers in America. A few months later, at the "Christmas Conference" in Baltimore, those societies were organized as a new denomination, the Methodist Episcopal Church.

44. May, *Enlightenment in America,* 76.

45. Isaac, *Transformation of Virginia,* 161–77.

46. Roger Finke and Rodney Stark, *The Churching of America, 1776–1990: Winners and Losers in Our Religious Economy* (New Brunswick, N.J.: Rutgers University Press, 1992), 54–56.

47. Quoted in Nelson, *Blessed Company,* 262.

48. William Fleetwood, *A Sermon Preached before the Society for the Propagation of the Gospel in Foreign Parts* (1711), quoted in Butler, *Awash in a Sea of Faith,* 137.

49. Annette Laing, " 'Heathens and Infidels'? African Christianization and Anglicanism in the South Carolina Low Country, 1700–1750," *Religion and American Culture* 12 (2002): 204–5, 214.

50. Nelson, *Blessed Company,* 259–72; and Butler, *Awash in a Sea of Faith,* 135–39.

51. Francis Le Jau, *The Carolina Chronicle of Dr. Francis Le Jau, 1706–1717,* ed. Frank W. Klingberg (Berkeley: University of California Press, 1956), 60–61. See also Laing, " 'Heathens and Infidels,' " 203.

52. Isaac, *Transformation of Virginia,* 68, 70; Butler, *Awash in a Sea of Faith,* 140–41; and Laing, " 'Heathens and Infidels,' " 197–217. See also Albert J. Raboteau, *Slave Re-*

ligion: The "Invisible Institution" in the Antebellum South (New York: Oxford University Press, 1978).

53. Laing, " 'Heathens and Infidels,' " 215–16.

54. May, *Enlightenment in America,* 70–71; Isaac, *Transformation of Virginia,* 171–72; and Butler, *Awash in a Sea of Faith,* 149–51.

3
THE CRISIS OF THE AMERICAN REVOLUTION: 1763–1783

The Church of England occupied a decidedly ambiguous place in American society on the eve of the war with Great Britain. On the one hand, it enjoyed
considerable prestige both as the established religious faith of the southern colonies and as the church of many of the wealthiest and most powerful citizens of
the North. Touting itself as an unwavering bulwark of British imperial power, the
church seemed to be in an especially favorable position for growth after the
successful conclusion of the Seven Years' War in 1763. Thanks to the outcome
of that conflict, American Anglicans were primed for expansion. They planned
not only to send missionaries into Catholic-controlled areas in Canada but even
to contest the Congregational religious establishment in New England.[1]

On the other hand, the very social and political forces that seemed so encouraging in 1763 were soon to bring the American branch of the Church of England
to the brink of extinction. Embracing powerful symbols of the British imperial
presence in the colonies—the monarchy, the episcopate, and the stately language
of the *Book of Common Prayer*—Anglican leaders purposely distanced themselves from other, more democratic sources of religious vitality and support during the political upheavals of the 1760s and 1770s. As a consequence, they were
hard-pressed to reestablish their denomination's position within the new cultural
environment created by the movement for American independence. With the coming of the American Revolution and the overthrow of the old colonial social order,
Anglicans faced an acute challenge to the religious tradition they had labored to
establish in America.[2]

THE CONFLICT OVER BISHOPS

No problem was more irksome to colonial Anglicans, especially the high
church party supported by the SPG, than the absence of a resident bishop.[3] Lacking the centralized authority that English bishops exercised, Anglicanism in the

colonies was forced to operate as a largely disunited collection of parishes under the distant supervision of the bishop of London. The church's attempt to procure an American episcopate, however, aroused sharp outcries from a diverse group of opponents, who envisioned it as an Anglican plot to overthrow the civil and religious rights of other Protestant colonists. As John Adams observed in the early nineteenth century, "the apprehension of Episcopacy" had contributed as much as any other cause to the coming of the Revolution. "The objection," he noted, "was not merely to the office of a bishop, though even that was dreaded, but to the authority of parliament," on which an Anglican episcopate would necessarily have been based.[4]

As early as 1638, William Laud, the archbishop of Canterbury, had considered a proposal to send a bishop to Puritan New England, and in 1672 a charter had been created that would have established both a diocese and a bishop in Virginia. Neither of those plans ever came to fruition, however. Throughout the 1670s and 1680s, when high church influence in England was at its peak, there was strong support for the creation of a colonial episcopate, but upheavals over religious and constitutional questions at the time of the Glorious Revolution prevented any concrete action from being taken. The founding of the SPG in 1701 again encouraged the drafting of schemes that would have led to the creation of an American episcopate. Although representatives of the society eventually won the support of Queen Anne for their plans, her death in 1714 and the accession of the unsympathetic George I to the English throne thwarted that plan as well.[5]

Over the next several decades, high church clergy continued to press the English government to establish a bishop in its American colonies. The publication of pamphlets and articles intensified during this period, and the campaign for an American episcopate eventually assumed a highly acrimonious, public profile. The controversy came to a head in the late 1760s. Following a meeting of Anglican clergy from the northern colonies at Elizabethtown, New Jersey, Thomas Bradbury Chandler composed a pamphlet entitled *An Appeal to the Public in Behalf of the Church of England in America* (1767). In it, he articulated familiar ecclesiastical arguments about the advantages of creating a colonial episcopate. In addition, he recalled the bloody days of the English Civil War, contrasting the loyalty of the Anglican bishops to the British crown with the regicide and disastrous experiment in republicanism perpetrated by the anti-episcopal Puritans. That same year, John Ewer, the Anglican bishop of Llandaff, preached to the annual gathering of the SPG in London. In his sermon, Ewer launched a caustic attack on the Puritans and their descendants, the Congregationalists of New England. When news of Ewer's sermon reached the colonies, Congregationalists and Presbyterians immediately interpreted both his statements and the sentiments espoused by Chandler's *Appeal* as evidence of a full-scale, coordinated assault on them by the hierarchy of the Church of England—an attack on their religious liberties as grave as the autocratic pretensions of Charles I.[6]

Seen within the context of the general imperial reorganization that followed the Seven Years' War, the ecclesiastical proposal touted by high church Anglicans like Chandler and Ewer caused understandable concern among Protestant religious dissenters both in America and in England. Having already tried to levy burdensome and unjust taxes upon the American populace, Congregationalists and Presbyterians wondered, would the British government next attempt to impose Anglican bishops?[7] Responding to Ewer and Chandler, Americans such as Charles Chauncy, a Congregational minister in Boston, and William Livingston, a Presbyterian lawyer in New York, argued that the Anglican campaign for a colonial bishop was just one more example of a continuing pattern of British despotism. According to Livingston, the introduction of a bishop would represent "an evil more terrible to every man who sets a proper value either on his liberty, property, or conscience than the so greatly and deservedly obnoxious Stamp Act" of 1765.[8] In his estimation, history demonstrated that ecclesiastical tyranny and political oppression invariably went hand-in-hand.[9]

Given the nature of religious institutions in the eighteenth century, Livingston's objections were not unreasonable. Although some advocates of the colonial episcopate sought to reassure their opponents that American bishops would exercise spiritual, not temporal, authority, that presumption was contrary to the actual practices of the Church of England at that time. Episcopacy was then so entwined within the fabric of the British government that, with the exception of a handful of nonjuring bishops, no Anglican prelate in the 1760s would have considered the possibility of functioning outside the temporal jurisdiction of the state.[10] Anglican bishops had always wielded civil and political powers, and monarchy and episcopacy had, indeed, been mutually supportive since the controversy with Puritanism during the reign of Elizabeth I.[11]

In the end, the campaign for an American bishop failed not simply because of the fears of non-Anglicans but because many politicians (especially Whigs and those who sympathized with Protestant dissenters both at home and in the colonies) and even some Anglican moderates began to question the feasibility of the plan. Officials of the British government, for example, recognized the extreme volatility of the American situation and, in the wake of the Stamp Act riots, were loath to inflame public opinion further by introducing a bishop. Although the clergy who served as SPG missionaries in the northern colonies strongly favored the creation of an episcopate, clergy and laity in the middle and southern colonies were far less enthusiastic. Some Anglicans, such as William Smith and Richard Peters of Philadelphia, thought the church would function more efficiently if several commissaries, rather than a single bishop, were sent to the colonies. Others, such as Thomas Gwatkin and Samuel Henley of Virginia, believed it was inappropriate for clergy in the North to apply for a bishop without the backing of the civil authorities in their colonies. Since the legislatures of Massachusetts and Connecticut supported Congregational churches, not the Church of England, the church-state union on which Anglican bishops depended could not have been easily replicated in New England. Finally, lay leaders in Virginia and other southern colonies recognized the negative impact that the introduction of a bishop would have had on them. In the absence of a bishop, laity were free to exercise fully autonomous control over the affairs of their churches.[12]

ANGLICAN LOYALISTS

Inasmuch as the prewar debate over bishops caused conflict even among Anglicans, it is hardly surprising that the Church of England in America divided more than any other denomination over the War for Independence itself. Like their fellow colonists, American Anglicans covered a broad spectrum of political views—from patriots on the left, to neutralists and conciliators in the center, to loyalists on the right. The paradoxes within Anglicanism in the revolutionary era are quite clear. About three-quarters of the signers of the Declaration of Independence were Anglican laymen, yet throughout the war loyalism had a decidedly Anglican tinge.[13] The greatest leaders of the revolutionary cause—statesmen such as Thomas Jefferson, George Washington, Patrick Henry, Alexander Hamilton, and John Jay—were members (at least nominally) of the Church of England, yet in some towns and villages "Tory" and "Anglican" were virtually synonymous.

Large numbers of Anglican clergy also had loyalist sympathies—a political stance that was generally linked to the relative *weakness* of the Church of England in the colonies where the loyalists served. In New England, for example, where Anglicanism was not established, Anglican clergy depended on the SPG rather than on their parishioners for financial support. Thus, when the war broke out, Anglicans continued to seek direction from the authorities in England who paid them, not from people at home who were leading the military revolt against the British government. Conversely, Anglicans were usually the most committed to the patriot cause where the Church of England was strongest, because in those colonies the clergy were maintained by local, not British governmental, sources.[14]

Although a precise calculation of the political views of all Anglican laypeople is not possible, a tally of the orientation of the approximately three hundred clergymen in America between 1776 and 1783 has been compiled. According to the historian Nancy Rhoden, over 80 percent of the clergy in colonial New England, New York, and New Jersey were loyalists, while less than 23 percent of the clergy in the four southern colonies adopted that stance during the war with Great Britain.[15] In New England, where Anglicans were a small minority among Congregationalists and where the SPG had helped found most of the parishes, all Anglican clergy except two (Edward Bass of Newburyport, Massachusetts, and Samuel Parker of Boston) were loyalists. In New York, and especially in the lower four counties where Anglicanism was established, only one priest (Samuel Provoost) was a patriot. For most of the war, the city of New York served as a British military stronghold and as refuge for prominent loyalists, many of whom belonged to the Church of England. And in New Jersey, where all of the clergy were SPG missionaries, all but one of the clergy (Robert Blackwell, who served as a chaplain in the Continental Army) took the British side.[16]

[handwritten marginalia] many paid by SPG + oath to King — Loyalty Crown

Another reason why so many Anglican clergymen remained loyal to Great Britain is contained in the oaths taken by each minister of the Church of England at the time of his ordination. According to the canons of 1604, Anglican clergy were required to affirm that the king "within his realms of England, Scotland, and Ireland, and all other his dominions and countries, is the highest power under God; to whom all men . . . do by God's laws owe most loyalty and obedience, afore and above all other powers and potentates in earth."[17] When he was ordained, each Anglican deacon or priest was obliged publicly to swear allegiance to the king, recognizing his authority as head of both church and state in Great Britain. Furthermore, the 1662 Act of Uniformity bound clergy to use the official liturgy of the Church of England whenever they led public worship.[18] This provision required the verbatim reading of services in the *Book of Common Prayer,* which included prayers for the king, for the royal family, and for Parliament. In the service of Holy Communion, for example, the priest was obliged to say the following prayer:

Almighty God, whose kingdom is everlasting, and power infinite; Have mercy upon the whole Church; and so rule the heart of thy chosen servant *George,* our King and Governor, that he (knowing whose Minister he is) may above all Things seek thy honour and glory: And that we, and all his subjects (duly considering whose authority he hath) may faithfully serve, honour, and humbly obey him, . . . through Jesus Christ our Lord. . . . *Amen.*[19]

Since Anglican clergy observed these oaths and prayers with great seriousness, they faced a crisis of conscience as soon as the revolt against Great Britain began. During 1775 and 1776, the Continental Congress issued a series of decrees ordering churches to observe specific days of fasting and prayer on behalf of the American cause. Although some loyalist clergy braved the consequences and refused to observe the fast days, most reluctantly held services. When they read the prayer book liturgy with its required prayers for the king, however, disturbances inevitably ensued. On July 4, 1776, when the Declaration of Independence was adopted, the dilemma faced by Anglicans grew even worse. After that date, the actions of Congress, supported by subsequent state laws, made prayers for the king and Parliament acts of treason. Whichever way the clergyman turned, he faced condemnation. Until such time as he was released from obedience to his ordination vows, he would be guilty of betraying his oath to the king if he prayed for the American cause. But if he remained faithful to the traditions of the Church of England, he risked both fines and imprisonment at the hands of American patriots.[20]

While ordination vows represented the chief reason, several other considerations also compelled Anglican clergy to become loyalists. The men supported by the SPG, for instance, were liable for dismissal by the society if they expressed any hint of disloyalty.[21] Another important factor was the unbending respect for political and ecclesiastical authority that was characteristic of Anglicanism. Although some Anglican loyalists sympathized with the grievances of their fellow colonists, they did not think that gaining independence through a violent revolt was at all justifiable.[22] Related to this conservative political attitude was a fear that the Revolution was fundamentally a neo-Puritan plot to destroy Anglicanism in the colonies. This concern was especially evident in New England, where British defeat left Anglicans at the mercy of the Congregational religious establishment. In Massachusetts and Connecticut, Anglicans tended to see clear parallels between the American Revolution and the English Civil War, when Puritans had not only executed the king and the archbishop of Canterbury but also outlawed Anglicanism itself.[23]

Sensing the potential hardship and disruption that lay ahead, some Anglican clergy who opposed independence started leaving the colonies before 1776. This group of emigrants included such prominent clergy as Thomas Bradbury Chandler and Myles Cooper, president of King's College in New York. On the same day that Paul Revere received his famous signal from the steeple of Christ (Old North) Church in Boston, the rector of the parish, Mather Byles, resigned his position. As threats intensified, increasing numbers of clergy fled to Britain, to Canada, and to American areas still under British military control, where some (e.g., Samuel Seabury of New York and Jonathan Odell of New Jersey) joined loyalist regiments as chaplains. Most of the Anglican clergy who remained in the colonies after the Declaration of Independence also decided, albeit reluctantly, to suspend services until they could perform them in accordance with the *Book of Common Prayer* and without interference from the patriot governments. By the summer of 1776, Anglican church doors were closing throughout America. At the end of the year, a missionary informed the SPG leadership that in the four colonies of Pennsylvania, New Jersey, New York, and Connecticut, the only Anglican churches still open were those in Philadelphia, one or two in rural Pennsylvania, those in British-controlled New York, and two parishes in Connecticut.[24]

The closing of churches did not mean that Anglican loyalists were left entirely without opportunities for worship. Clergy who did not flee from the colonies continued to minister to their congregations as best they could, using churches or private homes. In other parishes, lay readers, who were not bound by oath to perform prayer book liturgies verbatim, read the services of Morning and Evening Prayer and delivered printed homilies. In addition, at least one church in Massachusetts hired a non-Anglican clergyman to lead worship. A few Anglican clergy, moreover, defiantly continued to hold services. John Beach of Connecticut not only conducted worship throughout the war but also swore that he would continue praying for the king until the rebels cut out his tongue. And Charles Inglis of Trinity Church in New York persisted in reading the royal prayers even when George Washington was in the congregation and when a patriot militia company stood by, observing the service. In addition, those who were willing either to omit or to modify the royal prayers were usually able to read the prayer book liturgy without interference from revolutionaries. Samuel Tingley, an SPG missionary who served in Delaware and Maryland, handled the prayers for the king in a highly pragmatic fashion. Rather than praying "O Lord, save the King," he said instead, "O Lord, save those whom thou hast made it our especial Duty to pray for." God, he thought, would understand what was intended by those words.[25]

Because the members of virtually all Anglican parishes wished to continue public worship whenever possible, clergymen sought to obtain permission from the SPG and the bishop of London to hold prayer book services without including the royal prayers. Thomas Chandler, who had fled to England in 1775, acted as an intermediary between Anglicans in America and the leadership of the church in London during the war. Chandler advised loyalist clergy as early as 1779 that, despite the inability of English officials to grant *formal* permission to drop the prayers for the king, they would not object to their omission as long as the clergy did not begin praying for the American Congress instead. As news about this temporary accommodation spread, Anglican churches in New England and the middle colonies gradually began to reopen.[26]

Although their treatment was comparatively lenient for those times, Anglican loyalists nevertheless suffered for their views. Numerous laity were tarred and feathered or forced to "ride the Tory rail," and clergy, especially in New England, became prime targets of mobs roaming the countryside in search of targets for harassment. The average loyalist rector who remained in his parish, in fact, ran the risk of having his house ransacked, his library and private papers destroyed, and his livestock killed or stolen.[27] In Maryland in 1775, for instance, Jonathan Boucher attempted both to pray for the king and to preach against the evils of revolution. After being locked out of his church, burned in effigy, and threatened with bodily harm, he decided to take two pistols with him into the pulpit. When seized by a group of patriots while trying to preach on loyalism, Boucher saved himself by pointing one of those pistols at the head of the mob's leader. Such intimidation and indignities eventually convinced him, however, to abandon his parish position and leave for England in September 1775.[28]

Because many Anglican clergy refused to obey local laws by taking oaths of allegiance to Congress or by praying for the patriot cause, government authorities had the right to place them under arrest and to seize their property. The Massachusetts legislature passed a statute forbidding any preaching that might dissuade colonists from supporting the movement for independence. Since the law carried a 50-pound penalty—a sum roughly equivalent to a priest's annual stipend from the SPG—most clergymen felt enough pressure simply to discontinue services.[29] These threatened penalties exacted a grave toll: many clergy lost their possessions; others had to remain separated from their families for long periods of time; and others suffered physical infirmities that troubled them for the rest of their lives. Despite numerous hardships, most loyalist clergy chose to remain true to their religious calling. As William Clark, an SPG missionary in Dedham, Massachusetts, wrote in 1777, "by vows, oaths, and subscriptions, which have been made on Earth and recorded in heaven I am obliged to act as a dutiful subject of . . . King George the Third, and to the constant use of the Liturgy of that Church of which under God he is the head."[30]

The South — north Carolina
South Carolina
Georgia

ANGLICAN PATRIOTS

As the foregoing discussion suggests, there was a very close connection between membership in the Church of England and loyalist sympathies among Americans living in the northern colonies when the War for Independence began. This trend was almost exactly reversed, however, in the southern colonies, especially in Virginia, where many of the principal leaders of the Revolution were Anglicans.

In Virginia in the early 1770s, the Church of England was still firmly established by law and lay vestries continued to exercise control over the affairs of their parishes. George Washington, for instance, was a vestryman, a pewholder, and a regular (albeit decidedly rationalistic) Anglican churchgoer. In spite of his institutional ties to the Church of England, however, Washington saw no conflict between his religious faith and his commitment to the revolutionary cause. As a layperson, of course, he did not have to swear a religious oath to support and pray regularly for George III—a fact that helps explains why a far higher proportion of Anglican laity in the South became patriots in comparison to the clergy. Nevertheless, most of the clergy in Virginia either wholeheartedly supported the Revolution or assumed a neutral position during the war, while only about one in five remained loyal to Great Britain.[31] Unlike their high church colleagues in the North, who emphasized the theological and liturgical distinctiveness of Anglicanism, the clergy of Virginia tended to be as deistic in their religious sentiments as the local gentry on whom their salaries were dependent. Thus, when prominent church members such as Washington, Patrick Henry, and others led their colony into revolt, the Anglican clergy were generally willing to bless their efforts.[32]

A popular (though perhaps apocryphal) story recounts the dramatic decision of the Anglican clergyman John Peter Gabriel Muhlenberg of Woodstock, Virginia, to join the Continental army. Serving at an Anglican parish in the colony's backcountry, Muhlenberg not only took the lead in organizing the Committee of Safety in his county but also accepted appointment as the colonel of the local militia. One Sunday morning in early 1776, after preaching a rousing sermon on Ecclesiastes 3:1 ("To every thing there is a season, and a time to every purpose under the heaven," KJV), Muhlenberg threw off his vestments and revealed the militia uniform he was wearing underneath. Then, summoning the men of his congregation to join him in the fight against the British, he marched down the aisle and out of the church. So strong was his commitment to the patriot cause that he later became a brigadier general and commanded troops at several major battles during the war.[33] In defense of his military activities, Muhlenberg declared, "I am a clergyman, it is true, but I am a member of society as well . . . , and my liberty is as dear to me as to any man."[34]

Needless to say, not all Anglican clergy in the South took as active a role in the war as Muhlenberg, but the majority in North Carolina, South Carolina, and Georgia still were patriots—the strongest support coming from South Carolina, where the Church of England was most solidly established. The laity, moreover, strongly backed the Revolution, and 8 of the 10 signers of the Declaration of Independence from those colonies were Anglicans.[35] Maryland, on the other hand, represents something of an anomaly. The majority of Anglican laity there were patriots. And since Maryland supported an Anglican church establishment, one might have expected that a significant portion of the colony's 58 clergy would have supported the Revolution as well. In fact, only 11 took that position. This can be explained, however, by the existence of a strong high church faction in Maryland before the war. Many clergy not only had looked to England for an American episcopate but also had been at odds with the colonial legislature over salaries and lay control of the church.[36]

During the war with Great Britain, most of the patriot clergy in the South were able to keep their churches open and continued to function as they had in peacetime, at least in areas controlled by American forces. Distinguished from their loyalist colleagues by their willingness to accept the new political and ecclesiastical realities of post-1776 America, Anglican patriots enthusiastically preached on and prayed for the success of the Revolution. Despite occasional harassment by British troops, including the destruction and commandeering of church buildings, these clergy generally did not undergo much persecution. Besides ministering to their own congregations, a few even provided pastoral care in neighboring parishes that lacked clerical leadership after the departure of loyalist rectors.[37]

The one major theoretical problem faced by patriot clergymen was the interpretation of the strictures of the ordination oath to "bear faith and true allegiance to the King's Highness."[38] In reaching the conclusion that this oath was no longer binding on them, some clergy argued that biblical precepts about a Christian's need to obey those in civil authority (e.g., Romans 13:1–7) referred to the British king only when he governed in accordance with the laws and constitution of his nation.[39] Other clergy, claiming that they recognized the Continental Congress as the only valid governing authority in America, pointed to the precedent set during the Glorious Revolution in England less than a hundred years before. At that time, bishops and priests of the Church of England (with the notable exception of the nonjurors) had transferred their solemn oaths of allegiance from the deposed king, James II, to the new monarchs, William and Mary. Because the legislature of Virginia not only required adult males to swear an oath of allegiance to the commonwealth but also threatened any officeholder who refused, including parish rectors, with removal from his position, patriot clergy could justifiably claim that their ordination oaths to George III had been superseded by those new laws.[40] Finally, many patriot clergy concluded that their calling was first and foremost a religious and spiritual one: they were not just political functionaries but priests and pastors to whom ordinary people looked for the ministrations of the church. This justification attracted a number of wavering clergy (e.g., Edward Bass and Samuel Parker of Massachusetts, Thomas John Claggett of Maryland, and Samuel Tingley of Delaware) who might otherwise have had qualms about violating their ordination oaths.[41]

In considering the ideas and activities of Anglican patriots during the Revolution, the career of William White of Pennsylvania is particularly instructive. A member of a prominent Philadelphia family, White served as assistant to Jacob Duché, the rector of Christ Church in Philadelphia, at the outbreak of the war. Although Duché initially backed the American side and was even the original chaplain of the Continental Congress, he reversed his position after the British army captured his city in 1777. White, however, remained a patriot, and he fled to Maryland during the occupation of Philadelphia. He returned when the British abandoned the city in June 1778, and because Duché opted to follow the retreating army, White was chosen to be his successor both as chaplain of Congress and rector of Christ Church. Despite his readiness to offer prayers for the king until the Sunday immediately preceding the Declaration of Independence, White willingly altered the prayer book texts to reflect the new political situation in America in mid-1776. As he later explained, a priest's promise to pray for the king had to be understood within the context of his "pastoral duty generally." Thus, White thought it was reasonable for Anglicans to remove the royal prayers if there was "an external necessity" such as the forming of a new nation, and if the recitation of those prayers did not involve any essential "Christian duty."[42]

DISESTABLISHMENT   *The 1ˢᵗ amendment 1791*

The American Revolution and its aftermath had a profound effect not only on individual Anglicans as they tried to choose between competing political and ecclesiastical allegiances but also on the church's institutional presence in the colonies. The most crucial development that occurred within all American Christian denominations in this period was the elimination of governmental control over religious affairs. Thomas Jefferson, who along with James Madison was the chief architect of the First Amendment to the Constitution, believed that the conflict with Great Britain was a struggle against all "Lords Temporal or Spiritual"— against bishops as well as against tax commissioners, royal governors, and other symbols of British tyranny. Although the passage of the First Amendment in 1791 did not immediately resolve all questions about the relationship of religion and government in the United States, it effectively ended the church establishment system that had been in effect throughout the colonial period and (in Jefferson's words) helped erect "a wall of separation between Church and State." A double guarantee was put into place: henceforth, government would do nothing either to favor or to inhibit "the free exercise" of religion in the United States. The responsibility of promoting religious institutions and beliefs, therefore, no longer belonged to society as a whole but to individuals. In addition to requiring churches to depend on only the voluntary contributions of committed laypeople, this new arrangement tended both to favor religious bodies that were democratically governed and to discourage formalism in worship and theology.[43]

Despite the benefits that ultimately resulted from disestablishment, the process itself proved to be extremely difficult for Anglicans, who had been so thoroughly implicated and involved in the old system. In every colony where the Church of England had been established before 1776, the denomination was quickly stripped of its privileged position, as revolutionary governments and new state constitutions terminated the tax-based financial support on which it had traditionally depended. Ironically, in those places where Anglican support for the revolutionary cause was the strongest, the denomination had also been the most firmly entrenched before the war and thus lost the most in material terms in the late 1770s. Maryland, Virginia, and North Carolina suspended the payment of salaries to Anglican clergy in 1776, and Georgia and South Carolina followed suit in 1777 and 1778 respectively. And in 1777 the act that had established the Church of England in the New York City area was repealed. While several of those colonies continued to offer general support to *all* Protestant churches until the mid-1780s, Anglicans no longer held any advantage over rival denominations such as the Baptists and Presbyterians.

Although Congregationalists rather than Anglicans faced the main challenge of disestablishment in the New England states, the outcome of the war still did little to advance the position of the Church of England there. On the one hand, the legal status of Anglicanism vis-à-vis the various state governments in New England remained officially unchanged in the 1780s: Anglicans (along with Baptists, Methodists, and others) were simply recognized as official dissenters from the truncated state religious establishments that Massachusetts, Connecticut, and New Hampshire continued to maintain. On the other hand, the financial support and supervision that Anglican clergy had received from London during the colonial era abruptly came to an end with the arrival of peace. Because the SPG charter did not allow the funding of missions outside the British empire, all clergy, loyalist and patriot alike, lost their stipends after Great Britain officially recognized American independence in 1783. Despite complaints from a number of clergy, who felt betrayed by the church and government to whom they had remained loyal throughout a very perilous and uncertain time, the policies of the SPG were not altered in any way to accommodate the tenuous position of Anglicans in New England.[44]

Although exact figures are not available, approximately 80,000 loyalists left the 13 American colonies during the revolutionary era. Most emigrated to the Maritimes and to other parts of Canada, while some went to the West Indies, to Africa, and to Great Britain.[45] The fact that so many loyalists moved to the Maritime provinces not only doubled the total population of the region but thereafter significantly strengthened the position of the Church of England in Canada. Charles Inglis, an SPG missionary and outspoken advocate of an American episcopate, abandoned his position at Trinity Church in New York in 1783 and fled to London. Thanks to his political and ecclesiastical connections in England, he was later chosen to be the bishop of Nova Scotia, thus becoming (in 1787) the first colonial bishop of the Church of England. Although the Nova Scotia legislature formally established the Church of England, opposition from other Protestants prevented a full recreation of the British model. As a result, Inglis was given authority to exercise "all Manner of Jurisdiction, Power, and Coercion *Ecclesiastical*" in his diocese, but unlike bishops in England, he held no significant civil or temporal powers.[46]

Inglis's personal success and the advancement of the Church of England in Canada serve to highlight, in fact, the severe weakness of Anglicanism in the United States. The financial support on which the American church had once depended was now completely gone, and in every state except Connecticut, most parishes were either shut down or lacking clerical leadership. As an aristocratic and tradition-bound denomination awash in a sea of democratic freedoms, Anglicanism was desperately struggling to survive as the revolutionary era came to a close.[47]

NOTES

1. Peter M. Doll, *Revolution, Religion, and National Identity: Imperial Anglicanism in British North America, 1745–1795* (Madison, N.J.: Fairleigh Dickinson University Press, 2000), 177–84.

2. David L. Holmes, "The Episcopal Church and the American Revolution," *HMPEC* 47 (1978): 261; and *AR*, 106–7.

3. The terms "high church" and "high churchman," which were used to describe those who opposed the Puritan-Calvinist wing of the Church of England, began to appear in Anglican circles in the late seventeenth century. High church Anglicans tended to emphasize the importance of the episcopate, strict adherence to the prayer book, and the superiority of the Church of England to other forms of Protestantism.

4. Quoted in Patricia U. Bonomi, *Under the Cope of Heaven: Religion, Society, and Politics in Colonial America* (New York: Oxford University Press, 1986), 200.

5. *HPEC*, 96–98.

6. Doll, *Revolution, Religion, and National Identity,* 191–92; and Bonomi, *Under the Cope of Heaven,* 203–5.

7. Nancy L. Rhoden, *Revolutionary Anglicanism: The Colonial Church of England Clergy during the American Revolution* (New York: New York University Press, 1999), 37.

8. William Livingston, *The American Whig* (March 14, 1768), in *A Documentary History of Religion in America,* vol. 1, ed. Edwin S. Gaustad (Grand Rapids, Mich.: Eerdmans, 1993), 247.

9. Jon Butler, *Awash in a Sea of Faith: Christianizing the American People* (Cambridge: Harvard University Press, 1990), 198.

10. After the abdication of James II and the Glorious Revolution of 1688–89, six Anglican bishops and several hundred priests in England and Scotland remained loyal to the Stuart royal line and refused to take the required oath of allegiance to the new monarchs, William III and Mary II. These clergy, who were known as "nonjurors," were deprived of their livings and were forced to function without any support from the British government.

11. Rhoden, *Revolutionary Anglicanism,* 47, 52; and Doll, *Revolution, Religion, and National Identity,* 181–87.

12. Rhoden, *Revolutionary Anglicanism,* 40–46.

13. *HPEC,* 113.

14. Holmes, "Episcopal Church and the American Revolution," 265.

15. Rhoden, *Revolutionary Anglicanism,* 88–89. With no religious establishment of any kind and with little overt hostility between the Church of England and other denominations, the Anglican clergy in Pennsylvania and Delaware were about equally divided in their loyalties.

16. Holmes, "Episcopal Church and the American Revolution," 265–66, 282.

17. "Canons of 1604," in *The Anglican Tradition: A Handbook of Sources,* ed. G.R. Evans and J. Robert Wright (Minneapolis, Minn.: Fortress, 1991), 186.

18. "The Act of Uniformity" (1662), in *Anglican Tradition,* 243.

19. Quoted in Holmes, "Episcopal Church and the American Revolution," 290.

20. Holmes, "Episcopal Church and the American Revolution," 269–70.

21. Stipends were withdrawn from at least three Anglican clergymen who took the American side during the war: Edward Bass (Massachusetts), Robert Blackwell (New Jersey), and Samuel Magaw (Pennsylvania/Delaware)—see William Stevens Perry, ed., *Historical Collections Relating to the American Colonial Church,* 5 vols. (Hartford, Conn.: n.p., 1870–78), III: 602–40.

22. For a full analysis of the political philosophy of Anglican loyalists, see Robert McCluer Calhoon, *The Loyalists in Revolutionary America, 1760–1781* (New York: Harcourt Brace Jovanovich, 1973), 218–65.

23. See, for example, William H. Nelson, *The American Tory* (Oxford: Clarendon, 1961), 85–91; Wallace Brown, *The King's Friends: The Composition and Motives of the American Loyalist Claimants* (Providence: Brown University Press, 1965), 29, 281–82; and William Warren Sweet, "The Role of Anglicans in the American Revolution," *Huntington Library Quarterly* 9 (1947): 52. According to one loyalist, the men serving in American patriot regiments were "the descendants of Oliver Cromwell's army"—see Margaret Wheeler Willard, ed., *Letters on the American Revolution, 1774–1776* (Boston: Houghton Mifflin, 1925), 120.

24. For the report of closed churches, see Charles Inglis to Secretary of the SPG, October 31, 1776, in John Wolfe Lydekker, *The Life and Letters of Charles Inglis* (London: Society for Promoting Christian Knowledge, 1936), 160–61. See also Walter Herbert Stowe, "A Study in Conscience: Some Aspects of the Relations of the Clergy to the State," *HMPEC* 19 (1950): 305–7.

25. Samuel Tingley to SPG, March 5, 1782, quoted in Rhoden, *Revolutionary Anglicanism,* 108. See also Bruce E. Steiner, *Samuel Seabury, 1729–1796: A Study in the High Church Tradition* (Athens: Ohio University Press, 1971), 184–85; Stowe, "Study in Conscience," 306–7; Walter H. Stowe, "The Reverend Abraham Beach, D.D.," *HMPEC* 3 (1934): 91; Nelson R. Burr, *The Anglican Church in New Jersey* (Philadelphia: Church Historical Society, 1954), 373–415; Lorenzo Sabine, *Biographical Sketches of Loyalists of the American Revolution,* 2 vols. (Boston: Little, Brown, 1864), I: 154, 563–64; and Charles Mampoteng, "The New England Anglican Clergy in the American Revolution," *HMPEC* 9 (1940): 267–304.

26. Rhoden, *Revolutionary Anglicanism,* 113; and Stowe, "Reverend Abraham Beach," 90–91.

27. Holmes, "Episcopal Church and the American Revolution," 276–77. S.D. McConnell, *History of the American Episcopal Church, 1660–1915,* 11th ed. (Milwaukee: Morehouse, 1916), 210–11, provides a concise summary of the sufferings of loyalist clergy during the war.

28. Jonathan Boucher, *Reminiscences of an American Loyalist, 1738–1789,* ed. Jonathan Bouchier (Boston: Houghton Mifflin, 1925), 104–41.

29. Rhoden, *Revolutionary Anglicanism,* 107.

30. Quoted in Stowe, "Study in Conscience," 309.

31. Rhoden, *Revolutionary Anglicanism,* 88–89.

32. Henry F. May, *The Enlightenment in America* (New York: Oxford University Press, 1976), 70–72; and Holmes, "Episcopal Church and the American Revolution," 267–68, 278–79.

33. John K. Nelson, *A Blessed Company: Parishes, Parsons, and Parishioners in Anglican Virginia, 1690–1776* (Chapel Hill: University of North Carolina Press, 2001), 101–2.

34. Quoted in Rhoden, *Revolutionary Anglicanism,* 100.

35. For South Carolina, see Frederick Dalcho, *An Historical Account of the Protestant Episcopal Church in South Carolina* (Charleston: E. Thayer, 1820); and Brown, *King's Friends,* 227, 377 n. 67. For North Carolina, see Michael T. Malone, "Sketches of the Anglican Clergy Who Served in North Carolina during the Period 1765–1776," *HMPEC* 39 (1970): 399–429. And for Georgia, see Harold E. Davis, *The Fledgling Province: Social and Cultural Life in Colonial Georgia, 1733–1776* (Chapel Hill: University of North Carolina Press, 1976), 229–30; and Henry Thompson Malone, *The Episcopal Church in Georgia, 1733–1957* (Atlanta: Diocese of Georgia, 1960).

36. Charles A. Barker, *The Background of the Revolution in Maryland* (Hamden, Conn.: Archon, 1967), 359–67; Nelson, *American Tory,* 107–9; Brown, *King's Friends,* 172–73; and Rhoden, *Revolutionary Anglicanism,* 89.

37. Holmes, "Episcopal Church and the American Revolution," 280–83.

38. Quoted in Holmes, "Episcopal Church and the American Revolution," 289.

39. For a typical sermon by a patriot reinterpreting Romans 13, see David Griffith, "Passive Obedience Considered: In a Sermon Preached at Williamsburg, December 31st, 1775," *HMPEC* 44 (1975): 77–93.

40. Rhoden, *Revolutionary Anglicanism,* 108.

41. Holmes, "Episcopal Church and the American Revolution," 279.

42. William White, *Memoirs of the Protestant Episcopal Church in the United States of America* (Philadelphia: S. Potter, 1820), 61. See also Edgar L. Pennington, "The Anglican Clergy of Pennsylvania in the Revolution," *Pennsylvania Magazine of History and Biography* 63 (1939): 412–29; and Robert W. Prichard, *The Nature of Salvation: Theological Consensus in the Episcopal Church, 1801–73* (Urbana: University of Illinois Press, 1997), 8–9.

43. Edwin Scott Gaustad, *A Religious History of America,* new rev. ed. (San Francisco: Harper and Row, 1990), 115–20 (quotations on 120); *RHAP,* 382; and Butler, *Awash in a Sea of Faith,* 258–68.

44. Rhoden, *Revolutionary Anglicanism,* 118.

45. For estimates of the number of loyalist emigrants, see Brown, *King's Friends,* 250 (about 80,000); Morton Borden and Penn Borden, eds., *The American Tory* (Englewood Cliffs, N.J.: Prentice-Hall, 1972), 13 ("some 75,000 to 100,000"); Philip Carrington, *The Anglican Church in Canada: A History* (Toronto: Collins, 1963), 40–41 (47,000 in Canada); and Judith Fingard, *The Anglican Design in Loyalist Nova Scotia, 1783–1816* (London: Church Historical Society S.P.C.K., 1972), 39–43 (20,000 in Nova Scotia and Cape Breton).

46. Mark A. Noll, *A History of Christianity in the United States and Canada* (Grand

Rapids, Mich.: Eerdmans, 1992), 128–29; and Doll, *Revolution, Religion, and National Identity,* 229–35 (quotation on 235—emphasis added), 240–41.

47. Robert Bruce Mullin, *Episcopal Vision / American Reality: High Church Theology and Social Thought in Evangelical America* (New Haven: Yale University Press, 1986), 3–6; and *HPEC,* 123–24.

4

REORGANIZATION IN A NEW NATION: 1783–1811

The changed social and cultural circumstances of postrevolutionary America required religious groups that had once been closely linked to Great Britain to transform themselves into denominations capable of self-government in a new nation. At the same time that political and intellectual leaders were formulating constitutions for the federal government and for the individual states, clergy and laity in Christian denominations were active in the restructuring of their churches.[1] For example, English jurisdiction over American Catholicism was officially ended in June 1784, when John Carroll of Maryland was appointed superior of the church's mission in the United States. In December of that year, the Methodist Episcopal Church was similarly organized as a denomination distinct from the Church of England. Anglicans, too, were involved in a process of institutional reorganization. The situation was particularly difficult for them, however, because the war had brought their denomination to a point of almost total collapse. In a relatively brief period, Anglican parishes in America had lost thousands of members as many loyalists fled to Canada and England and patriots ashamed of the denomination's loyalist taint left the church. In the face of these losses, church leaders sought to refashion the denomination by preserving the distinctive theological and liturgical features of Anglicanism yet shedding those elements that had always bound it to the British government.

THE LEADERSHIP OF WILLIAM WHITE

The most influential figure in this complex process was William White, who, as rector of Christ Church, Philadelphia, occupied a highly favorable position in which to affect the future direction of his denomination. White himself had known and worked with many of the "founding fathers" of the United States—men like George Washington, Benjamin Franklin, Alexander Hamilton, and James Madison. What those leaders were accomplishing in the political sphere, he hoped to duplicate within the councils of his church.[2] In 1782 he published an important pamphlet, *The Case of the Episcopal Churches in the United States Considered,* in which he offered ideas about how his denomination might reconstitute itself after the Revolution. Although Anglicans in America had once been guided and supported by the bishop of London, the English crown, and the religious establishment in each colony, ecclesiastical authority now needed to be based entirely on voluntary associations. White proposed the creation of a three-tiered system of church government, with conventions composed of clergy and laity making decisions at each level (local, regional, and national). Although he expected that the new church would retain the historic order of bishop, priest, and deacon, White also stressed that its clerical leaders would have to exercise their powers in a democratic fashion.[3]

White was assisted in these organizational efforts by one of his former teachers, William Smith, who then served as a parish rector in Maryland. Beginning in 1780, Smith had convened gatherings of clergy and laity to reconstitute and regularize the functioning of the church in his state. The Maryland legislature responded to this initiative by granting title to properties formerly owned by the Church of England to Smith's synod. In 1783, Anglican conventions in both Maryland and Pennsylvania met and affirmed principles that White had proposed: the usefulness of a democratic form of church governance, the importance of sharing power equally between laity and clergy, and the necessity of organizing a convention to pass legislation and to oversee the church's business at the national level. The two state conventions also emphasized that worship in the "Protestant Episcopal Church" ought to conform as closely as possible to worship in the Church of England. In 1784, Episcopalians under White's leadership met, first in New Jersey in May and then five months later in New York. Delegates at those gatherings passed a series of resolutions similar to the ones adopted by the Maryland and Pennsylvania conventions, and they agreed to hold an initial meeting of the church's "general convention" in Philadelphia in September 1785.

Despite the progress that was made in 1783 and 1784, three critical questions about the future role of Episcopal bishops remained unanswered. First, as White was keenly aware, many of his fellow church members were strongly opposed to the concept of an episcopate. Americans had rid themselves of a king in 1776, and in the popular mind bishops not only were associated with the "immoderate power" wielded by kings but seemed to be fundamentally "anti-republican."[4] Second, the gentry who controlled parish affairs in the southern states had always resisted the involvement of English prelates in their churches. During the colonial period, in fact, laity in the South had openly opposed the introduction of a bishop, who of necessity would have curtailed the ecclesiastical powers they exercised. Third, even if Americans accepted the ministry of bishops in their churches, there was still one major impediment: no English prelate was likely to consecrate an American as bishop because that man would be legally incapable of taking the required oath of allegiance to the British king.

The majority of Anglican church leaders in America thought that forming a national denominational structure ought to precede the selection and consecration of a bishop, but they also understood the pressing need for new clergy to serve in the United States. Toward that end, the convention of the church in Maryland had dispatched two ministerial candidates—Mason Locke Weems and Edward Gantt Jr.—to England to seek ordination as priests. When they arrived in England in late 1782, however, they were stymied by their inability to swear allegiance to George III. As Weems and Gantt sat inactive in England, White's *Case* posited a solution to the predicament that Americans faced. White suggested that, as a temporary expedient, a presbyterian system might be instituted wherein three priests, rather than one bishop, would lay hands upon American ordinands, thus circumventing English bishops altogether. This practice had been employed in the earliest Christian communities, and Thomas Cranmer, Richard Hooker, and other leading Anglican divines had also recognized its theoretical validity.[5] Although White's pragmatic approach seemed sensible under the circumstances, this proposal soon occasioned the first major controversy within the still disunited Episcopal Church.

SAMUEL SEABURY AND THE HIGH CHURCH TRADITION

In contrast to White, high church Anglicans such as Samuel Seabury, a former SPG missionary in New York, believed that the episcopate was the foundation upon which any Christian organization had to be erected. In his eyes, bishops were part of the very essence of the church. Seabury asserted that the church, rather than being an association of religious individuals who had chosen to join together and organize themselves for fellowship and worship, had been "established by the Apostles, acting under the commission of Christ, and the direction of the Holy Ghost." Its framework, therefore, could not be "altered by any power on earth, nor indeed by an angel from heaven."[6] As successors of the apostles, bishops also represented one of the fundamental links to the first-century church. As Thomas Bradbury Chandler, one of Seabury's high church allies, complained, irresponsible people like White were ready to sacrifice "genuine Episcopacy . . . on the Altar of Ecclesiastical Republicanism"; if they were allowed to do that, the spiritual groundwork of the Anglican tradition in America would be irrevocably undermined.[7]

Deeply concerned about the strategy that White and Smith were pursuing in Pennsylvania and Maryland, a small group of Connecticut clergymen met secretly in the village of Woodbury in March 1783 to discuss the reorganization of the church in their state. They chose two priests as potential candidates for the episcopate: Jeremiah Leaming of New York and Samuel Seabury. Although Leaming did not accept his election, the strong-willed Seabury did. In June he set sail for England in search of three bishops—the minimum required by canon law—who would consecrate him as a bishop for America. When he reached London, he won the initial support of the archbishop of Canterbury and other officials, but two serious impediments prevented them from approving his consecration: first, he was unable to take an oath of allegiance to the king; and second, his election by a gathering of clergy, rather than by a state convention, meant that he did not have the necessary support of the *civil* government in Connecticut. Unable to circumvent the ecclesiastical system in which they operated (i.e., the right of the crown to exercise ultimate control over church affairs), the English bishops concluded that they had no warrant to authorize the consecration of an Anglican clergyman who lacked the sanction of his nation's civil authorities.[8]

After a year of unproductive negotiations with members of the English hierarchy, who advised him that only an act of Parliament would give them license to consecrate him, Seabury journeyed northward and met with bishops of the Episcopal Church of Scotland. Since Presbyterianism, not Anglicanism, was the legally established faith in Scotland, the bishops of the nonjuring Scottish Episcopal Church were free of the legal constraints imposed on English bishops, and they agreed to consecrate Seabury. Prior to that event, Seabury signed an agreement in which he not only acknowledged that the episcopate was a "sacred office . . . independent of all lay powers" but also promised to make every effort to have the liturgical practices and beliefs of the Episcopal Church of Scotland adopted by the American church.[9] Seabury's consecration took place in Aberdeen on November 14, 1784. In his sermon, John Skinner, one of the consecrators, emphasized that the true church, founded by Jesus Christ, existed as "a society entirely distinct by itself, without being incorporated into, or any way defended by the state."[10] Although the establishment of Christianity under the emperor Constantine in the fourth century had marred the church's original purity, the Episcopal clergy of Scotland and Connecticut were committed to restoring the church to its primitive state, neither protected by civil powers nor controlled in any way by laity.

Returning to the United States in the spring of 1785, Seabury started to organize his church by summoning a convocation of the clergy in Connecticut. At this August gathering, he ordained four candidates to the diaconate—the first American clergy ordained since the beginning of the Revolution. As word about the existence of an American bishop spread, many other prospective ordinands appealed to Seabury for assistance.[11] However, rapprochement between the two major factions in the church—Seabury's and White's—still seemed quite unlikely. Low church Episcopalians, who believed strongly in the importance of lay participation in the governance of the church, simply did not trust Seabury and his high church views about the prerogatives of clergy. As Americans, many of them also resented the fact that he received a pension from Great Britain for his services as the chaplain of a loyalist regiment. Further complicating the situation was the disapproval expressed by English church leaders about Seabury's consecration by schismatic bishops in Scotland. The presence of a bishop in Connecticut with Seabury's attitudes and credentials, therefore, complicated rather than resolved the organizational dilemmas that Anglicans were facing.[12]

A NEW CONSTITUTION AND A NEW PRAYER BOOK

In late September and early October of 1785, lay and clerical representatives from seven states (Delaware, Maryland, New Jersey, New York, Pennsylvania, South Carolina, and Virginia) met at Christ Church, Philadelphia, for the first General Convention of the Episcopal Church. The churches in North Carolina and Georgia were too weak to send delegates, and none attended from the three New England states (Connecticut, Massachusetts, and Rhode Island) because there were no provisions for Bishop Seabury to preside. In a 10-day meeting, the 24 lay representatives and 16 clergy under the leadership of William White and William Smith accomplished three major tasks:

1. They produced a draft version of the church's constitution. It was presbyterian in character and included a plan for triennial meetings of the General Convention with lay and clerical representatives attending from every state. The church in each state was also to have its own bishop, who in addition to his liturgical duties (ordaining clergy and confirming new members) would serve on an ex officio basis at meetings of the General Convention.

2. They drafted an American version of the 1662 *Book of Common Prayer* from which all references to the British sovereign were deleted. The committee in charge of the prayer book revision also made several decidedly liberal theological changes. They eliminated the Athanasian Creed, the Nicene Creed, and the phrase "He descended into Hell" in the Apostles' Creed; and in the baptismal service, they removed reference to the concept of spiritual regeneration as well as the mandatory use of the sign of the cross. (Because these theological modifications were intended to please evangelical Episcopalians, Seabury and his high church colleagues in New England deemed all of them unacceptable.)

3. They devised a plan to obtain the consecration of bishops from the Church of England. The convention sent a petition to the archbishops of Canterbury and York, asking them to support those in the United States who, professing "the same religious principles" as members of the Church of England, wished "to retain the venerable form of Episcopal government handed down to them . . . from the time of the Apostles."[13]

The General Convention met again in two sessions in 1786: at Philadelphia in June and at Wilmington, Delaware, four months later. Although some delegates at the first session attempted to have Seabury's consecration declared invalid, William White sponsored a somewhat more irenic proposal that recognized his episcopal orders but prevented him from exercising ecclesiastical authority outside of Connecticut.[14] At the second session, the convention received confirmation that its earlier petition to the Church of England had been successful, for Parliament had at last passed legislation that allowed the archbishops of Canterbury and York to consecrate candidates for the episcopate who were not British citizens. In response to this parliamentary action, the convention authorized Samuel Provoost, the rector of Trinity Church in New York, and White to travel to London, where on February 4, 1787, they were consecrated by four English bishops.

With the consecration of White and Provoost, Episcopalians had completed the initial stage of their denominational reorganization. By 1787, the church had three bishops as well as a proposed constitution and prayer book. Fundamental questions about church polity, however, still separated the leadership in the middle and southern states from Seabury and the clergy of New England. Was the Episcopal Church to be governed democratically, with clergy and laity sharing equal responsibility for its guidance, or did an "episcopal" church have to be under the direct authority and control of bishops? The inability to agree over the church's creeds also reflected a potentially serious theological division. If church members disagreed about the essentials of the Christian faith, the future unity of the denomination was in doubt. Given the circumstances that existed in 1787, Episcopalians in the United States might well have remained at odds, split perhaps into two separate denominations.[15]

Despite the gravity of the situation they faced, White and Seabury were eventually able to reach a compromise on the principles that divided them. The next General Convention assembled in 1789 in Philadelphia. White presided at the first session (July–August), and while no representatives from New England were present, Seabury contacted William Smith in an advance effort to promote unity. In response to Seabury's gesture, the convention quickly passed a resolution recognizing the legitimacy of his Scottish consecration. The first session of the 1789 convention also agreed to modify its own structure by creating a separate "House of Bishops." This arrangement not only provided the bishops with an assembly separate from the "House of Deputies," in which the convention's clerical and lay delegates met, but also gave them a partial veto over any action proposed by the deputies. This decision successfully addressed a concern raised both by the English consecrators of White and Provoost and by the New England clergy, who objected to the fact that American bishops lacked many of the prerogatives traditionally exercised by Anglican prelates. Like the United States Constitution, which was ratified during the same period, the constitution of the Episcopal Church was designed to reflect republican political ideals, especially the notion of a "mixed" government that balanced the competing interests of various political constituencies.[16]

In September 1789, at the beginning of its second session, the convention made further concessions to Seabury and the New Englanders. It increased the bishops' veto power over the House of Deputies (the proportion of deputies required to override a veto by the House of Bishops was raised from 60 to 80 percent), and it gave the bishops the right to originate (as well as to reject) legislation. Largely appeased by these decisions, Bishop Seabury and clerical deputies from Connecticut and Massachusetts then joined the convention as it completed its work. Delegates from all the states formally approved both the church's constitution and the body of laws known as the "canons." They also adopted a final version of the American *Book of Common Prayer* and made its use obligatory throughout the denomination. The 1789 prayer book incorporated material that some Episcopalians had earlier attempted to delete. The word "regeneration" was restored to the prayers in the baptismal service, and though clergy were given permission to omit the sign of the cross, that liturgical action was retained as an element within the rite of baptism. Finally, despite Seabury's reluctant assent to the removal of the Athanasian Creed, his high church faction was successful in incorporating both the Nicene Creed and the controversial reference to Christ's descent into hell in the Apostles' Creed into the new prayer book.

When the General Convention adjourned in October 1789, the various state churches (they were not called "dioceses" until 1838) had at last achieved a measure of organizational unity. However, full liturgical independence from England did not come until three years later. Out of deference to leaders of the Church of England, who remained concerned about the validity of Seabury's nonjuring Scottish orders, White and Provoost agreed not to join him in consecrating other bishops until a third American had been consecrated within the _English_ line of succession. This condition was met in 1790, when the archbishop of Canterbury and two other bishops consecrated James Madison as the first bishop of Virginia. Then, in 1792, Madison joined White, Provoost, and Seabury in consecrating Thomas John Claggett bishop of Maryland—an event that formally united the English and the Scottish episcopal lines in the United States.

ABSALOM JONES AND ST. THOMAS AFRICAN EPISCOPAL CHURCH

As white church leaders were reconstructing the institutional identity of Anglicanism after the Revolution, African Americans under the direction of Absalom Jones were similarly engaged in organizing what was not only the first black Episcopal parish but also the first black congregation of any denomination in the United States. Like his white counterparts, Jones greatly valued the ecclesiastical heritage of Anglicanism, and he recognized both the importance and the limitations of American democracy. As the first African American who served as a priest in the Episcopal Church, Jones's life and ministerial career also illustrate how the harsh realities of racial prejudice remained as strong in the churches as in other organizations in the young republic.[17]

Born a slave in Delaware, Jones was brought by his master to Philadelphia in 1762. Thanks to the influence of Quaker abolitionist sentiment in that city, he was able to obtain an education, and working diligently in his master's store, he eventually purchased his own freedom. By the mid-1780s, he was also a prominent member of the group of black worshippers who belonged to St. George's Methodist Church. Since John Wesley and the Methodists were officially opposed to slavery, St. George's attracted a significant number of African Americans, including the popular itinerant preacher Richard Allen. In 1787 Allen attempted to create a separate congregation for black Methodists, but when the white clergy of St. George's objected, he formulated another plan. Along with Jones, he organized the Free African Society as an independent association—technically not a church—that included black Philadelphians without regard to their denominational affiliation.[18]

While plans for the Free African Society went forward, Allen continued his ministry at St. George's. As the only black minister in the city, he drew so many African Americans to the church that whites began to have trouble finding seats. First, the parish's white leadership decided that black congregants would be allowed to sit only at the back and on the sides of the church building. Then, when the lack of space made that arrangement unsuitable, African Americans were told to sit by themselves in a new gallery constructed above the main floor. Before this seating plan could be put into operation, however, the church's black membership rebelled. One morning, when a white usher spotted Allen and Jones kneeling at a spot where they were not supposed to be, he tried to have them pulled to their feet in the middle of prayers. This precipitated a mass exodus of the church's black membership. This group soon found a temporary building and raised enough funds to ensure that they could continue to meet and hold services.

The Free African Society remained independent until 1794. After Allen left and founded Bethel Church (which later became the "mother" congregation of the African Methodist Episcopal Church), Jones assumed sole leadership of the society. Recognizing that most of its members wished to establish some official denominational ties, Jones encouraged them to vote on the issue of affiliation, and they elected to become Episcopalians rather than Methodists. Although Christ Church had started a ministry to African Americans in Philadelphia in 1758, the formality of Anglican worship, the paternalistic attitudes of the local aristocracy who belonged to the parish, and the seating restrictions that were placed on them had dissuaded black worshippers from joining the Church of England at that time. However, resentment at how African Americans had been treated by white Methodists at St. George's, as well as Jones's conservative nature and sense of formality, convinced the congregation of the value of joining the Episcopal Church.[19]

The parish adopted the name St. Thomas African Episcopal Church, and Jones was licensed by Bishop White to serve as its lay reader. However, because Jones did not know Greek or Latin—a prerequisite for ordination in the Episcopal Church—the parish had to petition the Pennsylvania diocesan convention to dispense with the language requirement and allow him to be ordained. Although the convention concurred with the parish's request, thus enabling Jones to be ordained a deacon (in 1795) and a priest (in 1804), this decision came at a high price. The convention ruled that, due to St. Thomas's "peculiar circumstances at present," it would not be entitled to the same privileges as other Episcopal parishes in the state, that is, being allowed to send a clergyman and elected lay representatives to the annual convention of the diocese. Whereas the members of the Pennsylvania convention of 1795 probably meant their decision to be only a temporary one, the restriction they placed on Jones's parish remained in effect long after his death in 1816. In fact, St. Thomas's was not allowed to participate fully in the life of its diocese until after the outbreak of the Civil War.[20]

AN UNCERTAIN FUTURE

In his study of the changes in Christianity in the United States in the late eighteenth and early nineteenth centuries, the historian Nathan Hatch observes that Americans living at that time straddled a boundary between two worlds—an older world, premised on attitudes reflecting deference, patronage, and respect for the established order, and a newer one, in which people considered themselves capable of thinking and acting on their own without reference to traditional authority.[21] The founders of the Episcopal Church certainly experienced the awkwardness of this position, for they faced the daunting task of preserving the distinctive heritage of Anglicanism while simultaneously transforming it into an "American" denomination. Although some lay Anglicans were prominent revolutionary leaders, the average American still regarded Anglicanism as fundamentally alien to the culture of their young nation. The polity of the Episcopal Church reflected American democratic ideals, but many elements of its worship—the archaic language of prayer, the aesthetic principles represented in liturgical forms, the use of the church year as a way of marking time, and the bodily actions of bowing and kneeling—continued to evoke the old-world traditions of hierarchy and subordination from which the colonies had declared their independence in 1776.[22]

Thus, in spite of the achievements of Episcopal leaders in restoring stability to their denominational affairs, the church's prospects at the end of the eighteenth century seemed uncertain—even dismal. In 1790, in a nation of four million people, the Episcopal Church had perhaps ten thousand adherents, and its growth over the next two decades proved to be extremely slow. In a country that was overwhelmingly rural, the denomination's strength lay in urban areas, principally among the middle and upper classes. The vast number of poorer folk, however, found the experiential faith of the Methodists and the Baptists far more appealing than the formal worship of the Episcopalians. Despite the desire of Absalom Jones and his congregation to join the Episcopal Church, black Christians, too, understood both the inherently egalitarian potential of the evangelical denominations and the elitist pretensions of Anglicanism.[23] Finally, anti-British feeling was increasing rather than abating, and it reached its peak during the War of 1812—a sentiment that worked against the rapid revival of American institutions closely identified with England.[24]

In the individual states, the status of the Episcopal Church seemed even more uncertain. New Jersey lacked a bishop until 1815, North Carolina till 1823, and Georgia till 1841; Massachusetts had a bishop for only 6 of the 22 years between 1789 and 1811.[25] In Virginia, less than 40 percent of the 107 Episcopal parishes that existed in 1784 were able to support ministers between 1802 and 1811. In 1802 the Virginia General Assembly declared that the denomination's colonial-era properties belonged to the state, and it authorized the sale of the church's glebe farms for public benefit—an action that led to the financial collapse of the diocese. In Maryland as well, half of the parishes remained vacant at the turn of the nineteenth century.[26] No delegation from North Carolina reached the General Convention until 1817, and after the death of Nathaniel Blount in 1816, the state had no Episcopal clergy at all.[27] In Georgia, Christ Church, Savannah, was the only parish still active in the 1790, and the state's Episcopalians were not represented at the General Convention until 1823.[28] After examining these circumstances, one modern-day commentator observed that the Episcopal Church more "closely resembled an executor settling the bankrupt estate of the old Anglican establishment than the heir of a rich and vital religious tradition."[29]

The church's theological position was equally unsettled at this time. Samuel Provoost and James Madison, the bishops of New York and Virginia respectively, were virtual deists who were highly suspicious of the historic creeds of Christianity. Samuel Seabury of Connecticut, on the other hand, was staunchly committed to retaining use of all the ancient creeds in worship; militant in his anti-Protestant views, he disliked both Calvinism and evangelical teachings on conversion. William White of Pennsylvania occupied a middle ground between the very extreme positions represented by his three episcopal colleagues. Yet despite his desire to attain a theological consensus within his denomination, he favored the adoption of a low church, rationalistic understanding of the church, not unlike Provoost's and Madison's views.[30]

Although religious interest in the United States was generally low in the early 1790s, a significant rise of enthusiasm did occur among segments of the Protestant population between 1795 and 1810—the beginnings of what came to be known as the Second Great Awakening. The leadership of the Episcopal Church, however, was little affected by this resurgence of spiritual zeal. Indeed, while Timothy Dwight, Congregational minister and president of Yale College, was stirring up a celebrated revival among students in New Haven in 1798, Samuel Provoost was whiling away his time translating the writings of Italian poet Torquato Tasso. The contrast between the evangelical vigor of the one clergyman and the intellectual languor of the bishop of New York graphically illustrates the troubled condition of the Episcopal Church at the end of the nineteenth century. Provoost, in fact, became convinced that the Anglican tradition in America would die out with the old colonial families. Disheartened and in poor health, he resigned his position in 1801 and retired to the country to study botany.[31]

NOTES

1. Robert T. Handy, *A History of the Churches in the United States and Canada* (New York: Oxford University Press, 1977), 145–46.

2. Charles C. Tiffany, *A History of the Protestant Episcopal Church in the United States of America,* 3rd ed. (New York: Scribner's, 1907), 299–300.

3. William White, "The Case of the Episcopal Churches in the United States Considered," in *DW,* 2–14. Frederick V. Mills Sr., *Bishops by Ballot: An Eighteenth-Century Ecclesiastical Revolution* (New York: Oxford University Press, 1978), 183–89, provides a useful summary of White's *Case* and of reactions to it. On White's achievement and

governing principles, see also the helpful précis provided by R. William Franklin in *SPCK,* 32–33; and Gregory A. Hotchkiss, "The Revolutionary William White and Democratic Catholicity," *AEH* 70 (March 2001): 40–74.

4. White, "Case of the Episcopal Churches," 8.

5. *Ibid.,* 10–11. American Methodists, still technically members of the Church of England, confronted a similar dilemma in 1784. John Wesley was very troubled that there were so few clergy, whether Anglican or Methodist, to administer the sacraments in America. Following the same logic as White, he recruited two other English priests, and styling themselves a "Primitive presbytery," they ordained three men. Wesley then authorized the new clergy to form themselves into a presbytery and to ordain other Methodist ministers as soon as they reached America—see Dee E. Andrews, *The Methodists and Revolutionary America, 1760–1800: The Shaping of an Evangelical Culture* (Princeton, N.J.: Princeton University Press, 2000), 65–67.

6. Quoted in Nancy L. Rhoden, *Revolutionary Anglicanism: The Colonial Church of England Clergy during the American Revolution* (New York: New York University Press, 1999), 139.

7. Quoted in Rhoden, *Revolutionary Anglicanism,* 140. See also Peter M. Doll, *Revolution, Religion, and National Identity: Imperial Anglicanism in British North America, 1745–1795* (Madison, N.J.: Fairleigh Dickinson University Press, 2000), 14–20.

8. Doll, *Revolution, Religion, and National Identity,* 221–22. Although the "Enabling Act" of August 1784 allowed Americans to be ordained to the diaconate and priesthood without swearing an oath of allegiance to the king (thus clearing the way for the ordination of Mason Weems and Edward Gantt Jr.), it made no provision for the consecration of bishops.

9. "Concordat of Bishop Seabury and the Nonjuring Scottish Bishops, His Consecrators, 1784," in *DW,* 15–16.

10. Quoted in Doll, *Revolution, Religion, and National Identity,* 227.

11. Describing himself as the "Bishop of All America," Seabury eventually ordained 26 clergymen, most of whom came from states other than Connecticut—see *HEC,* 89.

12. Bruce E. Steiner, *Samuel Seabury, 1729–1796: A Study in the High Church Tradition* (Athens: Ohio University Press, 1971), 167. See also *HEC,* 89–90, 95.

13. "To the Most Reverend and Right Reverend the Archbishops of Canterbury and York, and the Bishops of the Church of England, 1785," in *DW,* 22–23.

14. *HPEC,* 134.

15. *HEC,* 95.

16. *BHEC,* 54–56.

17. Harold T. Lewis, *Yet with a Steady Beat: The African American Struggle for Recognition in the Episcopal Church* (Valley Forge, Pa.: Trinity Press International, 1996), 27–30.

18. Carol V. R. George, *Segregated Sabbaths: Richard Allen and the Emergence of Independent Black Churches, 1760–1840* (New York: Oxford University Press, 1973), 40, 51.

19. *Ibid.,* 37–38, 52, 58.

20. George F. Bragg, *History of the Afro-American Group of the Episcopal Church* (Baltimore: Church Advocate Press, 1922), 59–68 (quotation on 63).

21. Nathan O. Hatch, "The Democratization of Christianity and the Character of American Politics," in *Religion and American Politics: From the Colonial Period to the 1980s,* ed. Mark A. Noll (New York: Oxford University Press, 1990), 93–94.

22. Robert Bruce Mullin, "Denominations as Bilingual Communities," in *Reimagining Denominationalism: Interpretive Essays,* ed. Robert Bruce Mullin and Russell E. Richey (New York: Oxford University Press, 1994), 167.

23. Nathan O. Hatch, *The Democratization of American Christianity* (New Haven: Yale University Press, 1989), 102–13.

24. Tiffany, *History of the Protestant Episcopal Church,* 385–87.

25. *BHEC,* 59.

26. Hatch, *Democratization of American Christianity,* 60.

27. Sarah McCulloh Lemmon, "Nathaniel Blount: Last Clergyman of the 'Old Church,' " *North Carolina Historical Review* 50 (1973): 363; and *HEC,* 97–98.

28. *HEC,* 97.

29. Ralph Morrow, quoted in Hatch, *Democratization of American Christianity,* 60.

30. Robert W. Prichard, *The Nature of Salvation: Theological Consensus in the Episcopal Church, 1801–73* (Urbana: University of Illinois Press, 1997), 11–12.

31. Mark A. Noll, *A History of Christianity in the United States and Canada* (Grand Rapids, Mich.: Eerdmans, 1992), 166–69; Robert Bruce Mullin, *Episcopal Vision / American Reality: High Church Theology and Social Thought in Evangelical America* (New Haven: Yale University Press, 1986), 3, 6, 24; and *MM,* 28.

5
UNITY, DIVERSITY, AND CONFLICT IN ANTEBELLUM AMERICA: 1811–1865

The first half of the nineteenth century was one of the most remarkable periods of institutional expansion in the history of American Christianity. Although formal membership in every major denomination declined precipitously after the Revolution, reaching all-time lows in the 1790s, the churches revived rapidly over the next three decades. Thanks to the revivals of the Second Great Awakening, populist leaders mounted vigorous campaigns not only to evangelize but also to reform the American people. Between 1780 and 1860, Baptists, Methodists, Presbyterians, Lutherans, and Roman Catholics all experienced gains that far surpassed the increase in the population as a whole, and important new religious movements such as the Disciples of Christ and the Mormons sprang into being. Following the war against Great Britain, a new spirit of egalitarianism allowed women and African Americans to assume positions of religious authority when—to the consternation of traditionalists—they were sometimes permitted to preach and to pray in public. As the French writer Alexis de Tocqueville noted following his tour of the United States in the early 1830s, religious institutions and beliefs played a far greater role in American society than anywhere else in the civilized world.[1]

Despite the success that most denominations enjoyed during the antebellum period, both the Episcopalians and the Congregationalists—the two religious bodies that had been legally established throughout the seventeenth and eighteenth centuries—experienced relatively slow growth, lagging behind the rise of the population as a whole.[2] In some ways, it was not surprising that these historic denominations underwent difficulties. The idea of a hierarchical, ordered society was then under attack, and in all areas of American life—politics, law, education, medicine, and religion—traditional elites faced severe challenges. Even Devereux Jarratt, who had once worked closely with Methodists in Virginia, lamented the leveling attitude of postrevolutionary America that was allegedly spawned by unlettered "tinkers and tailors, . . . and country mechanics of all kinds."[3] Confronted by the extraordinary religious enthusiasm and cultural ferment of the era of "the common man," Episcopalians struggled to adapt themselves as the social, theological, and liturgical sensibilities they valued fell more and more into disfavor.

THE HOBARTIAN SYNTHESIS

Although the Episcopal Church was virtually moribund during the first decade of the nineteenth century, the fortunes of the denomination began to improve markedly in the 1810s and 1820s with the emergence of a new generation of leaders who had no memories of the colonial Anglican establishment. The most important of these figures was John Henry Hobart, the bishop of New York, who was born a few months after the outbreak of hostilities with Great Britain. While studying for the ordained ministry under the tutelage of William White, he was introduced to and profoundly influenced by a number of high church Anglican writers, who emphasized the church's divine origins and the necessity of the historic episcopate.[4] In 1801 he was ordained to the priesthood and accepted a call to become assistant minister at Trinity Church, New York, where Benjamin Moore served both as rector and as bishop of the diocese. After Moore suffered an attack of paralysis in 1811, Hobart was elected assistant bishop of New York, thereby raising the high church party to a prominent position within the still-developing denomination.

High church advocates had traditionally viewed the time between the apostolic age of the first century and the rise of the papacy in the fifth century as the era when the church, tiny but pure, had most accurately reflected and upheld the teachings of the New Testament. This was the era, they said, when the core beliefs of Christianity had been articulated in the creeds and when the polity and essential liturgical practices of the church had been regularized. Relying on a static, almost fundamentalist approach to knowledge about the historical past, high church Anglicans grounded their faith both in the veracity of what they assumed had been taught in the patristic period and in the ability of the church to keep that theological heritage intact over the centuries. As Hobart declared at the opening service of the 1814 General Convention, Episcopalians should take pride in their adherence to "a system which, exhibiting the faith once delivered to the saints and bearing the stamp of apostolic authority, must be the best calculated . . . to extend in its purity the kingdom of the Redeemer, and to advance most effectually the salvation of man."[5] In his estimation, the Episcopal Church was not simply one among many American denominations; it was the true church that had been safeguarding the doctrine, ministry, and worship of apostolic Christianity for eighteen hundred years.[6]

Not surprisingly, Hobart's lofty image of the church set him at odds with other American Christians. These differences were most clearly revealed in debates about the meaning of the rite of baptism. One of the hallmarks of evangelical Protestantism was the belief that religious conversion involved the experience of divine grace, which was manifested publicly when a person sought to be baptized and performed acts of piety and benevolence. When speaking about baptism, evangelicals usually envisioned it as part of a conscious response to God's initiative in regenerating a believer's soul. For Hobart and high church Episcopalians, on the other hand, piety could not be separated from liturgical forms. Regeneration was necessarily grounded in the sacrament of baptism—an objective rite that was not dependent upon human emotions for its efficacy. Infants and young children became members of the church when they were baptized, and through a process of religious nurture and education, they gradually came to live as Christians. Although Hobart certainly agreed with his evangelical contemporaries about the importance of divine grace, repentance, and personal faith, he did not think those qualities were prerequisites for baptism; they were conveyed instead through participation in the ongoing life of the church.[7]

Hobart's ecclesiastical and theological views also provoked a lengthy controversy with other Episcopalians about their participation in interdenominational voluntary societies, which were organized to further the educational, missionary, and reform concerns of evangelical Protestants in antebellum America. Many of these societies were dedicated to the printing and distribution of the Bible. The Philadelphia Bible Society, for example, was organized in 1808, and in rapid succession state societies were formed in Connecticut, Massachusetts, New York, and New Jersey. Although prominent low church Episcopalians such as William White and New York judge William Jay participated enthusiastically in this movement, Hobart vigorously opposed it. He argued that, since the episcopate represented the defining characteristic of the church, involvement in "mixed societies" (i.e., organizations whose membership was drawn from a number of denominations) would inevitably undermine Episcopal uniqueness. Rather than working ecumenically with other Protestants, Hobart instead was involved in the founding of the New York Bible and Common Prayer Book Society, which was controlled by Episcopalians only. This society was committed to distributing copies of the prayer book and the Bible, for in Hobart's estimation, the biblical word could never be separated from the liturgical life of the church.[8]

As the historian Robert Bruce Mullin observes, Hobart's ecclesiology "not only set the method for . . . theology but also defined the scope" it took among his followers in the Episcopal Church. Hobart maintained that any question not explicitly discussed in the scriptures or in the councils of the early church was not worthy of consideration by church members. Underlying this belief was a radical separation of the concerns of the church from those of the state. The church was a *spiritual* institution, he insisted, and it had no interest in political matters. Such beliefs were sometimes taken to absurd extremes, however. For example, when De Witt Clinton, the governor of New York, died suddenly in 1828, Hobart refused to allow his clergy to speak about his death from their pulpits. The eulogizing of a public figure, he announced, threatened the independence of the church from political affairs. Later in the nineteenth century, high church Episcopalians also distanced themselves from important social issues such as abolitionism and temperance reform. True to Hobart's principles, they argued that, because those movements were unknown in the patristic age, they were essentially irrelevant to the church's mission.[9]

The moral as well as practical shortcomings of this system notwithstanding, the Episcopal Church grew steadily throughout New York State during the years in which Hobart was bishop. Hobart's emphasis on historic continuity and ecclesiastical order doubtless provided a sense of stability during a period of social and religious upheaval. Since one-quarter of all Episcopal clergy at this time were converts from other denominations, it is likely that the Hobartian synthesis also attracted ministerial candidates who were troubled by the subjective nature of faith and worship in American religion during the heyday of evangelical revivalism. The claim that their church had never wavered from the teachings of the apostles gave Episcopal clergy an unshakeable sense of certainty about the authority they exercised.[10]

THE EVANGELICAL PARTY

Although the organization of the Methodist Episcopal Church in 1784 had siphoned off a significant portion of the evangelical constituency that existed within colonial Anglicanism, a sizeable evangelical party surfaced again in the Episcopal Church at the beginning of the nineteenth century. Episcopal evangelical vitality was centered in the mid-Atlantic states, especially in Virginia, where the once-dying church was revived by the efforts of clergy such as William Holland Wilmer, William Meade, and Richard Channing Moore, the bishop of the diocese. The "Eastern diocese" (all the New England states except Connecticut) also was an area where evangelicals were strong throughout the lengthy episcopate (1811–1843) of Alexander Viets Griswold. Episcopal evangelicals tended to come from the nation's social elite rather than from the middle and working classes to which Methodists and Baptists usually belonged. The Episcopal Church thus offered influential, well-educated, and financially secure men and women an opportunity to experience a religion of the heart.[11]

Like many American evangelicals, Alexander Griswold experienced a religious crisis at a key moment in his adult life. Although his preaching had once been cold and formalistic, he believed his consecration to the episcopate had inspired "more serious thoughts of duty as a minister of Christ." Starting in 1812, Griswold also became aware of "the appearance of increased seriousness" among his parishioners at St. Michael's Church in Bristol, Rhode Island, where he served as rector. "There was little or no laughing, or merry salutation among the people" at the end of Sunday services, he noticed. Instead, the people left the church "silent and thoughtful," and some even "were anxious to know what they should do to be saved."[12] Griswold cared far more about encouraging spiritual earnestness than about promoting the claims of the Episcopal Church. He thus welcomed interaction with members of other denominations who shared his views on the necessity of conversion and personal piety. He was very critical of high church

Episcopalians, however, and he thought their passion for defending "the distinctive principles" of Anglicanism tended to lead to the "neglect of the essential doctrines of Christ."[13]

In one of the earliest formal statements of evangelical ideas—an influential devotional book entitled *The Episcopal Manual* (1815)—William Wilmer, then rector of St. Paul's Church, Alexandria, Virginia, reiterated Griswold's criticism and concerns. As Wilmer observed in his introduction, Episcopalians often found themselves torn between two dangerous extremes. Some members of the church felt tempted to "undervalue her order and her institutions," while others, by focusing only on "externals," permitted "the spirit and essence of the gospel to evaporate." He hoped his manual would enable Episcopalians to achieve a balanced spirituality—one that not only upheld "the dignity of our institutions, and the excellence of our doctrine and worship," but also inculcated "that power of godliness, without which all our doings are nothing worth."[14]

Wilmer was also the founding editor of the *Washington Theological Repertory*, a journal that vigorously espoused the platform of the evangelical party during the 1820s. According to an article in the magazine's inaugural issue, "the indispensable prerequisites for admission into Heaven" consisted of assent to six doctrinal principles: (1) the perfection of God; (2) the sinfulness of humankind; (3) salvation from sin through the atonement of Jesus Christ; (4) the power of God's grace to convert the human heart; (5) the necessity of a personal religious experience; and (6) the responsibility to conform one's life to the Christian gospel.[15] Evangelical theology began with the premise that, since human nature was utterly corrupted by sin, men and women were incapable of achieving salvation through their own efforts and had to rely entirely on divine grace. Although high church clergy often charged the evangelicals with being more Calvinist than Anglican in their theological orientation, evangelicals retorted that their faith was not derived from the teachings of John Calvin but from the Bible. As such, their beliefs represented "the common doctrine of all the reformed churches" and were "interwoven with the very rudiments of Christianity."[16]

Despite their intellectual debates with high church colleagues about the value and meaning of particular doctrines, evangelicals believed that true Christianity was concerned primarily with the heart, not the mind—with personal holiness rather than with rational assent to theological propositions. To gain entrance into God's kingdom, the sinner needed to experience a new birth—a sense of the heart "strangely warmed," to use John Wesley's well-known phrase. Conversion was the axis around which a Christian's spiritual life revolved, and salvation depended upon a person's ability to *feel* and respond to the transforming power of divine love. While some Christians might argue that their souls had been saved by formalistic means such as baptism or attendance at church, evangelicals trusted in a vital, heartfelt faith as evidence of their salvation. Alexander Griswold expressed these sentiments poetically in the hymn "Holy Father, Great Creator," which he composed in 1835: "Holy spirit, Sanctifier, / Come with unction from above. / Touch our hearts with sacred fire, / Fill them with the Savior's love." As the final verses of Griswold's hymn suggested, Christians ought continually to pray, "Great Jehovah, great Jehovah, / Form our *hearts* and make them thine."[17]

EARLY MISSIONARY ACTIVITY

Thanks to the religious enthusiasm generated by the Second Great Awakening and the rapid expansion of the United States westward across the Appalachian mountains, a tremendous rise of interest in missionary activity prevailed among American Protestants in the early nineteenth century. Although missionary work had once been dependent upon the initiative of nearby congregations and their members, distances were becoming too great and new settlements too numerous to be managed by individual pastors and evangelists. In 1810, only one in seven Americans lived west of the Appalachians, but by 1820 the proportion had risen to one in four. Between 1816 and 1821, moreover, five new western states— Alabama, Illinois, Indiana, Mississippi, and Missouri—had entered the Union.

In response to tremendous growth on the American frontier, Presbyterian, Baptist, and Methodist evangelists began to organize "camp meetings"—mass outdoor religious gatherings that drew thousands of people together over the course of several days. The famed camp meeting at Cane Ridge, Kentucky, in August 1801, for example, attracted over ten thousand worshippers (a crowd approximately five times the population of the largest city in Kentucky at that time), and an estimated three thousand participants were said to have experienced conversion. Despite the immediate successes that the camp meetings achieved, church leaders were interested not simply in converting individuals but in founding and strengthening congregations. All of the major Protestant denominations also formed voluntary societies during this period to support a more systematic approach to their evangelistic efforts. The first of these associations, the New York Missionary Society, was founded by Presbyterian, Baptist, and Dutch Reformed church members in 1796, and various denominations in other states quickly followed suit. Concern for domestic missions soon sparked similar interest in the foreign mission field. In 1810 a group of Congregational clergy in Connecticut and Massachusetts organized the American Board of Commissioners for Foreign Missions, which dispatched the first group of American missionaries to Asia two years later.

Still disorganized at the outset of the nineteenth century, the Episcopal Church was relatively slow to join this expansionist movement. Although the 1792 General Convention had appointed a committee to discuss the support of Episcopal missionaries on the frontier, the church took no action at the national level. In 1808, Bishops White of Pennsylvania and Claggett of Maryland circulated a pastoral letter reminding Episcopalians of their obligation to evangelize the West, but again little was actually done. Church members in South Carolina took the first concrete steps for their denomination when they founded the Society for the Advancement of Christianity. The goal of the society was to sponsor missionaries, to aid candidates for the ordained ministry, and to distribute Bibles, prayer books, and religious tracts throughout the state. South Carolina Episcopalians also organized the Protestant Episcopal Missionary Society of Charleston (1819), which supported missionaries in remote western areas of the state, and the Protestant Episcopal Female Domestic Missionary Society (1821), which provided religious instruction for the city's poor residents. These efforts led to the creation of other new organizations. Philadelphia Episcopalians, for example, formed a Society for the Advancement of Christianity in 1812, and two of its clerical missionaries, Jackson Kemper and William Augustus Muhlenberg, were active in the creation of parishes in central and western Pennsylvania. As Muhlenberg reported with dismay in 1816, some Episcopalians in frontier areas had been forced to join the Methodist Episcopal Church because no clergy of their own denomination were available to minister to them.[18]

Evangelicals under the leadership of Alexander Griswold eventually took the initiative in organizing a national missionary program for the Episcopal Church. In 1815 Griswold began corresponding with Josiah Pratt, a representative of the Church Missionary Society (CMS), which had been founded by Anglican evangelicals in the late eighteenth century. Pratt advised Griswold that the most effective way of encouraging U.S. evangelism would be to form a voluntary society similar to the CMS—a project to which his organization would gladly contribute funds.[19] Pratt's proposal helped stimulate the 1820 General Convention to create the Domestic and Foreign Missionary Society (DFMS) of the Protestant Episcopal Church, which any dues-paying Episcopalian could join. Although many evangelicals did so, a shortage of both funds and missionaries handicapped the DFMS, and despite modest success on the domestic front, foreign efforts were virtually nonexistent during the first 15 years of the society's existence.[20]

When it became clear that the voluntary system had been a failure, several members of the DFMS board of directors proposed an alternative plan. According to Charles Pettit McIlvaine, the bishop of Ohio, it was the responsibility of the *whole* church to proclaim God's word to the world. "The Church is a Missionary Society, in its grand design, in the spirit and object of its Divine Founder," McIlvaine argued. As a consequence, "every member of the Church, by the vows of that baptism in which he was consecrated to Christ . . . , stands committed and pledged to take part . . . in promoting the Gospel to the ends of the earth."[21] Although McIlvaine was himself an evangelical, he rejected the cooperative, interdenominational model originally favored by other evangelical Episcopalians. Joining with high church leaders such as George Washington Doane of New Jersey, he instead urged the adoption of a separate denominational approach to missionary work. This proposal was approved by the DFMS board of directors and officially adopted at the 1835 General Convention: henceforth, the Episcopal Church was itself a missionary society to which every Episcopalian by virtue of his or her baptism belonged. In addition, the convention appointed two committees (one for domestic mission, one for evangelism overseas) with the assumption that high churchmen would direct the domestic field while evangelicals would control the foreign one—an agreement that evangelicals later regretted as high church influence spread quickly throughout newly organized dioceses in the Midwest during the mid-nineteenth century.[22]

The 1835 General Convention also authorized the consecration of missionary bishops to serve in areas where the Episcopal Church was not yet formally established. Rather than having to form a diocese and then elect a bishop, Episcopalians in America's western territories were to receive the ministrations of a bishop, chosen by General Convention, who would lead them in evangelism and in the founding of parishes. (This policy was consistent with the views of high church Episcopalians, who believed that bishops, as heirs of the apostles, had a divinely ordained duty to lead Christian missionary endeavors.) Jackson Kemper, a high church Episcopalian who had studied for the ordained ministry under John Henry Hobart, was chosen as the denomination's first missionary bishop in 1835, and his responsibilities eventually included the states of Indiana, Iowa, Kansas, Minnesota, Missouri, Nebraska, and Wisconsin. As George Washington Doane proclaimed at Kemper's consecration service, "You are to go out, in the Saviour's name, *the first Missionary Bishop* of this Church. Going with the office, go in the spirit, of an Apostle . . . [and] preach the gospel of salvation to a ruined world."[23] Three years later Leonidas Polk of Tennessee was consecrated as the church's second missionary bishop, with responsibility for Arkansas and the Indian Territory (later Oklahoma), and in 1844 William Jones Boone of South Carolina was appointed to serve in China as the denomination's first foreign missionary bishop.

THE RISE OF TRACTARIANISM

Ever since the sixteenth century, when the ties between the English church and the papacy were severed, Catholic and Protestant elements within the Anglican Church had had an uneasy relationship. The tensions became particularly pronounced in the mid-1830s with the emergence of the Tractarian (or Oxford) movement in England. After reaching the United States in the late 1830s, Tractarianism quickly intensified ongoing debates between evangelical and high church Episcopalians about matters of belief and ritual.

The Tractarian movement began in July 1833 at Oxford, when John Keble, Anglican priest and professor at Oriel College, delivered a sermon on "national apostasy," in which he lamented the state of religious affairs in Great Britain. Keble was especially distressed by what he regarded as the unwarranted interference of Parliament in ecclesiastical matters, and he called for the Church of England to be free of state control. Keble's address encouraged a group of priests and scholars with like-minded high church views (Edward Bouverie Pusey and John Henry Newman being the most notable) to band together for mutual support at Oxford. Publishing a series of 90 *Tracts for the Times* between 1833 and 1841, these men sought to reclaim the catholic theological and devotional heritage of their church. However, in contrast to the traditional high church, which cast the church mainly in static terms as a preserver of apostolic order and authority, Tractarianism was primarily concerned about fostering piety and a sense of holiness. Thus, as several historians have observed, the Tractarians' emphasis on religious *feeling* had a great deal in common both with the contemporary Romantic movement and with evangelical Protestantism.[24] Whatever their intentions, the leaders of the Oxford movement were roundly condemned by mainstream Anglicans, and in the 1840s Newman and several other disillusioned Tractarians left the Church of England and became Roman Catholics.

The appearance of the first *Tracts* edition in the United States in 1839 caused an outcry among evangelical Episcopalians. Charles McIlvaine, for instance, charged that the Tractarians' theological assumptions were "downright Popery."[25] Tractarianism, he declared, represented "a systematic abandonment of the vital and distinguishing principles of the Protestant faith, and a systematic adoption of that very root and heart of Romanism, whence has issued . . . all its ramified corruptions and deformities." As such, Tractarian theology was contrary both to traditional Anglican teaching and to the scriptural doctrine of justification by faith.[26] Since fears of Roman Catholicism peaked among American Protestants in the late 1830s and early 1840s, McIlvaine's ideas were well received not simply in the Episcopal Church but in other Protestant denominations as well.

Conflicts involving Episcopal clergy sympathetic to the Oxford movement also shook the church during this period. One of these controversies concerned Arthur Carey, a student at the General Theological Seminary in New York, where interest in Tractarian teaching was especially high.[27] When the time arrived for him to be ordained in 1843, his evangelical rector, who doubted Carey's orthodoxy, refused to give the necessary consent. Although Carey was eventually ordained by Benjamin Tredwell Onderdonk, the bishop of New York, two out of the eight clergy who examined him prior to his ordination officially disassociated themselves from the bishop's actions. In addition, several evangelical bishops in other dioceses questioned their colleague's decision because they believed Carey's Tractarian views were tantamount to Roman Catholicism and ought to have disqualified him from being ordained in the Episcopal Church.

As a result of the Carey case, evangelicals and even some traditional high churchmen began to fear that their denomination had come under attack from the forces of obscurantism and ignorance. According to John Henry Hopkins, the bishop of Vermont, the Tractarians' fundamental error was believing that "the visible Church is the reservoir of all spiritual influences; that grace is given by her and *only through her instrumentality*."[28] Although evangelicals attempted to have the General Convention of 1844 condemn the alleged errors of Tractarianism, they failed to convince the House of Deputies that Anglican theological standards were actually threatened by the movement. The House of Bishops, on the other hand, did issue a pastoral letter affirming Episcopalians' belief in the Protestant doctrine of justification by faith and roundly condemning "the blasphemous doctrine of Transubstantiation and the abominable idolatries" of the Roman Catholic mass.[29] Evangelicals were also successful in bringing two pro-Tractarian bishops, Benjamin Onderdonk and his brother, Henry Ustick Onderdonk of Pennsylvania, to trial on charges of immorality and intemperance. Each man was eventually convicted and suspended from his episcopal duties.[30]

Whereas the cases of Carey and the two Onderdonks reveal as much about the prejudices of nineteenth-century evangelicals as they do about the attractions of Roman Catholicism to high church Episcopalians, one prominent American Tractarian leader voluntarily renounced his membership in the Episcopal Church during this period of controversy. Beginning in 1844, Levi Silliman Ives, the bishop of North Carolina, came under scrutiny from evangelicals in his diocese who accused him of favoring such Catholic customs as the making the sign of the cross in worship and prayer. Ives responded to criticism by reaffirming his commitment to the devotional reforms introduced by the Tractarians. "Churches are beginning to assume a more Church-like appearance—to be more in keeping with their divine and holy purpose," he said, while "the reverence of both clergy and people is manifestly increasing" because of the Tractarian influence.[31]

Ives's response infuriated evangelicals, and the dispute over Catholic influences within the Episcopal Church soon became a matter for public debate throughout North Carolina. Evangelical writers also whipped up anti-Catholic hysteria by linking Tractarianism to predatory sexual behavior. Focusing on the practice of auricular confession, which Ives was encouraging within his diocese, evangelicals charged that it allowed lascivious priests to use the intimacy of the confessional as a means of seducing vulnerable female penitents.[32] Such venomous attacks eventually took their toll on Ives. After being granted a leave of absence for travel in 1852, he wrote to members of his diocese from Italy and announced his conversion to Roman Catholicism—an event that further demonstrated to evangelicals the dangers inherent in permitting clergy with Tractarian views to minister in the Episcopal Church.[33]

SISTERHOODS AND WOMEN'S RELIGIOUS ORDERS

One of the most significant long-term consequences of the spread of Tractarian influences was the revival of the monastic tradition both in England and in the United States in the 1840s. Because women seeking full-time involvement in the life and work of the church had been allowed few options prior to the nineteenth century, it is not surprising that religious orders for women were the first ones organized. Edward Bouverie Pusey, a leading figure in the Oxford movement, was instrumental in promoting this trend, which began when he received the profession of English churchwoman Marion Hughes in 1841. True to the reform-minded religious temper of the time, these Anglican sisterhoods were oriented far more to charitable than to contemplative pursuits, and the women who joined them generally dedicated themselves to practical activities such as teaching, nursing, reforming prostitutes, and offering other forms of social ministry.[34]

While clergymen were usually responsible for the founding of sisterhoods in England, women led the way in the United States. According to Anne Ayres, who founded the first American order (the Sisterhood of the Holy Communion), there was a pressing need for religiously committed women to aid "the miserable young vagrants in our streets, in the thousand wretched houses within view of our comfortable dwellings, in our prisons, our penitentiaries, our hospitals." Constituting "a household united by their mutual love to Christ," a "true Christian sisterhood" could put the talents of Episcopalians to good use, she thought, in rescuing the degraded from their misery.[35] Ayres gained the support of William Augustus Muhlenberg, rector of the Church of the Holy Communion in New York, and after making her own personal commitment to religious service in 1845, she formally organized the new sisterhood at his parish in 1852.

Ayres's order initiated a number of social service programs that were later imitated in other locations. Inspired by the Lutheran order of nursing deaconesses founded at Kaiserswerth in Germany in 1836, the sisters of the Holy Communion were also among the pioneers of the nursing profession in the United States. The order opened a 17-bed infirmary in New York in 1853, and five years later, Ayres assisted Muhlenberg in the establishment of St. Luke's Hospital. In keeping with its Lutheran model and out of deference to the Protestant sensibilities of most Episcopalians, who viewed sisterhoods as suspiciously "Roman," Ayres's society was not strictly speaking a religious order. Its members were only required to make a simple statement of commitment, usually for a three-year term rather than for life; each woman wore plain clothes, not a habit; and there was no strict devotional or liturgical schedule, but each day revolved around the performance of service-oriented tasks.[36]

Several other Episcopal women's orders were formed during the second half of the nineteenth century. The Community of St. Mary, for example, was founded in New York in 1865. Organized by Harriet Starr Cannon and a few women who wished to belong to a religious order that was more traditional than Ayres's sisterhood, the Community of St. Mary required women to take lifetime vows, to wear a habit, and to follow a regular schedule of daily worship. Cannon emphasized the need to combine prayer and service, and her sisters dedicated themselves to the performance of works of mercy that included nursing and education. In 1878, during the catastrophic yellow fever epidemic in Memphis, Tennessee, members of the order chose to care for the sick and dying rather than leave the city. Their sacrificial devotion gained national attention and helped pave the way for far greater acceptance of the idea of sisterhoods in the Episcopal Church.[37]

Historian Mary Sudman Donovan argues that religious sisterhoods were critical in expanding the vocational opportunities of American women in the nineteenth century. Living in ordered communities enabled the women to support one another in the demands of their calling, giving them "the strength to break custom, to walk where it was unacceptable for a lone woman to walk, to accept a task society felt a genteel lady ought to shun." The early sisterhoods, Donovan believes, also represented "the radical edge of ministry" in the church at that time. The orders helped provide for the needs of society's least-valued members—prostitutes, handicapped children, and homeless women— and they were conduits of charity through which alms collected in Episcopal parishes were dispensed to the poor. As teachers, the sisters also nurtured a social conscience in many of the upper-class young women whom they instructed. In sum, the sisterhoods identified important new areas of lay ministry, trained workers to serve in those fields, and provided meaningful roles in which Episcopal women could serve.[38]

THE MUHLENBERG MEMORIAL

At the 1853 General Convention, a group of clergy under the leadership of William Augustus Muhlenberg presented a "memorial" (petition) to the House of Bishops in which they raised questions about the relationship of the Episcopal Church to what they termed "the great moral and social necessities" of their day.[39] Muhlenberg was then a highly respected figure in the denomination, known for his broad-minded spirit and for his opposition to narrow sectarianism. Although he was a steadfast member of the evangelical party, he had not only supported the work of Anne Ayres's sisterhood but also introduced liturgical innovations such as weekly (rather than quarterly) celebrations of the Eucharist and the placing of candles on the altar at his parish in New York.[40] Muhlenberg and his colleagues feared that internal dissension caused by the ongoing conflict between high church and evangelical Episcopalians was starting to hinder the mission of their denomination. The Episcopal Church was socially too narrow, geographically too restricted, and liturgically too rigid, they suggested, to be effective in the critical evangelistic task of "preaching and dispensing the Gospel to all sorts and conditions of men." They sought to create instead a "system, broader and more comprehensive than . . . the Protestant Episcopal Church as it now is, . . . providing for as much freedom in opinion, discipline and worship as is compatible with the essential faith and order of the Gospel."[41]

Muhlenberg's group advanced two distinct reform proposals—one liturgical and the other ecumenical. First, they suggested changes that would introduce greater flexibility in the church's worship. At this time, worship on a typical Sunday morning consisted of the prayer book services of Morning Prayer, Litany, and Ante-Communion (the initial part of the Eucharist through the sermon), all read successively in one sitting. Clergy, Muhlenberg believed, needed to have the freedom to alter this liturgy as well as to use biblical lessons and prayers that were not available in the official 1789 *Book of Common Prayer.* The petitioners feared that, because of the manner in which Episcopal worship was conducted, it had little appeal either to "the low classes of our population" or to people who desired a liturgy that was aesthetically and emotionally appealing. Second, they urged the recruitment of clergy in other denominations, "sound in the faith" and "able ministers of the New Testament," who would be willing to be ordained by Episcopal bishops but who would not be required to follow all the distinctive "prescriptions and customs" of the Episcopal Church. An ecumenical gesture like that would not only extend the reach of the Episcopal Church but also represent a major step toward effecting the union of all Protestants in the United States.[42]

The House of Bishops responded by appointing a special commission of five

Ecumenism

bishops to study the document and to present a report at the next General Convention. They knew that the memorial mainly reflected the concerns of Episcopal evangelicals, who for many years had been seeking greater liturgical flexibility in order to encourage more effective evangelism, especially on the frontier. Muhlenberg's plan also resonated with the evangelicals' desire for the unification of American Protestantism within an episcopal framework. High church clergy resisted the proposal, however, and argued that only a more determined expression of Anglican distinctiveness would truly further the spread of the gospel in the United States.[43]

The commission's 1856 report criticized the rigid organization and missionary failures of the Episcopal Church and urged a number of practical reforms: greater variety in worship services, acceptance of extemporaneous preaching (instead of the usual practice of reading from a manuscript), encouragement of the ministry of women in sisterhoods, greater attention to the religious instruction of children, and promotion of Christian unity.[44] Unfortunately, those suggestions were vigorously opposed by many members of the House of Deputies, who were profoundly disturbed by the bishops' eagerness for change. As a result of the deputies' intransigence, discussion of Muhlenberg's memorial was effectively dropped after the 1859 General Convention.[45]

THE EARLY MINISTRY OF ALEXANDER CRUMMELL

In his pathbreaking study, *The Souls of Black Folk* (1903), W. E. B. Du Bois devoted a chapter to the life and ministry of Episcopal priest Alexander Crummell. Both a scholar and an activist, Du Bois felt special affinity for Crummell. Not only had Du Bois's grandfather been active on the vestry of one of Crummell's parishes, but Du Bois himself was devoted to the same ideals of racial uplift and intellectual achievement in which Crummell had believed. Talented and combative, Crummell was a major figure in debates over race, education, and culture in the United States, and he was unquestionably one of the most important Episcopalians of the nineteenth century.[46]

Crummell grew up in New York City, where his family belonged to St. Philip's Church, founded in 1819 under the leadership of Peter Williams Jr. The second African American ordained to the Episcopal priesthood, Williams encouraged Crummell to seek ordination. When Crummell applied for admission to General Theological Seminary, however, Benjamin Onderdonk, the bishop of New York, blocked his application on the grounds that it was not suitable to have an African American enrolled at the seminary. Despite feeling humiliated by Onderdonk's undisguised racism, Crummell remained persistent, and he was eventually accepted as a candidate for the priesthood by Alexander Griswold of the Eastern diocese. During the 1840s, Crummell served in pastoral roles at small black congregations in New Haven, Providence, Philadelphia, and New York. He also became involved in the antislavery movement, but discouraged by the refusal of most white Episcopalians to support that cause, he sought the assistance of more sympathetic church leaders in England instead. Anglican evangelicals had been instrumental in the outlawing of slavery in the British empire earlier in the century, and they fully endorsed Crummell's argument about the scandalous ways in which the gospel had been compromised by slaveholding American Christians.[47]

Cognizant of the difficulties inherent in continuing to serve in the United States, Crummell sought and was able to obtain a teaching position as an Episcopal missionary in Liberia, the newly independent West African nation organized as a haven for ex-slaves from the United States. Despite his initial opposition to the colonization of freed slaves, Crummell soon became an advocate of black nationalism in Africa. Unfortunately, this stance placed him at odds with John Payne, the missionary bishop of the Episcopal Church in Liberia. Whereas Payne and other whites wished to evangelize, not to empower, the people of Africa, Crummell envisioned the enterprise as an experiment in nation building and sought to free the Liberian church from the control of white Americans like Payne.[48] After several years of devoted but ultimately frustrating service, Crummell's school was virtually bankrupt, and in 1861 he was forced to return to the United States.

Crummell continued to work both with white supporters of the colonization movement and with the Liberian government to publicize the idea of black nationhood in Africa. In a series of speeches delivered in 1861 and 1862, for example, he sought to convince American audiences that Liberia was advancing inexorably toward civilization and prosperity. With the outbreak of the Civil War, moreover, the fortunes of U.S. blacks had started to improve dramatically. Crummell argued that, despite the harshness of slavery and racial prejudice, America had trained blacks well in the ways of Western civilization. As "God's *chosen* messengers to the valley of the Niger and its far interior," African Americans were now being called out of bondage to participate in the social and cultural "regeneration" of their ancestral homeland.[49] Wholeheartedly committed to this mission in Africa, Crummell hoped that Liberia would quickly become (in the words of one historian) "a sort of black Victorian England."[50] Like English-speaking white philanthropists, Crummell believed in the supremacy of European culture. Unlike his white contemporaries, however, he was confident of the ability of African Americans to appropriate that culture and with it to foster "the evangelization and enlightenment of heathen Africa."[51]

SLAVERY AND THE CIVIL WAR

In marked contrast to Crummell's optimistic perspective on black emancipation and advancement during the initial stages of the Civil War, the outbreak of hostilities was viewed with great ambivalence by most white Episcopalians. Despite the fact that the controversy over slavery had split the Presbyterian, Methodist, and Baptist churches along sectional lines in the antebellum period, the national leaders of the Episcopal Church attempted to keep their distance from the political and military crisis that tore their nation apart in 1861. As the great Boston preacher Phillips Brooks commented at that time, it was farcical to observe the "shilly-shallying" of his fellow Episcopalians, who seemed unsure "whether there was a war going on or not, and whether if there was it would be safe for them to say so."[52] The Civil War challenged the institutional fabric of Anglicanism in America. Like the American Revolution, it revealed how estranged many of the church's clerical leaders were from the mainstream.

Although the institution of slavery existed, stable and unquestioned, in all parts of the United States at the close of the eighteenth century, various intellectual, social, and economic factors led both to its abolition in the North and to its expansion in the South over the first decades of the nineteenth century. By the 1830s, most members of the southern upper and middle classes were, if not slaveholders themselves, related by blood or marriage to slaveholders. Among church people, a significant percentage of the slaveholding population in the South were Episcopalians, and two of the largest slaveholders in the country—Leonidas Polk of Louisiana and Stephen Elliott of Georgia—were Episcopal bishops. In the 1820s and 1830s, moreover, a principled defense of slavery on religious grounds began to emerge in the churches. To counter the jibes of antislavery advocates, apologists for the South's "peculiar institution" asserted that slavery was not a moral or political evil (as abolitionists claimed) but a blessing for master and slave alike. Slavery had clearly been sanctioned in biblical times, its proponents argued, and in modern times it had become a "great missionary institution—one arranged by God," which empowered Christians in Europe and America to rescue the souls of thousands of Africans from heathenism.[53] In addition, because of the providential nature of American slavery, Christian masters and mistresses claimed that they bore a weighty responsibility for the education and evangelization of the Africans they owned.[54]

Despite its obvious usefulness to whites in the South, the religious defense of slavery was by no means strictly southern in origin.[55] In fact, many of its assumptions dovetailed neatly with the social ideas of high church Episcopalians in the North. Whereas the evangelical reform impulse of the Second Great Awakening helped give birth to abolitionism in the 1830s, several of the high church party's key concerns—its emphasis on the church's ancient, spiritual roots; its concomitant indifference to secular and political affairs; and its general disdain for individualism and moral perfectionism—predisposed significant numbers of Episcopal clergy to regard anyone who condemned slavery with suspicion. Two clergymen in the North were particularly outspoken in this regard: New York priest Samuel Seabury (grandson and namesake of the church's first bishop), who straightforwardly endorsed slavery in his *American Slavery . . . Justified by the Law of Nature* (1861); and John Henry Hopkins, the bishop of Vermont, whose *Bible View of Slavery* (1861) not only affirmed the legitimacy of slaveholding but also supported the right of the southern states to secede from the Union in its defense.[56] Although a few evangelical Episcopalians, such as New York judge William Jay, condemned both the inherent sinfulness of slaveholding and clergy like Seabury and Hopkins for being its "reckless and unblushing champions," most white church members considered slavery, even if morally suspect, to be no more eradicable than poverty or drunkenness.[57]

When hostilities began in earnest in the summer of 1861, the vast majority of individual Episcopalians patriotically supported the war effort of their nation. They enlisted as soldiers and as chaplains; they visited and nursed the troops; they distributed Bibles and spiritual reading in army camps; and they prayed both for military victory and for the safety of their loved ones in battle. Two factors, however, tended to make the involvement of southern white Episcopalians in the conflict more extreme than that of northerners. First, whites in the South faced the potential destruction of their society and its economy, and they clearly had more to lose if the Confederacy was defeated. Second, the evangelical party was relatively strong in the South, especially in key areas such as Virginia. For that reason, the apolitical attitudes fostered by high church theology had little sway over the thinking of the average southern Episcopalian. Thus, when Stephen Elliott declared from his pulpit at the outset of the war that southern Christians needed to take up arms and resist "the infidel and rationalistic principles which are . . . substituting a gospel of the stars and stripes for the gospel of Jesus Christ," he expressed a view—both practical and religious—with which most white evangelicals in his region agreed.[58]

After the secession of the southern states and the formation of the Confederate States of America, Episcopal leaders in the South organized a new church body. In a pastoral letter to members of his diocese in January 1861, Leonidas Polk explained that because their state had withdrawn from the federal Union a few weeks before, that action had effectively removed Louisiana Episcopalians from the jurisdiction of the church in the United States. Despite wishing to remain on good terms with U.S. Episcopalians, Polk emphasized that it was necessary for southern Episcopalians to "follow our Nationality." Just as American Anglicans had formally separated from the Church of England at the conclusion of the Revolution, so Episcopalians in the Confederacy needed to create their own national church in 1861.[59]

Following Polk's advice, Episcopal leaders held preliminary gatherings and eventually established the Protestant Episcopal Church in the Confederate States of America—a denomination whose constitution, canon laws, prayer book, and organization almost exactly mirrored those of the church in the United States. After the Confederate Episcopal Church held its first General Council (the term chosen instead of "General Convention") in November 1862, delegates at the meeting released a statement enunciating the principles that guided their work. Among the themes they emphasized was slavery's crucial role in the moral and religious elevation of the people of Africa. Although hindered for many years by the "hateful and infidel pestilence" of abolitionism, Confederate Episcopalians maintained, white southerners finally had the freedom to make slavery into the evangelistic instrument that God had ordained it to be. The church had a responsibility, they said, both to preach the gospel faithfully to enslaved Africans and to ensure that slaveholders viewed the people they owned as "not merely so much property, but . . . a sacred trust" conferred on them by God.[60]

White Episcopalians in the North, on the other hand, were decidedly more circumspect in endorsing the Union cause than their colleagues in the South were about speaking on the Confederate war effort. The Civil War had been raging for more than a year when the General Convention assembled in October 1862. Although that meeting occurred soon after the momentous Union victory at Antietam and Abraham Lincoln's subsequent release of the Emancipation Proclamation, neither the House of Bishops nor the House of Deputies believed it wise to comment on those events. There were understandable reasons for this reticence. Bishops on both sides of the conflict had been friends before the outbreak of fighting and continued to pray for one another in spite of their wartime separation. Moreover, Episcopal leaders in slaveholding border states such as Maryland, who felt the special strain of trying to keep the pro-northern and pro-southern factions in their dioceses ecclesiastically united, insisted on distinguishing between the support they offered the Union as *private* citizens and their political neutrality as officials of the *church*. And while evangelicals (e.g., Charles Pettit McIlvaine of Ohio) were strongly antislavery and pro-Union, high church clergymen (e.g., John Henry Hopkins of Vermont) saw the war against slavery as a continuation of the same dubious moral crusade they had been opposing since the 1830s. Thus, the 1862 General Convention attempted to speak as diplomatically as possible on the war: condemning the Confederate rebellion in traditional theological and biblical terms but reserving comment both on the politically divisive issue of abolitionism and on the creation of the new Confederate denomination. As the bishops remarked in their pastoral letter about the conflict, "to hate rebellion, so uncaused, is duty; but to hate those engaged therein, is the opposite of Christian duty."[61]

With the defeat of the Confederate armies and the emancipation of four million African Americans in the spring of 1865, white Episcopalians again confronted a severe ecclesiastical crisis. Although the failure of Confederate nationhood theoretically meant the end of the Confederate Episcopal Church, church leaders in the South were not at all sure they wished to return to their former denomination. However, because of the conciliatory efforts of John Henry Hopkins (then the presiding bishop), Henry C. Lay, the bishop of Arkansas, and Thomas Atkinson, the bishop of North Carolina, were encouraged to attend the October 1865 General Convention. The southern bishops were generally well received by the clergy and laity in attendance. Despite the efforts of a few members of the House of Deputies to pass a resolution offering thanks for Union victory in the war, the assembly followed Hopkins's irenic approach and adopted a statement simply thanking God for the return of peace and the prospective restoration of unity within the church. This response so pleased Atkinson and Lay that they quickly wrote other southern bishops, praising northerners for carefully avoiding subjects—namely, military defeat and the destruction of slavery—that "might give us pain."[62] As a result, when the second General Council of the Confederate Episcopal Church met in November 1865, the denomination resolved that every southern diocese was free

to resume its former status within the church in the United States, thereby officially terminating its existence.

Unlike white Episcopalians, African American Episcopalians did not find harmony in the denomination after the war. Between 1865 and 1870, thousands of
African Americans in the South left the Episcopal church and other white-
controlled denominations to which they had been compelled to belong while
enslaved. Although white church leaders seemed astounded by what the bishop
of Louisiana called "the strange defection of this people from our fold," most
black Episcopalians simply wished to escape from the racial paternalism and
coercion that were adjuncts of the gospel once preached to them by slaveholders.[63]
Concerned about this trend and about the rapid decline of membership in some
southern dioceses, the 1865 General Convention established a "Protestant Episcopal Freedman's Commission," giving it an evangelistic mandate to recapture
the African Americans who had deserted the Episcopal Church at the time of
emancipation. Since the clergy and laypeople who worked for this organization
were no less paternalistic in their views about black potential than most other
white Episcopalians, the commission enjoyed only minimal success, and it was
forced to disband in 1878.[64]

NOTES

1. Mark A. Noll, *A History of Christianity in the United States and Canada* (Grand
Rapids, Mich.: Eerdmans, 1992), 163–64; Jon Butler, *Awash in a Sea of Faith: Christianizing the American People* (Cambridge: Harvard University Press, 1990), 268–70; and
Nathan O. Hatch, *The Democratization of American Christianity* (New Haven: Yale University Press, 1989), 3–5.

2. Butler, *Awash in a Sea of Faith,* 270.

3. Quoted in Hatch, *Democratization of American Christianity,* 21–23 (quotation on
21).

4. Robert Bruce Mullin, *Episcopal Vision / American Reality: High Church Theology
and Social Thought in Evangelical America* (New Haven: Yale University Press, 1986),
18–22. Personal factors also affected Hobart's ecclesiastical views: in 1800 he married
Mary Chandler, daughter of Thomas Bradbury Chandler, one of the great high church
leaders of colonial Anglicanism.

5. John Henry Hobart, "The Origin, the General Character, and the Present Situation
of the Protestant Episcopal Church in the United States of America, 1814," in *DW,* 55.

6. Hobart, "Origin, the General Character," 47; and Mullin, *Episcopal Vision / American Reality,* 41–42, 66–71.

7. Robert W. Prichard, *The Nature of Salvation: Theological Consensus in the Episcopal Church, 1801–73* (Urbana: University of Illinois Press, 1997), 22, 87–89; and Mullin, *Episcopal Vision / American Reality,* 61–66, 72–74.

8. Diana Hochstedt Butler, *Standing against the Whirlwind: Evangelical Episcopalians
in Nineteenth-Century America* (New York: Oxford University Press, 1995), 43–44, 46–47;
and Mullin, *Episcopal Vision / American Reality,* 50–58.

9. Mullin, *Episcopal Vision / American Reality,* 70 (source of quotation), 86–90.

10. *Ibid.,* 91–94.

11. Butler, *Standing against the Whirlwind,* 4–15.

12. Quoted in *MM,* 37.

13. Quoted in Butler, *Standing against the Whirlwind,* 15.

14. William Holland Wilmer, *The Episcopal Manual* (1815), quoted in *MM,* 60.

15. "Prospectus," *Washington Theological Repertory* (1819), quoted in Butler, *Standing against the Whirlwind,* 29.

16. "Editorial," *Washington Theological Repertory* (1821), quoted in Butler, *Standing against the Whirlwind,* 29.

17. *The Hymnal 1982,* hymn 368 (emphasis added). See also Butler, *Standing against the Whirlwind,* 32–34.

18. *HPEC,* 194–97.

19. *MM,* 124–25.

20. Butler, *Standing against the Whirlwind,* 76.

21. Charles Pettit McIlvaine, "The Missionary Character and Duty of the Church" (1835), quoted in Butler, *Standing against the Whirlwind,* 77.

22. *HPEC,* 217.

23. George Washington Doane, "The Missionary Bishop, September 25, 1835," in *DW,* 119.

24. Owen Chadwick, ed., *The Mind of the Oxford Movement* (Stanford, Calif.: Stanford University Press, 1960), 11; and G.C. Faber, *Oxford Apostles: A Character Study of the Oxford Movement* (Harmondsworth, U.K.: Penguin, 1954), 134–35.

25. Charles Pettit McIlvaine, "The Oxford Tracts" (1839), quoted in Butler, *Standing against the Whirlwind,* 103.

26. Charles Pettit McIlvaine, "Oxford Divinity Compared, 1841," in *DW,* 57.

27. The idea of establishing a national or "general" seminary for the theological training of clergy was adopted at the 1817 General Convention. Through the efforts of John Henry Hobart, the school was eventually opened in New York in 1822, thus becoming the first seminary of the Episcopal Church.

28. Quoted in *HPEC,* 238.

29. Quoted in *HPEC,* 240.

30. For background on Henry Onderdonk, see David L. Holmes, "The Making of the Bishop of Pennsylvania, 1826–1827," *HMPEC* 41 (1972): 225–62 and 42 (1973): 171–97.

31. L. S. Ives, *A Pastoral Letter Addressed to the Clergy and Laity of His Diocese* (1849), quoted in Richard Rankin, *Ambivalent Churchmen and Evangelical Churchwomen: The Religion of the Episcopal Elite in North Carolina, 1800–1860* (Columbia: University of South Carolina Press, 1993), 160.

32. Rankin, *Ambivalent Churchmen and Evangelical Churchwomen,* 162.

33. *HPEC,* 244–45.

34. Sheridan Gilley, "The Church of England in the Nineteenth Century," in *A History of Religion in Britain: Practice and Belief from Pre-Roman Times to the Present,* ed. Sheridan Gilley and W. J. Sheils (Oxford: Blackwell, 1994), 298.

35. Anne Ayres, *Evangelical Sisterhoods* (1867), quoted in *DC,* 29.

36. *DC,* 31–37.

37. Rima Lunin Schultz, "Woman's Work and Woman's Calling in the Episcopal Church: Chicago, 1880–1989," in *Episcopal Women: Gender, Spirituality, and Commitment in an American Mainline Denomination,* ed. Catherine M. Prelinger (New York: Oxford University Press, 1992), 38; and *DC,* 37–42. In contrast to the women's orders, monastic institutions for men were not only fewer in number but also later in organiza-

82   THE EPISCOPALIANS

tion—the first being the establishment of an American branch of the English Society of St. John the Evangelist in Boston in 1872.

38. *DC,* 50–51 (quotations on 50).

39. "Muhlenberg Memorial, 1853," in *DW,* 209.

40. *HEC,* 150–51.

41. "Muhlenberg Memorial, 1853," in *DW,* 209–10.

42. Mullin, *Episcopal Vision / American Reality,* 181–82; and "Muhlenberg Memorial, 1853," in *DW,* 209–10 (source of quotations).

43. Butler, *Standing against the Whirlwind,* 140–41.

44. "Preliminary Report on the Memorial, 1856," in *DW,* 212–24.

45. *HAEC,* 287–88.

46. W. E. B. Du Bois, *The Souls of Black Folk* (Chicago: A. C. McClurg, 1903), 215–27; Wilson Jeremiah Moses, *Alexander Crummell: A Study of Civilization and Discontent* (Amherst: University of Massachusetts Press, 1992), 30; and J. R. Oldfield, "Introduction," in *Civilization and Black Progress: Selected Writings of Alexander Crummell on the South,* ed. J. R. Oldfield (Charlottesville: University Press of Virginia, 1995), 2.

47. Carl R. Stockton, "Conflict among Evangelical Brothers: Anglo-American Churchmen and the Slavery Controversy, 1848–1853," *AEH* 62 (1993): 509–11.

48. Oldfield, "Introduction," 7.

49. Alexander Crummell, "The Progress and Prospects of the Republic of Liberia" (1861), in *Destiny and Race: Selected Writings, 1840–1898,* ed. Wilson Jeremiah Moses (Amherst: University of Massachusetts Press, 1992), 165–66, 173–74 (quotation on 174).

50. Oldfield, "Introduction," 9.

51. Crummell, "Progress and Prospects of the Republic of Liberia," 174.

52. Quoted in Alexander V. G. Allen, *Life and Letters of Phillips Brooks,* vol. 1 (New York: E. P. Dutton, 1901), 428.

53. Stephen Elliott, quoted in Janet Duitsman Cornelius, *Slave Missions and the Black Church in the Antebellum South* (Columbia: University of South Carolina Press, 1999), 185.

54. George W. Freeman, "The Rights and Duties of Slave Holders, November 27, 1836," in *DW,* 187.

55. See, for example, Larry E. Tise, *Proslavery: A History of the Defense of Slavery in America, 1701–1840* (Athens: University of Georgia Press, 1987).

56. Mullin, *Episcopal Vision / American Reality,* 111–13, 198–99, 206–11.

57. William Jay, *Miscellaneous Writings on Slavery* (1853), quoted in Butler, *Standing against the Whirlwind,* 149; and S. D. McConnell, *History of the American Episcopal Church, 1600–1915,* 11th ed. (Milwaukee: Morehouse, 1916), 360–63.

58. Stephen Elliott, *The Silver Trumpets of the Sanctuary* (1861), quoted in James W. Silver, *Confederate Morale and Church Propaganda* (1957; reprint, New York: Norton, 1967), 45–46.

59. Leonidas Polk, "Pastoral Letter of Bishop Leonidas Polk, January 30, 1861," in *DW,* 157–58. Polk himself, who had been trained as a soldier at West Point before entering the ordained ministry, took a leave of absence from his bishop's post and accepted a general's commission in the Confederate army. Although he intended to return to his diocese when the war was over, he was killed in battle in 1864.

60. "Pastoral Letter of House of Bishops, Protestant Episcopal Church in the Confederate States of America, November 22, 1862," in *DW,* 164–73 (quotations on 170).

61. "Pastoral Letter of the House of Bishops, Protestant Episcopal Church, 1862," in

DW, 158–64 (quotation on 164); McConnell, *History of the American Episcopal Church,* 261–69; and Mullin, *Episcopal Vision / American Reality,* 201–5.

62. Thomas Atkinson and Henry C. Lay, quoted in DuBose Murphy, "The Spirit of a Primitive Fellowship: The Reunion of the Church," *HMPEC* 17 (1948): 446.

63. Joseph Wilmer, quoted in Hodding Carter and Betty Werlein Carter, *So Great a Good: A History of the Episcopal Church in Louisiana and of Christ Church Cathedral, 1805–1955* (Sewanee, Tenn.: University Press, 1955), 154; and William E. Montgomery, *Under Their Own Vine and Fig Tree: The African-American Church in the South, 1865–1900* (Baton Rouge: Louisiana State University Press, 1993), 126–27.

64. H. Peers Brewer, "The Protestant Episcopal Freedman's Commission, 1865–1878," *HMPEC* 26 (1957): 361–81; and J. Carleton Hayden, "After the War: The Mission and Growth of the Episcopal Church among Blacks in the South, 1865–1877," *HMPEC* 42 (1973): 403–27. One of the lasting contributions made by the church commission was the founding of several educational institutions (most notably, St. Augustine's College in Raleigh, North Carolina) for African Americans.

6
SOCIAL AND INTELLECTUAL CHALLENGES: 1865–1918

In the five decades between the end of the Civil War and the beginning of World War I, Episcopalians and other Americans witnessed tremendous changes in their society. During this period, the United States, once a predominantly agricultural nation, was transformed into a manufacturing one, and by the early twentieth century the center of the country's population had shifted from rural villages to cities. Between 1860 and 1900, approximately fourteen million immigrants, the majority coming from southern and eastern Europe, entered the United States. Most of them (as well as thousands of African Americans migrating from the South) flooded into urban areas in the Northeast and Midwest. These cities soon harbored masses of people—Roman Catholics, Jews, and Eastern Orthodox— who lived wholly outside the world of the Protestant churches. In addition to the social dilemmas associated with such demographic upheavals, theological challenges raised by the expansion of scientific knowledge forced Protestant church leaders to reconcile traditional biblical teachings with new ideas about natural selection and evolution.[1]

Although the Episcopal Church had sometimes seemed estranged from the social and religious culture of antebellum America, it flourished institutionally in the decades after the Civil War. Holding influential and powerful positions, Episcopalians were often at the forefront of economic and intellectual change, while significant numbers of wealthy Americans were attracted to the stability of a denomination that still represented English customs and ecclesiastical traditions. Because of the lingering ideals of Anglican establishmentarianism, Episcopal leaders also remained committed to the principle that the church had a responsibility to strengthen and unite its society. Thus, out of a desire to alleviate suffering and to minimize disorder, Episcopalians initiated some of the most important institutional expressions of the social gospel movement in the United States.[2]

THE BROAD CHURCH MOVEMENT

Reacting against the strident tone that so often marked the relationship between low church evangelicals and high church Tractarians, a third church party emerged as a force within Anglicanism in the mid-nineteenth century. In contrast to the moralistic individualism of the evangelicals and the narrow ecclesiasticism of the Tractarians, the new "broad church" party stressed the importance of tolerance, comprehensiveness, and rationality. The term "broad church" was first used by clergy in the Church of England in the early 1850s to indicate the type of theological milieu they wished to encourage—a church "not High or Low, but Broad," as one English priest said.[3] This movement represented the Anglican version of the "modernist impulse," which so profoundly influenced European and American religious bodies in the late nineteenth century. Like modernist thinkers in other denominations, the Episcopal broad church party believed in both the adaptation of religious ideas to contemporary culture and the progress of human society toward realization of the kingdom of God.[4]

The greatest of the first generation of broad church leaders was English priest Frederick Denison Maurice. A highly independent, anti-dogmatic thinker, Maurice was deprived of his professorship at King's College, London, in 1853 for denying the doctrine of the eternal punishment of sinners in hell. Along with Charles Kingsley, he also popularized the idea of social Christianity. Emphasizing the importance of the incarnation and the unity of society under the fatherhood of God, Maurice sought to apply Jesus' religious teachings to everyday economic and political affairs. Another early expression of broad church principles appeared in the controversial collection of articles entitled *Essays and Reviews,* published in 1860. Although roundly condemned by evangelicals and Tractarians alike, the small group of English clergy who contributed to that work called into question such beliefs as the existence of miracles and eternal damnation, and they argued that the Bible should be studied freely and critically "like any other book."[5]

As had happened earlier in the century with Tractarianism, the broad church movement first appeared in the Church of England but then caught the attention of Episcopalians in the United States. Phillips Brooks, who served prominently in the church in Boston, first as the rector of Trinity Church and later as the bishop of Massachusetts, was the broad church party's leading American spokesperson from the 1870s through the early 1890s. Brooks had been raised within the Episcopal evangelical tradition, but according to his biographer Alexander V. G. Allen (himself a broad churchman), he began to feel uncomfortable with many of its theological positions by the time of the Civil War. Evangelicals tended not only to be dogmatic but also to distrust the intellect, Allen contended, "as though its existence were rather a dangerous thing to the . . . Christian faith." Brooks was especially troubled by his classroom experiences as a student at the Virginia Theological Seminary in Alexandria, which had been founded by evangelical Episcopalians in the 1820s. The teachers at that seminary, he claimed, believed that a man needed to renounce all intellectual speculation and inquiry if he wanted to be an effective preacher.[6]

Brooks and other clergy who supported the broad church movement organized a series of yearly conferences for the discussion of key issues relating to the life of the church. Alexander H. Vinton, an evangelical who had once been Brooks's rector at St. Paul's Church in Boston, presided at the first meeting of these "church congresses" in 1874. The Episcopalians who formulated the church congress idea believed that ordinary ecclesiastical conventions, both diocesan and national, usually did not address crucial questions about the church's mission but too easily became sidetracked by liturgical and bureaucratic minutiae. They sought to foster instead both an appreciation of the life of the mind and the expression of a variety of viewpoints within their denomination.[7]

At the 1874 meeting of the church congress, for example, a priest with liberal theological views spoke on the importance of tolerating divergent doctrinal opinions, while a high church priest countered with a paper advocating clear limits on what Episcopalians might teach and believe. Invitations to speak were also extended to people engaged in various special ministries in the church. Thus, 1875 congress participants included William Welsh, a layman who served as head of the Congressional Board of Indian Commissioners; Thomas Gallaudet, a priest who was the leading figure in the church's ministry among the deaf; Henry Benjamin Whipple, the bishop of Minnesota, who was active in the mission to American Indians; and Samuel Isaac Joseph Schereschewsky, the missionary bishop of Shanghai. Although harshly criticized by some diehard conservatives, who denounced "Episcopal Unitarians, who with the Prayer Book in hand teach views directly opposed it," broad church Episcopalians continued to sponsor meetings of the church congresses through the mid-1930s.[8]

The general openness of Episcopalians to intellectual inquiry helped them avert some of the worst doctrinal controversies that divided other Protestant denominations in this period. One of the most widely publicized heresy trials in American history led to the suspension of the noted Old Testament scholar Charles Augustus Briggs from the Presbyterian ministry in 1893. After he was expelled from the Presbyterian Church, Briggs found a home in the Episcopal Church, and he was eventually ordained an Episcopal priest. Briggs was especially impressed by the ability of the Anglican tradition to overcome inherent tensions between its Protestant and Catholic elements. He believed that, as the most theologically inclusive religious body in the United States, the Episcopal Church one day might not only absorb all the other Protestant denominations but also bridge the even broader gulf separating Protestantism from Roman Catholicism.[9]

Despite Briggs's praise, the Episcopal Church was not entirely free of doctrinal disputes and charges of heresy against its most outspoken broad church leaders. For instance, when Phillips Brooks was elected bishop of Massachusetts in 1891, a few high church clergy in other dioceses attempted unsuccessfully to block his consecration. That same year, Howard MacQuery, a rector in Canton, Ohio, was suspended from the ordained ministry for denying the doctrine of the Virgin Birth in a book he wrote about evolution. Another significant heresy trial took place in 1906, when Algernon Sidney Crapsey, rector of St. Andrew's Church in Rochester, New York, was condemned for his heterodox views. Well known for his commitment to ministry among the urban poor, Crapsey had published a series of lectures entitled *Religion and Politics* (1905), in which he argued that Christians should become involved in social reform. While that position was not particularly controversial, he also maintained that Episcopalians needed to rethink their belief in such ancient doctrines as the Trinity and the Virgin Birth. Convicted of heresy in the diocese of Western New York, Crapsey resigned from his position as a priest but continued to write and lecture on religious subjects.[10]

Thanks to his position as a renowned preacher at a fashionable parish in Boston, Phillips Brooks was the unquestioned standard-bearer of the broad church movement of his generation. Brooks's intellectual contributions, however, were far less impressive than those of William Porcher DuBose, who labored in comparative obscurity for nearly five decades as a professor of theology at the University of the South in Sewanee, Tennessee.[11] DuBose had been an officer in the Confederate army during the Civil War, and after being wounded in battle and captured by the Union forces, he experienced a religious conversion. Ordained a priest in 1866, he served for a short period in a parish in South Carolina before going to "Sewanee" in 1871 as chaplain of the newly opened college, where he remained until his death in 1918.

Central to DuBose's thinking—and true to the theological modernism of the late nineteenth century—was his desire to interpret the relationship between God and creation. How was belief in divine transcendence to be reconciled with the incarnation and with the continuing presence of God in the church and in the world? Speaking at the 1878 meeting of the church congress, DuBose argued that there could be "no manifestation . . . of the Divine except in and through the human."[12] Knowledge of God and theological reflection, therefore, were closely related to the everyday experiences of ordinary men and women. Moreover, because of his belief in a gradual process of theological discovery, DuBose did not think that any single denomination was capable of fully grasping the gospel on its own. He was ecumenical in outlook and distrustful of those who claimed to be the only Christians who possessed the truth.[13] Finally, DuBose accepted the theory of biological evolution and linked it to Christian teaching about the incarnation. As he wrote in 1907, "there is no real break between the natural and the supernatural"—"earth and heaven are one continuous life" in Jesus Christ, through whom God's spirit is progressively communicated to humanity.[14]

THE CHICAGO-LAMBETH QUADRILATERAL

As the thinking of Briggs and DuBose suggests, broad church Episcopalians were generally receptive to the idea of reuniting with other Christian denominations. Connected with this theoretical interest in ecumenism, however, was the assumption that the Episcopal Church was the religious body best suited to direct the formation of a united "Church for Americans."[15] Proponents of church union pointed out that the Episcopal Church had many superior qualities: it was a strong national denomination that, unlike the Presbyterians, Methodists, Baptists, and Lutherans, was not officially divided on either sectional or ethnic lines; it was solidly established in cities; its membership included a disproportionately high number of the nation's corporate and governmental leaders; it upheld a traditional, though not theologically rigid faith; and its polity, democratic as well as hierarchical, reflected both ancient and modern sensibilities.

Although a few Episcopalians advanced proposals touting American Protestant unity prior to the Civil War (e.g., William Augustus Muhlenberg's 1853 memorial), the most noteworthy contribution was advanced by William Reed Huntington later in the century. Then rector of a parish in Worcester, Massachusetts, Huntington preached to his congregation in January 1870 about the ecumenical strategy he thought Episcopalians should adopt. According to Huntington, Anglican beliefs could be reduced to four key tenets: (1) the Old and New Testaments as the church's authoritative scriptures; (2) the primitive creeds (Apostles' and Nicene) as the church's rule of faith; (3) the two sacraments (baptism and the Eucharist) ordained by Jesus himself as the essential acts of Christian worship; and (4) the episcopate as the cornerstone of church government. To be successful in conversations with other denominations, Episcopalians needed to emphasize these central elements of the Anglican tradition. Huntington hoped that his "quadrilateral" would not only avoid the complexities of such Reformation statements as the Thirty-nine Articles, the Augsburg Confession, and the Westminster Confession but also appeal to many liberal-minded Roman Catholics in the United States.[16]

Writing in the optimistic spirit that inspired many Americans in the northern states immediately after the Civil War, Huntington stated that national unity—ecclesiastical as well as political—was both desirable and achievable. He elaborated further on his theological and social views in his two major works, *The Church-Idea: An Essay towards Unity* (1870) and *A National Church* (1898). Huntington did not think that either Roman Catholicism or Protestantism was capable of embodying the full richness of Christianity. While he admitted that all Christians were unlikely to be subsumed into one already existing religious organization, he still believed that the Episcopal Church represented the most effective means of unity. It not only embodied the fundamentals of Christian faith and practice but also, unlike Roman Catholicism, was racially and ethnically pure—the "Church of the Anglo-Saxon . . . a plant of hardy growth, . . . true as steel."[17] Because of these theological and cultural advantages, Huntington argued that his denomination had a critical role to play in shaping the country's moral character. He also encouraged Episcopalians to think of themselves as the de facto "national church" or "Church of America"—a hegemonic vision eventually incarnated in the construction of the National Cathedral in Washington, D.C., at the beginning of the twentieth century.[18]

As a result of Huntington's efforts, the House of Bishops of the Episcopal Church officially adopted his four principles of church unity at the meeting of the 1886 General Convention in Chicago. In their statement, the bishops expressed their wish to take steps "to heal the unhappy divisions of Christendom, . . . to more fully develop the Catholic idea of the Church of Christ, . . . [and] to enter into brotherly conference with all or any Christian Bodies seeking the restoration of the organic unity of the Church."[19] Two years later, at the start of the third Lambeth conference in England, Henry Whipple of Minnesota presented Huntington's quadrilateral to the international gathering of Anglican bishops.[20] "No one branch of the Church," he averred, "is absolutely by itself alone the Catholic Church; all branches need reunion" to make the church complete. "At a time when every form of error and sin is banded together to oppose the Kingdom of Christ," he said, "the world needs the witness of a united Church."[21] After the bishops debated the merits of church unity, they too accepted (in slightly modified form) the document now known as the Chicago-Lambeth Quadrilateral.[22]

Over the next few years, Episcopalians presented the Quadrilateral to the leaders of 18 church bodies. Most responses to that ecumenical proposal were neither enthusiastic nor hostile. The emphasis on scripture in the first article, while acceptable to Christians generally, was clearly more characteristic of Protestant views than of Roman Catholic ideas about ecclesiastical authority. The inclusion of the Nicene Creed, on the other hand, appealed to the Eastern Orthodox and Roman Catholics but implicitly undermined the Protestant principle of *sola scriptura*. The focus on only two sacraments was decidedly Protestant, while recognition of the historic episcopate meant that the clergy of most Protestant denominations would have to be re-ordained by Episcopal bishops before being allowed to lead worship in Episcopal parishes. Thus, despite the ostensible wish to encourage ecumenism, the Chicago-Lambeth Quadrilateral proved to be no more acceptable as a basis for church union than the Muhlenberg memorial had been several decades before. Episcopalians simply were extending to other Christians a formal invitation to close down their churches and join the Episcopal Church.[23]

ANGLO-CATHOLICISM AND THE REFORMED EPISCOPAL SCHISM

According to John Henry Newman, the original objective of the Oxford movement had been to restore knowledge of the Catholic faith within Anglicanism. Relying mainly on the circulation of *Tracts for the Times,* the leaders of the movement hoped to convince their fellow Anglicans that the teachings of the early church fathers and of seventeenth-century high church theologians had relevance to the ongoing life of the English church. At the beginning of the Catholic revival in the Church of England, therefore, the Tractarians had little interest in changing the ceremonial practices of worship. However, by placing increased emphasis on the importance of apostolic succession—ancient, divinely ordered, hierarchical authority—and by tapping into the aesthetic sensibilities of the contemporary Romantic movement—the desire for beauty, reverence, and heightened feelings of the sublime—"Anglo-Catholics" gradually introduced more ornate forms of ritual and clerical dress, patterned self-consciously on medieval models. Through the efforts of the English priest John Mason Neale and of members of the Camden Society of Cambridge, high church Anglicans not only examined the architecture and rituals of the pre-Reformation church but also advocated the wearing of vestments (e.g., chasubles and cassocks) that had fallen into disuse in the seventeenth century. A new interest in Gothic architecture similarly emerged in the 1840s, when U.S. architects such as Richard Upjohn of Boston began to build impressive buildings—Trinity Church, New York (completed in 1846) being the most notable—in that style.[24]

Although William Augustus Muhlenberg did not consider himself Anglo-Catholic and was opposed to elaborate rituals of "the Romish type," he was responsible for introducing a number of liturgical innovations in the places where he served in the 1830s and 1840s. Muhlenberg stressed the need for beauty in worship. This emphasis included the placing of candles and flowers on the altar as well as the hanging of evocative images of the Virgin Mary and of the crucified Jesus in the nave and sanctuary of the church.[25] Muhlenberg's liturgical concerns were also closely related to his hope that the Episcopal Church would become more accessible and attractive to ordinary Americans—an idea clearly expressed in his 1853 memorial.[26]

The modest aspirations of the first proponents of ritualism notwithstanding, the increasing presence and visibility of such innovations within the Episcopal Church became a significant source of conflict in the 1860s. Over the next two decades, Anglo-Catholics gradually introduced a host of liturgical changes into worship in their parishes and dioceses: stone altars (rather than wooden tables), eucharistic vestments, crucifixes, elevation of the communion bread and wine, bowing and genuflection, prayers to saints and prayers for the dead, incense, choir processions, and the like. Whereas Anglo-Catholics believed that such practices had been commonplace in the mid-sixteenth century and had not been offensive to the earliest English reformers, evangelical Episcopalians and even some older high churchmen were shocked by what they regarded as a "Romanizing" trend. In tandem with their liturgical objections, the opponents of ritualism also feared that the rising tide of Catholicism in their denomination was part of a larger conspiracy, inspired by the papacy, to undermine American religious and political liberties. Thus, when Charles Pettit McIlvaine, the evangelical bishop of Ohio, spoke out against ritualism in 1864, he was concerned about far more than the way churches were furnished or clergy were dressed. The Anglo-Catholics' plan "to promote a taste for a ceremonial sensuous religion," he declared, was "the very essence of Popery."[27]

This controversy further escalated in 1866, when John Henry Hopkins, the presiding bishop of the church, published a small book (bearing on its cover the provocative image of a smoking censer) entitled *The Law of Ritualism*. In an attempt to resolve the dispute between evangelicals and Anglo-Catholics, Hopkins affirmed that many of the liturgical practices desired by the ritualists had been legally mandated by the church when the first English Prayer Book was published in 1549. In fact, he argued, because the statutes supporting those rituals had never been officially repealed, they were still applicable in the Episcopal Church.[28]

A few months later, a group of 24 evangelical bishops responded angrily to Hopkins's claims. They denied his assertion that the canon law of the Church of England continued to have validity in the Episcopal Church, and they declared that the Anglo-Catholics' use of candles, incense, and genuflection was tantamount to the acceptance of Roman Catholic doctrines about the Mass. At the same time, the most extreme members of the evangelical party charged that the 1789 *Book of Common Prayer* represented a major problem for the church and needed quick revision. Calls for prayer book revision reached their height with the publication of Franklin Rising's *Are There Romanizing Germs in the Prayer Book?* (1868). There were, indeed, "Romanizing germs" in the church's worship, Rising concluded, and the only way to ensure "a purely evangelical Liturgy" would be to "agitate, agitate, AGITATE" for a thorough overhaul of the *Book of Common Prayer.*[29]

In keeping with these concerns, evangelicals sought latitude to omit parts of the prayer book that they believed were contrary to the teachings of the Bible. One of the phrases to which they strenuously objected was the pronouncement in the baptismal service that "this child is regenerate." Baptism was a *sign* of spiritual regeneration, they maintained, but the rite itself could not save, since salvation ultimately depended upon the baptized person's faith and trust in God's grace. Because of this theological assumption, evangelical clergy routinely omitted references to "regeneration" when they officiated at baptisms.[30]

In 1869, Charles Edward Cheney, an evangelical rector in Chicago, became locked in a bitter dispute over baptismal regeneration with his bishop, Henry John Whitehouse. Whitehouse had earlier offended evangelicals by asserting his acceptance of two controversial high church beliefs: the real presence of Christ in the Eucharist and spiritual regeneration in the sacrament of baptism. In response, Cheney and a group of evangelicals issued a statement censuring Whitehouse for "*unprotestantizing* this Protestant Episcopal Church, corrupting her doctrine, debasing her worship, and over-turning her long-established rites, ceremonies, and usages."[31] As bishop, however, Whitehouse had the final say in this dispute. Condemning Cheney for his refusal to read the words of the baptismal service exactly as they were printed in the prayer book, he deposed Cheney from the priesthood in 1871.

With these quarrels as backdrop, proposals both for the creation of church canons governing ritual and for the revision of the prayer book were brought forward at the General Conventions of 1868 and 1871. At the 1868 convention, evangelicals introduced a resolution that would have banned the use of eucharistic vestments, candlesticks, crucifixes, and other Anglo-Catholic practices, but their proposal failed to win wide approval. Following the convention, the House of Bishops did release a carefully worded pastoral letter that avoided specific references to Anglo-Catholicism but affirmed the Protestant nature of the English Reformation and condemned unequivocally "the unscriptural and uncatholic pretensions of the Bishop of Rome."[32] The banning of Anglo-Catholic ceremonial practices was again considered at the 1871 convention. After a lengthy and rancorous debate, the resolution was defeated when the House of Deputies refused to concur with the affirmative vote of the House of Bishops. Although the convention eventually accepted an alternative resolution that left decisions regarding rituals and vestments in the hands of individual diocesan bishops (the majority of whom were sympathetic to the evangelical cause), some evangelicals nevertheless felt so downcast by this decision that they began talking about seceding from the Episcopal Church.[33]

In the midst of the debates over ritualism, James DeKoven, a clerical member of the House of Deputies, vigorously espoused the Anglo-Catholic position. DeKoven had earlier served in Wisconsin as a professor at Nashotah House, a seminary founded in 1842 in support of Anglo-Catholic missionary efforts on the northwestern frontier. After leaving Nashotah House in 1859, he became warden of Racine College, where he encouraged a host of so-called "advanced" ceremonial practices.[34] Concerned about the evangelicals' effort to restrict the range of doctrinal and liturgical beliefs in the Episcopal Church, DeKoven delivered a memorable speech to his fellow deputies in 1871. He defended ritualism on three grounds. First, he noted that many Anglo-Catholic practices not only were used in the early church (the elevation of the communion bread and wine) but also were ancient and biblical in origin (the use of incense in worship). Second, he suggested that beliefs such as the real presence of Christ in the eucharistic elements strengthened the religious commitment of the Christian faithful. And third, he argued that a "broad, Catholic, tolerant charity" was needed to encourage the spread of Christianity throughout all segments of American society.[35]

In the end, sharp disagreements over the meaning of liturgical rituals and texts—theological differences intensified by latent anti-Catholic prejudices—tore the institutional fabric of the Episcopal Church in a way that the moral issue of slavery had failed to do only a few years before.[36] In protest against the supposed Catholic threat to the Protestant traditions of Anglicanism, a group of 8 clergymen and 19 laymen under the leadership of George David Cummins, the assistant bishop of Kentucky, organized a new denomination—the Reformed Episcopal Church—in New York on December 2, 1873. (A few days later, Cummins consecrated Charles Cheney as the first new bishop in the denomination.) The Reformed Episcopal leaders adopted a "Declaration of Principles" remarkably similar to the ones first proposed by William Reed Huntington as a basis for ecumenical relations. They affirmed their belief in the Old and New Testaments, the Apostles' (but not the Nicene) Creed, the two sacraments of baptism and the Lord's Supper, and episcopacy ("not as of Divine right, but as a very ancient and desirable model of Church polity"). Moving beyond Huntington, however, the Reformed Episcopalians condemned various "erroneous and strange doctrines" over which they had recently been fighting with Anglo-Catholics: Christ's presence in the communion bread and wine, baptismal regeneration, celebration of communion on an "altar" instead of "the Lord's Table," and designation of clergymen as "priests." Finally, Cummins announced his intention to encourage other freedom-loving Americans to join his denomination so that the Reformed Episcopal Church might present a united Protestant front against the menacing specters of Romanism and atheistic unbelief.[37]

Despite Cummins's aspirations—not unlike those of broad church Episcopalians in the same period—to oversee the creation of a pan-Protestant "national church," the founding of the Reformed Episcopal Church did not lead to a full-scale exodus either of evangelicals from the Episcopal Church or of Congregationalists, Presbyterians, Methodists, or Baptists from their own denominations. In fact, most evangelical Episcopalians who had once been Cummins's allies denounced his actions, and the handful of clergy who joined him were, like Cheney, men seriously at odds with their bishops. As a result of the Reformed Episcopal schism, low church Episcopalians began to reaffirm the "Episcopal" part of their religious identities, while Cummins's new denomination not only remained numerically small but also became increasingly less "Anglican" over the next several decades.[38]

THE WOMAN'S AUXILIARY

In the aftermath of the Civil War, as the male leaders of the Episcopal Church wrangled and divided over churchmanship issues, Episcopal women increasingly found opportunities to unite in the exercise of their ministries in the church. Even though most American churchgoers were women and women had been the mainstays of church life ever since the seventeenth century, ordained leadership remained almost exclusively a male province in American Christianity in the mid-nineteenth century. Although a few women had been ordained in the Congregational, Unitarian, and Universalist churches, in most denominations women not only were barred from seeking ordination but also were excluded from participation in the governance of their parishes and denominations. In the 1860s and 1870s, however, significant changes began to occur in the formal religious activities of women in the United States. Despite the stereotype of the middle-class Victorian woman entrusted exclusively with the care of family and home, women began to press for more active religious roles, extending their domestic responsibilities into the work of missionary and moral reform societies. Following the Civil War, every major Protestant denomination organized a national women's organization, and in 1874 the influential, interdenominational Women's Christian Temperance Union also was founded.[39]

Among Episcopalians, the Protestant Episcopal Freedman's Commission sponsored the first extensive use of churchwomen in a mission field, sending them to work as teachers among African Americans in the postbellum South. The establishment of the Bishop Potter Memorial House in Philadelphia in 1867 also offered instruction to prepare women both for social service work in urban parishes and for missionary work on the western frontier. Moreover, in an effort to draw together and encourage the missionary concerns of Episcopal women at the national level, Mary Abbot Emery helped organize a major new agency that the General Convention officially established in 1871: the Woman's Auxiliary to the Board of Missions of the Episcopal Church. This voluntary association of church-women recruited missionaries, trained teachers, and raised funds through a regular system of giving. Despite some limitations—auxiliary leaders were not permitted either to serve on the Board of Missions itself or to exercise full administrative control over their organization—the auxiliary offered Episcopal women a centralized organization to support their involvement in religious work outside their homes.[40]

The leadership provided by four members of the Emery family had a major impact on the achievements of the auxiliary throughout its first 45 years. Mary Abbot Emery, who served as general secretary from 1872 to 1876, accomplished a great deal in a relatively brief period. For example, she was successful in uniting several local missionary organizations run by women (e.g., the Indian Aid Association of Baltimore, the Dakota League of Massachusetts, and the Hartford Bureau of Relief) into a cohesive national structure. She also developed a system for the distribution of missionary boxes containing clothing, books, medical supplies, and other materials needed by workers in the field, and she worked out a fund-raising plan that provided support not only for missionary clergy but also for the many girls' secondary schools that were opened in the West at that time. And through her extensive correspondence, she bolstered the morale of missionaries by sending them numerous letters of sympathy and encouragement.[41]

In 1876 Mary Emery resigned from her position with the auxiliary when she married A. T. Twing, the secretary for domestic missions of the Episcopal Church. She was succeeded by her younger sister, Julia Chester Emery, who led the organization for the next 40 years. Two other sisters, Susan Lavinia Emery and Margaret Theresa Emery, also assisted in the auxiliary's work—the former as editor of a children's magazine about missions, the latter as coordinator of the missionary box program. When her husband died in 1882, Mary Emery Twing again assumed a role in the organization. Serving as "honorary secretary" until 1901, she focused on developing and publicizing vocational opportunities for women in the church. While maintaining a veneer of submissiveness that did not overtly threaten the male hierarchy of their denomination, the Emery sisters were able to extend considerably the formal influence of women within the official circles of the Episcopal Church.[42] As Julia Emery emphasized in her 1916 report to the Board of Missions, women were eager to be enlisted to work "under their rectors and Bishops and the organized authorities of the Church." For those women, the auxiliary was not simply a bureaucratic organization but "a reminder, a co-operator, and a vehicle" through which they could engage themselves in strengthening the general missionary efforts of their church.[43]

At the end of the nineteenth century, several other women's organizations were founded that complemented the work of the auxiliary. For example, with the encouragement of Julia Emery, the 1889 General Convention established the

United Offering (later called the United Thank Offering) as a supplement to the funds donated by churchwomen to the Board of Missions. The United Offerings of 1892 and 1895 were used to endow the work of missionary bishops, while the Offering of 1898 was designated exclusively for the training and support of women serving as missionaries. Because they retained substantial control over the money raised through the United Offering, female Episcopalians began to respond with increasing enthusiasm to its triennial appeals: their contributions grew dramatically from $21,000 in 1892, to $243,000 in 1910, and then to $669,000 in 1922. The Church Periodical Club was another important women's organization founded in this period. In 1888, a group of women led by Mary Drake Fargo launched this club at the Church of the Holy Communion in New York City. Working closely with the Woman's Auxiliary, the club sent periodicals and reading materials to various domestic mission stations, including schools for Indians in the West and African Americans in the South.[44]

SOCIAL GOSPELS

Despite having high hopes about the fruits of their victory in the Civil War, northern Protestants were bitterly disappointed by the realities of life in the United States after 1865. Rather than entering the millennial era that some expected, Americans instead endured a Gilded Age of tawdry materialism and corrupt politics. Outraged and distressed by what they were experiencing, church leaders attempted to confront the myriad problems of late-nineteenth-century America through a diverse and loosely structured movement that became known as the "social gospel."[45]

At the conservative end of the spectrum of religious responses to the Gilded Age was the combination of old-fashioned Protestant moralism and laissez-faire economic doctrine expounded by Pittsburgh industrialist Andrew Carnegie. In his famous essay "The Gospel of Wealth" (1889), Carnegie argued that Christian civilization was founded upon three social principles: the sacredness of private property, the virtue of unfettered competition, and the acceptability of wealth accumulation. Anyone who worked diligently and lived a good life, he maintained, would be materially rewarded by God. A corollary to Carnegie's "gospel" was the belief that, since God was the creator of all things, those who were blessed with material success had a responsibility to be good stewards of their possessions by sharing them with others. Thus, an emphasis on charity became commonplace in conservative Protestant social thought—a virtue that Carnegie's own philanthropic endeavors exemplified.[46]

Although Carnegie himself was not a member of the Episcopal Church, several broad church Episcopalians were influential in the development and implementation of the ideas he popularized. For instance, William Graham Sumner, the principal American proponent of social Darwinism—the application of evolutionary theories about the "survival of the fittest" to human communities—began his professional career as an Episcopal priest. A theological liberal, Sumner served as the rector of a church in Morristown, New Jersey, in the early 1870s. During that period, he struggled to reconcile the contradictions he perceived between the teachings of religion and the teachings of science. He eventually abandoned both the priesthood and his religious faith after accepting an academic position at Yale University. As a sociologist, he insisted on the rightfulness of the human struggle to accumulate wealth, and he used that idea as a reason to chastise reformers who urged governmental intervention in the problems of the poor. "If we do not like the survival of the fittest we have only one possible alternative, and that is the survival of the unfittest," he wrote. "The former is the law of civilization, the latter is the law of anti-civilization."[47]

While most Episcopal clergy serving comfortably in well-to-do parishes were apt to agree with Carnegie and Sumner that the rich deserved to be rich, some of them tempered that view by reminding church members about the need for Christian stewardship. William Lawrence, the bishop of Massachusetts, presents a particularly intriguing case. Raised in a privileged environment, he once said that the gospel could be reduced to two key principles: "that man, when he is strong, conquers Nature," and that, "in the long run, it is only to the man of morality that wealth comes."[48] Over time, however, he learned to feel more sympathy for working-class Americans, though he still tended to refer to them in patronizing and paternalistic terms.[49] Lawrence chaired the commission that was appointed by the 1901 General Convention to study "the relations of capital and labor." In the report it eventually presented, Lawrence's commission re-emphasized the principle that, whereas wealth was a divine gift, "its proper use" represented "a religious duty." As the report concluded, "the menace of the idle poor . . . is not more serious than the menace of the idle rich whose extravagant pleasures corrupt not only their own ideals, but set false ones for the poor."[50]

In the middle of the spectrum of nineteenth-century social gospels stands the so-called institutional church movement, which arose in urban Protestant parishes in the 1890s. Although the social-service ministries sponsored by William Augustus Muhlenberg provided an early model of the institutional church, William Stephen Rainsford brought the idea to perfection during his work as rector of St. George's Church in New York. When Rainsford arrived at St. George's in 1888, the parish was in a moribund state. It was located in a declining neighborhood, and most of its wealthiest members had left for other parishes. However, with the backing of a small group of patrons led by the prominent financier J.P. Morgan, Rainsford soon transformed St. George's into a center of vigorous preaching and social service. Rainsford insisted that the old system of pew rents should be abolished so that people of all social ranks could freely attend the church. Although Morgan sometimes grumbled at his rector's views, he also admired his steadfast commitment to the gospel imperative to succor the needy. Opening up the facilities of the parish to people in the community, St. George's sponsored wide-ranging social programs: a boys' club, girls' and women's organizations, a trade school, a cadet battalion, and a gymnasium.[51]

Episcopalians also made significant contributions to Christian ministry in urban areas through the work of various women's organizations, the Girls' Friendly Society being the most notable. Founded in England, the Girls' Friendly Society came to the United States in 1877 when Emily M. Edson, a member of St. Anne's Church in Lowell, Massachusetts, established a chapter of the organization at her parish. Edson was concerned about the fate of young women working in the textile mills in her area, and she convinced other women in her church to meet regularly with the millworkers. She hoped that "watching over the [workers], making friends with them, bringing them to the notice of the clergyman of the parish, and taking an interest in their welfare" would benefit them "in the most exposed and trying period of their lives."[52] Two other chapters were soon formed in Massachusetts, and by 1885 the society had not only spread to Maryland and New York but also formed a central governing council. Adopting the rules of the English association prohibiting anyone "who has not borne a virtuous character" from joining the society, Episcopal women set up educational programs, lending libraries, and classes in needlework, and they engaged the young women with whom they met in discussing topics such as "Good Manners" and "Good Taste."[53]

Concurrent with this trend, Episcopal Church leaders made tentative but definite steps toward the professionalization of the denomination's women workers. In September 1857, William Whittingham, the bishop of Maryland, "set apart" (though he pointedly did not "ordain") Adeline Blanchard Tyler and five other women as the first American deaconesses. Serving at St. Andrew's Church in Baltimore, the deaconesses ministered as nurses to the sick and dying in the city. In succeeding decades, bishops in other dioceses followed Whittingham's example. In 1864 in Tuscaloosa, Alabama, Richard Hooker Wilmer set apart three women as deaconesses; eight years later, Abram Littlejohn of Long Island established an order of deaconesses in his diocese, empowering seven women "to serve the widow and the orphan, the sick and the destitute, the wretched and the distressed."[54] Although the exact status of deaconesses within the ordained hierarchy of the church later proved controversial, the women who served in that role at the end of the nineteenth century managed a variety of social service tasks.[55] They directed programs in large parishes influenced by the institutional church movement, where space was available for health clinics, schools, recreational activities, and other programs for working-class Americans. Deaconesses also served in settlement houses, worked as matrons in church hospitals and children's homes, held positions at girls' schools, and labored in far-flung missionary outposts in Japan and China.

Finally, at the most progressive end of the social gospel spectrum, a small but highly influential group of Episcopalians envisioned the complete transformation of American society through the auspices of the church. Unlike evangelical Protestant reformers, who in the antebellum period had attacked slavery and alcoholism for contaminating the sanctity of the individual will, these socially radical Episcopalians were often inspired by Anglo-Catholic sacramental views and stressed both the corporate nature of the church and the responsibility of Christians for all of society.[56]

Emphasizing the vital interconnection between church and society, the econ- omist Richard T. Ely touted one of the key principles of the Christian socialist movement in England: the idea that "the real English Church . . . is the English nation."[57] Like William Reed Huntington, Ely longed for the creation of a national church, allied with the government, that would foster an activist religious ethos in the United States. For the right-thinking and truly dedicated Christian, he wrote in 1899, "salvation means . . . a never-ceasing attack on every wrong institution, until the earth becomes a new earth, and all its cities, cities of God."[58] Another Episcopalian who joined Ely in affirming the importance of Christian socialism was the priest William Dwight Porter Bliss. A contributor to the founding of several organizations, including the Church Association for the Advancement of the Interests of Labor, Bliss defined Christian socialism as "the application to society of the way of Christ" and the creation of "a socialism based on Christ."[59]

A disciple of Bliss and a professor at Wellesley College, Vida Scudder was arguably the most influential promoter of Christian socialist ideas in the early twentieth century. The author of numerous articles and books, she insisted on the compatibility of biblical teaching and socialist tenets. A socialist society would be in harmony with the kingdom that God intended to establish on earth, she maintained, for it would allow working people the freedom to seek and to satisfy their need for "union with the Eternal."[60] Scudder mixed radical political views with a fondness both for the mysticism of the Middle Ages (when Western society was formally united under the authority of the church) and for Anglo-Catholic sacramentalism. She was intensely involved in the work of the Society of the Companions of the Holy Cross, a group of Episcopal laywomen dedicated to intercessory prayer and active engagement in the social problems of the day. At their meetings, the Companions gathered not only to pray together and to study the Bible but also to hear reports about workers' strikes and to offer support to labor unions.[61] Scudder's theological convictions, like those of many Episcopa- lians committed to Christian socialism, were based on the doctrine of the incar- nation. The fact that God had become incarnate in human flesh indicated that there was no separation between the social and the spiritual dimensions of the Christian faith.[62]

INDIAN MISSIONS

The hope of obtaining land had brought the first group of European colonists to America in the seventeenth century, and that same dream continued to impel their descendants westward in the eighteenth and nineteenth centuries. Following the acquisition of vast amounts of territory between the Mississippi River and the Pacific coast in the 1840s, white Americans quickly sought to take possession of and exploit those western areas. In concert with the expansion of the United States, Christian missionaries also began to evangelize native peoples in the ter- ritories of the upper Midwest.

One of the most notable of those missionaries was James Lloyd Breck, who moved to Minnesota in 1850 to work among the Ojibwe Indians. Breck hoped to win native converts by combining the fervor for missions that was typical of evangelical Episcopalians with an Anglo-Catholic emphasis on liturgy and ritual. At the Gull Lake mission he founded in 1852, worship took place in a rustic log church with a hanging cross and open Gothic windows. In his account of a service at the church in the mid-1850s, Breck stressed the order and solemnity of worship as the native congregants sang familiar Episcopal hymns and repeated the words of the *Book of Common Prayer*, translated into their own language.[63] Breck left the northern missions in 1857 and moved to Faribault in southern Minnesota, where he founded a boarding school (now called Shattuck-St. Mary's School) for the religious training of Ojibwe and Dakota children. His work in the northern part of the state, however, was continued and expanded by Bishop Henry Whipple and by John Johnson Enmegabowh, an Indian converted to Christianity by Methodists and later ordained an Episcopal priest.

Whipple advocated the protection and support of the Ojibwe and Dakota throughout his lengthy episcopate (1859–1901). Concerned about the well-being of the native people in his diocese, he defended them against the fraud and deception that often characterized U.S. Indian policy, and he convinced the 1871 General Convention to create a commission to defend the Indians' rights—an interest that earned him the Ojibwe name "Straight Tongue." Yet like many of his white contemporaries, Whipple was motivated by the paternalistic assumption that native people would ultimately convert to Christianity and become fully assimilated into *his* culture. Thus, whereas Episcopal missionaries at the White Earth reservation acted as watchdogs of the U.S. Indian Bureau and even recruited men to work with them as deacons—but, tellingly, not as priests—these white Episcopalians simultaneously undermined the traditional rhythms and bonds of Indian life.[64] According to Joseph Gilfillan, the Episcopal archdeacon who coordinated mission activities at White Earth, a concerted program of evangelization represented the most effective means of "civilizing" the Indians. "No power on earth" could do it better, he claimed, than the native Indian missionary, whose ability to interact with his people in their own language accomplished what "guns and pistols and the United States army" were not capable of doing.[65]

In 1871 the House of Bishops created the missionary district of Niobrara (comprising present-day South Dakota and western Nebraska), and a year later William Hobart Hare, rector of a parish in Philadelphia, was elected bishop of that territory. Although some white settlers already lived in the area, Hare's primary responsibility was to evangelize the Indians of the Sioux territory—a task at which he was quite successful. By the time of his death, about one-half of the 25,000 Indians in South Dakota were baptized and active in the work of the mission. "The civilization of our western Indians is due more largely to you than to any other man," the mayor of Sioux Falls, South Dakota, remarked to Hare in 1909.[66] Although this observation was intended to praise Hare unreservedly, it also hints at the two-sided aspect of his evangelistic program—a mission that placed emphasis not only on conversion to the Christian faith but also on assimilation to

Euro-American culture. Toward that end, Hare established in his missionary district four boarding schools where Indian children, uprooted from their families in nearby reservations, learned basic vocational skills. They were trained to hold steady but menial jobs under the tutelage of the white elite—a strategy comparable to what Episcopalians had devised among the Ojibwe in Minnesota.

MINISTRY AMONG AFRICAN AMERICANS

Episcopalians, black as well as white, who were involved in the evangelization of African Americans in the South faced similar questions about the broader cultural implications of their work. Few white leaders in the church considered African Americans to be their equals, and they feared the consequences of not closely controlling the religious affairs of black people. The trustees of Virginia Seminary, for instance, knew that "qualified" black men needed an education to become priests, but they did not want African American students to enroll at their school in Alexandria. As a result, they sponsored the creation of a separate black seminary in Petersburg, Virginia. Named in honor of the first Episcopal missionary bishop in Liberia, the Bishop Payne Divinity School began operations in 1878 and thereafter became the principal training ground for black Episcopal clergy in the South.[67]

In the period immediately after the Civil War, a number of parishes composed of former slaves in the southern states attempted to become affiliated with the Episcopal dioceses in which they were geographically located. White bishops and priests, who generally believed in the need to offer paternalistic oversight to black church members, tended to favor the admission of those parishes into their dioceses. White laypeople, on the other hand, usually obstructed those plans. Thus, when representatives of several African American parishes applied for admission into the diocese of South Carolina in 1875, white laity voting at the diocesan convention blocked their petition. Following this decision, six black congregations in South Carolina chose to remove themselves from the jurisdiction of the Episcopal Church, and they joined the recently organized Reformed Episcopal Church instead.[68]

By the early 1880s, when southern states were beginning to pass racial segregation laws, white Episcopalians were keenly aware of the dilemma they faced in relation to the ecclesiastical status of African Americans. A few years before, the Methodist Episcopal Church, South, had made the decision to establish a separate denomination for its African American members by organizing the "Colored Methodist Episcopal Church." Should the Episcopal Church, white Episcopalians asked themselves, similarly segregate its African American membership? To consider the implications of this idea, a group of bishops, priests, and laypeople from southern dioceses—all white men—assembled at the University of the South in July 1883. After several days of debate, delegates at the "Sewanee conference" rejected the idea of forming a new denomination but resolved instead to seek permission from the upcoming General Convention to create special missionary organizations into which the black Episcopalians of each southern diocese could be placed. If that plan passed, the conference members argued, white bishops would be able to maintain ecclesiastical control over African Americans without officially admitting either black parishes or black church people into their dioceses.[69]

This proposal outraged black Episcopalians, and under the leadership of Alexander Crummell, then rector of St. Luke's Church in Washington, D.C., they vigorously campaigned against it. When the next General Convention assembled in October 1883, the House of Bishops officially endorsed the Sewanee plan, but the proposal failed to win the necessary concurrence of the House of Deputies. The deputies maintained that, instead of segregating the black membership it already had, the church needed to make the evangelization of African Americans one of its highest priorities at the national level. The leadership in the southern dioceses generally chose to ignore this dictum, however, and they soon created segregated "colored convocations" to which their black parishes were assigned. Despite the protests of a handful of leaders in the North, the denomination as a whole had no way of preventing individual dioceses from adopting this racial strategy.[70]

Stymied by white church members, Alexander Crummell and other black Episcopalians banded together and formed the Conference of Church Workers among Colored People to lobby for recognition and respect in denominational affairs. Like many white clergy in the late nineteenth century, Crummell lamented the fact that few African Americans were interested in belonging to the Episcopal Church. Unlike his white colleagues, however, he understood the reason why blacks regarded the denomination with suspicion. What was needed, he thought, was the recruitment of a cadre of black leaders who not only were trained to minister to their own people but would be treated as equals by whites.[71]

Among the strongest supporters of this strategy was Anna Julia Cooper, the widow of an Episcopal priest and a teacher at St. Augustine's College in North Carolina. Born in slavery, Cooper knew the value of a good education and a vital religious faith in assisting the rise of black women and men in the South. The Episcopal Church, in fact, offered many advantages to African Americans. "Thinking colored men," she wrote, "almost uniformly admit that the Protestant Episcopal Church with its quiet, chaste dignity and decorous solemnity . . . is eminently fitted to correct the peculiar faults of worship—the rank exuberance and often ludicrous demonstrativeness of their people." Although white clergy often complained that African Americans were indifferent to the Episcopal Church, Cooper knew that this accusation was not true. Whites had created the problem themselves by discouraging and devaluing the involvement of blacks in church affairs. African Americans needed *priests* of their own race, she insisted, not the "perpetual colored diaconate" that patronizing whites had instituted.[72]

After Crummell's death in 1898, George Freeman Bragg, rector of St. James' First African Church in Baltimore, emerged as the principal leader of the Conference of Church Workers. Revising the strategy they had earlier adopted, black

Episcopalians now began to press southern bishops to allow African Americans to separate themselves voluntarily from "white" dioceses. If African Americans were going to be relegated to a separate, second-class status with practically no voice in church affairs, Bragg and others asked, why not let them create their own independent missionary jurisdictions and elect black bishops to oversee those organizations?[73]

At this stage, the Conference of Church Workers received some very unlikely support from William Montgomery Brown, the bishop of Arkansas. A committed proponent of social Darwinism, Brown believed that the best way to preserve the nation's racial purity was by keeping whites and blacks completely separated from one another. He also considered the paternalistic racial attitudes held by many of his fellow bishops to be outdated and hopelessly sentimental. Rejecting the traditional theological notion of "the fatherhood of God and the brotherhood of man" as an inadequate rationale for keeping African Americans within the Episcopal Church, he preferred to let black people sink or swim entirely on their own.[74] Because of his faith in the Darwinian concept of a perpetual struggle between the races for survival, Brown encouraged African Americans to establish a new denomination, and he even offered to participate in the consecration of black bishops to lead that church.[75]

The ideas advanced by Bragg and Brown were hotly debated at the next two General Conventions, and in 1910 a compromise was reached—one intended to retain African Americans within the church while granting them some of the autonomy and respect they were seeking. Officially amending the church's constitution, the 1910 General Convention voted to allow the consecration of suffragan (assistant) bishops in dioceses where factors such as the size of the geographical area (e.g., dioceses in western states), the size of the population (e.g., dioceses located in major urban areas), or the diversity of the population (e.g., dioceses in southern states) warranted the ministry of more than one bishop. Although several western and northeastern dioceses soon thereafter elected the suffragan bishops they needed, dioceses in the South—still wholly under the control of whites—resisted the thought of making a black man a bishop.

The situation was finally resolved in 1918, when the diocese of Arkansas (Bishop William Brown had resigned from his position in 1912) elected and consecrated an African American priest, Edward Thomas Demby, as its "suffragan bishop for colored work." A short time later, the diocese of North Carolina similarly chose Henry Beard Delany to lead its evangelistic work among African Americans. The raising of Demby and Delany to the episcopate, however, did not lessen the impact of racism on the church's life. On the one hand, the two black bishops were never fully supported by the Conference of Church Workers because they were thought to be too closely tied to the white establishment in their dioceses. According to George Freeman Bragg, no "constructive Negro . . . with respect to real ability" could have been elected bishop in the Episcopal Church, and he assumed that Demby and Delany had been chosen only because whites regarded each man as "a good and safe Negro."[76] On the other hand, the two men were given no appreciable power by white Episcopalians. They had little chance to make much of an impact on their dioceses, and no other African American was elected to serve as a bishop in the United States until the early 1960s.[77]

FOREIGN MISSIONS AND WORLD AFFAIRS

The rise of the United States as a world power at the end of the nineteenth century sparked a rapid increase in overseas missions sponsored by the American churches. In the wake of victory in the Spanish-American War and the initiation of an open-door policy with China, portions of Latin America and Asia became accessible for the first time both to American business interests and to the missionary endeavors of Western Christians. National aspirations and evangelistic concerns often seemed closely related. As President William McKinley remarked when speaking to a group of clergymen, his decision to annex the Philippines in 1898 was directly linked to his religious faith. After Americans gained military control of the islands, he prayed for divine guidance about the next step that should be taken. Concluding that it would not be proper either to give the islands back to Catholic Spain or to let the people of the Philippines rule themselves, McKinley realized that "there was nothing left for us to do but to take them all, and educate the Filipinos, and uplift and civilize and Christianize them, . . . as our fellow-men for whom Christ died."[78]

During this heady period of imperialist expansion, when Protestant leaders believed the evangelization of the world was truly within their reach, the Episcopal Church also sought to project itself overseas. Thomas March Clark, who served as presiding bishop of the denomination between 1899 and 1903, had set the tone for Episcopalians a few years earlier when he addressed the General Convention about the nature of the church's mission. There are no barriers to Christian evangelism, he asserted, for "nothing is foreign to the Church that pertains to humanity." Thus, "when the cry is heard on the wind from a perishing world, 'Come to our help!' . . . every faithful servant of Jesus asks, 'What can I do to rescue those who are perishing for lack of knowledge' " about the gospel?[79] In response to this ostensible call from people in other countries, Episcopalians planted missions in Brazil, China, Cuba, the Dominican Republic, Haiti, Hawaii, Japan, Mexico, Panama, the Philippines, and Puerto Rico, and the number of communicants of the denomination outside the United States rose dramatically from about 400 in 1880 to more than 28,000 in 1920.[80]

One of the most successful Episcopal missions was located in the Philippines, which became an important strategic outpost of the United States in the Far East. As soon as American troops captured the islands from Spain, the 1898 General Convention constituted the territory as a missionary district of the denomination. Because 80 percent of the population was at least nominally Roman Catholic, Episcopalians chose to direct their evangelistic work toward those who were not Christian—groups that included primitive headhunters in the mountains of northern Luzon as well as the Chinese community in Manila and the Muslims on the southern islands of the Philippines.[81]

The original missionaries were two army chaplains stationed on the islands with the soldiers, but their work was soon superseded by that of Charles Henry Brent, who served as the missionary bishop of the Philippines from 1901 until 1917. Brent was a strong proponent of "muscular Christianity," and like most English and American missionaries in that era, he recognized the need to "take up the White Man's Burden" and uplift the "lower races" by bringing them into contact with Anglo-Saxon cultural values.[82] Nevertheless, Brent also proved to be a capable and energetic religious leader, visiting remote sections of the islands, founding mission stations, and establishing schools. Viewing the inhabitants of the Philippines as "a fine people, with large possibilities," Brent and other missionaries believed that properly trained and taught Filipinos could adopt Western customs and thereby become good Episcopalians.[83]

The next position that Charles Brent assumed was chief of chaplains of the American Expeditionary Force in France in 1917. The military post that Brent occupied was symbolic of a tremendous change that had occurred in the relationship of the Episcopal Church to American society between the Civil War and World War I. By the time Congress approved a declaration of war against the Central Powers, Episcopalians had joined the majority of Americans of all faiths in unreservedly backing the Allied military effort. Denominations that had the closest ancestral ties to Great Britain were the ones most supportive of war in 1917, and few were more steadfast than the Episcopal Church. In stark contrast to its uncertain stance during earlier conflicts, the Episcopal Church had little difficulty in blessing what one rector in Washington, D.C., called "a crusade" and "a Holy War."[84] According to William T. Manning, then rector of Trinity Church, New York, "the soul of America never uttered itself more nobly and truly" than it had when entering battle against the "malignant power of [German] militarism."[85] And as the House of Bishops declared in October 1917, whenever a nation is at war "on behalf of justice, liberty and humanity . . . , the Church's station is at the front."[86]

Church agencies sent Bibles and other religious literature to the American troops, and more than two hundred Episcopal clergy left their parishes to become military chaplains during the war. So complete was Episcopalians' support of the war that when Paul Jones, the missionary bishop of Utah, openly expressed pacifist sentiments, he was strongly condemned throughout the church. Although he insisted that "German brutality and aggression" needed to be stopped, he did not think the church was justified either "in treating the sermon on the mount as a scrap of paper" or in abandoning its claim to universality by becoming "the willing instrument of a national government." Accusing his fellow Episcopalians of adopting an unchristian attitude—one that "savors too much of Mohammedanism with its policy of carrying religion by the sword"— Jones reluctantly resigned from his position as bishop in 1918.[87]

NOTES

1. *AR,* 243–45; and *RHAP,* 735–36.

2. Henry F. May, *Protestant Churches and Industrial America* (New York: Harper, 1949), 186; and *AR,* 264–65.

3. Arthur P. Stanley, quoted in *MM,* 285.

4. William R. Hutchison, *The Modernist Impulse in American Protestantism* (Cambridge: Harvard University Press, 1976), 2.

5. Benjamin Jowett, "On the Inspiration of Scripture" (1860), quoted in Josef L. Altholz, "A Tale of Two Controversies: Darwinism in the Debate over 'Essays and Reviews,' " *CH* 63 (1994): 51.

6. Alexander V. G. Allen, *Life and Letters of Phillips Brooks,* vol. 1 (New York: E. P. Dutton, 1901), 283; Gillis J. Harp, " 'We Cannot Spare You': Phillips Brooks's Break with the Evangelical Party, 1859–1873," *CH* 68 (1999): 932; and *MM,* 299.

7. *HEC,* 184–86; and *MM,* 311–13.

8. Quotation in *HPEC,* 307.

9. Mark S. Massa, *Charles Augustus Briggs and the Crisis of Historical Criticism* (Minneapolis: Fortress, 1990), 120–21, 124–25, 133–35.

10. *HPEC,* 311.

11. The University of the South was organized in 1857 through the efforts of three Episcopal bishops (Leonidas Polk of Louisiana, Stephen Elliott of Georgia, and James Hervey Otey of Tennessee) as a bastion of proslavery ideology during the sectional conflict preceding the Civil War. Because Union soldiers destroyed most of the school's property during the war, it did not open until the fall of 1868. A theological department for the training of clergy was also started in 1879.

12. William Porcher DuBose, "The Interpretation of the Bible" (1878), quoted in *William Porcher DuBose: Selected Writings,* ed. Jon Alexander (New York: Paulist, 1988), 23.

13. Robert Boak Slocum, *The Theology of William Porcher DuBose: Life, Movement, and Being* (Columbia: University of South Carolina Press, 2000), 110–13.

14. William Porcher DuBose, *The Gospel According to St. Paul* (1907), in *William Porcher DuBose,* 86; and *BHEC,* 124.

15. William Montgomery Brown, later the bishop of Arkansas, suggested this idea in his book *The Church for Americans* (1895)—see *HEC,* 188–89.

16. *HPEC,* 270–71.

17. William Reed Huntington, *The Church-Idea: An Essay towards Unity* (1870; reprint, Harrisburg, Pa.: Morehouse, 2002), 111–15 (quotation on 113).

18. Ian T. Douglas, *Fling Out the Banner! The National Church Ideal and the Foreign Mission of the Episcopal Church* (New York: Church Hymnal, 1996), 88–90; Richard G. Hewlett, "The Creation of the Diocese of Washington and Washington National Cathedral," *AEH* 71 (2002): 358–62, 378; and *HPEC,* 347. See also John F. Woolverton, "Huntington's Quadrilateral: A Critical Study," *CH* 39 (1970): 198; J. Robert Wright, "Heritage and Vision: The Chicago-Lambeth Quadrilateral," *ATR,* supplementary series no. 10 (1988): 10–11; Stuart H. Hoke, "Broken Fragments: William Reed Huntington's Personal Quest for Unity," *AEH* 69 (June 2000): 211–41.

19. "Chicago Quadilateral, 1886," in *DW,* 225–26.

20. The Lambeth conference is a decennial assembly, advisory rather than legislative in character, that every bishop in the worldwide Anglican Communion is eligible to attend. The first Lambeth conference took place in England in 1867.

21. Quoted in *ECUS*, 274.

22. The Chicago-Lambeth Quadrilateral of 1888 is still one of the official statements on ecumenical relations of both the Anglican Communion and the Episcopal Church.

23. Samuel McCrea Cavert, *The American Churches in the Ecumenical Movement, 1900–1968* (New York: Association Press, 1968), 28; *HPEC*, 347; and *AR*, 92–93.

24. Allen C. Guelzo, *For the Union of Evangelical Christendom: The Irony of the Reformed Episcopalians* (University Park: Pennsylvania State University Press, 1994), 58–59; *MM*, 359; and *HEC*, 148–50.

25. *MM*, 362–63 (Muhlenberg quoted on 363).

26. "Muhlenberg Memorial, 1853," in *DW*, 209.

27. Charles Pettit McIlvaine, *Righteousness by Faith* (1864), quoted in Diana Hochstedt Butler, *Standing against the Whirlwind: Evangelical Episcopalians in Nineteenth-Century America* (New York: Oxford University Press, 1995), 192–93.

28. *MM*, 373–76; and *HPEC*, 273.

29. Franklin S. Rising, *Are There Romanizing Germs in the Prayer Book?* (1868), quoted in Guelzo, *For the Union of Evangelical Christendom*, 66.

30. Butler, *Standing against the Whirlwind*, 193–95, 203–5.

31. Quoted in Guelzo, *For the Union of Evangelical Christendom*, 81. See also Butler, *Standing against the Whirlwind*, 205.

32. Quoted in *HPEC*, 274. The bishops were very concerned about what was taking place in the Roman Catholic Church at this time: preparations were being made for the pronouncement of papal infallibility, which took place at the meeting of Vatican Council I in 1870.

33. Guelzo, *For the Union of Evangelical Christendom*, 67–68; *HPEC*, 282–85; and *MM*, 376–87. See also "Pastoral Letter on Baptismal Regeneration and Eucharistic Adoration, 1871," in *DW*, 66–68.

34. *MM*, 326.

35. James DeKoven, "The Canon on Ritual, 1874," in *DW*, 73–77 (quotation on 76). According to the historian T. J. Jackson Lears, the Anglo-Catholic sacramental beliefs that Episcopalians like DeKoven defended allowed elite Americans in the late nineteenth century to protest against the rise of modern industrialism without fully rejecting the materialistic culture in which they lived—see T. J. Jackson Lears, *No Place of Grace: Antimodernism and the Transformation of American Culture, 1880–1920* (New York: Pantheon, 1981), 198–203.

36. *HPEC*, 285.

37. Guelzo, *For the Union of Evangelical Christendom*, 155–94 ("The Declaration of Principles," quoted on 155–56).

38. Butler, *Standing against the Whirlwind*, 211–12. In 1998, the Reformed Episcopal Church reported a membership of about 6,850 communicants.

39. *AR*, 246–47.

40. Pamela W. Darling, *New Wine: The Story of Women Transforming Leadership and Power in the Episcopal Church* (Cambridge, Mass.: Cowley, 1994), 18–21; and *DC*, 52–67.

41. *DC*, 68–75.

42. Darling, *New Wine*, 23–26.

43. Julia Chester Emery, "Forty-Fifth Annual Report of the Woman's Auxiliary to the Board of Missions, 1915–1916," in *DW*, 433.

44. *DC*, 76–78, 83–84; and *BHEC*, 77.

45. George M. Marsden, *Religion and American Culture* (San Diego: Harcourt Brace Jovanovich, 1990), 96–112.

46. Winthrop S. Hudson, *Religion in America: An Historical Account of the Development of American Religious Life,* 4th ed. (New York: Macmillan, 1987), 282–84.

47. William Graham Sumner, quoted in Sean Dennis Cashman, *America in the Gilded Age: From the Death of Lincoln to the Rise of Theodore Roosevelt,* 2nd ed. (New York: New York University Press, 1988), 58; and *RHAP,* 790.

48. May, *Protestant Churches and Industrial America,* 64–72; and *RHAP,* 789–90 (source of Lawrence quotation).

49. William Lawrence, *Memories of a Happy Life* (Boston: Houghton Mifflin, 1926), 47–49.

50. "Report of Joint Commission on the Relations of Capital and Labor, 1910," in *DW,* 326, 330.

51. Paul T. Phillips, *A Kingdom on Earth: Anglo-American Social Christianity, 1880–1940* (University Park: Pennsylvania State University Press, 1996), 70–71.

52. E. M. Edson, "The Girls' Friendly Society" (1886), quoted in *DC,* 85.

53. *DC,* 84–86 (Records of the Girls' Friendly Society, quoted on 85).

54. *HEC,* 158–59; and *DC,* 88–95 (*Form of Admitting Deaconesses to Their Office* [1872], quoted on 93). See also Barbara Brandon Schnorrenberg, "Set Apart: Alabama Deaconesses, 1864–1915," *AEH* 63 (1994): 469–90.

55. After debating the topic for 20 years, the General Convention passed a canon officially sanctioning the office of deaconess in 1889. It required that deaconesses be devout communicants who were unmarried (i.e., single or widowed), and it allowed them to resign from their office at any time. Deaconesses were expected to complete two years of training, and they served under the authority of a bishop or rector. However, since ordination was exclusively a male prerogative, and since deaconesses were meant to serve in only social service ministries, they were not assigned any functions in worship services. Their garb, which typically included a veil, starched collar and cuffs, and a cross, marked them as religious professionals dedicated to the service of others. Deaconess training schools— established in New York (1890), Philadelphia (1891), and Berkeley, California (1908)— offered courses in both academic (church history, theology, and biblical studies) and practical (household management, nurses' training, and office administration) subjects— see Mary Sudman Donovan, "Paving the Way: Deaconess Susan Trevor Knapp," *AEH* 63 (1994): 491–502; and *DC,* 95–122.

56. Lears, *No Place of Grace,* 200.

57. Richard T. Ely, "Church and State" (1890), quoted in Phillips, *A Kingdom on Earth,* 168.

58. Richard T. Ely, *Social Aspects of Christianity* (1899), in *A Documentary History of Religion in America,* vol. 2, ed. Edwin S. Gaustad (Grand Rapids, Mich.: Eerdmans, 1993), 129. See also Phillips, *A Kingdom on Earth,* 168–69.

59. W. D. P. Bliss, *Encyclopedia of Social Reform* (1908), in Ronald C. White Jr. and C. Howard Hopkins, *The Social Gospel: Religion and Reform in Changing America* (Philadelphia: Temple University Press, 1976), 168, 170.

60. Vida Scudder, *Socialism and Character* (Boston: Houghton Mifflin, 1912), 316. See also Gary Scott Smith, "Creating a Cooperative Commonwealth: Vida Scudder's Quest to Reconcile Christianity and Socialism, 1890–1920," *AEH* 52 (1993): 397–428.

61. *DC,* 148–50. The Companions were organized by Emily Malbone Morgan and Harriet Hastings in 1884.

62. Vida D. Scudder, *The Church and the Hour: Reflections of a Socialist Churchwoman* (New York: Dutton, 1917), 15–16, 37–39; Scudder, *Socialism and Character,* 349–55; and Lears, *No Place of Grace,* 209–15.

63. Michael D. McNally, *Ojibwe Singers: Hymns, Grief, and a Native Culture in Motion* (New York: Oxford University Press, 2000), 46, 48, 73; and James Lloyd Breck, "Indian Mission—Minnesota, 1854," in *DW,* 127–28.

64. David Pendleton Oakerhater, a Cheyenne convert to the Episcopal Church, was ordained to the diaconate in 1881 and served as the denomination's principal missionary in the Indian Territory (present-day Oklahoma) in the late nineteenth and early twentieth centuries. Despite his stature in the church, he was never allowed to be ordained a priest.

65. J. A. Gilfillan, "On the Wrong Way and the Right Way to Civilize the Indians" (1911), quoted in McNally, *Ojibwe Singers,* 89–91, 96–101 (quotation on 101).

66. Ferenc Morton Szasz, "The Episcopal Bishops and the Trans-Mississippi West, 1865–1918," *AEH* 69 (2000): 361–62; and *HPEC,* 263 (source of quotation).

67. G. MacLaren Brydon, *The Episcopal Church among the Negroes of Virginia* (Richmond: Virginia Diocesan Library, 1937), 8–12, 25–26; and Odell Greenleaf Harris, *The Bishop Payne Divinity School: A History of the Seminary to Prepare Black Men for the Ministry of the Protestant Episcopal Church* (Alexandria, Va.: Protestant Episcopal Theological Seminary, 1980), 1–10.

68. Herbert Geer McCarriar Jr., "A History of the Missionary Jurisdiction of the South of the Reformed Episcopal Church, 1874–1970," *HMPEC* 41 (1972): 197–220.

69. *An Account of the Conference on the Relation of the Church to the Colored People of the South, Held at Sewanee, Tennessee, July 25 to 28, 1883* (Sewanee, Tenn.: Wm. H. Harlow, [1883]), 3–14.

70. George F. Bragg, *History of the Afro-American Group of the Episcopal Church* (Baltimore: Church Advocate Press, 1922), 151–53, 305–7. See also Gardiner H. Shattuck Jr., *Episcopalians and Race: Civil War to Civil Rights* (Lexington: University Press of Kentucky, 2000), 12–14.

71. Alexander Crummell, "The Best Methods of Church Work among the Colored People," in *Civilization and Black Progress: Selected Writings of Alexander Crummell on the South,* ed. J. R. Oldfield (Charlottesville: University Press of Virginia, 1995), 155–62.

72. Anna Julia Cooper, *A Voice from the South* (1892; reprint, New York: Oxford University Press, 1988), 33–47 (quotations on 34, 39); and Kevin K. Gaines, *Uplifting the Race: Black Leadership, Politics, and Culture in the Twentieth Century* (Chapel Hill: University of North Carolina Press, 1996), 128–51.

73. George F. Bragg, *Afro-American Church Work and Workers* (Baltimore: Church Advocate, 1904), 16–30; and Shattuck, *Episcopalians and Race,* 20–22.

74. William Montgomery Brown, *The Crucial Race Question; or, Where and How Shall the Color Line Be Drawn,* 2nd ed. (Little Rock: Arkansas Churchman's Publishing, 1907), xi–xxx, 150–58, 162–65, 188–92, 245–49, 253–58, 266–70. Brown's extreme theological and social views—he later became a Communist and declared that the Christian faith was outmoded—eventually led to his being deposed from the episcopate in 1924.

75. Harold T. Lewis, *Yet with a Steady Beat: The African American Struggle for Recognition in the Episcopal Church* (Valley Forge, Pa.: Trinity Press International, 1996), 75–76, 102. In 1905 Brown hired an African American priest, George Alexander McGuire, to lead the segregated "colored work" program in his diocese. McGuire later became chaplain-general of Marcus Garvey's Universal Negro Improvement Association, and in 1921 he founded a new denomination, the African Orthodox Church, along the lines of

what the Conference of Church Workers and Brown had previously proposed—see Gavin White, "Patriarch McGuire and the Episcopal Church," *HMPEC* 38 (1969): 109–41.

76. Bragg, *History of the Afro-American Group,* 294.

77. David M. Reimers, "Negro Bishops and Diocesan Segregation in the Protestant Episcopal Church: 1870–1954," *HMPEC* 31 (1962): 231–42; Lewis, *Yet with a Steady Beat,* 78–81; and Michael J. Beary, *Black Bishop: Edward T. Demby and the Struggle for Racial Equality in the Episcopal Church* (Urbana: University of Illinois Press, 2001), 99–119. Although the Episcopal Church had earlier consecrated two black missionary bishops (James Theodore Holly for Haiti in 1874 and Samuel David Ferguson for Liberia in 1885), Edward Demby and Henry Delany were the first African Americans chosen to serve as bishops within the boundaries of the United States.

78. William McKinley, quoted in Mark A. Noll, *A History of Christianity in the United States and Canada* (Grand Rapids, Mich.: Eerdmans, 1992), 293.

79. Thomas March Clark, "The Mission of the Church: A Sermon Preached at the Opening of the General Convention . . . , October 3, A.D. 1883," in *DW,* 143–44.

80. *HEC,* 193–96.

81. *HPEC,* 336–38.

82. Clifford Putney, *Muscular Christianity: Manhood and Sports in Protestant America, 1880–1920* (Cambridge: Harvard University Press, 2001), 127–37.

83. Arun W. Jones, "A View from the Mountains: Episcopal Missionary Depictions of the Igorot of Northern Luzon, the Philippines, 1903–1916," *AEH* 71 (2002): 380–88, 406–10 (quotation on 382).

84. *RHAP,* 884.

85. William T. Manning, *Our Present Duty as Americans and Christians* (February 4, 1917), quoted in William H. Katerberg, *Modernity and the Dilemma of North American Identities, 1880–1950* (Montreal: McGill-Queen's University Press, 2001), 112.

86. "House of Bishops, Pastoral Letter, October 18, 1917," in *DW,* 342. See also *RHAP,* 883–84.

87. "The Forced Resignation of Bishop Paul Jones, October 17–18, 1917," in *DW,* 340–41.

7
EMERGENCE OF THE MODERN CHURCH: 1918–1958

Church modeling on Protestant silhouette (handwritten annotation)

In the wake of Allied victory in World War I, the hopes of Protestants in the United States seemed to reach new heights. Participation in the war had provided an unprecedented stimulus to piety, and church leaders were determined to maintain that trend in the 1920s. Just as their nation's successful military effort had demonstrated the value of organization and centralization, so Protestants recognized the importance of increased cooperation in meeting religious goals. The creation of the Federal Council of Churches in 1908—an effort designed to "bring the Christian bodies in America into united service for Christ and the world"—had represented an important first step toward the realization of a unified social mission.[1] The launching of the Interchurch World Movement (IWM) in 1919 was similarly intended to advance the cause of interdenominational unity by bringing all the benevolent and missionary agencies of American Protestantism together in a single evangelistic, educational, and fund-raising campaign. Reflecting the same idealism that inspired the creation of the League of Nations, the IWM offered (in the words of one of its founders) "the vision of a united church uniting a divided world."[2]

Despite the spirit of hopefulness that followed the war, the 1920s were also marked by a distinct sense of cultural crisis. The Bolshevik Revolution in Russia in 1917 and the advent of major labor strikes in the United States in 1919 not only spawned a "red scare" but also revived the expression of virulent nativist sentiments. The "Great Migration" of black southerners to northern cities increasingly angered white Americans and inspired an upsurge in white-on-black violence. Reborn in 1915, the Ku Klux Klan attained a peak of three million members in 1923, and its crusade against Roman Catholics, Jews, and immigrants (as well as African Americans) revealed the depth of conservative Protestant fears about social change. Even as liberal Protestants attempted to draw closer to one another in the first decades of the twentieth century, new theological fault lines materialized within their own denominations. Fierce battles between modernists and fundamentalists divided major denominations such as the Northern Baptist Convention and the Presbyterian Church in the U.S.A., and the Scopes trial of 1925 signaled the continuing hold of traditional cultural values on the nation's rural areas.[3]

Relatively untroubled by controversies that upset other American denominations, Episcopalians entered the 1920s in a supremely confident mood. Their church had experienced steady growth between 1880 and 1920—the number of its parishes doubling (from 4,151 to 8,365) and its membership tripling (from 345,433 to 1,075,820) in size. In fact, Episcopal leaders initially resisted participation in the Federal Council of Churches because they believed that their denomination was comprehensive enough by itself to become the "bridge church" into which all others would one day be united. The Episcopal Church, they thought, embodied the best aspects of Catholicism and Protestantism, tradition and modernity, diversity and unity—qualities that other Christians might soon have the wisdom to recognize. Since the denomination enjoyed considerable social prestige and occupied a position of historic importance in the Anglo-American world, Episcopalians assumed that they had a unique responsibility to dictate the course of ecumenical affairs.[4]

Ideas about bureaucratic efficiency also encouraged Episcopalians to modernize and expand their operations at the national level. The General Convention of 1919 passed a resolution that required the presiding bishop (formerly the senior diocesan bishop in the United States) to be elected by the House of Bishops for a renewable six-year term. At the same time, the convention established a 24-member National Council, chaired by the presiding bishop and composed of equal numbers of bishops, priests, and laymen. The council was given authority to coordinate the ongoing work of the denomination between triennial meetings of the General Convention. Finally, having seen the value of large-scale fund-raising drives during the war, Episcopalians initiated a nationwide campaign to identify the needs of their denomination and to increase its financial support. Through this effort, the 1919 convention aspired "to bring the spiritual and material resources of the Church to bear more effectively . . . upon her whole task as witness to the Master."[5]

THE FAITH AND ORDER MOVEMENT

Despite Episcopalians' general opposition to collaborating with other American Protestants through the Federal Council of Churches, Charles Henry Brent, bishop of the Philippines, emerged as a key figure in the early stages of the international ecumenical movement. Brent had become committed to the cause of church unity while attending the Edinburgh Missionary Conference in 1910, when twelve hundred delegates from various ecclesiastical traditions and countries gathered to discuss issues relating to worldwide Christian evangelism. "I was converted," he later reported. "I learned that something was working that was not of man in that conference; that the Spirit of God was . . . preparing a new era in the history of

Christianity."[6] With Brent's support, William T. Manning of New York introduced a resolution at the 1910 General Convention proposing the formation of another ecumenical conference at which vexing questions about "Faith and Order" (that is, doctrine and polity) could be discussed.

Although the idea of ecumenical participation was approved in principle by the Episcopal Church, the outbreak of war in Europe prevented the undertaking of any concerted action. Over the next few years, Manning himself backed away from ecumenism, for along with other Anglo-Catholics, he strongly disapproved of reuniting with Protestant denominations. Only the Roman Catholic, Orthodox, and Anglican churches, he contended, possessed the *true* faith and *authentic* order on which church unity ought to be based.[7] Meanwhile, Pope Benedict XV turned down requests for Roman Catholic participation in the nascent ecumenical movement. Like Episcopalians touting the importance of their own comprehensiveness as the foundation for Christian reunion, Benedict declared that all Christians had to reconcile themselves to his supreme authority as "the visible head of the Church."[8] In addition, many conservative Protestant denominations refused to participate in the Faith and Order movement because they feared it would inevitably undermine the distinctive theological beliefs to which they were committed.

Such opposition notwithstanding, four hundred Christians gathered at Lausanne, Switzerland, in 1927 for the first World Conference on Faith and Order. Delegates representing over one hundred Christian communions came from almost every part of the globe. Although the gathering did expose some serious theological disagreements among the participating churches, as a whole it was successful and represented a critical milestone in the development of the ecumenical movement. It addressed issues regarding evangelism, the nature of the church, a common confession of faith, ordained ministry, the sacraments, and the church's role in the world. The frank exchange of ideas at the conference as well as the experience of worshipping together led delegates to appreciate other traditions. As the French Reformed pastor Elie Gounelle observed, Lausanne was the first worldwide assembly of Christians that ended "without anathemas or excommunications," and as such it was "a new thing and a marvel."[9]

In poor health and nearing the end of his life, Brent was elected to preside at the first session of the conference. Reemphasizing the Anglican ideal of comprehensiveness, he lamented that most Christians were "devoted to the cult of the incomplete—sectarianism," thus denying "the Christ in a neighboring church." He urged participants at Lausanne to renounce that sectarian spirit and instead to keep the idea of Christian unity constantly in mind. It is only "by practicing unity," he concluded, "that we shall gain unity."[10]

As Brent's remarks suggest, the Lausanne conference helped bolster the commitment of Episcopalians to the formation of ecumenical relationships. They took part not only in the later Faith and Order conferences but also in the conferences on Life and Work (i.e., social policy), which began in 1925; and they joined the Church of England in establishing full communion with the Old Catholic Church in 1931.[11] These various international discussions eventually bore fruit in 1948, when the Episcopal Church became one of the founding members of the World Council of Churches.

THE FAILURE OF ECUMENICAL DIALOGUE WITH THE PRESBYTERIANS

Spurred by the success of the Lausanne conference, the 1928 General Convention adopted a proposal, which Brent introduced, establishing a commission to confer with representatives of the Methodist and Presbyterian churches about the possibility of ecclesiastical unification. Although Lutherans were also added to this group in 1931, neither they nor Methodists were prepared to engage seriously in such discussions. Since Lutherans in the United States were themselves separated along myriad ethnic and theological lines, and since Methodists were engaged in the process of healing the sectional division that had occurred in the 1840s, there was no realistic basis on which any Lutheran or Methodist denomination could consider union with the Episcopal Church. Presbyterians were similarly split, having divided into northern and southern branches during the Civil War, but the Presbyterian Church in the U.S.A. (the northern denomination) still decided to enter into talks with Episcopalians. Despite the enthusiasm expressed by a few Episcopal leaders who had been active in the international ecumenical movement, the series of meetings they held with the Presbyterians further revealed the ambivalence that most members of their denomination felt about union with other American Protestants.[12]

Edward Lambe Parsons, the bishop of California, was the principal Episcopalian involved with the unity commission. Raised a Presbyterian, he had studied at Union Theological Seminary in New York, where Charles Augustus Briggs had been his mentor. When Parsons's presbytery refused to ordain him, he (like Briggs) sought ordination in the theologically more diverse Episcopal Church. Parsons considered himself to be a "liberal evangelical." As he explained in 1934, liberal evangelicals stressed "the unity of all truth and the revelation in scientific and historical discovery of the wider meanings of the Personality of God." Armed with the wisdom provided by modern knowledge, Christians would no longer become "lost in dogmas, in institutions and in things," but they would be free to discover how otherwise antiquated religious practices and beliefs were "but the clothing of a deep and essential personal relationship" with the divine.[13]

Although a theological liberal like Parsons had no objection to pursuing union with the Presbyterians, other influential Episcopalians eventually derailed his efforts. In May 1938 the Presbyterian General Assembly accepted the invitation of the Episcopal commission to form a committee of their own and join actively in talks. Over the next decade, the meetings between the two commissions produced a number of tentative proposals for discussion, but the documents they released soon became the focus of intense debate among Episcopalians. The chief point of contention concerned an explicit affirmation of the spiritual and liturgical equality between Episcopal and Presbyterian clergy, for various reports made clear that Presbyterian teaching elders would not have to be re-ordained as priests by Episcopal bishops. The American Church Union, which had been formed in 1936 to promote Anglo-Catholic principles within the Episcopal Church, voiced especially strong opposition to that point. How could the church maintain its traditional faith and order, Anglo-Catholics asked, if such a plan was implemented? *The Living Church,* a popular Anglo-Catholic journal in the Midwest, also attacked the ecumenical proposals as an attempt by liberal Protestants to take over the Episcopal Church. In addition, Wallace E. Conkling, the bishop of Chicago, worked persistently to derail the proposal, while William Manning asserted that no Episcopalian could in good conscience accept any scheme to unite with the Presbyterians.[14]

Statements by leading pro-union Presbyterians inadvertently made matters worse during this period. Presbyterian traditionalists, who believed that John Calvin had restored the faith and polity of the New Testament after centuries of obscurantism and corruption, were fearful that liberals in their denomination might capitulate to high church Episcopalians about the importance of the episcopate. As a consequence, liberals addressed the concerns of their conservative colleagues by reemphasizing that the distinctive teachings and practices of Presbyterianism would remain intact after the merger. While these statements placated Presbyterian traditionalists, they deeply offended high church Episcopalians and made it difficult for the plan's proponents to claim that the concerns of Anglo-Catholics had been safeguarded during the negotiations.[15]

The continuation of the dialogue with the Presbyterians became one of the main subjects of deliberation at the 1946 General Convention. Whereas Episcopal advocates of union pressed for an affirmation of the ecumenical venture, some leading Anglo-Catholics worried that they might have to secede from their denomination if that course of action was upheld. There was no point in considering an ecumenical process, they said, that would "move us farther and farther away from any of the great historic Catholic Communions" and make the Episcopal Church "a laughing stock before the eyes of Christendom."[16] After considerable debate, the 1946 convention passed a resolution that, while not directly challenging the idea of union with the Presbyterians, effectively scuttled any further debate about its merits. In the resolution, the unity commission was directed to prepare a statement on ecumenical relations that was in harmony with the Chicago-Lambeth Quadrilateral—that is, that emphasized the importance of the historic episcopate. For its part, the Presbyterian General Assembly never brought the matter of church union to a vote, for the majority of Presbyterians bristled at the idea of bishops. Thus, while the decision of the Episcopal convention allowed negotiations with the Presbyterians to continue, the two sides had reached an impasse that brought their discussions to an end.[17]

RESPONSE TO THE GREAT DEPRESSION

As the noted journalist Walter Lippmann observed on the eve of the stock market crash of 1929, American society was becoming increasingly secular and irreligious. Broad cultural trends were pushing Americans to define themselves in terms of the things they owned and the pleasures they enjoyed. The social gospel, which had been vigorous in the mainline churches before World War I, declined dramatically in the 1920s; few Protestants even questioned, let alone condemned, the commercial character of their culture and the materialistic values it promoted.[18]

The collapse of the stock market came as a tremendous shock, therefore, to religious as well as to nonreligious Americans. Although significant numbers of Americans sought and found solace in organized religion during the hard times of economic depression, fundamentalist and Pentecostal churches such as the Assemblies of God and the Church of the Nazarene proved to be far more adept at attracting adherents than the Episcopal Church. Despite maintaining relatively steady membership figures throughout the 1930s, the combined receipts of Episcopal parishes fell from $44.7 million in 1927 to $30.6 million in 1934, and annual contributions for the denomination's foreign missions dropped from $2.25 to $0.96 per capita. In the decade following the market crash, many parishes had to reduce the salaries of their clergy, and some even had trouble making mortgage payments on their buildings.[19]

Responding to the appalling social crisis that confronted them, religious thinkers increasingly turned to the "neo-orthodoxy" espoused by leading Reformed theologians—for example, Karl Barth of Switzerland and Reinhold and H. Richard Niebuhr of the United States—who emphasized such traditional Protestant beliefs as the sovereignty of God, the moral depravity of humanity, and salvation in Jesus Christ. Episcopal theologians, too, were influenced by neo-orthodoxy and recognized the fundamental dichotomy between the church's ideals and those of a secular society. True to their Anglican establishmentarian roots, however, Episcopalians also highlighted the responsibilities of the institutional church in directing and reforming society. No Anglican spokesperson was more influential in this regard than William Temple, who served as the archbishop of York in England from 1929 to 1942. In the face of severe unemployment and the suffering of many working-class citizens, Temple stressed that the church needed to "make its voice heard in matters of politics and economics" by playing a central role in "the fulfilment of God's purpose in the world and beyond it."[20] Wherever social evils existed, Temple insisted, Christians had to work for a just political and economic order.[21]

In a pastoral letter released in November 1933, the House of Bishops of the Episcopal Church affirmed these Anglican social teachings by calling church members to contribute to "the happiness, peace and security" of their economically struggling nation. "Days of material anxiety are days of spiritual opportunity," the bishops remarked, for "though material values collapse, spiritual values remain unimpaired." They blamed many of the country's troubles on "the lowering of moral standards" during the world war and on a "malevolent and violent attack upon Christian institutions and the Christian faith" by America's cultural elite. Since they assumed the problem was fundamentally a spiritual one, the bishops' prescription for economic recovery involved religious as well as practical measures: establishing "a new order in which there shall be a more equitable distribution of material wealth [and] more certain assurance of security for the unemployed," and sharing "the world-wide vision of service given to us by Jesus Christ." "Let us prove our faith in practice," they urged, "and nothing can withstand the spiritual momentum that must follow."[22]

The bishops' call to militant Christian action pleased Vida Scudder of Wellesley College, who continued to be an advocate of the church's social responsibilities. In an article praising the pronouncements of the House of Bishops, Scudder stressed that "the whole Church should be on her knees these days praying quite concretely for definite ends." Since the fate of Western civilization appeared to be hanging in the balance, the response of Christians to the crisis might well save the day. Although Scudder did not mention them specifically, there were several Episcopalians who were active in the early stages of the New Deal: Franklin and Eleanor Roosevelt in the White House; Frances Perkins, the Secretary of Labor; and Henry A. Wallace, the Secretary of Agriculture. "*We* are the Church," she declared, "you, and you, and I"—great political leaders as well as ordinary people. Even as the present social order was being dramatically transformed, Christians could accelerate that process by studying the issues and by offering intercessory prayers. No one could foretell the outcome of the approaching revolution, Scudder concluded, but "we can rest assured that the Church advances toward effective triumph only if we her children march with the Cross of Christ before us."[23]

ISSUES OF WAR AND PEACE

Despite rushing headlong into war against the Central Powers in 1917, American church leaders recoiled from the memory of the conflict soon after the armistice was signed. Initial estimates revealed that the World War I had resulted in at least ten million dead and twenty million wounded worldwide. Most church leaders not only were shocked by the senseless butchery of modern warfare but also felt ashamed of their own role in demonizing Germany and urging America's entrance into battle. Chastened, almost every American denomination endorsed the creation of the League of Nations and vowed to work for international peace. As the bishops of the Episcopal Church declared in their pastoral letter of 1933, "disciples of the Prince of Peace . . . are bound by every solemn obligation to wage unremitting war against war."[24]

By the late 1930s, as the United States faced the prospect of participating in another European war, antiwar and pacifist sentiments remained strong in the American churches. Despite the well-documented brutality of the totalitarian regimes in Germany, Italy, and Japan, abhorrence of the even greater bloodshed that an actual war might bring induced religious leaders to oppose involvement in the affairs of other nations. The presiding bishop of the Episcopal Church, Henry St. George Tucker, had once been the missionary bishop of Japan, and he was outspoken about the need for American neutrality in the approaching conflict.

Although sharply critical of the concessions contained in the Munich Pact of 1938, Tucker insisted throughout 1939 that the United States should not be drawn into the conflict in Europe and Asia. Several weeks after the German invasion of Poland, a group of Episcopalians under the leadership of John Nevin Sayre, a priest who was active in the interdenominational Fellowship of Reconciliation, met in New York and formed the Episcopal Pacifist Fellowship. This organization, which contained about eight hundred members at its peak in the mid-1940s, offered strong support to conscientious objectors throughout World War II.[25]

By early 1941, however, when Nazi Germany seemed to be on the brink of victory over England, the majority of Episcopalians realized that they could no longer refuse to help their traditional allies in the British isles. Several months before the Japanese attack on Pearl Harbor, some Episcopal bishops began to call on fellow church member Franklin Roosevelt and the U.S. government to come to Great Britain's aid. At that time, Tucker described Hitler and the Nazis as "a cancerous growth" that had to be removed by force of arms. He not only decried Hitler's murderous campaign against the Jews but also called for efforts to provide asylum for Jewish refugees fleeing the Nazi forces in Europe. After the United States formally entered the war against the Axis powers in December 1941, Tucker envisioned the expanding conflict as a judgment by God on the sins of all nations—a bloody contest into which Americans should enter with an attitude of penitence rather than self-righteousness or vindictiveness.[26]

The war in the Pacific had a particularly devastating impact on Episcopalians' missionary work among Asians. In the Philippines, the two American bishops and almost all of the Episcopal missionaries were imprisoned after the Japanese captured the islands.[27] Since Episcopalians had also been involved in evangelistic efforts among Asian Americans on the West Coast, the wartime internment of citizens of Japanese descent similarly disrupted the church's domestic missionary activities. In January 1942, Presiding Bishop Tucker appointed Charles Shriver Reifsnider, who had served as a missionary in Japan, as the bishop in charge of the denomination's nine Japanese American congregations. Just a few weeks later, the U.S. government ordered the removal of people of Japanese ancestry from California and from parts of Washington, Oregon, and Arizona. As that military order was being implemented, Daisuke Kitagawa, a priest in Seattle, wrote an "Open Letter to Fellow Christians in the USA," in which he strongly objected to the eviction of his people from their homes and their relocation in internment camps. Despite this protest, even sympathetic Episcopalians such as Tucker and Reifsnider could do little to ameliorate the situation, though they did insist on continuing the church's ministry among those who were confined in the camps.[28]

After the war, the justice of placing Japanese Americans in internment camps was one of several controversial subjects addressed in a collection of essays entitled *Christianity Takes a Stand* (1946), edited by William Scarlett, the bishop of Missouri and chairman of the General Convention's Joint Commission on Social Reconstruction. Assigned the task of considering how the Episcopal Church might take the lead in creating "a better world for all peoples" after 1945,

Scarlett's commission articulated three principal objectives for which their denomination would aim: international peace (recognition of "the basic Christian principle of the unity . . . of all mankind in God"); interracial cooperation (acceptance of "the Jewish-Christian tradition that all mankind is one Family in God"); and economic justice (application of the belief that "the economic order exists to serve God by increasing the welfare of all men").[29] In his essay on the removal of Japanese Americans from the West Coast, Edward Parsons of California concluded that "every decent American must determine that nothing like it shall ever happen again in this 'land of the free.' "[30] Scarlett's volume also discussed other critical social issues such as the status of minorities in the United States (by Eleanor Roosevelt), methods for achieving full employment (by Frances Perkins), the relationship between the United States and the Soviet Union (by Reinhold Niebuhr), and the morality of the atomic bomb (by Arthur Holly Compton, a winner of the Nobel Prize in physics).

POSTWAR REVIVAL AND PARISH GROWTH IN THE SUBURBS

After two highly unsettled decades of economic depression and war, most Americans enjoyed a period of unprecedented prosperity from the late 1940s through the 1960s, when the average American earned more money, ate better, and generally lived more comfortably than his or her parents had. Although poverty still remained a serious problem for some citizens, millions also entered the ranks of the home-owning middle class. In a movement spurred by the postwar baby boom, Americans flooded into the suburbs—a trend further encouraged by the expansion of the automobile industry and by a rapid increase in government spending on roads and public schools.[31] According to one observer, the typical suburban development attracted people who wanted "to center their lives around the home and the family, to be among neighbors whom they can trust, . . . [and] to participate in organizations that provide sociability and the opportunity to be of service to others."[32]

Religious bodies were one of the most common organizations to which Americans flocked after World War II. The late 1940s witnessed an astounding surge in piety in the United States as new churches and synagogues were formed in the expanding suburbs. The Census Bureau reported in 1957 that 96 percent of the American population named a specific affiliation when asked, "What is your religion?" According to official membership statistics, moreover, over 60 percent of all Americans belonged to a church in the late 1950s—a dramatic increase over the number of churchgoers 30 years earlier.[33] The Episcopal Church also fared extremely well in this period. By 1960 there were nearly 3.3 million baptized Episcopalians: 1 in every 55 citizens was an Episcopalian, compared to just 1 in every 416 Americans in 1830. And despite the fact that in 1956—for the first time in its history—the denomination had more priests (7,889) than parishes

(7,200), it was estimated that several hundred more clergymen would soon be needed to keep up with the growing number of Episcopal congregations.[34]

While faring very well in statistical terms after the war, the Episcopal Church also saw its spiritual life revitalized through renewed attention to liturgy and theology. The growing interdenominational liturgical movement had a particularly strong effect on some parishes. Seeking the restoration of many of the practices of the early church, liturgical reformers emphasized certain key principles: (1) that worship is the work of the laity, not the performance of a single ordained person at the altar or pulpit; (2) that churches should have the simple design and spare ornamentation typical of the buildings in which Christians assembled for worship in the first and second centuries; and (3) that Christians should fully integrate Sunday morning worship into their everyday lives.[35]

In 1946 a group of Episcopal scholars, seminary faculty, parish clergy, and laity created an organization called Associated Parishes, which was dedicated to disseminating information about the liturgical movement throughout the church. Thanks to the efforts of Associated Parishes, congregations increasingly began to celebrate the Eucharist (rather than choral morning prayer with sermon) as the principal form of Sunday morning worship. Priests were also encouraged to use freestanding altars and to face worshipers when celebrating the Eucharist, thus highlighting the similarities between that service and Jesus' Last Supper. Standing replaced kneeling as the preferred posture for the congregation at prayer, and the explanation of biblical texts became the central focus of the sermon. In addition, laypeople, not clergy, were expected to read scripture lessons and to lead intercessory prayers. Although Associated Parishes was a voluntary association, not an official denominational agency, its members and the ideas they developed and popularized eventually transformed worship in the Episcopal Church.[36]

During the postwar period, clergy and laity alike developed a renewed interest in theology. Although neo-orthodoxy remained highly influential, the writings of Paul Tillich, a German theologian who had emigrated to the United States in 1933, represented the quintessential expression of American Protestant theological ideas in the 1950s. Tillich's existentialism articulated both the anxiety and the religious optimism of that era. Identifying religion as "ultimate concern," he offered guidance to well-educated Americans who did not want to pay an intellectual price for their spiritual commitment. Thus, Tillich emphasized that doubt is a necessary part of faith and that, without it, faith often becomes either fanatical or idolatrous.[37] His method of providing subtle answers for contemporary ethical questions stimulated the thinking of many Episcopalians. For instance, Clifford Stanley and Albert Mollegen, liberal evangelicals who served on the faculty of Virginia Seminary, were two of his most prominent American disciples.[38]

A number of Episcopal theologians also guided and enriched the religious imaginations of Americans during this period. Norman Pittenger, who taught at General Seminary and later at Cambridge University, introduced many students to process theology, a school of thought derived from the philosophy of Alfred North Whitehead and his pupil Charles Hartshorne. Challenging traditional meta-

alfred north whitehead - an evolving cosmos through which God acts persuasively.

physical thinking about an unchanging, omnipotent God, process theologians instead emphasized the notion of an evolving cosmos through which God acts persuasively, not coercively. Professor John Macquarrie of Union Seminary, who had converted to the Episcopal Church from Presbyterianism, was committed to developing "a new style natural theology." Strongly influenced by the New Testament scholarship of Rudolf Bultmann and the metaphysics of Martin Heidegger, Macquarrie sought to construct an intellectual "bridge between our everyday thinking and experience and the matters about which theologians talk," thereby relating religious discourse to all areas of human life.[39]

On a popular and less academic level, Episcopalians formed discussion groups to consider topics of general interest such as "Christianity and Modern Man," and they also read the works of important religious writers such as C. S. Lewis, Austin Farrer, E. L. Mascall, and Evelyn Underhill, all members of the Church of England. Reaching well beyond the members of his denomination, James A. Pike, dean of the Cathedral of St. John the Divine in New York, explored the implications of Christian beliefs on the religious television program he regularly hosted. Seabury Press, the church's newly established publishing house, also supported the religious education of adults in the books and materials it produced. One of its first publications was the *Church's Teaching Series,* which was meant to give Episcopalians a grounding in "the basic content of the Church's faith." Fearing that their denomination was failing to communicate the essentials of Christianity to its ever-increasing membership, the educators who devised the *Church's Teaching Series* intended not only to overcome the lamentable "religious illiteracy of our time" but also to demonstrate how there was a profound "difference between human ideals and divine commandments."[40] In addition to this series, which was designed for adults, the Christian education department of the Episcopal Church distributed a carefully prepared Sunday school curriculum for children. Entitled the *Seabury Series,* the curriculum focused on stories, both biblical and modern, that illustrated the complex ethical decisions faced by Christians in their daily lives.[41]

NEW URBAN MINISTRIES

Although church membership figures reached new heights in the 1950s and parishes were alive with activity, not all American Christians were pleased with the religious enthusiasm they witnessed. In the eyes of some critics, American society had become dominated by an empty "culture religion" that was nothing more than "faith in faith."[42] This problem was illustrated unwittingly by President Dwight Eisenhower in 1954, when he remarked that the United States "is founded on a deeply felt religious faith—and I don't care what it is."[43] The title of Gibson Winter's well-known book, *The Suburban Captivity of the Churches* (1961), coincd a phrase that encapsulated the despair felt by many clergy and theologians about the state of contemporary American religion. An Episcopal priest who had served in suburban congregations in the 1940s, Winter thought it tragic that at a time "when America's position of world leadership requires a prophetic church," churchgoers were concerned with only the conformist banalities of parish life: bazaars, bake sales, endless "functions," and virtual "enslavement" to the needs of their children.[44]

Because the exodus of middle-class whites to the suburbs and the resultant decline of downtown areas threatened the property values of many urban parishes, Protestant leaders in the late 1940s and early 1950s began to emphasize the need to re-evangelize the American city. The establishment of the interdenominational East Harlem Protestant Parish in New York was one of the first and most successful of these efforts. William Stringfellow, a lawyer and lay Episcopalian who worked as a legal counselor for the East Harlem Parish in the mid-1950s, wrote extensively about his experiences living in an impoverished neighborhood in upper Manhattan. Despite the squalor and misery that surrounded him, Stringfellow was convinced that inner-city settings such as East Harlem represented a particularly fruitful mission field. Influenced by the theological writings of Karl Barth and the German Lutheran martyr Dietrich Bonhoeffer, Stringfellow laid emphasis on the intimate relationship between God and the secular world. "The Christian faith is not about some god who is an abstract presence somewhere else," he insisted, "but about the living presence of God here and now, in this world, in *exactly* this world, as men . . . live and work in it."[45]

The most celebrated Episcopal inner-city ministry of the postwar period was organized and led by three priests: Paul Moore, C. Kilmer Myers, and Robert Pegram. The three men worked at Grace Church in Jersey City, New Jersey—a once prosperous parish that had lost most of its members during the "white flight" to the suburbs and was struggling to stay in operation in the late 1940s. Moore, Myers, and Pegram had been friends at General Seminary, and instead of priming themselves for jobs in affluent suburban settings like many of their classmates, they believed that the new generation of leaders in the Episcopal Church needed to identify themselves with the poor. Moore, who had been severely wounded in combat during World War II, also contrasted the virile character of urban ministry with the feminine, family-oriented milieu of Protestantism in the suburbs. Since God called Christians to redeem society, the true "battle line of the Church is the inner-city," he said, not "the matriarchal child-centered suburban parish," with which the majority of Episcopalians were comfortably affiliated.[46] Myers and Pegram were bachelors, and they shared the rectory on the Grace Church grounds with Moore, his wife Jenny, and the Moore children. The priests quickly instituted an "open rectory" policy and thus were in continuous contact with the struggles of the poor people who were their neighbors and parishioners. As Jenny Moore later observed about this experience, "the difference between a non-Christian and a Christian is that the former may work to alleviate suffering but that the latter attempts to share in it as well."[47]

Social ministries similar to the one in Jersey City—well-to-do Episcopalians making a conscious choice to live and work among the poor—were instituted in a number of urban areas in the Northeast in the 1950s. Myers, for example, was recruited by the rector of Trinity Church, New York, and asked to serve as vicar of St. Augustine's Chapel, a mission that Trinity supported on Manhattan's decaying Lower East Side. Thanks to his earlier work at Grace Church, Myers soon developed an effective outreach program, focusing on worship and recreation, with the neighborhood's juvenile delinquents and street gangs.[48] John Harmon, who became rector of St. John's Church in Roxbury (Boston's largest African American neighborhood) in 1952, organized a ministry similar to Myers's. Harmon was involved in the postwar liturgical movement, and in his sermons he underscored the historic relationship between Anglo-Catholic ritualism and social ministry in urban neighborhoods. He believed in Christ's mystical identification with those who were suffering, and he asked otherwise complacent church people to see how God's grace could be active even in places where they did not expect to discover it.[49]

Arthur Walmsley, a priest who also had served in urban parishes in the 1950s, substantially agreed with the analysis of the contemporary religious scene offered by colleagues such as Moore, Myers, and Harmon. Although Walmsley knew a revival of sorts was taking place in many Episcopal congregations, the therapeutic concerns that were so popular in suburbia—the "preoccupation with small-group, face-to-face relationships, family life, [and] the parish family"—were actually antithetical to the traditional Anglican emphasis on the social gospel. The average churchgoer, he observed, seemed to have forgotten that Christ came "not to redeem the Church but the world." As a result, few Episcopalians were willing to look beyond life in their local parishes to consider how they might become more involved in the social, political, and economic affairs of their nation.[50]

THE END OF RACIAL SEGREGATION IN THE CHURCH

In the early 1930s, African American scholars Benjamin Mays and Joseph Nicholson spent over a year collecting data about black religious institutions in the United States, eventually publishing their findings in *The Negro's Church* (1933). Mays and Nicholson's research provided extremely grim news for Episcopalians: less than 2 percent of all urban black churches were affiliated with the Episcopal Church, and in rural areas the percentage was less than 1 percent. Although there had been some growth in the black Episcopal population in the Northeast as African Americans migrated northward in the 1910s and 1920s, the number of black Episcopalians in the South had clearly declined during that same period.[51]

Faced with such dismal statistics, white leaders in the Episcopal Church were forced to give far greater attention to the relationship between African Americans and their denomination than they had ever done before. After several years of deliberation, the National Council of the Episcopal Church created a nationwide racial ministry under the direction of an "Executive Secretary for Negro Work." Bravid Harris, a black priest then serving as archdeacon of the "colored convocation" in the diocese of Southern Virginia, was appointed to the new position in

July 1943. At the same time, the council adopted a set of "Guiding Principles Designed to Govern the Church's Negro Work." Believing that Christian churches ought to embody "the reality of community as God intends it" by transcending all ordinary national, ethnic, and racial lines, the council resolved that the Episcopal Church would "break through the encirclement of racial segregation in all matters which pertain to her program . . . and lead the way towards the fulfillment of our Lord's desire that they all may be one."[52]

Although most white Episcopalians in the 1940s continued to accept the reality of racial segregation, many of them also hoped that their Negro work program would at least ameliorate the situation faced by black church members. However, as Episcopalians of all races looked more closely at the efforts of their denomination in the African American community, they saw an unsettling picture. The most disturbing news concerned Bishop Payne Divinity School in Petersburg, Virginia, where southern bishops had been sending black candidates for the ordained ministry for several decades. Reports about the seminary's dilapidated buildings and inadequate curriculum caused particular discomfort for those who still believed in the viability of a church-supported system of segregated education. After trying for several years to improve conditions in Petersburg, the trustees of the black seminary voted to close the school in May 1949. Because Virginia Theological Seminary had been instrumental in founding the seminary in 1878, the financial assets of Bishop Payne were transferred to Alexandria after its campus and property in Petersburg were sold. In addition, the color line was broken at Virginia Seminary in the fall of 1951, when John Walker of Detroit enrolled as the school's first African American student.[53]

Even as Episcopalians were voluntarily ending racial segregation in their seminaries in Virginia, two Supreme Court decisions accelerated the process of desegregation in other church institutions. In two separate rulings in June 1950, the Supreme Court questioned the constitutionality of maintaining "separate but equal" facilities for black students in colleges and graduate schools. Those rulings set the stage for a major conflict at the University of the South in Sewanee, Tennessee. At a meeting of representatives from dioceses in the southeastern United States in October 1951, a majority of the bishops, priests, and laypeople who were present declared that the School of Theology of the University of the South should no longer be segregated but should be open to seminarians of all races. However, when the trustees of "Sewanee" discussed that specific proposal a few months later, they decided that state segregation laws in Tennessee prevented them from opening the school to African Americans. The theology faculty immediately challenged that decision, and when the board of trustees refused to reconsider it, most of the faculty members resigned in protest.[54]

News about these events quickly spread throughout the denomination, and at the 1952 General Convention a resolution was passed condemning any Episcopal college or seminary that used race as a criterion for denying admission to students. The conflict further expanded in the winter of 1953, when James Pike was chosen by the Sewanee trustees to receive an honorary degree. Pike refused to accept the honor and instead issued a press release, in which he stated that he had no desire to hold a "doctorate in . . . white divinity" from Sewanee. If the University of the South were a Christian institution, he declared, it would have abolished its "apartheid policy" and defied the segregation laws that most Americans regarded as immoral.[55] Chastened by Pike's statements and embarrassed by the adverse publicity they had generated, the Sewanee trustees voted at their next meeting to open the School of Theology to African American applicants.[56]

Because of the scrutiny that the church's segregated system of theological education received in the late 1940s and early 1950s, liberal Episcopalians began to question other aspects of its "Negro work" agenda as well. One particularly telling criticism was advanced by Alger Adams, an African American priest in Yonkers, New York. Writing in *The Witness* (the church's most socially progressive journal) in the fall of 1951, Adams strongly condemned what he called "Church Jim Crow." He was especially critical of the principles the National Council had adopted when it instituted the Negro work program in 1943. Due to the official nature of those teachings, few Episcopalians bothered to question the existence of parishes that were organized along racial lines. Adams charged that, whereas church members ought to have been engaged in advancing the cause of American democracy on all fronts, "our spiritual blindness, our moral cowardice, and our double-tongued . . . mortal sin in not knowing good from evil" were preventing the racially inclusive teachings of Jesus Christ from being put into practice.[57]

As Adams was well aware, parishes composed exclusively of African Americans remained a fact of life in major northern cities as well as in most southern dioceses. Since the end of World War II, however, white Episcopalians had taken steps to desegregate the meetings of their diocesan conventions, thereby allowing African American clergy and the lay representatives of black parishes to become part of the church's decision-making process. Only the diocese of South Carolina continued to resist this trend. Although the issue of desegregation had first been raised there in 1945, segregationists were able to block the reform for several more years. Finally, with the urging of diocesan bishop Thomas Carruthers at the convention in May 1954, the white parishes of South Carolina ended the racial policy that had been in effect since 1875 by admitting St. Mark's Church, Charleston, and two other African American parishes into their convention fellowship.[58]

A far greater milestone in American race relations was reached just two weeks after the meeting of the South Carolina convention, when the Supreme Court handed down its landmark ruling on the *Brown* school segregation case. The justices unanimously ruled that separation on the basis of race was an inherently unequal arrangement that caused grave harm to black children. Several lay Episcopalians played prominent roles in the research and legal maneuvering that preceded the *Brown* decision: J. Waties Waring, a federal district judge in South Carolina who had initially questioned the constitutionality of the "separate but equal" principle in a court decision in 1951; Thurgood Marshall, the National Association for the Advancement of Colored People (NAACP) lawyer who had led the fight against racial segregation in a series of court cases covering several years; Pauli Murray, a lawyer who had compiled a painstaking study, *States' Laws on Race and Color* (1951), which aided Marshall and the NAACP in their legal battles with segregationists; and Kenneth and Mamie Clark, academic psychologists who provided crucial evidence of the negative effects of segregation on the personalities of African American children.[59]

Although the reaction of politicians and journalists to the *Brown* decision was predictably mixed, almost every major religious body in the United States quickly endorsed it, beginning with the Presbyterian Church in the United States (the southern Presbyterians) and the Southern Baptist Convention. Although the Episcopal Church was comparatively slow in making a pronouncement on the *Brown* decision, the first one it offered originated in a somewhat unlikely place. In June 1954, Duncan M. Gray Jr., a white priest who served on the Christian social relations committee of the diocese of Mississippi, prepared a statement discussing the Supreme Court ruling. Gray invoked a wide variety of religious authorities in support of desegregation, including biblical teachings on the fatherhood of God and official declarations of the Anglican Communion about the need for racial inclusiveness in the church. From the standpoint of both the Christian faith and American democracy, Gray concluded, Episcopalians were morally bound to support the *Brown* decision. This statement gained the attention of officials at the denomination's New York headquarters, and with Gray's assistance the National Council of the Episcopal Church adopted a resolution similar to his in December 1954. "The Court's ruling is more than a matter of law and order," the National Council declared; "it has to do with the will of God and the welfare and destiny of human beings" as well. Based, therefore, on "religious faith and democratic principles," the Supreme Court decision was unquestionably "just, right and necessary."[60]

CHANGING ROLES OF WOMEN

The first half of the twentieth century brought significant and visible changes in the roles exercised by women both in the churches and in American society as a whole. The evolving status of women in the United States, especially during the ratification process of the Nineteenth Amendment, was mirrored—albeit ambivalently—in actions of the Episcopal Church. Following the General Convention of 1919, when the organizational structure of the denomination was significantly reshaped, the Woman's Auxiliary chose to become an adjunct to the National Council rather than to the Board of Missions. This switch enabled the auxiliary to expand the scope of its bureaucratic oversight by including women who served as religious educators and social workers with those who were missionaries. The 1919 convention, however, defeated a resolution that would have given women the right to vote in church assemblies. Robert H. Gardiner, a lay deputy from Maine, proposed the removal of the word "laymen" from the laws governing diocesan representation at general conventions—a move that would have allowed both male and female Episcopalians to be elected to the House of

Deputies. Gardiner's resolution was defeated at the convention; furthermore, during a subsequent process of rewriting the church's canons, the words "male" and "laymen" were also inserted wherever terminology was ambiguous. These textual emendations made explicit the *exclusion* of women from the highest governing levels of the church.[61]

Fifteen years later, however, the opinions of General Convention delegates about female representation had changed a bit, and in 1934 the convention voted to allow the Triennial meeting of the Woman's Auxiliary to nominate, and the convention itself to elect, four women who would serve on the National Council.[62] The first four women who were chosen through this process took seats at the January 1935 meeting of the National Council: Elizabeth Matthews of the diocese of Southern Ohio, Eva D. Corey of the diocese of Massachusetts, Rebekah L. Hibbard of the diocese of Los Angeles, and Isabelle Lindsay Cain of the diocese of Upper South Carolina. Although the all-male General Convention still held the exclusive right to appoint women to the National Council, it never failed to approve the individuals whom the Triennial meeting nominated.[63]

As women were slowly achieving representation in the national leadership of the Episcopal Church, the number of women employed as missionaries of the denomination began to decline. In 1916, women made up 39 percent of the church's mission workers. These women belonged to a dedicated corps of educated professionals who generally enjoyed greater autonomy as missionaries, especially in remote foreign areas, than they would have had in parishes and dioceses at home. In fact, a 1924 survey on the position of women in the foreign mission field revealed that both the missionaries themselves and the native women to whom they ministered had a greater share in church governance than their counterparts in the United States.[64]

Although the number of women missionaries continued to be high until World War II, a precipitous drop occurred between 1940 (when there were 137 women in the foreign mission field) and 1970 (when there were only 14). The ending of British and American colonialism, coupled with the shifting of responsibility to indigenous church leaders, was one of the major factors in this decline. Another cause was the increasing clericalization of the foreign missionary force; bishops preferred to recruit clergy (by definition, male) rather than lay workers because priests were able to serve in a dual capacity—sacramental as well as secular—in the typically understaffed organization of a missionary diocese. A final reason for the decline related to the gradual absorption of the Woman's Auxiliary into the National Council after 1919. As one historian has observed, this decision meant that "the distinct women's voice in mission work . . . was increasingly lost in the larger bureaucratic machine of the National Council."[65]

The middle years of the twentieth century also witnessed a steady decline in the number of Episcopal deaconesses. The reduction began in the 1920s and continued for several decades thereafter. From a figure of 222 active deaconesses in 1930, the total fell to 164 in 1950 and to only 86 in 1960. This change was caused not only by the expanding range of places where women could work in

American society but also by the decreasing number of opportunities for these religiously trained women. In hospitals, for example, they were gradually replaced by secular nurses. The automobile, too, made it possible to combine several small, isolated congregations where deaconesses had once served, and the consolidated congregations usually hired clergymen rather than laywomen.[66]

Even as the number of women missionaries and deaconesses was declining, however, the hiring of professional church workers in more affluent, self-supporting parishes became quite popular. By the 1950s, clergy in suburban parishes were eager to hire women with solid theological training to direct their expanding Christian education and children's programs. One of the leading institutions involved in this movement was Windham House in New York City, which had opened in 1928 to train college-educated women for professional service in the church. Personnel shortages during the war years of the 1940s increased the need for women workers, and the growing demand for religious educators led to the creation of a Windham House program in that field. The school also sponsored a 1949 conference that led to the creation of the Association of Professional Church Workers. Windham House and its two sister schools—St. Margaret's House in Berkeley, California, and the Bishop Tuttle Training School (for African Americans) in Raleigh, North Carolina—had a tremendous impact on the shape of religious education in the Episcopal Church in the mid-twentieth century.[67]

Although women were still formally barred from membership in the House of Deputies, they had become increasingly visible as leaders and participants in many other areas of the church's life throughout the 1950s. Just as African Americans who were active in the civil rights movement were seeking integration into the social, political, and economic life of their nation, so Episcopal women were striving to be accepted as the equals of men within the official structures of their denomination. In an effort to dismantle the antiquated "separate sphere" in which they had been required to operate since the original formation of the Woman's Auxiliary, women pressed for an end to the subordinate status implied in their organization's name. This goal was finally achieved in 1958, when the National Council reorganized itself and gave the Woman's Auxiliary a new, self-consciously modern title: "the General Division of Women's Work." At the same time, the council recommended that parish and diocesan women's groups adopt the name "Episcopal Church Women"—a change that was meant to demonstrate the integral role played by women in all aspects of the denomination's mission and ministry.[68]

NOTES

1. Edwin Scott Gaustad, *A Religious History of America*, new rev. ed. (San Francisco: Harper and Row, 1990), 228–29 (quotation on 228); and *RHAP*, 896–99.

2. William A. Brown, *The Church in America* (1922), quoted in *RHAP*, 897.

3. George M. Marsden, *Religion and American Culture* (San Diego: Harcourt Brace Jovanovich, 1990), 180–85; and *RHAP*, 899–901.

4. William H. Katerberg, *Modernity and the Dilemma of North American Anglican Identities, 1880–1950* (Montreal: McGill-Queen's University Press, 2001), 114, 132–33.

5. George E. DeMille, *The Episcopal Church since 1900: A Brief History* (New York: Morehouse-Gorham, 1955), 24–36; *HAEC,* 351–52; and *HPEC,* 343 (source of quotation).

6. Quoted in Alexander C. Zabriskie, *Bishop Brent: Crusader for Christian Unity* (Philadelphia: Westminster, 1948), 145. See also *HPEC,* 351.

7. Katerberg, *Modernity and the Dilemma of North American Anglican Identities,* 113–15.

8. Quoted in Samuel McCrea Cavert, *Church Cooperation and Unity in America: A Historical Review, 1900–1970* (New York: Association Press, 1970), 19.

9. Quoted in Zabriskie, *Bishop Brent,* 173.

10. Quoted in David E. Sumner, *The Episcopal Church's History: 1945–1985* (Wilton, Conn.: Morehouse-Barlow, 1987), 134.

11. The Old Catholic Church had been organized by former Roman Catholics (principally in Germany, Austria, and Switzerland) who refused to recognize the decree on papal infallibility promulgated at Vatican Council I in 1870.

12. DeMille, *Episcopal Church since 1900,* 139, 151–52, 154, 159–62.

13. Edward Lambe Parsons, "The Liberal Evangelicals' Message in Our Church Today, 1934," in *DW,* 419. See also *HEC,* 212–13.

14. Charles Duell Kean, *The Road to Reunion* (Greenwich, Conn.: Seabury, 1958), 60–64; DeMille, *Episcopal Church since 1900,* 152–53; and Katerberg, *Modernity and the Dilemma of North American Anglican Identities,* 130.

15. DeMille, *Episcopal Church since 1900,* 152–53; and Kean, *Road to Reunion,* 66–72.

16. *Journal of the General Convention of the Protestant Episcopal Church* (1946): 664.

17. W. Stanley Rycroft, *The Ecumenical Witness of the United Presbyterian Church in the U.S.A.* (n.p.: Board of Christian Education of the United Presbyterian Church in the U.S.A., 1968), 147; and *HPEC,* 356.

18. Marsden, *Religion and American Culture,* 194–98.

19. *RHAP,* 919–20; and *HEC,* 205, 218–19.

20. William Temple, *Christianity and Social Order* (New York: Penguin, 1942), 7, 15.

21. Robert E. Hood, *Social Teachings in the Episcopal Church* (Harrisburg, Pa.: Morehouse, 1990), 44–49; and Paul T. Phillips, *A Kingdom on Earth: Anglo-American Social Christianity, 1880–1940* (University Park, Pa.: Pennsylvania State University Press, 1996), 279–85.

22. "House of Bishops, Pastoral Letter, November 9, 1933," in *DW,* 353–57.

23. Vida D. Scudder, "Social Problems Facing the Church in 1934," in *DW,* 357–61. See also *BHEC,* 151.

24. "House of Bishops, Pastoral Letter," in *DW,* 355; and Gerald L. Sittser, *A Cautious Patriotism: The American Churches and the Second World War* (Chapel Hill: University of North Carolina Press, 1997), 16–21.

25. *HEC,* 219–20.

26. Martin E. Marty, *Modern American Religion,* vol. 2 (Chicago: University of Chicago Press, 1991), 390; and David Hein, "Henry St. George Tucker," *ANB* 21, 896 (source of quotation).

27. *BHEC,* 155.

28. Linda Popp Di Biase, "Neither Harmony nor Eden: Margaret Peppers and the Exile of the Japanese Americans," *AEH* 70 (2001): 106–8, 116; and Joanna B. Gillespie, "Jap-

anese-American Episcopalians during World War II: The Congregation of St. Mary's Los Angeles, 1941–1945," *AEH* 69 (2000): 140–46.

29. *Journal of the General Convention of the Protestant Episcopal Church* (1943): 465–69.

30. Edward Lambe Parsons, "The Legacy of the Japanese American Evacuation," in *Christianity Takes a Stand: An Approach to the Issues of Today,* ed. William Scarlett (New York: Penguin, 1946), 89.

31. James T. Patterson, *Grand Expectations: The United States, 1945–1974* (New York: Oxford University Press, 1996), 61, 64–65, 71–72, 77.

32. Herbert Gans, *The Levittowners* (1982), quoted in Patterson, *Grand Expectations,* 76.

33. *RHAP,* 950–53.

34. *HEC,* 229; *BHEC,* 157; and Sumner, *Episcopal Church's History,* 199.

35. For further background, see Michael Moriarty, "William Palmer Ladd and the Origins of the Episcopal Liturgical Movement," *CH* 64 (1995): 438–51.

36. *HEC,* 240–41.

37. Robert S. Ellwood, *The Fifties Spiritual Marketplace: American Religion in a Decade of Conflict* (New Brunswick, N.J.: Rutgers University Press, 1997), 208–9.

38. *HEC,* 223.

39. John Macquarrie, *Principles of Christian Theology* (New York: Scribner's, 1966), 51; and *BHEC,* 159–60. See also Robert J. Page, *New Directions in Anglican Theology: A Survey from Temple to Robinson* (New York: Seabury, 1965).

40. Theodore O. Wedel, "The Church's Teaching: An Introduction, 1949," in *DW,* 380, 384–85.

41. *HEC,* 230–32; and Sumner, *Episcopal Church's History,* 74–84.

42. Will Herberg, *Protestant—Catholic—Jew: An Essay in American Religious Sociology,* new ed. (Garden City, N.Y.: Doubleday, 1960), 89, 258.

43. Dwight D. Eisenhower, quoted in *RHAP,* 954.

44. Gibson Winter, "The Church in Suburban Captivity," *Christian Century* 72 (1955): 1113–14 (source of first quotation); and Gibson Winter, *The Suburban Captivity of the Churches: An Analysis of Protestant Responsibility in the Expanding Metropolis* (Garden City, N.Y.: Doubleday, 1961), 79 (source of second and third quotations).

45. William Stringfellow, "Poverty, Piety, Charity and Mission," *Christian Century* 78 (1961): 584–85. See also William Stringfellow, *My People Is the Enemy: An Autobiographical Polemic* (New York: Holt, Rinehart, 1964), 3–32; and Robert S. Ellwood, *The Sixties Spiritual Awakening: American Religion Moving from Modern to Postmodern* (New Brunswick, N.J.: Rutgers University Press, 1994), 99–100, 124–25.

46. Paul Moore Jr., "Inner City—Battle Line," *Witness,* 31 March 1960, 7–10.

47. Jenny Moore, *The People on Second Street* (New York: Morrow, 1968), 136. See also Paul Moore, *Presences: A Bishop's Life in the City* (New York: Farrar, Straus, 1997), 104–31.

48. C. Kilmer Myers, *Light the Dark Streets* (Greenwich, Conn.: Seabury, 1957), 16–21, 147–53.

49. Gardiner H. Shattuck Jr., *Episcopalians and Race: Civil War to Civil Rights* (Lexington: University Press of Kentucky, 2000), 92.

50. Arthur E. Walmsley, "Not Blueprints, but Wrestling," *TLC,* 22 November 1959, 16–17.

51. Benjamin Elijah Mays and Joseph William Nicholson, *The Negro's Church* (1933; reprint, New York: Russell and Russell, 1969), v–vi, 210–14, 222, 230–36, 251, 312–13.

52. Minutes of the Meeting of the National Council of the Episcopal Church (February 9–11, 1943), quoted in Shattuck, *Episcopalians and Race,* 34–35. Harris's tenure as Executive Secretary for Negro Work proved to be relatively brief, for in 1945 he was elected bishop of the missionary district of Liberia. He was succeeded by Tollie Caution, the rector of an African American parish in New York.

53. Shattuck, *Episcopalians and Race,* 37–40. Ordained in 1954, Walker was eventually elected suffragan bishop of the diocese of Washington (D.C.) in 1971.

54. Donald Smith Armentrout, *The Quest for the Informed Priest: A History of the School of Theology* (Sewanee, Tenn.: School of Theology, University of the South, 1979), 279–306.

55. Quoted in Shattuck, *Episcopalians and Race,* 48.

56. Armentrout, *Quest for the Informed Priest,* 306–9.

57. Alger L. Adams, "Church Jim Crow: We Lag Far Behind," *The Witness,* 15 November 1951, 13–14.

58. Shattuck, *Episcopalians and Race,* 42–43, 54–55.

59. *Ibid.,* 59–63.

60. *Just, Right, and Necessary: A Study of Reactions to the Supreme Court Decision on Segregation* (New York: National Council, 1955), 1–44 (quotation on 37); and Will D. Campbell, *And Also With You: Duncan Gray and the American Dilemma* (Franklin, Tenn.: Providence House, 1997), 123–44.

61. *DC,* 162–64, 171–72.

62. Beginning in 1880, representatives of the Woman's Auxiliary met every three years in conjunction with the meeting of the General Convention. This gathering became known as the "Women's Triennial."

63. Pamela W. Darling, *New Wine: The Story of Women Transforming Leadership and Power in the Episcopal Church* (Cambridge, Mass.: Cowley, 1994), 71–72.

64. *DC,* 128–29, 134–39.

65. Mary Sudman Donovan, "Women as Foreign Missionaries in the Episcopal Church, 1830–1920," *AEH* 61 (1992): 16–35; and Ian T. Douglas, "A Lost Voice: Women's Participation in the Foreign Mission Work of the Episcopal Church, 1920–1970," *AEH* 61 (1992): 52 (source of quotation).

66. *HEC,* 236.

67. Fredrica Harris Thompsett, "The Genuine Vocations of Windham House Women, 1928–1967: An Overlooked Chapter in Episcopal Women's Leadership," *Journal of the Canadian Church Historical Society* 44 (2002): 139–61; and *HEC,* 216–17, 236–37.

68. Darling, *New Wine,* 86–88.

8
CHANGING TIMES: 1958–2003

The early twentieth century had been a relatively calm and successful period for the Episcopal Church, and like virtually every other American religious body, it had increased significantly in size immediately after World War II. In books, magazines, and newspapers, some writers even speculated that because of the denomination's many attractive features—a historic liturgy, an air of calm reasonableness, and a smooth blend of Catholic and Protestant elements—the Episcopal Church occupied a particularly enviable position in the American religious marketplace. Unfortunately, that observation proved to be far too optimistic, for between 1963 and 1988 the Episcopal Church lost over a million members—an unprecedented drop after nearly two centuries of steady institutional expansion. In fact, during that same 25-year period, as evangelical and theologically conservative churches experienced rapid growth, all mainline Protestant denominations reported astonishing losses in membership.[1] According to historians, the 1960s represented a crucial watershed in American religious life: James Findlay characterized the events of that tumultuous era as the "last hurrah" of the Protestant establishment, while Sydney Ahlstrom thought the decade marked the end of the long "Puritan Epoch" that had begun several centuries before.[2] In any case, along with American society as a whole, the Episcopal Church entered an extended period of transformation during the second half of the twentieth century.

THE CIVIL RIGHTS MOVEMENT

The single most important issue that Episcopalians faced during this period was the impact of the civil rights movement on the nation's political and religious life. At the 1958 General Convention, a coalition of liberal church members committed to civil rights activism presented a resolution condemning racial prejudice and calling their church to support efforts to end segregation in the South. Adopting the substance of this resolution, the convention affirmed belief in "the natural dignity and value of every man, of whatever color or race, as created in the image of God." The convention also encouraged church members "to work together, in charity and forbearance, towards the establishment . . . of full opportunities in fields such as education, housing, employment and public accommodations."[3] After the meeting, two white priests—Cornelius Tarplee, an employee of the denomination's National Council, and John B. Morris, the rector of a parish in South Carolina—agreed between themselves to keep pressure on church leaders about the civil rights issue. Morris and Tarplee's decision soon led them to organize the Episcopal Society for Cultural and Racial Unity (ESCRU). Founded in December 1959, ESCRU was dedicated to the principle that no division based upon race, ethnicity, or social class should exist within the Episcopal Church.[4]

The formation of ESCRU coincided with the beginning of an important stage in the civil rights movement as "sit-in" protests started to take place in southern cities in early 1960. A few weeks after the first sit-ins began in Greensboro, North Carolina, several employees of the National Council published a report declaring that Anglican social teaching recognized the Christian's duty to disobey unjust laws. This statement outraged white Episcopalians in the South, especially Charles C.J. Carpenter, the bishop of Alabama. " 'Civil disobedience,' " he charged, "is just another name for lawlessness," and the Episcopal Church was courting danger by giving more attention to sit-in protests than to preaching the gospel of Jesus Christ.[5] This outburst from a prominent southern bishop elicited a counterblast from the ESCRU leadership. Speaking for the organization, John Morris lambasted Carpenter and predicted that the civil rights movement would prove to be "a plumb-line in the South," dividing church leaders who were ready to implement their denomination's racially inclusive teachings from those, like the bishop of Alabama, who aspired to be only "chaplains to the dying order of the Confederacy."[6]

Despite these biting words, Carpenter continued to oppose the civil rights movement. When racial protests spread to Birmingham (where the offices of the diocese of Alabama were located) in 1963, Carpenter again became the focus of attention among Episcopalians. Although Birmingham was generally regarded as the most racially divided city in the United States, white moderates were in the process of wresting political control from Eugene "Bull" Connor, the hard-line segregationist police commissioner. Worried that further challenges from black groups might hinder the moderates' efforts to ameliorate the Jim Crow system, white political and religious leaders tried to convince Martin Luther King Jr. to halt the civil rights demonstrations he was organizing in Birmingham. When King refused to follow this advice, Carpenter and seven other white clergymen released a public letter criticizing him for heightening racial tensions in their city. Infuriated by this statement, King responded in the now-celebrated "Letter from Birmingham Jail" by rebuking the white clergy for ignoring the Bible's message of justice for people of all races.[7]

Pressure from white church leaders in the South prevented the National Council of the Episcopal Church from taking a definitive stand on the civil rights movement prior to 1963. The statements of individual staff members and of ESCRU spokespersons sometimes were newsworthy, but they did not represent the official position of their denomination. However, as the brutality of Bull Connor and other segregationists in Birmingham was gradually exposed by daily television news reports, the national leadership of the denomination at last felt comfortable in speaking out. In May 1963 Arthur Lichtenberger, the church's presiding bishop, released a pastoral letter addressing the racial turmoil in Alabama. This letter, which was circulated widely in the secular press as well as in the church, spoke of the need for Christians to affirm the value of the upheavals then occurring throughout the South by joining hands "across lines of racial separation, in a common struggle for justice."[8] The civil rights movement gained even wider support in the church a few months after the publication of Lichtenberger's pastoral letter. At a special meeting in August 1963, the House of Bishops not only endorsed civil rights legislation then being debated in Congress but also encouraged church members to take part in the upcoming March on Washington in support of that legislation. As a result of the bishops' statement, numerous Episcopal dioceses and parishes sent large groups to participate in the march on August 28.[9]

One of the most dramatic confrontations between civil rights advocates and segregationists took place in April 1964, when the wives of three Episcopal bishops (Esther Burgess, wife of John M. Burgess, the suffragan bishop of Massachusetts; Mary Peabody, wife of Malcolm E. Peabody, the retired bishop of the diocese of Central New York; and Hester Hocking Campbell, wife of Donald Campbell, a former suffragan bishop of Los Angeles) challenged segregation laws in St. Augustine, Florida.[10] The day after the three women arrived in St. Augustine, they attempted to eat breakfast together at a segregated restaurant but were refused service when the restaurant manager realized that Esther Burgess was a "Negro." Although they complied with the manager's request that they leave the restaurant, the women were later arrested for taking part in an interracial protest at a nearby motel. Photographs of the well-dressed Episcopalians standing behind bars in a Florida jail cell immediately appeared in the national press. Seventy-two-year-old "Grandmother Peabody" received special attention not only because of her age but also because she was the mother of Endicott Peabody, the governor of Massachusetts. When the three women were released on bail and returned home, they were greeted with expressions of admiration and support from church officials.[11]

The climax of the national civil rights movement occurred in March 1965, when Martin Luther King summoned religious leaders throughout the country to come to Selma, Alabama, and demonstrate their solidarity with the struggles of African Americans. Over five hundred Episcopalians eventually joined the huge entourage of civil rights workers that gathered at Selma. At the conclusion of the great Selma-to-Montgomery march, King praised that veritable "pilgrimage of clergymen and laymen of every race and faith" who poured into Alabama "to face danger at the side of its embattled Negroes."[12] Many of the Episcopalians who traveled to Selma also attempted to desegregate worship at St. Paul's Church, the Episcopal parish in the city. Although they were initially turned away by ushers guarding the entrance to the building, an interracial contingent of ESCRU members eventually gained access to worship at the church several weeks later.[13]

Among the ESCRU volunteers involved in the desegregation of St. Paul's were Judith Upham and Jonathan Daniels, two white seminarians studying at the Episcopal Theological School in Cambridge, Massachusetts. During the spring of 1965, Upham and Daniels stayed in Selma and met repeatedly with white church leaders to discuss the need for racial integration throughout the diocese of Alabama. Although Upham had to work elsewhere that summer, Daniels committed himself to helping register black voters in rural areas outside of Selma. While working with the Student Nonviolent Coordinating Committee, Daniels was murdered on August 20, 1965. His sacrifice on behalf of racial justice was officially recognized by the Episcopal Church in 1991, when the General Convention passed a resolution adding his name to the list of martyrs in the denomination's calendar of "Lesser Feasts and Fasts."[14]

POLITICAL RADICALISM AND CONSERVATIVE BACKLASH

Despite the passage of federal legislation guaranteeing basic political rights to black southerners, most African Americans in 1965 still had not achieved even a measure of social and economic equality with whites—a fact starkly demonstrated by the explosion of rioting in several major American cities in the late 1960s. As members of a denomination that was relatively strong in urban areas, Episcopalians could not afford to ignore this growing unrest, and as a consequence church leaders responded swiftly to the next stage of America's ongoing racial crisis.

Alarmed by the disastrous riots in Detroit and in Newark, New Jersey, during the summer of 1967, John Hines, who had succeeded Arthur Lichtenberger as presiding bishop in 1965, decided that unprecedented action was required. In his opening sermon at the General Convention that assembled in September of that year, Hines called privileged Episcopalians to take their place "humbly and boldly, alongside . . . the dispossessed and oppressed peoples of this country for the healing of our national life."[15] He then introduced a proposal designed to appropriate $9 million over a three-year period (a figure equivalent to approximately one-quarter of the denomination's operating budget at that time) for the empowerment of the nation's poorest citizens. Hines's bold proposal was passed almost unanimously by the church's bishops and deputies; dubbed the General Convention Special Program (GCSP), it began operations in January 1968.[16]

Acting with the haste he thought the situation required, Hines made two critical errors in organizing GCSP. His first error was failing to include African American clergy who were already engaged in ministry among the poor in the program's staff. At the same time, Hines allowed Tollie Caution, then the senior black official on the national staff of the Episcopal Church, to be summarily dismissed from his position. Although a number of black Episcopalians thought Caution was the

most qualified person to lead GCSP, Hines believed that his relatively conservative approach to social issues would be detrimental to the radical program Hines
envisioned. Caution's dismissal and the insensitive manner in which it was handled brought an immediate outcry from African American clergy in northeastern
dioceses. Their feelings of anger and betrayal quickly sparked the creation of a
new organization, now called the Union of Black Episcopalians (UBE), in February 1968. The clergy who founded the UBE resolved that their organization
always would fight for the full inclusion of African Americans at every level in
the church's decision-making process.[17]

Hines's second error was underestimating the ability of his fellow bishops to
undermine decisions of the national Episcopal Church. Although a local bishop
was supposed to be consulted whenever a GCSP grant was distributed within the
geographical boundaries of his diocese, GCSP staff understandably resisted this
courtesy because they did not want conservative whites in southern dioceses
interfering with their program of black empowerment. Conservatives argued,
however, that because the Episcopal Church was a federation of independent
dioceses, the central administrative staff in New York had no authority to act in
a diocese against the wishes of its bishop. As a result of this fundamental disagreement over the nature of power in the church, national meetings of the denomination soon became the scenes of strident debates between conservatives
who objected to GCSP grants to radical groups and liberals who supported the
basic focus of the program. Opposition to GCSP came not only from individual
bishops but also from the newly formed Foundation for Christian Theology. Organized at a parish in Victoria, Texas, the Foundation was dedicated to presenting
"a Christian challenge to those who presume to . . . involve the Church in the
social, political, and economic activities of our times." Quickly gaining a national
constituency, the organization became a persistent critic of Hines and other liberal
church leaders.[18]

This polarization over social issues reached a crisis point when the church
assembled for a Special General Convention in August 1969. Because so much
business had remained unfinished following the 1967 General Convention, the
denomination temporarily interrupted its pattern of triennial gatherings and scheduled an additional meeting during an in-between year. The 1969 convention had
barely come to order, however, when it was interrupted by a group of black
militants demanding that the Episcopal Church hear their concerns. Declaring that
whites had no right unilaterally to set the agenda for the whole denomination,
Paul Washington, rector of the Church of the Advocate in Philadelphia, spoke
eloquently in favor of giving the militants a hearing. When whites objected to
this idea, Washington led a walkout of African Americans from the convention
floor. Although some black deputies left with reluctance—this was the first General Convention to include significant numbers of African American representatives—the demonstration had its intended effect. The agenda having shifted away
from the discussion of internal denominational affairs, delegates turned their attention to issues in the larger society. According to one liberal priest who was at

the convention, the willingness of the delegates to shift their focus demonstrated that the Episcopal Church was no longer "the comfortable upper middle-class version of respectable Christianity" it had always been.[19]

The Special General Convention of 1969 also witnessed one of the first major antiwar protests in the Episcopal Church. Throughout the meeting, antiwar activists stood at the back of the convention hall and read aloud the names of American soldiers killed in Vietnam. Several clergy who had been prominent in civil rights activities—C. Kilmer Myers, the bishop of California; his erstwhile colleague Paul Moore, the suffragan bishop of Washington; and Malcolm Boyd, a former college chaplain then serving as a member of the ESCRU staff—had recently turned their energies to protesting American involvement in the Vietnam war. During the convention, Myers also staged a takeover of the podium similar to the black militants' actions: two military deserters appeared without warning and asked the church to give them sanctuary. When the deputies refused to consider their request, separate groups—one white, one black—rose and turned their backs on the rest of the convention.[20]

Although conservative Episcopalians believed they had been outmaneuvered by radicals at the 1969 convention, they soon exacted their revenge. With dissatisfaction and anger growing among white church members, conservatives organized themselves and vowed to fight both the work of GCSP and the liberal outlook of the Hines administration at the next General Convention. Since the denomination not only was starting to experience a significant decline in membership but also had been forced to cut its annual budget by $1 million in 1970, GCSP proved to be an easy target for dissidents to attack that year. Both the funds available to the program and the freedom of its staff to distribute them were sharply curtailed at the 1970 General Convention. Although the program continued to function for three more years, it had little support from anyone in the church at the grassroots level, and it was formally terminated with only minimal protest in 1973. The decision to end GCSP led the editors of one conservative journal to express thanks that "a give-away program that smacked more of Lady Bountifulism than of apostolic Christianity" had finally been eliminated from the budget of their church.[21]

At the same time, as the operation of GCSP was being scuttled, John Hines decided to retire prematurely from his position as presiding bishop. While Hines was continuing to insist that the church needed to engage in societal reform efforts, he was succeeded in 1974 by John M. Allin, the bishop of Mississippi. A conservative in every way, Allin had resisted the involvement of church-sponsored civil rights groups in his state throughout the 1960s. He also believed that his principal task as presiding bishop was to repair the unraveling institutional life of his denomination. Allin argued that, as "a rag-tag, disorganized, poorly educated group of middle-class Americans," most Episcopalians had been woefully unprepared for the ambitious social gospel crusade to which John Hines and other liberal leaders had summoned them in the late 1960s.[22]

THE ORDINATION OF WOMEN

Prior to the nineteenth century, most Christian organizations, with the exception of radically egalitarian groups such as the Friends and the Shakers, did not offer the same opportunities for leadership to women as they did men. Although by the mid-nineteenth century a few decentralized liberal denominations (e.g., the Congregationalists, the Unitarians, and the Universalists) permitted women both to be ordained to the ministry and to serve as lay leaders in congregations, American denominations generally excluded women from those positions until the twentieth century. The northern Presbyterians, for example, did not fully endorse women's ordination until 1957, and the southern Presbyterians waited until 1964. In most dioceses of the Episcopal Church, in fact, women could not even serve on parish vestries until the 1950s, and as late as the 1960s they were usually not allowed to preach, to administer communion, to serve as ushers, or to represent their parish at the annual convention of the diocese.

Inspired by the successes of the civil rights movement, some Episcopal women in the mid-1960s began to complain that they, like African American men, were excluded from the most important decision-making bodies of the church. Between 1943 and 1964, in fact, every meeting of the General Convention had rejected a resolution that would have allowed women to serve in the House of Deputies. The social ferment of the 1960s, however, made the question of women's equality more urgent. As activist Episcopal lawyer Pauli Murray observed in 1965, "the evil of antifeminism (Jane Crow)" was identical to "the evil of racism (Jim Crow)," and the moral obligation to ensure the rights of both women and blacks was part of "the fundamental and indivisible issue of human rights."[23] Finally, at the 1967 General Convention, as male Episcopalians sought to aid the empowerment of poor Americans by instituting GCSP, they offered a similar advance to the women of the church by voting to make them eligible for election as convention deputies—a constitutional change that went into effect at the beginning of the 1970 General Convention.

Even as Episcopal women at last gained the right to become lay representatives at church councils, voices began to be raised advocating the need for them to take the next step by seeking ordination as deacons, priests, and bishops. Although the order of deaconess had officially been recognized in 1889, the church's canons stipulated that a deaconess was not a "deacon"—the first level of ordained ministry, still reserved exclusively for men. Many decades later, however, in an effort to encourage the recruitment of more women as deaconesses, the General Convention amended this rule. A new canon, adopted in 1964, not only allowed married women to become deaconesses but also stated that deaconesses were "ordered" rather than "set apart" (the old terminology) for ministry in the church. Recognizing the implications of this change in language, James Pike, the bishop of California, announced in 1965 that he intended to recognize deaconess Phyllis Edwards as a deacon and list her as a member of the clergy in the diocesan records. Pike's action forced the church to consider the status of deaconesses again, and as a result, the General Convention of 1970 passed a new canon that eliminated all distinctions between male deacons and female deaconesses, thereby allowing women to seek diaconal ordination.[24]

Since the diaconate had usually been regarded as only a brief transitional stage prior to a man's ordination to the priesthood, Episcopal leaders also debated whether the tradition of an all-male priesthood should similarly be abolished. Although the committees appointed to study the issue reported that there were no clear theological or biblical grounds on which to deny the priesthood to women, that idea still seemed a bit too radical to most people in the Episcopal Church, and the proposal was narrowly defeated at the 1970 General Convention at the same time that the admission of women to the diaconate was approved.[25] When the next General Convention assembled in 1973, proponents again offered a resolution that would have permitted the ordination of women to the priesthood. At that point they had every reason to be hopeful because, at its meeting in November 1972, the House of Bishops had endorsed women's ordination "in principle." In addition, American society was rapidly being transformed by the women's movement, and for an increasing number of people, the absence of women from church leadership positions was beginning to seem odd. Once more, however, the proposed legislation on women's ordination failed to pass the House of Deputies. Although the majority of lay and clerical deputies at the 1973 General Convention voted in favor of women's ordination, the vote failed to carry because of a parliamentary technicality.[26]

Supporters of women's ordination were bitterly disappointed by the results of the 1973 convention. Some women who had been ordained deacons after the 1970 convention feared that the canon enabling them to be ordained priests might never be passed. Reaching the conclusion that (as deacon Suzanne Hiatt stated) their "vocation was not to continue to ask for permission to be a priest, but to *be* a priest," these women started to develop a strategy for gaining ordination without the approval of the General Convention.[27] A pivotal moment occurred in New York in November 1973, when several of those deacons met with the bishops who most strongly supported their cause. The bishops said they were unwilling to ordain the women until they had received approval from the church as a whole at the General Convention. "That came as a shock," Suzanne Hiatt reported, "but it was a crucial step in our claiming of our own authority. These were our friends and allies, but since they could go no further we had to go on without them."[28]

In December 1973 five women who had been at that meeting and who served as deacons in the diocese of New York took the next step. They attended the annual service when their bishop ordained all the eligible deacons in his diocese to the priesthood. Since Paul Moore, a leading liberal, had become the bishop of New York in 1972, the women thought he might ordain them alongside the five male candidates. Although Moore allowed them to join the five men in reciting the ordination vows, he ultimately declined to lay his hands on their heads at the actual moment of ordination. The women and many in the congregation then walked out of the service in protest. In a formal statement delivered by the five women, they charged that "peace in the House of Bishops is more important than justice; that the law of man, established by church conventions, is more compelling than the Gospel of the Lord."[29] Moore later said that he could barely keep his hands from going forward to touch the women's heads. However, since the canons of the church prevented him from taking that action, he felt as if "my hands were literally tied behind my back."[30]

During the first half of the next year, discouragement and restlessness grew among those who most strongly supported women's ordination. In an address at his school's commencement in early June, Harvey Guthrie, the dean of the Episcopal Theological School, threatened to resign unless the trustees of his seminary added an ordained woman to the faculty. A few days later, Charles V. Willie, the vice-president of the House of Deputies, remarked in a sermon that he thought the church's ban on the ordination of women was completely unjust. Bishops, he declared, should simply ordain all qualified persons without regard to the candidate's sex. And at an ordination service in mid-June, Edward G. Harris, the dean of the Philadelphia Divinity School, called the bishops of the Episcopal Church to ordain women to the priesthood without any further delay.[31]

By July 1974, supporters of women's ordination had decided to schedule an ordination service in which women deacons would be advanced to the priesthood. On July 19 three bishops—Daniel Corrigan, retired suffragan of Colorado; Robert DeWitt, who had just resigned as bishop of Pennsylvania; and Edward Welles, retired bishop of West Missouri—dispatched a letter to their episcopal colleagues stating their intention to ordain 11 women to the priesthood. Corrigan, DeWitt, and Welles emphasized that the service they were planning, though contrary to the legal niceties of the Episcopal Church, would be "an act of obedience to the Spirit."[32] The 11 women ordinands also wrote a general letter to all Episcopalians in which they declared their commitment "to bring closer to reality the Pauline promise that 'there is neither male nor female for we are all one in Christ Jesus.' "[33] Meanwhile, Lyman Ogilby, who had just succeeded DeWitt as the bishop of Pennsylvania (and in whose jurisdiction the planned ordination was scheduled to take place), stated that any Episcopal clergyman who participated in the service would be violating the rules of his church and would be subject to disciplinary action.[34]

Firmly committed to the principle of equal rights for women, the supporters of women's ordination went ahead with their plans. The service was held on July 29, 1974, at the Church of the Advocate in Philadelphia, the parish where Suzanne Hiatt served as a deacon and where Paul Washington, the civil rights advocate who had led the black walkout at the Special General Convention five years before, was rector. Before a congregation of nearly two thousand supporters and a few protesters, 11 women, including Hiatt, were ordained priests by Bishops DeWitt, Corrigan, and Welles.[35] In his sermon at the service, Charles Willie declared: "As blacks refused to participate in their own oppression by going to the back of the bus in 1955 in Montgomery, women are refusing to cooperate in their own oppression by remaining on the periphery of full participation in the Church in 1974 in Philadelphia."[36] Hiatt later described the ordinations as a "Spirit-filled occasion," when "the bishops told the women to take authority as priests in the church of God." Looking back on the event, she remarked that it was "the only way for women to have done it. Our ordination was on our terms, not the church's terms. We saw ourselves as deacons proceeding in obedience to the insistence of the Holy Spirit."[37]

The ordination of the "Philadelphia 11" caused a severe crisis in the Episcopal Church. In response to this challenge to hierarchical authority in the church, Presiding Bishop John Allin called an emergency meeting of the House of Bishops. At that gathering the bishops not only decried the actions of Corrigan, DeWitt, and Welles but also declared that "the necessary conditions for valid ordination to the priesthood in the Episcopal Church" had not been fulfilled at the service in Philadelphia.[38] Allin and the other bishops also advised Episcopalians not to recognize the 11 women as priests until the next General Convention could decide on their ecclesiastical status. The women responded by questioning the right of the House of Bishops to declare their ordinations invalid. At the same time, Charles Willie resigned his post as vice-president of the House of Deputies as a gesture of protest. The bishops, he charged, were far more concerned about "procedure, authority, and discipline" than about "love and justice."[39] Other supporters openly flouted the bishops' attempts to suppress the 11 new priests. Suzanne Hiatt and Carter Heyward, for example, received faculty appointments at the Episcopal Divinity School, where in March 1975 they began to celebrate the Eucharist in the school's chapel.[40] And on September 7, 1975, George W. Barrett, the retired bishop of Rochester, further heightened the crisis in the church by ordaining four more women to the priesthood at a service in Washington, D.C.[41]

Since the existence of 15 women ministering actively as priests represented a serious threat to the institutional unity of the denomination, debate at the 1976 General Convention centered on the women's status. After some initial discussion about the proper parliamentary procedures to follow, both houses of the convention voted to recognize (effective on January 1, 1977) the eligibility of women to serve in all three orders of ordained ministry—the diaconate, the priesthood, and the episcopate. In separate deliberations, the bishops decided to require each of the "Philadelphia 11" and the "Washington 4" to be "regularized" in a public service acknowledging the fact that she had already been validly ordained as a priest. Although a sizable block of bishops and priests, most of whom were staunch Anglo-Catholics, remained fervent in their opposition to the idea that a woman could be a "priest," approximately one hundred women priests had been ordained and were actively functioning in the Episcopal Church by the end of 1977. By 1979, moreover, almost three hundred women, serving in 72 of the church's 93 dioceses, had been ordained to the priesthood.[42]

The final barrier to the full participation of women in ordained ministry fell in February 1989, when Barbara C. Harris (who, as a lay leader, had carried the cross at the head of the procession into the Church of the Advocate on July 29,

1974) was consecrated suffragan bishop of Massachusetts. Despite the continued resistance of a few Anglo-Catholic traditionalists who vociferously protested her election, Harris's consecration symbolized how much the church's old order had changed in a relatively short time.[43] Four years later, Jane Holmes Dixon became the second woman bishop in the Episcopal Church when she was consecrated suffragan bishop of Washington. And in 1993 Mary Adelia McLeod became the first female diocesan bishop when she was elected by the convention of the diocese of Vermont.

CONTROVERSY OVER SEXUALITY AND GAY RIGHTS

Soon after General Convention approved the ordination of women to the priesthood, another major controversy surfaced within the Episcopal Church. One of the first women to be ordained a priest was Ellen Barrett, a deacon serving in the diocese of New York. Although Paul Moore, the diocesan bishop, knew that Barrett was a lesbian when he ordained her to the diaconate, he did not believe that her sexual orientation alone was sufficient to bar her from the ordained ministry. However, because she was the first co-president of Integrity, a recently formed organization for gay Episcopalians, Barrett's sexual orientation was widely known throughout the church. As soon as Moore ordained her in 1977, howls of protest were heard not only in New York but also in many other dioceses. Moore reported that he received 42 letters from fellow bishops commenting on his action: 10 positive, and 32 negative. As William Frey, the bishop of Colorado, remarked, there were "far more constructive ways to show pastoral concern for homosexuals than by attempting to bless that which God offers to redeem."[44] Despite the many objections he heard, Moore concluded that it was not Barrett's sexual orientation but her candor about it that troubled many of her most vocal detractors.[45]

This ecclesiastical controversy about sexual orientation reflected the growth of the wider gay liberation movement throughout American society in the late 1960s and early 1970s. Although urban Anglo-Catholic parishes had always been regarded as havens for gay Episcopalians, the sexual revolution of the 1960s brought questions about the role of gays and lesbians in the church to the surface. After the first national convention of Integrity, held in Chicago in 1975, the dean of the cathedral in that city emphasized that Integrity members were loyal Episcopalians who simply wanted "to come to terms with their own sexuality as churchmen and not [as] pariahs and untouchables."[46] The 1976 General Convention was the first to address this issue directly when it ruled that "homosexual persons are children of God" who deserved pastoral care in the church and legal protection in society.[47] The conflict that arose over Ellen Barrett's ordination, however, forced bishops and deputies at the next General Convention to speak in far more concrete terms about gay Episcopalians' status. The 1979 convention attempted to reach a compromise on the subject by differentiating between homosexual orientation (deemed to be acceptable) and homosexual *activity* (deemed to be unacceptable). The resolution also forbade the ordination of anyone, gay or straight, who was engaged in sexual relations outside of marriage. Although several liberal bishops indicated that they had no intention of abiding by such restrictions in their dioceses, the 1979 General Convention did at least bring a measure of peace, albeit short-lived, to the explosive sexuality issue.[48]

When Edmond Lee Browning, the bishop of Hawaii, was elected to succeed John Allin as presiding bishop at the 1985 General Convention, his initial remarks to the church suggested that his administration would be far more progressive and open to change than Allin's. Browning emphasized that diversity was one of the strengths of the Episcopal Church, and he declared that there would be "no outcasts" in the church as long as he was presiding bishop.[49] Encouraged by the climate of tolerance that Browning was attempting to create, gay and lesbian Episcopalians pressed for full inclusion in the church. They argued not only that the ordination process should be open to them but that clergy should also be allowed to bless same-sex couples who were living in committed, monogamous relationships.[50]

John S. Spong, bishop of the diocese of Newark (northern New Jersey) and one of the most outspoken critics of the church's traditional teachings on sexuality, caused a considerable stir in December 1989 when he ordained Robert Williams, an openly gay man, to the priesthood. Unfortunately, in the remarks he made to the press soon after his ordination, Williams embarrassed both Spong and the leaders of Integrity who supported him by ridiculing gays living in monogamous relationships, calling them traitors to the gay liberation movement. When Williams refused to apologize for his remarks, he was removed from the position he held at his diocese's outreach ministry to gays and lesbians in Newark. Other bishops angrily censured Spong for having ordained Williams.[51]

Whereas conservative opponents of the ordination of gays and lesbians viewed the bishops' condemnation of Spong as a reaffirmation of the church's statement on homosexuality at the 1979 General Convention, liberals regarded the matter as simply an unfortunate case involving one very tactless and immature gay priest. Soon after Spong's censure, therefore, the leadership in Newark authorized Walter Righter, the assistant bishop of the diocese, to ordain Barry Stopfel, a gay man living in a committed relationship, to the diaconate. This ordination service took place in September 1990. In response, a coalition of conservative bishops brought formal charges of heresy against Righter for willfully violating the church's theological teachings on sexuality and for flaunting its rules on ordination. The accusations against Righter were eventually endorsed by 76 active and retired bishops, one-quarter of all the church's bishops.

After a lengthy judicial process culminating in a May 1996 decision, a church court composed of eight bishops exonerated Righter of the charges that had been brought against him. In its majority opinion, the court drew a distinction between "core doctrines"—essential, unchangeable Christian truths that were expressed in ancient documents such as the Nicene Creed—and mere "doctrinal teachings" that change over time, such as the church's views on social issues (e.g., slavery, divorce, contraception). For a "doctrinal teaching" to be binding on Episcopal clergy, the court maintained, there had to be a canon or General Convention resolution that clearly expressed the intentions of the church on that matter. The court ruled, therefore, that Righter had not violated any core doctrine of Christianity when he ordained Stopfel and that the Episcopal Church had no doctrinal teaching that unequivocally forbade the ordination of homosexuals. Although this decision was bitterly condemned in conservative circles, it effectively upheld the independence of individual bishops and dioceses in deciding who would or would not be ordained within any jurisdiction.[52]

The Episcopal Church, of course, was not the only American denomination then struggling with issues regarding sexuality. In 1997 the Presbyterian Church (U.S.A.) approved a rule requiring all unmarried ministers, deacons, and elders to be celibate, and three years later the denomination passed a similar resolution banning same-sex unions. In 1999 the Churchwide Assembly of the Evangelical Lutheran Church in America (ELCA) voted to continue the denomination's general policy of forbidding the ordination of noncelibate homosexuals. A year later, the United Methodist Church (the nation's second-largest Protestant body) voted to uphold its policies against both same-sex unions and the ordination of sexually active homosexuals. Although there was dissent and even an occasional act of defiance within all these denominations, the United Church of Christ and the Unitarian Universalist Association were the only major Protestant bodies that officially encouraged the ordination of gay and lesbian church members at the end of the twentieth century.

The early years of the twenty-first century witnessed significant gains in the rights of homosexual persons as Canada followed Denmark, the Netherlands, and Belgium in moving to legalize gay marriage, and the U.S. Supreme Court issued a landmark decision that struck down a Texas state law banning private consensual sex between adults of the same sex. These historic actions in 2003 formed part of the North American backdrop to a dramatic series of events in which the General Convention of the Episcopal Church in the United States consented to the election of the denomination's first openly gay bishop.

The larger historical setting of this General Convention decision also included two widely reported events within the Anglican Communion. In 1998 the Lambeth Conference of Anglican bishops from around the world passed a resolution that, in effect, accepted gay persons as full members of the church but said that homosexual conduct was incompatible with scripture and therefore that gays should remain celibate. Also, just two months before the 2003 General Convention of the Episcopal Church, an openly gay—but celibate—priest in the Church of England withdrew his acceptance of nomination to the see of Reading because, he said, his consecration might damage the unity of the Church, including the Anglican Communion.

Meeting in Minneapolis, Minnesota, in August 2003, delegates to the General Convention voted to confirm the election of the Reverend Canon V. Gene Robinson, a 56-year-old divorced father of two who for 13 years had been living in a committed relationship with a male partner. In approaching this new challenge, the Episcopal Church continued to wrestle with issues of scriptural interpretation, theological ethics, institutional identity, and authority. Its decisions had implications not only for its own self-understanding but also for its relations with the other 37 provinces in the 77-million-member Anglican Communion and for its future relations with the Roman Catholic Church, the Eastern Orthodox churches, and other churches, both conservative and liberal.

At the time of his election as bishop coadjutor of New Hampshire, Robinson, a graduate of the University of the South and General Theological Seminary, had served for 15 years as Canon to the Ordinary (assistant to the bishop) in the diocese of New Hampshire. A highly regarded and well-respected figure in his diocese, Robinson won the required majority support at the General Convention of both the House of Deputies and the House of Bishops. The vote in the House of Deputies was by orders. In the lay order, diocesan delegations voted 63 yes, 32 no, and 13 divided. The clergy voted 65 yes, 31 no, and 12 divided. In the House of Bishops, the vote was 62 in favor, 43 opposed. Presiding Bishop Frank T. Griswold was one of the bishops voting to ratify Robinson's election as bishop.

Despite pleas by church officials for unity and peace, this decision continued to be highly controversial. Opponents of the election of an openly gay bishop argued that this action divided the Episcopal Church both from other Anglicans around the world and from the church's traditional teaching on marriage and sexuality. The presiding bishop acknowledged that many Anglicans would see this decision as a historic departure from biblical teachings and the church's traditional practice. He hoped, however, that the members of the Episcopal Church could learn to live within "the tension of disagreement."[53] He told the 2003 convention delegates, "It is my conviction that different points of view can be held in tension within the church without issues of sexuality becoming church dividing."[54] Without question, many Episcopalians knew at the end of this triennial gathering that Griswold now faced the most significant challenge of his presiding episcopate.

The response of the archbishop of Canterbury, the Anglo-Catholic theologian Rowan Williams, reflected his anxiety for the future of the Anglican Communion. A liberal who personally supported the ordination and appointment of homosexual clergy, Williams nonetheless expressed his concern that the decision of the Episcopal Church in the United States would "inevitably have a significant impact on the Anglican Communion throughout the world." Undoubtedly having in mind millions of more traditional Anglicans in Africa, Asia, Latin America, and elsewhere, he warned that "we need as a church to be very careful about making decisions for our part of the world which constrain the church elsewhere."[55] Following the Episcopalians' vote at their General Convention, the spiritual leader of the world's Anglicans spoke of "difficult days" ahead for members of the global Communion.[56]

Bishop-elect Robinson termed his election "a huge leap for gay and lesbian folk in the church," and certainly his many supporters in the American branch of

Anglicanism viewed his election as an important step toward greater openness and inclusiveness, that would benefit all members of the Episcopal Church.[57] But both Archbishop Williams and Bishop Griswold had to work strenuously in the days that followed to prevent a major schism.

TRADITIONALIST RESURGENCE

In the wake of the many changes and upheavals that occurred in the late twentieth century, the Episcopal Church became almost as fractured as American society at large, with numerous conservative groups forming to counter what they perceived to be the prevailing liberal tendencies of their denominational leadership. While many Americans undoubtedly joined the Episcopal Church because of its relative openness to contemporary attitudes and ideas, even more people became disenchanted with it because they were offended by the progressive social and theological positions it adopted after the mid-1960s. As one particularly acerbic critic complained, the motto of the modern Episcopal Church had essentially become "trendier than thou."[58]

The first major traditionalist organization to be formed during this period was the Society for the Preservation of the Book of Common Prayer (now known as the Prayer Book Society of the Episcopal Church). As its name suggests, this society was founded to impede the attempts of Episcopalians to revise the *Book of Common Prayer*. Although the original American Prayer Book of 1789 had undergone minor revisions in 1892 and 1928, liturgical scholars recognized as early as the 1940s that more thorough changes were going to be needed. They believed that the 1928 prayer book was no longer adequate for the modern church: its archaic sixteenth-century language confused more people than it compelled, and emphases in many of its services and prayers did not reflect either contemporary Christian theology or the ideas of the twentieth-century liturgical movement. Between 1967 (when the General Convention approved an updated eucharistic rite for trial use) and 1979 (when the new edition of the *Book of Common Prayer* was officially adopted), parishes in the Episcopal Church experienced much liturgical experimentation and—in some cases—heated controversy.[59]

Although many Episcopalians were pleased with the revisions that were introduced in the late 1960s, others objected strenuously to changes that occurred both in the order and in the language of their familiar Sunday morning services. Just as the shift from Latin to contemporary English had shocked American Catholics after Vatican II, so the use of contemporary rather than Elizabethan English in worship profoundly troubled Episcopalians. As one church member remarked, "now we are asked to speak to God in the same impertinent inflections we use with . . . our telephone operators." That fact, he complained, was not only offensive in itself but also indicative of an "effort to weaken the faith."[60] Resentment against the ongoing revision of the 1928 prayer book inspired a group of Episcopalians to gather in May 1971 on the campus of the University of the South, where they organized the Prayer Book Society. Despite their ability to rally sup-port from many ordinary church members, the leaders of the Prayer Book Society were unable to convince more than a handful of bishops, clergy, and convention deputies to side with them. After usage of the 1979 *Book of Common Prayer* became solidly established in parishes in the early 1980s and ceased being a subject of serious debate, the Prayer Book Society decided to widen the focus of its criticisms. As a result, the society began to focus on its opposition to the ordination of women and the movement of gay and lesbian Episcopalians from the margins to the mainstream of the church's life.[61]

Opposition to the ordination of women proved to be the catalyst that sparked the formation of another major traditionalist group in the mid-1970s. The Evan-gelical and Catholic Mission (ECM) was founded in December 1976 under the leadership of Stanley Atkins, the bishop of the diocese of Eau Claire in Wisconsin. Organized in the wake of the affirmation of women's ordination at the 1976 General Convention, the ECM was intended to provide a "supportive ecclesial entity *within* the Episcopal Church" for Anglo-Catholics and others who objected to the convention's decision.[62] The ECM claimed to be "evangelical" because it affirmed the primary authority of the Bible, and it claimed to be "catholic" because it adhered to the traditions of the ancient, apostolic church. As a result of this dual emphasis, it focused not only on matters of church polity (the presence of women in the ordained ministry) but also on broader issues involving sexuality (e.g., abortion, divorce, homosexuality). Following the election of Barbara Harris as the suffragan bishop of Massachusetts, the ECM reorganized itself in June 1989 as the Episcopal Synod of America. Motivating this name change was the idea that the new synod would represent a national organization, under the direc-tion of conservative male clergy, with which traditionalists in any diocese could choose to affiliate.[63]

A third major traditionalist group came into being in 1987: Episcopalians United for Revelation, Renewal, and Reformation. Evangelical rather than Anglo-Catholic, Episcopalians United was led by Harry Griffith, a layman who was then head of the Anglican Fellowship of Prayer. As its name suggested, Episcopalians United had three primary concerns: adherence to the revelation of God in the Bible, renewal of the church through worship and prayer, and moral reformation of society. "Our Church has been under constant assault . . . from a steady stream of radical groups who have forced change after change," the leaders of the new organization asserted. The identity of those various radicals was clear to the tra-ditionalists: "social activists . . . liberal liturgical thinkers . . . radical feminists . . . [and] gay and lesbian lobbies" who were trying to take control of the church.[64]

In addition to traditionalist organizations whose members remained within the Episcopal Church, a number of schismatic bodies were formed during the 1960s and 1970s. These groups included the Anglican Orthodox Church (1963), the American Episcopal Church (1968), the Anglican Episcopal Church of North America (1972), and the Anglican Church of North America (1977), which later became the Anglican Catholic Church. Since the total number of adherents in all these schismatic groups was never more than thirty thousand, the Episcopal Church experienced its greatest losses through the silent defection of individual members either to other major denominations or, more likely, to no church at all.[65]

While some conservative Episcopalians sought the support of organizations with strong political as well as theological agendas, others found respite from the social activism of their church's national leadership within less confrontational movements of spiritual renewal. Beginning in the early 1960s, growing numbers of evangelical Episcopalians reported that they had experienced the "baptism of the Holy Spirit," manifested in glossolalia (speaking in tongues) and spiritual healing. Episcopalians, Roman Catholics, and mainline Protestants who received these gifts usually referred to themselves as "charismatics" in order to differentiate their movement from established Pentecostal denominations such as the Assemblies of God. The charismatic phenomenon in the Episcopal Church first gained public attention in April 1960, when Dennis Bennett, the rector of St. Mark's Church in Van Nuys, California, announced from his pulpit that he and 70 other parishioners had begun to speak in tongues. This revelation caused an uproar in Bennett's parish and eventually forced him to leave his position. A commission appointed to investigate the impact of the growing charismatic movement in the diocese of California concluded that there was "no scriptural warrant for making it normative for all Christians."[66] Bennett, on the other hand, declared that it was "important that the Spirit be allowed to work freely" in an otherwise religiously indifferent Episcopal Church.[67]

As hundreds of other Episcopalians underwent similar Spirit-filled experiences, a few congregations emerged as major national centers of charismatic renewal in the Episcopal Church: the Church of the Redeemer in Houston, Texas, under the leadership of W. Graham Pulkingham; St. Paul's Church in Darien, Connecticut, under the leadership of Everett "Terry" Fullam; and St. Luke's Church in Bath, Ohio, under the leadership of Charles Irish. Formal organizations such as Cursillo and Faith Alive also helped spark the rise of evangelical enthusiasm throughout the church, and by the 1970s almost every Episcopal diocese had at least one parish that described itself as "renewed." This movement further coalesced with the formation of the Episcopal Charismatic Fellowship, now called the Episcopal Renewal Ministries, at a conference in Dallas in 1973. This increasing interest in spiritual renewal and evangelism did have a social dimension: many evangelical and charismatic Episcopalians became active in such community service ministries as feeding the hungry and working with the homeless. However, unlike their more liberal contemporaries, evangelicals and charismatics preferred to articulate their faith in personal rather than political terms.[68]

The early years of the twenty-first century saw renewed vigor and activity within a number of traditionalist Episcopal bodies. At the 2003 General Convention, for example, the American Anglican Council, a conservative group, maintained a strong presence, with more than two hundred volunteers in attendance. This organization led the opposition to legislation to approve blessings for same-sex unions and the election of Gene Robinson as bishop coadjutor of New Hampshire.[69]

INCREASING ETHNIC AND RACIAL DIVERSITY

The long-standing association between Anglicanism and the American white Anglo-Saxon Protestant establishment notwithstanding, expectations about the ethnic and racial makeup of the Episcopal Church received a vigorous challenge during the final quarter of the twentieth century as increasing numbers of African Americans, Asian Americans, Hispanic Americans, and American Indians began to exercise leadership roles at the national level.[70]

A key moment in this struggle for greater inclusiveness in the church occurred in the early 1970s. Although the GCSP was a well-intentioned attempt by liberal whites to empower black groups *outside* the church, the dismissal of Tollie Caution in 1967 had also terminated the denomination's 30-year black ministries program. Since African Americans were the largest minority group in the Episcopal Church (roughly 5 percent of the church's membership), the lack of a national staff officer in charge of evangelism in the black community was a critical problem. However, thanks to strong pressure from the UBE at the 1973 General Convention, John Allin, the newly elected presiding bishop, was made to see the advantages of restoring the "Black Desk" position at denominational headquarters in New York. As a result of Allin's discussions with the UBE, Franklin D. Turner was chosen to lead the reinstated Office of Black Ministries and the presiding bishop gave his support to the development of an affirmative action program for the hiring of other African American staff members.[71] Between 1971 and 1991, moreover, 13 African Americans (including Turner himself) were elected to the episcopate in dioceses within the United States, while Charles Radford Lawrence II also served as the first black president of the House of Deputies from 1976 to 1985.[72]

Another important area that received renewed attention was the church's ministry among American Indians. William Hobart Hare had been revered by most Episcopalians in South Dakota in the late nineteenth and early twentieth centuries, but his evangelization strategy consisted of bringing to Indians both the "good news" of the Christian gospel and the bad news of cultural assimilation. According to one present-day observer in the diocese of South Dakota, the church once tried "to transform Indians into persons who would think about and worship God the same way the English did."[73] Changes started to occur in the mid-twentieth century, however, as Episcopalians placed greater emphasis on ministry to so-called racial minorities. In the mid-1950s, for example, Vine Deloria, a member of the Standing Rock Sioux tribe, served as the church's executive secretary for Indian work—a position similar to the one exercised by Tollie Caution on behalf of African Americans. After leaving his position on the national staff of the denomination, Deloria also directed the missionary work of the diocese of South Dakota in the 1960s.[74]

Episcopalians had often done a better job than other denominations in employing the Dakota language in church services and in raising up a native ministry. A century after Hare's episcopate, in fact, some bishops were even touting the benefits of Indian ritual and spirituality for use in the Episcopal Church. For instance, Indian ritual was commonplace during the 1980s and 1990s at services in Calvary Cathedral in Sioux Falls, South Dakota. Craig Anderson, who served as bishop of that diocese from 1984 to 1992, saw clear parallels between Christian liturgical practices and Indian ritual (e.g., the relationship between confirmation and the traditional naming ceremony; the use of the Indians' honoring song as a way to remember Christian saints; the burning of sweetgrass instead of incense in worship; the employment of the sweat lodge ceremony at times of fasting). All those rites, Anderson said, served as correctives to the majority culture in the United States by calling people "back to [their] senses," to "a renewed sense of incarnation," to a fresh understanding of "what it is to be a part of this planet."[75]

This openness to Native American spirituality was also matched by a stronger commitment both to the recruitment of clergy and to new evangelistic strategies among American Indians. In 1971 Harold Stephen Jones, the suffragan bishop of South Dakota, became the first Native American to be elected to the episcopate, and between 1974 and 1989 the number of American Indian priests and deacons in the church tripled. Another highly significant milestone was the creation of the Navajoland Area Mission out of portions of Arizona, New Mexico, and Utah in 1979. Steven T. Plummer, who in 1976 had been the first Navajo ordained to the priesthood, was consecrated as bishop of the new diocese in 1990.[76] Finally, at a reconciliation ceremony held in November 1997 in Jamestown, Virginia, the Episcopal Church formally apologized for the atrocities that Anglicans had committed against Indians in colonial times. Symbolizing the church's penitential attitude, the service of reconciliation included the use of American Indian music, dance, and prayers.[77]

ECUMENICAL RELATIONS

One of the most ambitious ecumenical proposals of the twentieth century was presented by Eugene Carson Blake, the stated clerk of the United Presbyterian Church. Preaching at the invitation of Bishop James Pike at Grace Cathedral, San Francisco, in December 1960, Blake suggested that four major denominations—the United Church of Christ, the Methodist Church, Pike's Episcopal Church, and his own United Presbyterian Church—unite to form a single ecclesiastical body that could claim to be "truly catholic, truly reformed, and truly evangelical."[78] Pike strongly supported Blake's proposal, and within two years the Consultation on Church Union (COCU) was organized in response to the initiative. Eventually, nine Protestant denominations joined COCU, and over the succeeding decades representatives from each church carried on discussions and issued reports about the desirability of church union.

Despite these hopeful initial efforts, plans for the merger of the churches were eventually abandoned as changes in American society in the 1960s and 1970s encouraged an interest in pluralism and diversity rather than in unity.[79] By the end of the twentieth century, COCU evolved instead into Churches Uniting in Christ—a plan designed to allow each denomination to retain its own unique polity and liturgical traditions while simultaneously sharing in communion and working in a common social mission with the other churches. Although Episcopalians had often been uneasy about how COCU proposed to handle the role of bishops, at the 2000 General Convention the Episcopal Church did pledge to continue its participation in the COCU dialogue.[80]

A more promising endeavor than COCU was the effort of Episcopalians to achieve full communion with the ELCA, the largest Lutheran body in the United States. In the colonial era, Anglicans and Swedish Lutherans in the mid-Atlantic region had enjoyed very cordial relations, and their clergy had engaged in pulpit exchanges and attended one another's meetings. Lutherans and Episcopalians had also discussed plans of union in the early nineteenth century, and the publication of the Chicago-Lambeth Quadrilateral encouraged ecumenical conversations between representatives of the Episcopal Church and various Lutheran bodies in the 1880s and 1890s.[81] Although in the twentieth century Lutherans focused on healing internal theological and ethnic rifts—at one time there were over 60 separate Lutheran church bodies—rather than on engaging in ecumenical conversations, the formation of the ELCA in 1988 at last freed church members to undertake serious discussions with Roman Catholics and Episcopalians.

The initial series of talks between Lutherans and Episcopalians had begun in 1969 and culminated in a eucharistic celebration at Washington National Cathedral in January 1983. During that celebration, representatives of the Episcopal Church and of the three Lutheran denominations that eventually formed the ELCA (the Lutheran Church in America, the American Lutheran Church, and the Association of Evangelical Lutheran Churches) agreed both to recognize the authenticity of all four religious bodies as "a Church in which the Gospel is preached and taught" and to permit their clergy to stand together at the altar in common celebrations of the Lord's Supper.[82] Further discussions, which took place between 1983 and 1991, resulted in two important documents: "Toward Full Communion" and the "Concordat of Agreement." Those texts indicated that "full communion" would be premised on a mutual sharing of gifts, not on an organizational merger. The churches would be interdependent in doctrine and ministry while remaining autonomous in structure, and clergy would be able to officiate at services in one another's churches without Episcopalians being required to subscribe to the Augsburg Confession or Lutherans being required to receive ordination by an Episcopal bishop. In addition, bishops from each denomination would agree to participate in the consecrations of bishops from the other church, so that all ELCA bishops would eventually stand in the same historic line of succession that Episcopalians claimed to have maintained.[83]

After the two reports were published, the denominations debated the strengths and weaknesses of what had been proposed. In the summer of 1997, both churches were prepared to decide (Episcopalians at their General Convention in July, Lutherans at their Churchwide Assembly in August) whether to accept the Concordat of Agreement. Before votes were taken, however, strong voices of opposition to the concordat were heard, especially among Lutherans. The main Lutheran objection echoed what Presbyterians had said during their discussions with the Episcopal Church in the 1940s: the concordat required Lutherans to recognize and accept the historic episcopate.[84] Episcopalians who opposed the concordat (mainly Anglo-Catholics) also objected to the way it dealt with the episcopate. They focused, however, on a provision temporarily eliminating the requirement that clergy had to be ordained by a "duly qualified" bishop in the historic succession. This provision, Episcopal critics argued, eliminated a fundamental principle of Anglican faith and practice.[85]

Despite such objections, most observers thought the Concordat of Agreement represented a remarkably balanced and effective compromise with numerous benefits. For instance, rather than competing against one another in sparsely populated rural areas or in inner-city neighborhoods, Lutherans and Episcopalians could coordinate their pastoral and evangelistic efforts and perhaps even form united parishes. Such joint endeavors would not only boost the morale of small congregations but also provide demonstrable evidence of the importance of Christian unity.[86] As one Lutheran pastor observed, in the future there would be "no excuse for building a Lutheran church on one corner of the street and an Episcopal church on the other."[87]

Although Episcopalians voted overwhelmingly in favor of the concordat at the General Convention in July 1997, the ELCA defeated the proposal at its Churchwide Assembly in August. The majority of Lutheran representatives at the assembly supported the concordat, but a two-thirds majority was required for passage, and the measure fell short by just a handful of votes. As the debates prior to the vote suggested, the major stumbling block had been the historic episcopate. The main opposition to the concordat came from congregations that were steeped in the confessional pietism prevalent in Lutheranism in the upper Midwest.[88]

Despite the defeat of the Concordat of Agreement in 1997, ecumenists from the two denominations recommitted themselves to achieving full communion. In the spring of 1998, the Lutherans released a document ("Called to Common Mission: A Lutheran Proposal for a Revision of the Concordat of Agreement") in which the issue of the episcopate was again discussed, but in terms more acceptable to traditional Lutheran views about ordained ministry.[89] After further discussion and revision of the document, "Called to Common Mission" was officially adopted by the ELCA in August 1999. Although Anglo-Catholics again objected strenuously to provisions that downplayed distinctive Anglican teachings on the episcopate, the agreement was also ratified by Episcopalians at the General Convention of 2000.[90] Having at last achieved consensus on full communion, the Episcopal Church and the ELCA made plans to celebrate this achievement in a joint service at the Washington National Cathedral in January 2001.

DENOMINATIONAL IDENTITY AT THE END OF THE MILLENNIUM

By the year 2000, membership in the Episcopal Church had leveled off at slightly more than 2.3 million. Despite the declining size of their denomination, Episcopalians in the 1990s exhibited a far better appreciation of their religious identity than they had 30 years earlier, when membership figures were at their peak. With decline and loss came a renewed attention to Anglicanism's unique theology and spirituality—an outlook reminiscent of the early nineteenth century, when unfashionable ideas about hierarchy and tradition set the Episcopal Church apart from the nation's democratic, reform-oriented religious culture.[91]

According to James Fenhagen, a former dean of General Theological Seminary, three key elements—comprehensiveness, personal holiness, and holy worldliness—have always defined "the Anglican way."[92] These emphases, he suggests, continued to make the Episcopal Church distinctive among the major American Christian denominations at the end of the second millennium.

"Comprehensiveness" reflects the ideal of the *via media,* originally formulated during the reign of Elizabeth I—a blend of Catholic and Protestant elements and a refusal to impose rigid doctrinal tests on church members. As a consequence, Anglicans have usually accepted anyone into their fellowship who is at least minimally orthodox and willing to participate in prayer book worship. The spirit of comprehensiveness, on the other hand, has sometimes masked moral laxity, doctrinal confusion, and the very exclusion of the minority views it is intended to protect.

The "personal holiness" theme has been manifested in the interweaving of corporate worship and individual prayer with a sense of beauty, joy, and religious awe. The quest for personal holiness, however, has occasionally degenerated into a narcissistic turning inward, a self-absorption, a focus merely on the *feeling* of being holy. At its worst, it has also fostered an unhealthy fixation on aesthetics and meaningless ritual.

Finally, "holy worldliness" has meant that Anglicanism cherishes the divine presence in everyday affairs, seeing value in the physical as well as in the spiritual, in pleasure as well as in suffering. At times, however, this quality has amounted to little more than the deification of the status quo, the sacralization of the social institutions of the nation's ruling elite. The idea of holy worldliness has also led to the compartmentalization of life into sacred and secular realms, so that the practice of the faith is thought to have no relevance to economic or political affairs outside of the church's splendid Gothic edifices.

Throughout the history of the Episcopal Church, and certainly in the lives of leading Episcopalians, these core elements of the Anglican way have been amply displayed. The last third of the twentieth century was an era of rapid social change that affected Episcopalians as much as all Americans. Despite the many heated debates and arguments that divided them during this period, Episcopalians still found much to appreciate in the traditions of their denomination—an institution whose structure of governance, forms of worship, and fluid approach to theology provided a vital alternative for churchgoers on the American religious scene at the beginning of the third millennium.

NOTES

1. *HEC,* 249–50; *AR,* 357, 362; and Gardiner H. Shattuck Jr., "Should the Episcopal Church Disappear? Reflections on the Decade of Evangelism," *ATR* 73 (1991): 177–78.

2. James F. Findlay Jr., *Church People in the Struggle: The National Council of Churches and the Black Freedom Movement, 1950–1970* (New York: Oxford University Press, 1993), 224; and *RHAP,* 1079.

3. *Journal of the General Convention of the Protestant Episcopal Church* (1958): 319 (source of quotation); and Gardiner H. Shattuck Jr., *Episcopalians and Race: Civil War to Civil Rights* (Lexington: University Press of Kentucky, 2000), 94–97.

4. John L. Kater Jr., "The Episcopal Society for Cultural and Racial Unity and Its Role in the Episcopal Church, 1959–1970" (Ph.D. diss., McGill University, 1973), 27–34.

5. Charles C. J. Carpenter, "Memorandum to Officers and Members of the National Council" (April 7, 1960), quoted in Shattuck, *Episcopalians and Race,* 103; and "Study by 2 Episcopalian Groups Voices Sympathy for Sitdowns," *NYT,* 31 March 1960, 27.

6. John B. Morris, "Statement Given Press," 9 April 1960, quoted in Shattuck, *Episcopalians and Race,* 103.

7. S. Jonathan Bass, *Blessed Are the Peacemakers: Martin Luther King Jr., Eight White Religious Leaders, and the "Letter from Birmingham Jail"* (Baton Rouge: Louisiana State University Press, 2001), 110–30.

8. "Time to Act! A Statement by the Presiding Bishop," *TLC,* 2 June 1963, 7–8.

9. Shattuck, *Episcopalians and Race,* 129–32.

10. When he was consecrated suffragan bishop in 1962, John Burgess became the first African American to exercise episcopal jurisdiction over white church members. He later became the first black diocesan bishop in the Episcopal Church.

11. Robert K. Massie, "Don't Tread on Grandmother Peabody," *Saturday Evening Post,* 16 May 1964, 74–76; Esther J. Burgess, "Witness at St. Augustine, Florida," *Church Militant,* May 1964, 2–3; and Hester H. Campbell, *Four for Freedom* (New York: Carlton, 1974), 8–11, 73–82.

12. Martin Luther King Jr., "Our God Is Marching On!" in *A Testament of Hope: The Essential Writings of Martin Luther King, Jr.,* ed. James Melvin Washington (San Francisco: HarperSanFrancisco, 1986), 228.

13. Shattuck, *Episcopalians and Race,* 154–56.

14. Charles W. Eagles, *Outside Agitator: Jon Daniels and the Civil Rights Movement in Alabama* (Chapel Hill: University of North Carolina Press, 1993), 36–59, 79–87, 127–30, 163–84, 224–49.

15. John E. Hines, quoted in Kenneth Kesselus, *John E. Hines: Granite on Fire* (Austin, Tex.: Episcopal Theological Seminary of the Southwest, 1995), 261.

16. Shattuck, *Episcopalians and Race,* 175–80.

17. Harold T. Lewis, *Yet with a Steady Beat: The African American Struggle for Recognition in the Episcopal Church* (Valley Forge, Pa.: Trinity Press International, 1996), 155–61; and Edward Rodman, *Let There Be Peace among Us: A Story of the Union of Black Episcopalians* (Lawrenceville, Va.: Brunswick, 1990), 4–10.

18. "Foundation for Christian Theology Formed," *TLC,* 18 September 1966, 6–7 (source of quotation); and Shattuck, *Episcopalians and Race,* 195–203.

19. John M. Krumm, "Miracle Convention of 1969," *Witness,* 2 September 1969, 7 (source of quotation); "An Act of Faith," *Episcopalian,* October 1969, 8–17, 22–29, 32–38, 56; and Paul M. Washington, *"Other Sheep I Have": The Autobiography of Father Paul M. Washington,* ed. David McI. Gracie (Philadelphia: Temple University Press, 1994), 86–96.

20. Paul Moore, *Presences: A Bishop's Life in the City* (New York: Farrar, Straus, 1997), 204–6; Michael B. Friedland, *Lift Up Your Voice Like a Trumpet: White Clergy and the Civil Rights and Antiwar Movements, 1954–1973* (Chapel Hill: University of North Carolina Press, 1998), 144, 148, 178, 201, 219; and Shattuck, *Episcopalians and Race,* 194.

21. "GCSP Liquidated—At Long Last," *TLC,* 18 November 1973, 13.

22. John M. Allin, quoted in "The Third John and the 23rd PB," *Episcopalian,* November 1973, 20; and Shattuck, *Episcopalians and Race,* 202–13.

23. Pauli Murray, *Pauli Murray: The Autobiography of a Black Activist, Feminist, Lawyer, Priest, and Poet* (Knoxville: University of Tennessee Press, 1989), 362. Murray later became the first African American woman to be ordained an Episcopal priest.

24. Pamela W. Darling, *New Wine: The Story of Women Transforming Leadership and Power in the Episcopal Church* (Cambridge: Cowley, 1994), 107–13.

25. *Ibid.,* 114–17.

26. David E. Sumner, *The Episcopal Church's History: 1945–1985* (Wilton, Conn.: Morehouse-Barlow, 1987), 19–21; and Darling, *New Wine,* 119–21. On particularly controversial questions, the rules of the convention required that each diocesan delegation (four clergy and four laity) should be divided into its lay and clerical parts. For the vote in either of the two parts to be counted as affirmative, at least three of the four deputies in that group had to vote for the resolution. A divided vote (2–2), furthermore, was counted as a *negative.* Thus, the vote for women's ordination in the clerical order of the House of Deputies was 50 dioceses "yes," 43 "no," and 20 divided; in the lay order of the house, it was 49 dioceses "yes," 37 "no," and 26 divided. But because each divided delegation represented a negative vote, the motion was defeated.

27. Suzanne R. Hiatt, quoted in Darling, *New Wine,* 123 (emphasis added).

28. Suzanne R. Hiatt, "How We Brought the Good News from Graymoor to Minneapolis: An Episcopal Paradigm," *Journal of Ecumenical Studies* 20 (1983): 580.

29. Quoted in Carter Heyward, *A Priest Forever: One Woman's Controversial Ordination in the Episcopal Church* (1976; reprint, Cleveland: Pilgrim, 1999), 59.

30. Moore, *Presences,* 293.

31. Don S. Armentrout, "Ministry in the History of the Episcopal Church," *Sewanee Theological Review* 38 (1995): 250; Hiatt, "How We Brought the Good News," 580; and Mary S. Donovan, *Women Priests in the Episcopal Church: The Experience of the First Decade* (Cincinnati: Forward Movement, 1988), 7.

32. Daniel Corrigan, Robert DeWitt, and Edward Welles II, quoted in Alla Bozarth-Campbell, *Womanpriest: A Personal Odyssey* (New York: Paulist, 1978), 123.

33. Merrill Bittner et al., quoted in Bozarth-Campbell, *Womanpriest,* 125.

34. Armentrout, "Ministry in the History of the Episcopal Church," 251.

35. The other women ordained were Merrill Bittner, Alla Bozarth-Campbell, Allison Cheek, Emily Hewitt, Carter Heyward, Marie Moorefield, Jeannette Piccard, Betty Bone Schiess, Katrina Welles Swanson, and Nancy Hatch Wittig.

36. Quoted in Bozarth-Campbell, *Womanpriest,* 135–36.

37. Hiatt, "How We Brought the Good News," 581. See also Darling, *New Wine,* 127–32.

38. Quoted in Armentrout, "Ministry in the History of the Episcopal Church," 253.

39. Quoted in Armentrout, "Ministry in the History of the Episcopal Church," 254.

40. The 1974 merger of the Philadelphia Divinity School with the Episcopal Theological School (ETS) in Cambridge, Massachusetts, had formed a new seminary, the Episcopal Divinity School, which was located on the former ETS campus.

41. Eleanor Lee McGee, Alison Palmer, Elizabeth Rosenberg, and Diane Tickell were the women who were ordained at that service.

42. Sumner, *Episcopal Church's History,* 26–30; and Darling, *New Wine,* 136–40.

43. Darling, *New Wine,* 173–80.

44. Quoted in Sumner, *Episcopal Church's History,* 65.

45. Moore, *Presences,* 259.

46. James E. Carroll, quoted in Sumner, *Episcopal Church's History,* 64.

47. Quoted in Sumner, *Episcopal Church's History,* 65.

48. *HEC,* 268–70; and Sumner, *Episcopal Church's History,* 66–67.

49. Edmond Browning, "Address to General Convention, 1985," in *DW,* 603.

50. *HEC,* 287.

51. Darling, *New Wine,* 201–7; and *HEC,* 287–89.

52. Ed Stannard, "Court Dismisses Charges against Bishop," *Episcopal Life,* June 1996, 1, 10, 12–13; and *HEC,* 289–93. Episcopal conservatives did win a victory two years later at the 1998 Lambeth Conference, when the worldwide gathering of Anglican bishops affirmed traditional teachings on sexuality and rejected homosexual practice as incompatible with scripture.

53. Frank Griswold, quoted in David Skidmore, "Bishops Approve Robinson," Episcopal News Service on-line, 6 August 2003. <http://www.episcopalchurch.org/ens>

54. Frank Griswold, quoted in Jeffrey Steenson, "Tension High at Convention's Opening," *TLC,* 17 August 2003, 9.

55. Rowan Williams, quoted in *ibid.*

56. Rowan Williams, quoted in "Anglicans Warned over Gay Bishop," BBC on-line, 6 August 2003. <http://www.co.uk/bbc>

57. Quoted in *ibid.* The same General Convention also passed a resolution recognizing "that local faith communities are operating within the bounds of our common life as they explore and experience liturgies celebrating and blessing same-sex unions." This resolution stopped short of authorizing liturgies for such services, but both proponents and opponents of services blessing same-sex unions saw this resolution as a step toward official authorization of such liturgies.

58. Paul Seabury, "Trendier Than Thou," *Harper's,* October 1978, 39.

59. John Booty, *The Episcopal Church in Crisis* (Cambridge, Mass.: Cowley, 1988), 29–32; and Sumner, *Episcopal Church's History,* 107–15.

60. Walter Sullivan, quoted in Sumner, *Episcopal Church's History,* 113.

61. *HEC,* 253–54; and Sumner, *Episcopal Church's History,* 113.

62. Quoted in Darling, *New Wine,* 151.

63. *Ibid.,* 151–52, 182–84, 212–13.

64. *Ibid.,* 152–54 (quotation on 153).

65. *AR,* 363–64.

66. Quoted in Booty, *Episcopal Church in Crisis,* 81.

67. Quoted in Sumner, *Episcopal Church's History,* 122.

68. *HEC,* 264–67; and Sumner, *Episcopal Church's History,* 120–30.

69. "Convention Briefs," *TLC,* 17 August, 2003, 10.

70. According to one popular but overstated study of the social and financial power wielded by Episcopalians, "the Englishness, formality, . . . and fundamental conservatism of the Episcopal religion have nurtured and accompanied the development of a distinctly upper-class way of life and system of values that have dominated American business, law, and politics for 100 years"—Kit and Frederica Konolige, *The Power of Their Glory: America's Ruling Class—The Episcopalians* (New York: Wyden, 1978), 26.

71. Rodman, *Let There Be Peace among Us,* 37–42; and Lewis, *Yet with a Steady Beat,* 166–67.

72. *HEC,* 294–96.

73. Stephen M. Hall, quoted in David Hein, "Episcopalianism among the Native Americans of South Dakota," paper presented at the Annual Meeting of the American Academy of Religion, New Orleans, November 1990, 1–2. A revised version of this paper has been published as "Episcopalianism among the Lakota/Dakota Indians of South Dakota," *Historiographer* 40 (Advent 2002): 14–16.

74. Virginia Driving Hawk Sneve, "Pastor to Indians and Non-Indians: Vine Deloria," *TLC,* 12 December 1999, 14.

75. Quoted in Hein, "Episcopalianism among the Native Americans," 6; and Owanah Anderson, *400 Years: Anglican / Episcopal Mission among American Indians* (Cincinnati: Forward Movement, 1997), 294. Although Indian clergy in South Dakota have often favored the use of native dance and song in Episcopal services, they have usually opposed the introduction of *religious* practices such as the sacred pipe—Hein, "Episcopalianism among Native Americans," 8.

76. *HEC,* 263–64, 300.

77. "Episcopal Church Apologizes to Indians," *Christian Century* 114 (1997): 1119–20.

78. Quoted in Sumner, *Episcopal Church's History,* 138.

79. Robert S. Ellwood, *The Sixties Spiritual Awakening: American Religion Moving from Modern to Postmodern* (New Brunswick, N.J.: Rutgers University Press, 1994), 54.

80. "Planning for Greater Unity," *Christian Century* 116 (1999): 175–76; "Role of Bishops Remains in Question in Plan for Unity of Nine Churches," *TLC,* 21 February 1999, 6; Paul A. Crow Jr., "Still on Pilgrimage," *Christian Century* 116 (1999): 380–82; Michael Kinnamon, "Ecumenical Rebirth," *Christian Century* 117 (2000): 526–27; Jean Caffey Lyles, "Dealing with Rebels," *Christian Century* 117 (2000): 781. For a thorough critique of the Consultation on Church Union as it existed in the late 1970s, see *A Communion of Communions: One Eucharistic Fellowship,* ed. J. Robert Wright (New York: Seabury, 1979), 52–53, 89–94.

81. Nelson H. Burr, "The Early History of the Swedes and the Episcopal Church in America," *HMPEC* 7 (1938): 113–32; Joyce L. White, "The Affiliation of Seven Swedish Lutheran Churches with the Episcopal Church," *HMPEC* 46 (1977): 171–86; and Don S. Armentrout, "Lutheran-Episcopal Conversations in the Nineteenth Century," *HMPEC* 44 (1975): 167–87. See also Suzanne Geissler, *Lutheranism and Anglicanism in Colonial New Jersey: An Early Ecumenical Experiment in New Sweden* (Lewiston, N.Y.: Mellen, 1988).

82. "Lutheran-Episcopal Dialogue, September 1982," in *DW,* 490.

83. For a full discussion of the dialogue between Lutherans and Episcopalians, see David Hein, "The Episcopal Church and the Ecumenical Movement, 1937–1997: Presbyterians, Lutherans, and the Future," *AEH* 66 (1997): 4–29.

84. "The Dissenting Report of Lutheran-Episcopal Dialogue, Series III," in *Lutheran-Episcopal Dialogue, Series III,* ed. William A. Norgren and William G. Rusch (Minneapolis: Augsburg, 1991), 111.

85. "Introduction," in *Inhabiting Unity: Theological Perspectives on the Proposed Lutheran-Episcopal Concordat,* ed. Ephraim Radner and R. R. Reno (Grand Rapids, Mich.: Eerdmans, 1995), 5, 7. The phrase "duly qualified" appears in the "Preface to the Ordination Rites," *Book of Common Prayer* (1979), 510.

86. Janet Irwin, "Episcopal-Lutheran Unity at the Grassroots," *TLC,* 18 February 1996, 8; Ed Stannard, "Historic Vote Offers Closer Lutheran Bonds," *Episcopal Life,* September 1996, 10; J. Robert Wright, "Differing Gifts of Lutherans," *TLC,* 16 January 2000, 13. For examples of joint efforts undertaken by the two churches during that period, see Malin Foster, "Technically Two Parishes but with One Heart," Mary Lee B. Simpson, "Neither Fish nor Fowl, Parish Just a Success," and Julie Nelson, "Both Faith Groups Learn Ages-Old Native Tradition," in *Episcopal Life,* September 1996, 10–12.

87. Lowell Almen, quoted in Jeffrey Steenson, "True Accord: Episcopalians and Lutherans Agree on Full Communion," *TLC,* 30 July 2000, 10.

88. "Roller Coaster in Philadelphia," *Lutheran,* October 1997, 10; and Richard E. Koenig, "The ELCA Assembly: Now and Not Yet," *Christian Century* 114 (1997): 780–82.

89. Gustav Niebuhr, "Lutherans Reconsider Episcopal Concordat," *NYT,* 30 November 1997, 25; and "ELCA Revises Ecumenical Proposal," *Christian Century* 115 (1998): 424.

90. Roderick James Thompson and Armand Kreft, "Old Proposal Was Better Than the New One," *TLC,* 14 November 1999, 19–20; and Steenson, "True Accord," 10.

91. Robert Bruce Mullin, "Denominations as Bilingual Communities," in *Reimagining Denominationalism: Interpretive Essays,* ed. Robert Bruce Mullin and Russell E. Richey (New York: Oxford University Press, 1994), 167.

92. James C. Fenhagen, *The Anglican Way* (Cincinnati: Forward Movement, 1981).

Part Two
A BIOGRAPHICAL DICTIONARY OF LEADERS IN THE EPISCOPAL CHURCH

A

AYRES, ANNE (3 January 1816, London–9 February 1896, New York). *Education:* Unknown. *Career:* Teacher, New York, 1836–45; religious sister, 1845–52; founding sister, Sisterhood of the Holy Communion, New York, 1852–96.

Anne Ayres, the founder of the first religious sisterhood in the Episcopal Church, was born in London in 1816. Little is known about her early life, but she came to New York with her father when she was 20 years old. She found employment as a teacher of young girls from well-to-do families, one of them the niece of William Augustus Muhlenberg,* an Episcopal clergyman. Highly impressed by a sermon that Muhlenberg preached, Ayres decided to devote her life to the work of the church. In a private ceremony at which Muhlenberg officiated, she formally dedicated herself to Christian service in November 1845. Seven years later, when he was rector of the Church of the Holy Communion in New York, Muhlenberg sponsored the founding of the Sisterhood of the Holy Communion, of which Ayres was the "First Sister."

Although Ayres's order was the first Protestant sisterhood formed in the United States, it was organized in a manner different from the typical Roman Catholic order. Its members did not take lifetime vows, but each woman pledged to remain unmarried and to serve for renewable three-year terms. The order had no monastic rule, and while there was a prescribed form of dress, members did not wear a traditional religious habit. The sisters served principally as nurses, first at a small infirmary at the Church of the Holy Communion, and later at St. Luke's Hospital, which Muhlenberg helped organize in 1858. Ayres had charge of both the nursing and the household administration at the hospital. In 1865 Muhlenberg undertook a new venture, St. Johnland (a "Christian industrial community") on Long Island, where Ayres also devoted considerable time to managing social service ministry to the poor.

In her later years, Ayres served as a companion, nurse, and secretary to Muhlenberg. When he died in 1877, she withdrew from her work at St. Luke's Hospital but continued to serve at St. Johnland. She edited two volumes of Muhlenberg's essays and speeches, published as *Evangelical and Catholic Papers* (1875–77), and she composed a full biography of her friend and mentor. Although the Sisterhood of the Holy Communion never became large and ultimately went out of existence in 1940, Ayres is credited with inspiring the revival of the religious life in the Episcopal Church. She died at St. Luke's Hospital in New York in 1896.

Bibliography

A. *Thoughts on Evangelical Sisterhoods* (New York, 1862); *Practical Thoughts on Sisterhoods* (New York, 1864); *Evangelical Sisterhoods* (New York, 1867); *The Life and Work of William Augustus Muhlenberg* (New York, 1880).
B. *DAB* 1, 452–53; *DC,* 29–37; *EDC,* 35; *FD,* 59–65; *NAW* 1, 74–75; *Churchman,* 15–22 February 1896; *N.Y. Herald,* 12 February 1896; *TLC,* 22 February 1896; H. Boone Porter Jr., *Sister Anne: Pioneer in Women's Work* (New York, 1960).

B

BLAIR, JAMES (May 1656?, Alvah, Scotland–18 April 1743, Williamsburg, Va.). *Education:* M.A., University of Edinburgh, 1673; studied theology with William Keith and Laurence Charteris, Edinburgh, 1673–79. *Career:* Minister, Cranston, Scotland, 1679–82; clerk, Rolls Office, London, 1682–85; rector, Varina (Henrico), Va., 1685–94; president, College of William and Mary, 1693–1743; rector, Jamestown, Va., 1694–1710; rector, Bruton Parish Church, Williamsburg, Va., 1710–43.

James Blair, the founder and first president of the College of William and Mary, was born in Banffshire, Scotland. Educated at the strongly Calvinist Marischal College (now the University of Aberdeen) and at the University of Edinburgh, Blair was episcopally ordained in 1679 as a minister in the Church of Scotland. He served Cranston Parish until 1682, when he was removed for refusing to take the Test Oath acknowledging the English king, James II, a Roman Catholic, as the heir to the British throne and the head of the Scottish church. Blair then proceeded to London, where he served for three years in a secular post as clerk to the Master of the Rolls. During this period he formed a lasting friendship with Henry Compton, the Anglican bishop of London, who appointed him missionary to a rural parish in Henrico County in the colony of Virginia.

In 1687, two years after his arrival in Virginia, Blair married Sarah Harrison, the daughter of an influential planter. This marriage into the local gentry increased Blair's prominence. In 1689 he became the first colonial priest to be designated a commissary, which meant that he was deputized by the bishop of London to provide discipline and direction to the Anglican clergy in Virginia. An energetic leader, Blair set up a convocation system, called annual conferences, and worked vigorously to improve the moral climate of his parish. He also attempted to establish ecclesiastical courts and to bring about better financial arrangements for clergy through the standardization of the value of the tobacco in which they were paid. The results of these efforts were meager, however, as he proved more effective in drawing attention to existing problems than in removing them.

Out of Commissary Blair's concern for the religious condition of his colony grew his plan for the College of William and Mary, the first Anglican institution of higher education in America and the second college (after Harvard) to be established in the colonies. In 1690 Blair brought together the colony's clergy, about 24 men, and formed a plan to start a college that would provide Christian learning for local young men and thereby ensure an educated ministry. In 1691 he traveled to England, where he worked hard for two years to win support for his enterprise. He finally secured the college's charter in 1693 and was named its president for life. Despite various setbacks, Blair managed to establish the College of William and Mary as the most vital and important center of academic excellence in the southern colonies prior to the American Revolution. This college provided a large number of the Virginia-born Anglican clergy who served in the colony before the American Revolution, and it educated such political leaders as Thomas Jefferson, James Monroe, and John Marshall.

In 1695, when his college was first opening its doors, Blair moved from Jamestown to Middle Plantation, which he and the colony's lieutenant governor in 1699 persuaded the General Assembly to rename Williamsburg and to designate as the capital of the colony. As the Anglican commissary and as a college president, he was the most influential figure in Virginia after the royal governor. In 1710 Blair also became rector of Bruton Parish in Williamsburg, where he served until his death in 1743.

Bibliography

A. *Our Saviour's Divine Sermon on the Mount . . . Explained, and the Practice of It Recommended in Divers Sermons and Discourses,* 5 vols. (London, 1722); 4 vols. (London, 1740).

B. *AAP* 5, 7–9; *ACAB* 1, 281; *ANB* 2, 914–15; *DAB* 2, 335–37; *DARB,* 57–58; *DCA,* 165–66; *EDC,* 50; *NCAB* 3, 231–32; *SH* 2, 196; *SPCK,* 83–84; G. MacLaren Brydon, "James Blair, Commissary," *HMPEC* 14 (1945): 85–118; P.G. Scott, "James Blair and the Scottish Church: A New Source," *WMQ,* 3rd ser., 33 (1976): 300–308; Parke Rouse Jr., *James Blair of Virginia* (Chapel Hill, N.C., 1971); J.E. Morpurgo, *Their Majesties' Royall Colledge of William and Mary in the Seventeenth and Eighteenth Centuries* (Williamsburg, Va., 1976).

BLISS, WILLIAM DWIGHT PORTER (20 August 1856, Constantinople, Turkey–8 October 1926, New York). *Education:* Robert College, Constantinople; Phillips Academy, Andover, Mass.; B.A., Amherst College, 1878; B.D., Hartford Theological Seminary, 1882. *Career:* Minister of Congregational churches in Denver, Colo., and South Natick, Mass., 1882–85; Episcopal lay reader, Lee, Mass., 1885–87; rector, Grace Episcopal Church, Boston, 1887–90; priest-in-charge, Mission (later Church) of the Carpenter, Boston, 1890–94; traveling lecturer, Christian Social Union, 1894–98; rector, Church of Our Savior, San Gabriel,

Calif., 1898–1902; rector, Amityville, N.J., 1902–6; special investigator, U.S. Bureau of Labor, 1907–9; rector, West Orange, N.J., 1910–14; student, pastor, and Young Men's Christian Association worker in Switzerland, 1914–21; rector, St. Martha's Episcopal Church, New York, 1921–25.

William D. P. Bliss, a priest and social reformer, was born in Constantinople, Turkey, in 1856. The son of missionaries, he grew up as a Congregationalist and served briefly as a minister in Congregational churches in Colorado and Massachusetts. However, after studying the Anglican tradition, he was so impressed by its catholicity and theological breadth that he decided to join the Episcopal Church and become a priest. His first Episcopal congregation was located in Lee, Massachusetts, a factory town, where he became acquainted both with the working condition of the local laborers and with their general alienation from the church. In 1890 he founded an experimental inner-city church community called the Mission of the Carpenter in Boston. In that parish setting he attempted to apply the teachings of the New Testament to urban problems. As one of the leading advocates of the social gospel, Bliss joined the Knights of Labor and even turned down a nomination to become the Labor Party's candidate for lieutenant governor of Massachusetts in 1887.

Strongly influenced by Anglican social theorists such as Charles Kingsley and F. D. Maurice, Bliss believed that the Episcopal Church had a responsibility to exercise leadership in American society. Throughout his ministry, he lectured widely about Christian socialism, and he organized publicity campaigns and initiated local programs on behalf of the labor movement. He participated as well in the creation of several larger social gospel organizations, such as the Church Association for the Advancement of the Interests of Labor (1887) and the Society of Christian Socialists (1889). Bliss also made significant contributions as a writer and editor. He assisted the well-known Congregationalist reformer Josiah Strong in the production of his series, *Studies in the Gospel of the Kingdom;* he edited both *The Dawn* (1889–96), which was the magazine of the Society of Christian Socialists, and *The American Fabian* (1895–96); and he compiled materials for the massive *Encyclopedia of Social Reform* (1897).

In all of his efforts, Bliss remained dedicated to socialism, by which he meant the collective ownership and cooperative operation of land and capital for the good of all. However, he never confused a socialist utopia with the kingdom of God, nor did he think that social activism could replace Christian faith and participation in the sacraments. A Christocentric realist, he emphasized that salvation is possible only through the redemption achieved by Christ's atonement. As he commented in his *Handbook of Socialism* (1895), "no Socialism can be successful unless rooted and grounded in Christ, the Liberator . . . the Head of Humanity." The Christian church, Bliss held, is "the world's first, greatest, and necessary International."

After leaving the Church of the Carpenter in 1894, Bliss served in a number of pastoral capacities in California, New Jersey, New York, and Switzerland. He died in New York City in 1926.

Bibliography

A. *A Handbook of Socialism* (London, 1895); *The Encyclopedia of Social Reform* (New York, 1897).
B. *ANB* 3, 31–32; *DAB* 2, 377–78; *DARB*, 61–62; *DCA*, 168–69; *EDC*, 51; *NCAB* 20, 91–92; *SH* 2, 204; *SPCK*, 84–85; *NYT*, 9 October 1926; Christopher L. Webber, "William Dwight Porter Bliss (1856–1926): Priest and Socialist," *HMPEC* 28 (1959): 9–39; Richard B. Dressner, "William Dwight Porter Bliss's Christian Socialism," *CH* 47 (1978): 66–82; Charles Howard Hopkins, *The Rise of the Social Gospel in American Protestantism, 1865–1915* (New Haven, 1940), chap. 10; Howard H. Quint, *The Forging of American Socialism: Origins of the Modern Movement* (Columbia, S.C., 1953).

BOUCHER, JONATHAN (12 March 1738, Blencogo, England–27 April 1804, Epsom, England). *Education:* Schools at Bromfield and Wigton. *Career:* Tutor, Port Royal, Va., 1759–62; served churches in King George and Caroline Counties, Virginia, 1762–70; in Anne Arundel and Prince George's Counties, Maryland, 1770–75; and in Paddington and Epsom, England, 1775–1804.

Jonathan Boucher, an Anglican clergyman and outspoken loyalist during the American Revolution, was born in Blencogo in Cumberland County in northern England. He left England in April 1759 to become the tutor of a gentleman's sons at Port Royal, Virginia. Desiring to improve his position in society and having been assured of the rectorship of Hanover Parish in King George County, Virginia, he journeyed back to England in 1762 to be ordained a priest. A few months after his return to America, he moved to St. Mary's Parish, Caroline County, Virginia, where he became a tobacco planter and ran a small school. In 1770 he was appointed rector of St. Anne's Parish in Annapolis, Maryland. At Annapolis he led an active life: presiding over meetings of a literary organization known as the Homony Club, establishing a warm friendship with Governor Robert Eden, drafting legislation and writing speeches for the governor, and serving as chaplain to the lower house of the Maryland Assembly. In November 1771 Eden appointed him to the lucrative rectorship of Queen Anne's Parish in Prince George's County. This additional living enabled him to purchase a large amount of land ideally suited for growing tobacco, and he quickly established himself as a well-to-do planter. His position was further enhanced through his marriage in June 1772 to Eleanor Addison, who belonged to a prominent Maryland family.

Throughout the period of his service in Virginia, Boucher appeared to be more of an American Whig than a Tory, for he opposed both the Stamp Act (which he called "oppressive and illegal") and the Townshend Acts. In Maryland, however, his prosperous economic circumstances, his friendship with members of the colonial establishment, and his commitment to an American episcopate helped his inherent conservatism emerge. In the early 1770s, he also engaged in a personal battle over the church establishment and the clerical salary system in Maryland. He opposed passage of the Vestry Act of 1773, which allowed citizens the option of paying their clergy in cash rather than in tobacco, and he was outraged when his own parishioners refused to pay the tobacco assessment that was owed to him. This conflict further strengthened Boucher's opposition to revolution and social change.

As an Anglican clergyman, Boucher believed that his ordination oath required unwavering loyalty to the British king. As he grew more and more unpopular in the colony, he imagined that armed patriots were threatening his life, and he kept loaded pistols beside him in the pulpit. In September 1775 Boucher and his wife left Maryland for England, never to return. He had lost almost everything, and his first years in England were particularly difficult. Friends procured for him the curacy of Paddington and a pension from the British government, and he added to his income by tutoring and writing for journals. During the last 19 years of his life he served as vicar of Epsom in Surrey, where he died in 1804.

Bibliography

A. *A View of the Causes and Consequences of the American Revolution* (London, 1797); *Reminiscences of an American Loyalist, 1738–1789,* ed. Jonathan Bouchier (Boston, 1925).

B. *AAP* 5, 211–14; *ANB* 3, 235–37; *DAB* 2, 473–75; *EDC,* 55; *NCAB* 9, 123; *WWWA* Historical vol. 1607–1896, 65; Philip Evanson, "Jonathan Boucher: The Mind of an American Loyalist," *Maryland Historical Magazine* 58 (1963): 123–36; Ralph Emmett Fall, "The Rev. Jonathan Boucher, Turbulent Tory (1738–1804)," *HMPEC* 36 (1967): 323–58; Anne Y. Zimmer and Alfred H. Kelly, "Jonathan Boucher: Constitutional Conservative," *Journal of American History* 58 (1971): 897–922; Anne Young Zimmer, *Jonathan Boucher: Loyalist in Exile* (Detroit, 1978).

BOYLE, SARAH PATTON (9 May 1906, near Charlottesville, Va.–21 February 1994, Arlington, Va.). *Education:* Tutored privately at home. *Career:* Housewife and mother; writer of articles and books.

Sarah Patton, a civil rights activist and theological writer, was born on her family's farm outside of Charlottesville, Virginia, in May 1906. Her father, Robert W. Patton, was a priest and the director of the American Church Institute for Negroes, an agency of the Episcopal Church that supported the vocational education of African Americans in the South. Like other elite southern white women of her generation, "Patty" (as she was known to friends and family) was schooled at home. In 1932 she married E. Roger Boyle II, a professor of drama at the University of Virginia in Charlottesville. The mother of two children, she supplemented her family's income by selling paintings and articles to women's magazines. Although she had drifted away from the Episcopal Church when she was a young woman, exploring alternative forms of spirituality, she became an active churchgoer again in the late 1940s.

Boyle wrote about her spiritual transformation in *The Desegregated Heart*

(1962), an autobiographical account of her involvement in the early stages of the civil rights movement in her home state. The catalyst for her religious conversion was the successful suit by Gregory Swanson, an African American, to gain admission to the racially segregated law school of the University of Virginia in 1950. Inspired by Swanson's action, Boyle wrote articles in favor of racial integration in several national magazines, and in 1956 the White Citizens' Council targeted her for harassment by placing a burning cross on her front yard. As a result of her well-meaning efforts to challenge racial mores in Virginia, she not only felt cut off from her white friends, who did not share her liberal views on civil rights, but also was treated suspiciously by African Americans, who viewed her as simply a privileged white paternalist. Boyle also sensed that she and her husband were growing emotionally distant—a process of alienation that eventually led to their divorce. She called God "the only permanent thing left in my life." Boyle's lengthy, step-by-step account of her spiritual awakening during the 1950s earned her a reputation as a spiritual leader and lay theologian, and *The Desegregated Heart* was read in church discussion groups and Christian fellowship gatherings on college campuses.

After the publication of her book, Boyle achieved recognition from civil rights groups such as the National Association for the Advancement of Colored People and the Southern Christian Leadership Conference. She participated in the March on Washington in August 1963, and in June 1964 she was jailed for several days during protest demonstrations against segregation in St. Augustine, Florida. After her divorce in 1965, she moved to Arlington, Virginia. By 1966, as the interracial harmony of the civil rights movement began to dissipate, Boyle saw that her optimistic message of human and Christian "brotherhood" had become outdated, and she withdrew from public life. Still a woman of deep personal faith, her final years were devoted to confronting ageism in American society—a story recounted in her final autobiographical work, *The Desert Blooms* (1983). Boyle died in Arlington in February 1994.

Bibliography

A. Papers at the library of the University of Virginia, Charlottesville; "A Voice from the South," *Christian Century* 69 (1952): 1471–73; "Southerners Will *Like* Integration," *Saturday Evening Post,* 19 February 1955, 25, 133–34; "Spit in the Devil's Eye: A Southern Heretic Speaks," *Nation* 183 (1956): 327–29; *The Desegregated Heart: A Virginian's Stand in Time of Transition* (1962; reprint, Charlottesville, Va., 2001); *For Human Beings Only* (New York, 1964); *The Desert Blooms: A Personal Adventure in Growing Old Creatively* (Nashville, 1983).
B. *EDC,* 56; *FD,* 237–45; Kathleen Murphy Dierenfield, "One 'Desegregated Heart': Sarah Patton Boyle and the Crusade for Civil Rights in Virginia," *Virginia Magazine of History and Biography* 104 (1996): 251–80; Joanna Bowen Gillespie, "Sarah Patton Boyle's Desegregated Heart," in *Beyond Image and Convention: Explorations in Southern Women's History,* ed. Janet L. Coryell et al. (Columbia, Mo., 1998), 158–83; Jennifer Rittenhouse, "Speaking of Race: Sarah Patton Boyle and the 'T.J. Sellers Course for Backward Southern Whites,'" in *Sex, Love, Race: Crossing*

Boundaries in North American History, ed. Martha Hodes (New York, 1999), 491–513; Fred Hobson, *But Now I See: The White Southern Racial Conversion Narrative* (Baton Rouge, La., 1999), 61–71.

BRAGG, GEORGE FREEMAN JR. (25 January 1863, Warrenton, N.C.–12 March 1940, Baltimore). *Education:* Studied at St. Stephen's Parish and Normal School, Petersburg, Va.; graduated from Bishop Payne Divinity School, Petersburg, Va., 1886. *Career:* Vicar, Holy Innocents mission (later, Grace Church), Norfolk, Va., 1887–91; rector, St. James' First African Church, Baltimore, 1891–1940.

George Freeman Bragg Jr., a priest and early civil rights leader, was born in slavery in Warrenton, North Carolina, in January 1863. His parents, George Freeman and Mary Bragg, were devoted members of Emmanuel Church in Warrenton. Following their emancipation in 1865, the Bragg family moved to Petersburg, Virginia, where with the assistance of the Protestant Episcopal Freedman's Commission they were involved in the founding of St. Stephen's Church. Bragg studied at the parish school operated by the staff of St. Stephen's, and in 1879 he entered its theological department (later renamed Bishop Payne Divinity School). After being suspended from classes in 1880 because the rector of St. Stephen's, a former Confederate army officer, found him "wanting in the virtue of humility," Bragg spent several years promoting educational and political opportunities for African Americans in post-Reconstruction Virginia. Returning to Bishop Payne in 1885, he graduated the next year and was ordained to the diaconate in January 1887.

Bragg's parish ministry began in Norfolk, Virginia, where he organized Holy Innocents mission and founded the Industrial School for Colored Girls. Because of racial discrimination, southern bishops customarily required African Americans to serve in the diaconate for at least five years. However, thanks to his native abilities as well as to his persistence in securing support from influential whites, Bragg was ordained a priest in December 1888 after slightly less than two years as a deacon. Successful in his efforts in Norfolk, he was called to be rector of St. James' First African Church, the oldest black Episcopal parish in the South, in 1891. Although St. James was virtually moribund at that time, Bragg quickly revived the congregation. Over the next 10 years, St. James' not only became a self-supporting parish but also purchased a rectory and erected a new church building. By the 1930s it had over five hundred communicants and was one of the strongest black parishes in the Episcopal Church. Besides serving at St. James' for nearly five decades, Bragg was general secretary and historiographer of the Conference of Church Workers among Colored People. In that position he advocated the creation of a racial missionary district in which black Episcopalians could manage their own church affairs with minimal interference from whites—a plan that was repeatedly rejected at meetings of the General Convention during the early twentieth century.

In addition to his considerable work as a priest and pastor, Bragg was active in the African American community both locally and nationally. He organized the Committee of Twelve, a group of black leaders that campaigned against whites' attempt to disenfranchise African Americans voters in Maryland. He was also an original member of the Niagara Movement, founded in 1905, which was the precursor of the National Association for the Advancement of Colored People. In addition, Bragg edited and published materials with his own press throughout most of his adult life. Beginning as a young man in 1882, he published the *Lancet,* a pro-Republican paper concerned with politics in Virginia. In 1886 he founded another paper, the *Afro-American Churchman,* later known as the *Church Advocate,* which served both as the parish newspaper of St. James' Church and as the unofficial organ of the Conference of Church Workers among Colored People. Finally, Bragg wrote more than 20 pamphlets and books released under the imprint of the Church Advocate Press, his own publishing house. His longest and most important work, *History of the Afro-American Group of the Episcopal Church* (1922), is still an indispensable guide to the early history of black clergy, laypeople, and parishes.

Bragg remained the rector of St. James' Church until his death. He died in Baltimore in March 1940 after a brief illness.

Bibliography

A. Papers at the Schomburg Center for Research in Black Culture in New York, at the Moorland-Spingarn Research Center at Howard University, and at Virginia State University in Petersburg; *Afro-American Church Work and Workers* (Baltimore, 1904); *A Bond Slave of Christ: Entering the Ministry under Great Difficulties* (Baltimore, 1912); *History of the Afro-American Group in the Episcopal Church* (Baltimore, 1922); *Heroes of the Eastern Shore: Absalom Jones, the First of the Blacks* (Baltimore, 1939).

B. *ANB* 3, 398–99; *DANB,* 57–58; *EAAR,* 111–12; *EDC,* 56; WWWA 3, 97; *Afro-American,* 16 March 1940; "Personal: George F. Bragg, Jr.," *Journal of Negro History* 25 (July 1940): 399–400; J. Carleton Hayden, " 'For Zion's Sake I Will Not Hold My Peace': George Freeman Bragg, Jr., Priest, Pastor, and Prophet," *Linkage,* October 1986, 10–11, 23; Mildred L. McGlotten, "Rev. George Freeman Bragg: A Negro Pioneer in Social Welfare," (M.A. thesis, Howard University, 1948).

BRECK, JAMES LLOYD (27 June 1818, Philadelphia County, Pa.–30 March 1876, Benicia, Calif.). *Education:* Studied at Flushing Institute, Long Island, N.Y.; B.A., University of Pennsylvania, 1838; B.D., General Theological Seminary, 1841. *Career:* Missionary in Wisconsin, 1841–50; in Minnesota, 1850–67; in California, 1867–76.

James Lloyd Breck, a priest and one of the greatest missionary leaders of the Episcopal Church, was born in Pennsylvania in 1818. An Anglo-Catholic, his beliefs were shaped initially by his experiences at William Augustus Muhlenberg's* liturgically advanced Flushing Institute. He also attended General Theological Seminary, where he was introduced to the ideas of the Oxford movement.

While he was a student at the seminary, an address by Bishop Jackson Kemper* inspired him to undertake missionary work in the West, and after graduation, he headed to the sparsely settled Wisconsin territory with two of his former classmates, William Adams and John Henry Hobart Jr. The men first settled in 1841 at Prairie Village, now Waukesha, Wisconsin, where they built St. John's Church in the Wilderness. The next year they moved to Nashotah Lake and founded Nashotah House seminary on a 500-acre tract in the forest 28 miles west of Milwaukee. All three were seeking an opportunity to live out their priestly vocations in a quasi-monastic setting. They were successful in accomplishing that goal at Nashotah, and by the fall of 1844 there were 30 students in residence.

Breck gave fully of himself to the tasks of a missionary in Wisconsin, traveling thousands of miles to develop schools, to preach the gospel, and to administer the sacraments. Seeking new challenges, however, he moved to Minnesota in 1850. He worked first in St. Paul, where he attempted to found a religious order, and then he served for five years among the Ojibwe Indians. He also established educational, agricultural, and missionary centers at Crow Wing and Leech Lake. In 1857 he settled at Faribault and the next year founded the Seabury Divinity School and boarding schools for the religious training of Ojibwe and Dakota children. Like most missionaries of that period, Breck sought not only to bring Indians to the Christian faith but also to instill in them a way of life that whites called "civilized."

In October 1867 Breck traveled by ship to San Francisco to carry out further missionary work on the Pacific coast. He took with him a party of 17 missionaries: 5 clergymen, 7 candidates for the ministry, and 5 women. Settling at Benicia, they confronted a tremendous challenge because the area had a large population that was growing quickly, while the Episcopal Church was, as Breck put it, "*fifteen years behindhand in this work.*" Throughout his ministry, Breck had focused on three related areas: education, including theological training for ordination; evangelism, through personal contacts and regular worship; and spiritual formation, with the development of a disciplined religious life. This pattern continued in California. At the time of his death, the Pacific Coast Mission included five congregations and a college with both a grammar school and a divinity school attached to it.

After Breck died in Benicia in March 1876, his body was transported back to Wisconsin for burial at Nashotah House.

Bibliography

A. "Indian Mission—Minnesota, 1854," in *DW*, 126–29; *The Life of the Reverend James Lloyd Breck, D.D., Chiefly from Letters Written by Himself*, ed. Charles Breck (New York, 1883).

B. *ANB* 3, 453; *BB*, 80–81; *DAB* 3, 3–4; *DARB*, 73–74; *DCA*, 183–84; *EDC*, 58; *WWWA* Historical vol. 1607–1896, 72; William P. Haugaard, "The Missionary Vision of James Lloyd Breck in Minnesota," *HMPEC* 54 (September 1985): 241–51; Theodore I. Holcombe, *An Apostle of the Wilderness: James Lloyd Breck, D.D., His*

Missions and Schools (New York, 1903); Owanah Anderson, *400 Years: Anglican / Episcopal Mission among American Indians* (Cincinnati, 1997), chap. 3.

BRENT, CHARLES HENRY (9 April 1862, Newcastle, Ont., Canada–27 March 1929, Lausanne, Switzerland). *Education:* A.B., Trinity College, Toronto, 1884; read for holy orders, 1884–86. *Career:* Master, Trinity College School, Port Hope, Ont., 1884–86; organist and curate, St. John's Church, Buffalo, N.Y., 1886–87; priest, St. Andrew's Mission, Buffalo, N.Y., 1887–89; novice, Society of St. John the Evangelist, Boston, 1889–91; assistant minister, St. Stephen's Mission, Boston, 1891–1901; first bishop of the missionary district of the Philippine Islands, 1901–17; president, First International Opium Commission, Shanghai, 1909; senior headquarters chaplain, American Expeditionary Force, France, 1917–18; bishop, diocese of Western New York, 1918–29; bishop-in-charge, American Episcopal churches in Europe, 1926–28.

A bishop and ecumenical leader, Charles Henry Brent was born in Newcastle, Ontario, in 1862. He graduated from Trinity College, Toronto, in 1884 and then studied privately for the ordained ministry. He was ordained a deacon in March 1886 and a priest in March 1887. After serving briefly in parishes in Buffalo, New York, he lived and worked for three years as a novice of the Society of St. John the Evangelist, an Episcopal religious order in Boston. Leaving the order in 1891, he served for the next 10 years as an assistant priest at St. Stephen's Mission, an inner-city church in Boston. During this period, his ministry and writings became widely known, and he was later asked to deliver the Paddock lectures at General Theological Seminary in 1904 and the Noble lectures at Harvard in 1907.

In 1901 Brent was elected missionary bishop of the Philippine Islands by General Convention. Arriving in Manila in May 1902, he began to organize the work of his denomination in a country that had recently been seized by the United States from Spain. Over the next 15 years he ministered to the large American and British population, including military personnel and government officials, and he started a mission for Chinese expatriates. He also oversaw the founding of the Cathedral of St. Mary and St. John and built hospitals and schools. In addition to his efforts with Episcopalians and Anglicans, Brent cooperated with representatives of other religious traditions, both Christian and non-Christian. Unwilling to follow the course of Protestant missionaries who attempted to lead the native population away from their allegiance to Roman Catholicism, he limited the outreach of his denomination to the non-Christian populations of the Philippines: the animistic Igorot tribes in northern Luzon and the Muslim Moros in the southern islands. As a high church Episcopalian, he viewed evangelization as a lengthy process that inculcated in "backward" peoples not only Christian beliefs but also a civilized lifestyle. For years he also worked strenuously, but with little success, to eliminate the opium trade in Asia.

During World War I, Brent served both as a representative of the War Council of the Young Men's Christian Association and (at the invitation of General John

J. Pershing) as chief of chaplains for the American Expeditionary Force. He was elected the fourth bishop of the diocese of Western New York in October 1917, and he took up his duties there in February of the next year. Awakened to the need for ecumenical cooperation by his experience in the Philippines and inspired by the 1910 World Missionary Conference in Edinburgh, which he attended as a delegate, Brent became a pioneering figure in the early stages of the movement for church unity. Seeking to facilitate discussions between the various Christian communions about significant questions of theology and polity, Brent presided at the first session of the World Conference on Faith and Order, the historic 10-day meeting that was held in Lausanne, Switzerland, in 1927.

Brent's last public appearance was as a representative of the Episcopal Church at the enthronement of Cosmo Gordon Lang as archbishop of Canterbury. Several months later, in March 1929, he suffered a severe heart attack and died while in Lausanne.

Bibliography

A. *With God in the World* (New York, 1899); *The Consolations of the Cross* (New York, 1902); *The Splendor of the Human Body* (New York, 1904); *Adventure for God* (New York, 1905); *Liberty and Other Sermons* (New York, 1906); *Prisoners of Hope and Other Sermons* (New York, 1915); *The Mount of Vision* (New York, 1918); *The Commonwealth: Its Foundations and Pillars* (New York, 1930); *Things That Matter: The Best of the Writings of Bishop Brent,* ed. Frederick Ward Kates (New York, 1949).

B. *ANB* 3, 481–83; *DAB* 21, 115–17; *DCA,* 184–85; *EDC,* 58; *NCAB* 26, 482–83; *SH* 2, 260; *SPCK,* 88–93; *WWWA* 1, 135; Eugene C. Bianchi, S.J., "The Ecumenical Thought of Bishop Charles Henry Brent," *CH* 33 (1964): 448–61; Arun W. Jones, "A View from the Mountains: Episcopal Missionary Depictions of the Igorot of Northern Luzon, the Philippines, 1903–16," *AEH* 71 (2002): 380–410; Emma J. Portuondo, "The Impact of Bishop Charles Henry Brent upon American Colonial and Foreign Policy, 1901–1917," (Ph.D. diss., Catholic University of America, 1968); Eleanor Slater, *Charles Henry Brent: Everybody's Bishop* (Milwaukee, 1932); Alexander C. Zabriskie, *Bishop Brent: Crusader for Christian Unity* (Philadelphia, 1948); George E. DeMille, *The Episcopal Church since 1900* (New York, 1955).

BRIGGS, CHARLES AUGUSTUS (15 January 1841, New York–8 June 1913, New York). *Education:* Graduated from the University of Virginia, 1857–60; Union Theological Seminary (N.Y.), 1861–63; University of Berlin, 1866–69. *Career:* Presbyterian minister, Roselle, N.J., 1870–74; professor of Hebrew and cognate languages, Union Theological Seminary (N.Y.), 1874–91; Edwin Robinson professor of biblical theology, Union Seminary, 1891–1904; professor of theological encyclopedia and symbolics, Union Seminary, 1904–13.

Charles Augustus Briggs, a controversial biblical scholar, was born in New York City in 1841. Educated at the University of Virginia, he experienced a religious conversion during a college revival and decided to enter the Presbyterian ministry. He served briefly in a New York regiment at the outbreak of the Civil War and then enrolled at Union Theological Seminary in 1861. After graduating from Union, he studied abroad for three years at the University of Berlin. When he returned to the United States in 1869, Briggs became the pastor of the Presbyterian church in Roselle, New Jersey. In 1874 he was appointed professor of Hebrew at Union Seminary, where he remained until his death nearly four decades later.

Briggs helped found the *Presbyterian Review,* a highly regarded journal of theology that he initially co-edited with A. A. Hodge, a professor at Princeton Theological Seminary. Briggs's studies in Germany had led him away from the conservative scholasticism of the dominant Princeton school and toward an appreciation of the historical-critical method of biblical study. In his inaugural lecture at Union in September 1876, he claimed that the scripture scholar could honor the Bible as the word of God while still employing the tools of historical science. He also rejected the doctrine of biblical infallibility, replacing it with the idea of "plenary inspiration": despite the errors in it, the Bible is still an inspired and reliable guide to Christian faith and practice. This position not only brought him into conflict with Hodge and other Princeton faculty who believed in the inerrancy of the scriptures but also led him to resign as editor of the *Review* in 1889.

In November 1890 the board of directors of Union Seminary transferred Briggs to a newly established professorship in biblical theology. In his inaugural address on "The Authority of Holy Scripture" (January 1891), Briggs argued that God was revealed through "three great fountains of divine authority—the Bible, the Church, and the Reason"; each could be a means of grace. He also condemned the idea of biblical inerrancy, and he discussed redemption as a process that extended beyond earthly life in a middle state between death and the final judgment. This address caused a considerable stir in the press. Although Briggs's views were fully supported by the presbytery of New York, the Union board of directors, and the seminary faculty, the Presbyterian General Assembly of 1891, which was under the control of conservatives with ties to Princeton Seminary, voted to disallow his appointment to the chair in biblical theology. Moreover, after a series of church trials, he was convicted of heresy and in 1893 suspended from the ministry by the General Assembly. In response, Union Seminary severed its formal ties with the Presbyterian Church, thereby denying to the General Assembly jurisdiction over faculty appointments.

No longer comfortable as a Presbyterian, Briggs was increasingly attracted to the theological broadness of the Episcopal Church, and in 1899 he was ordained a priest by Henry C. Potter,* the bishop of New York. Although this action aroused the indignation of conservative Episcopalians who opposed Briggs's scholarly methodology, his ordination symbolized the acceptability of the critical study of scripture within mainstream circles in the Episcopal Church. Briggs continued to write and to teach as the first non-Presbyterian member of the Union faculty. During the last decade of his life, he was involved in promoting the future reunion of churches. Poor health forced him to retire from full-time academic work in 1910, and he died three years later at his seminary residence in New York.

Bibliography

A. *The Authority of Holy Scripture: An Inaugural Address* (New York, 1891); *The Bible, the Church, and the Reason: The Three Great Fountains of Divine Authority* (New York, 1892); *The Messiah of the Gospels* (New York, 1894); *The Messiah of the Apostles* (New York, 1895); *General Introduction to the Study of Holy Scripture* (New York, 1899); *History of the Study of Theology,* 2 vols. (New York, 1916).

B. *ACAB* 1, 374; *ANB* 3, 535–36; *DAB* 3, 40–41; *DARB,* 76–77; *DCA,* 188; *EARH,* 80–82; *EDC,* 58–59; *MCTA,* 319–23; *NCAB* 7, 318–19; *NCE* 2, 802; *SH* 2, 270–71; *NYT,* 9 June 1913; Max Gray Rogers, "Charles Augustus Briggs: Heresy at Union," in *American Religious Heretics,* ed. George H. Shriver (Nashville, 1966); Mark Stephen Massa, *Charles Augustus Briggs and the Crisis of Historical Criticism* (Minneapolis, Minn., 1990); Richard L. Christiansen, *The Ecumenical Orthodoxy of Charles Augustus Briggs* (Lewiston, N.Y., 1995).

BROOKS, PHILLIPS (13 December 1835, Boston–23 January 1893, Boston). *Education:* B.A., Harvard College, 1855; B.D., Virginia Theological Seminary, 1859. *Career:* Rector, Church of the Advent, Philadelphia, 1859–62; rector, Holy Trinity Church, Philadelphia, 1862–69; rector, Trinity Church, Boston, 1869–91; bishop, diocese of Massachusetts, 1891–93.

Arguably the greatest preacher in the history of the Episcopal Church, Phillips Brooks was born in Boston in 1835. After his ordination in 1859, he served in Philadelphia for 10 years as rector of two different parishes. Returning to Boston in 1869, he began a lengthy and highly successful tenure at Trinity Church. After their church building was destroyed by the fire that devastated downtown Boston in 1872, Brooks and the Trinity congregation relocated to the city's newly developed Back Bay section. At that site, he oversaw the construction of a magnificent building designed by the architect H. H. Richardson. Constructed in a Romanesque rather than Gothic revival style, the new church in Copley Square featured a massive pulpit that provided an impressive setting for Brooks's preaching. Thoroughly devoted to the parish ministry, Brooks declined offers to serve as dean of the Episcopal Theological School (1866) and as professor and chaplain at his alma mater, Harvard University (1881), and he remained at Trinity Church for over 20 years.

During the Civil War, Brooks loyally supported the Union war effort and pressed for the abolition of slavery. Although he was hardly radical in his own political views, he was very critical of his fellow Episcopalians in the North who refused either to condemn secession or to discuss the social issues that had led to the outbreak of war. His sermon following the assassination of the sixteenth president, "The Character, Life, and Death of Abraham Lincoln," brought him accolades from across the United States. He also gained national attention with his poem, "O Little Town of Bethlehem," written for the Sunday school children of his parish in Philadelphia following a Christmas Eve service he attended in Palestine in 1865. Sung to Lewis Redner's music, the hymn's simple, peaceful beauty appealed to many Americans in the aftermath of the Civil War.

Brooks was one of the leading broad church Episcopalians of his day, and his theological liberalism and social conservatism were well suited to the affluent parish where he served. As a theological liberal, he believed in the essential goodness of humanity, and he consistently stressed a person's potential for spiritual growth rather than his or her innate sinfulness. In the pulpit he was not ostentatious but warmly persuasive and earnest. He preached rapidly, almost conversationally, yet his words were carefully chosen and aesthetically refined. Holding a view of the preacher as one who brings "truth through personality," as he said in his famous "Lectures on Preaching" at Yale University in 1877, Brooks attempted to show how faith is relevant to everyday existence. He embraced a pragmatic approach to religious truth, and he emphasized ethical behavior over strict adherence to orthodoxy. Never a theological trailblazer, he was strongly influenced by the thinking of Samuel Taylor Coleridge, Frederick Denison Maurice, and Horace Bushnell.

Brooks was elected bishop of the diocese of Massachusetts in April 1891. A preacher of Christian tolerance, his eagerness to enter into cordial relations with other denominations caused concern among Anglo-Catholics, who actively opposed his election to the episcopate. This dispute in the Episcopal Church received extensive coverage in the Boston newspapers, which regularly backed their local pastor against his Anglo-Catholic opponents. Brooks's election was eventually confirmed, and he was consecrated bishop at Trinity Church in October 1891. Barely more than a year into his tenure as bishop, however, he died in January 1893. On the day of his funeral, businesses closed throughout Boston as thousands of people gathered to watch his funeral procession move through the city. Brooks was later memorialized by the noted sculptor Augustus St. Gaudens, who depicted him in his preaching gown with Jesus standing at his back, laying his hand dramatically on Brooks's shoulder.

Bibliography

A. Papers at Houghton Library of Harvard University; "A Sermon on the Nature of the Church," *Theology Today* 12 (1955): 57–67; *Lectures on Preaching* (New York, 1877); *The Influence of Jesus* (New York, 1879); *Sermons Preached in English Churches* (New York, 1883); *Twenty Sermons* (New York, 1886); *The Light of the World* (New York, 1890); *Essays and Addresses: Religious, Literary, and Social,* ed. John Cotton Brooks (New York, 1895); *The Law of Growth* (New York, 1902).
B. *ANB* 3, 623–25; *DAB* 3, 83–88; *DARB,* 80–81; *DCA,* 191–92; *EARH,* 82–83; *EDC,* 59; *NCAB* 2, 304; *SH* 2, 274; *SPCK,* 93–97; *NYT,* 24 January 1893; Jerome F. Politzer, "Theological Ideas in the Preaching of Phillips Brooks," *HMPEC* 33 (1964): 157–69; Gillis J. Harp, "The Young Phillips Brooks: A Reassessment," *Journal of Ecclesiastical History* 49 (1998): 652–67; Robert B. Slocum, "The Social Teaching of Phillips Brooks," *ATR* 84 (2002): 135–46; Alexander V. G. Allen, *Life and Let-*

ters of Phillips Brooks, 2 vols. (New York, 1900); William Lawrence, *The Life of Phillips Brooks* (New York, 1930); Raymond W. Albright, *Focus on Infinity* (New York, 1961); John F. Woolverton, *The Education of Phillips Brooks* (Urbana, Ill., 1995); David B. Chesebrough, *Phillips Brooks: Pulpit Eloquence* (Westport, Conn., 2001).

C

CASE, ADELAIDE TEAGUE (10 January 1887, St. Louis, Mo.–19 June 1948, Boston). *Education:* B.A., Bryn Mawr College, 1908; M.A., Columbia University, 1919; Ph.D., Columbia University, 1924. *Career:* Teacher, St. Faith's School, Poughkeepsie, N.Y., 1908–9; librarian, national headquarters of the Episcopal Church, New York, 1914–16; instructor, New York Training School for Deaconesses, 1917–19; instructor (later professor), Teachers College, Columbia University, 1919–41; professor of Christian education, Episcopal Theological School, 1941–48.

A religious educator and the first woman to be appointed professor at an Episcopal seminary, Adelaide Case was born in St. Louis, Missouri, but raised in New York City. After graduation from Bryn Mawr College, she taught briefly at an Episcopal boarding school in Poughkeepsie, New York. Although poor health prevented her from working regularly for several years, she was able to enroll in the doctoral program at Teachers College of Columbia University in 1917. During this period, she also taught at the New York Training School for Deaconesses. After receiving her Ph.D. from Columbia in 1924, she became a faculty member in the religious education department of Teachers College, eventually rising to the rank of full professor and department chair. In 1941 she joined the faculty of the Episcopal Theological School (ETS) in Cambridge, Massachusetts, where she served until her death.

In her teaching and writing, Case consistently upheld two principal concerns: the need for "progressive" methods of religious education and the importance of Christian social ethics. She believed that "education, when it becomes socially dangerous [to the status quo], is surely beginning to be socially useful." In her first book, *Liberal Christianity and Religious Education* (1924), she related John

Dewey's progressive educational philosophy to the religious instruction of children, stressing the advantages of encouraging intelligent reasoning rather than dogmatizing. As she wrote in an article in 1929, denominations needed to assist in the creation of "a seven-day plan for religious education which will utilize the public school, the home, the playground, and the church school, integrating the religious aspects of all these experiences and directing them toward the realization of Christian purposes."

In addition to her academic responsibilities, Case was involved with organizations such as the Religious Education Association, the Student Christian Movement, the Federal Council of Churches, the Episcopal Pacifist Fellowship, and the Church League for Industrial Democracy (later known as the Episcopal League for Social Action). Within the Episcopal Church she served on several commissions of the Woman's Auxiliary and of the National Council, and between 1946 and 1948 she also was a member of the National Council itself. A liberal Catholic, she quietly espoused the idea of women's ordination and took a regular turn on the faculty's preaching schedule at ETS. Although there were many barriers to the involvement of women in the church, she encouraged the expansion and development of vocational opportunities for them through her involvement as a board member of Windham House in New York.

The physical problems that troubled Case as a young woman eventually took their toll on her health. She died in a Boston hospital at the age of 61.

Bibliography

A. *Liberal Christianity and Religious Education: A Study of Objectives in Religious Education* (New York, 1924); *As Modern Writers See Jesus: A Descriptive Bibliography of Books about Jesus* (Boston, 1927); *Seven Psalms: Suggestions for Bible Study, Meditation, and Group Worship* (New York, 1935); *The Servant of the Lord: A Devotional Commentary on the Servant Songs in Second Isaiah* (New York, 1940).

B. *ANB* 4, 530–31; *EDC,* 72; *NAW* 1, 301–2; *Religious Leaders of America,* ed. J.C. Schwarz, vol. 2 (1941–1942) (New York, 1941), 198; *NYT,* 20 June 1948; Charles L. Taylor Jr., "Adelaide T. Case: An Appreciation," *TLC,* 8 August 1948, 11; Sydney Temple, ed., *Peace Is Possible: Essays Dedicated to the Memory of Adelaide T. Case* (Deep River, Conn., 1949).

CHANDLER, THOMAS BRADBURY (26 April 1726, Woodstock, Conn.–17 June 1790, Elizabethtown [now Elizabeth], N.J.). *Education:* B.A., Yale College, 1745; studied theology with Samuel Johnson, 1745–47. *Career:* Schoolteacher, Woodstock, Conn., 1745–47; lay reader and catechist, St. John's Church, Elizabethtown, N.J., 1747–51; rector, 1751–90.

A missionary of the Society for the Propagation of the Gospel in Foreign Parts (SPG) and a highly regarded clerical leader of the colonial church, Thomas Bradbury Chandler was raised in a Congregational family in Connecticut. While a student at Yale College, he was strongly influenced by the Anglican ethos that prevailed during the presidency of Timothy Cutler,* and following his graduation, he studied theology under the Anglican clergyman Samuel Johnson.* Although too young for ordination, he was appointed a lay reader and catechist at St. John's Church, Elizabethtown, New Jersey, in 1747. After being ordained to the priesthood in 1751, he became rector of St. John's—a parish with which he remained affiliated for the rest of his life. Chandler caused some consternation among his parishioners in 1763 when he refused to allow the evangelist George Whitefield* to speak in the church. This opposition was rooted in his social and ecclesiastical conservatism: he feared that Whitefield's preaching would disrupt parish life.

Chandler was a forceful advocate of bishops for the American church, continually emphasizing to his SPG superiors in London that an American episcopate would help bind the colonies to the mother country. Speaking for Anglican clergy in New York and New Jersey, he published the first of a series of controversial pamphlets on the subject of a colonial episcopate in 1767. He later engaged in a vigorous pamphlet debate with the Congregational clergyman Charles Chauncy, a militant opponent of bishops. From 1766 to 1775 Chandler also advocated the Tory cause, defending the laws and government of England and arguing against the foolishness of republicanism.

In May 1775 Chandler fled to New York and thence to England, where he remained for 10 years, separated from his wife and six children, who continued to live in Elizabethtown. While he was absent, St. John's Church suffered greatly as a result of the American Revolution. The congregation dispersed, the pews and floors were removed and burned, the building became a stable, and the organ pipes were ripped out and melted down for ammunition. Upon Chandler's return to America in 1785, his failing health prevented him from carrying out all but the lightest of parochial duties. Although he was the first American chosen for the new Anglican bishopric of Nova Scotia, he was not able to accept the appointment. Suffering from cancer of the face, he eventually died in Elizabethtown in 1790. Chandler's high church principles remained influential long after his death, however, as his son-in-law, John Henry Hobart,* the bishop of New York, advanced many of his ideas in the early nineteenth century.

Bibliography

A. *An Appeal to the Public in Behalf of the Church of England in America* (New York, 1767); *The Appeal Defended; or, the Proposed American Episcopate Vindicated* (New York, 1769); *The Appeal Further Defended: In Answer to the Farther Misrepresentation of Dr. Chauncy* (New York, 1771); *The Life of Samuel Johnson* (New York, 1805).
B. *AAP* 5, 137–42; *DAB* 3, 616; *DARB,* 106–7; *EDC,* 82; *HPEC,* 105–16; Samuel Clyde McCulloch, "Thomas Bradbury Chandler: Anglican Humanitarian in Colonial New Jersey," in *British Humanitarianism: Essays Honoring Frank J. Klingberg* (Philadelphia, 1950), 100–23.

CHASE, PHILANDER (14 December 1775, Cornish, N.H.–20 September 1852, Jubilee, Ill.). *Education:* B.A., Dartmouth College, 1795. *Career:* Schoolteacher and Episcopal missionary in northern and western New York, 1795–99; served congregations in Poughkeepsie and Fishkill, N.Y., 1799–1805; rector, Christ Church, New Orleans, La., 1805–11; rector, Christ Church, Hartford, Conn., 1811–17; bishop, diocese of Ohio, 1819–31; president, Kenyon College, 1824–31; farmer and occasional missionary, Gilead, Mich., 1831–35; bishop, diocese of Illinois, 1835–52; presiding bishop of the Episcopal Church, 1843–52.

A bishop, missionary, educator, and low church leader, Philander Chase was the son of a prominent New Hampshire farmer and his wife. He was educated at Dartmouth College, where, influenced by the *Book of Common Prayer* and by a tract extolling the virtues of Anglicanism, he rejected the Congregationalism of his forebears and joined the Episcopal Church. After studying for the ordained ministry under the guidance of a priest in Albany, New York, he was ordained a deacon in 1798 and a priest in 1799. After serving churches in New York, Louisiana, and Connecticut, Chase became part of the flow of New Englanders migrating to Ohio after the War of 1812. To help serve the state's rapidly growing population, he began organizing new congregations, including churches in Zanesville and Columbus.

Although Chase was consecrated as the first bishop of Ohio in 1819, the meager financial resources of the diocese forced him to earn a living by engaging in secular pursuits, including operating a sawmill, running the local post office, and farming. Wishing to have institutions for the training of local clergy who were grounded in the principles of evangelical Anglicanism, Chase was successful in raising funds from aristocrats in Great Britain. With this money, he founded Kenyon College and Bexley Hall seminary in 1824. An industrious as well as autocratic leader, Chase served as president of both the college and the seminary while also performing his episcopal duties. In 1831, following the mandate of his diocesan convention that he could not be both bishop and college president, he resigned both offices and took up farming, first in Ohio and then in Michigan.

Accepting election as the first bishop of Illinois in 1835, Chase successfully labored to plant churches in the towns and rural areas of the state. In 1839 he founded Jubilee College, which was forced to close in 1862. During his last decade in office, he encountered resistance from clergy in Chicago who were attracted by the Tractarian movement. An old-fashioned low churchman, he rejected any deviation from the prayer book, whether by evangelical or by Anglo-Catholic innovators. As the senior bishop of his denomination, Chase served as the presiding bishop from 1843 until his death in 1852.

Bibliography

A. *Reminiscences of Bishop Chase: An Autobiography,* 2 vols. (Peoria, Ill., 1841–44; Boston, 1848).
B. *AAP* 5, 453–62; *ANB* 4, 736–37; *BB,* 74–75; *DAB* 4, 26–27; *DARB,* 110–11; *DCA,* 244; *ECUS,* 102–10; *EDC,* 85; *NCAB* 7, 1–2; *SBAE,* 85–88; Laura Chase Smith, *The Life of Philander Chase* (New York, 1903).

COIT, HENRY AUGUSTUS (20 January 1830, Wilmington, Del.–5 February 1895, Concord, N.H.). *Education:* Studied at Flushing Institute, Long Island, N.Y.; studied at the University of Pennsylvania, 1847–48; studied theology under Alonzo Potter. *Career:* Tutor and schoolteacher, 1848–54; missionary priest, diocese of Albany, 1854–56; rector, St. Paul's School, Concord, N.H., 1856–95.

An Episcopal priest and the first rector of St. Paul's School in Concord, New Hampshire, Henry Coit was born in Wilmington, Delaware, in 1830. The son of an Episcopal priest, he attended William Augustus Muhlenberg's* Flushing Institute on Long Island and the University of Pennsylvania. He served as a tutor in the family of Stephen Elliott, the bishop of Georgia, and as an instructor of Greek and Latin at the College of St. James, near Hagerstown, Maryland. He also helped run a parish school for boys in Lancaster, Pennsylvania. After deciding to enter the ordained ministry, Coit studied in Philadelphia under the direction of Alonzo Potter, the bishop of Pennsylvania. After his ordination to the priesthood in 1854, he undertook missionary work in the diocese of Albany, establishing several new congregations in Clinton County, New York.

Coit's fame derives from his long and exemplary service as the head of St. Paul's, one of the nation's preeminent Episcopal boarding schools. Founded by the Boston physician George Cheyne Shattuck Jr. at his summer estate two miles west of town, the school began operating in April 1856 with three boys, including Shattuck's two sons, in attendance. Coit and Shattuck had much in common and worked well together. Both men were high church Episcopalians. Believers in the doctrine of baptismal regeneration, they sought to build an environment in which the grace conferred at baptism was realized in a character transformed gradually through participation in the liturgy and spiritual disciplines of the Episcopal Church. In an antebellum culture strongly influenced by Protestant evangelicalism, with its emphasis on emotional conversion experiences, Shattuck and Coit launched a school with a decidedly different ethos. The chapel, whose rites were planned to be aesthetically rich and appealing, was the center of school life. Boys attended chapel services daily, and most of the school's masters were Episcopal clergy.

Coit himself was autocratic, austere, even unworldly, and he attempted, with varying degrees of success, to instill his own preference for simplicity and self-sacrifice in the sons of the urban elite: Morgans, Mellons, and Vanderbilts. Owen Wister, author of *The Virginian* (1902) and a graduate of St. Paul's, observed that Coit's recumbent marble statue in the school chapel was clothed in a monastic gown. This depiction was appropriate, he said, because the rector had been born "seven hundred years later than the days of his spiritual kin." In his last years, Coit even turned for spiritual solace to the Society of St. John the Evangelist, an Anglican religious community for men. It was said by many who had known him that his image, the tall priest in a long black coat, remained as a kind of abiding presence at the school long after his death. By the time of Coit's death in 1895, the school enrolled 345 boys and employed 36 masters, and it had become the model for numerous other American boarding schools.

Bibliography

A. Papers at St. Paul's School in Concord, N.H.; "An American Boys' School—What It Should Be" (1891), reprinted in James P. Conover, *Memories of a Great Schoolmaster (Dr. Henry A. Coit)* (Boston, 1906), 189–214; *School Sermons* (New York, 1909).

B. *ANB* 5, 183–84; *DAB* 4, 276–77; *EDC,* 106; *WWWA* Historical vol. 1607–1896, 114; Joseph H. Coit, *Memorials of St. Paul's School* (New York, 1891); James Carter Knox, *Henry Augustus Coit: First Rector of St. Paul's* (New York, 1915); Frederick Joseph Kinsman, *Salve Mater* (New York, 1922); Owen Wister, "Dr. Coit of St. Paul's," *Atlantic Monthly,* December 1928, 756–68; Arthur Stanwood Pier, *St. Paul's School, 1855–1934* (New York, 1934); August Heckscher, *St. Paul's School: The Life of a New England School* (New York, 1980).

COOPER, ANNA JULIA HAYWOOD (10 August 1858?, Raleigh, N.C.–27 February 1964, Washington, D.C.). *Education:* Graduated from St. Augustine's College, 1881; B.A., Oberlin College, 1884; M.A., Oberlin College, 1887; Ph.D., University of Paris, 1925. *Career:* Teacher, Wilberforce University, 1884–85; teacher, St. Augustine's College, 1885–87; teacher in Washington, D.C., 1887–1901; principal, M Street High School, Washington, D.C., 1902–6; teacher, Lincoln University, 1906–11; teacher, M Street (later Dunbar) High School, Washington, D.C., 1911–30; president, Frelinghuysen University, 1930–42; teacher, Frelinghuysen University, 1942–50.

Anna Julia Haywood Cooper, an author and educator, was born in Raleigh, North Carolina, probably in August 1858. Her mother, Hannah Stanley, was a slave, and her father was believed to be Fabius J. Haywood, the white man who was Hannah's master. Little is known about Anna's childhood, but after she was emancipated at the end of the Civil War, she entered St. Augustine's Normal School and Collegiate Institute (later St. Augustine's College), founded by the Episcopal Church to educate African Americans in Raleigh. Because there were so few teachers and because Anna herself was so gifted, she was allowed to tutor older students at the school. In 1877 she married George Cooper, an Episcopal priest, but he died after only two years of marriage. She completed her studies at St. Augustine's in 1881 and entered Oberlin College, from which she received a bachelor's degree in mathematics in 1884 and a master's degree three years later. She then moved to Washington, D.C., where she began a lengthy career as a teacher.

Between 1902 and 1906, Cooper served as the principal at the prestigious M Street High School, the only college preparatory school for African Americans in Washington. She was dismissed from her position in 1906, however, for refusing to lower the school's academic standards by switching to a program of vocational education. She then became a teacher at Lincoln University in Jefferson City, Missouri. When a new administration assumed control at M Street in 1911, Cooper was invited to return there as a teacher rather than as a principal. She accepted this offer and remained at the school for nearly 20 years. She began studying for a doctorate at Columbia University in 1914, but after traveling extensively in Europe during summer vacations, she eventually transferred her credits to the University of Paris. She completed her dissertation at the Sorbonne in 1925. In that work, entitled "L'Attitude de la France à l'égard de l'esclavage pendant la Révolution" (later published in English as *Slavery and the French Revolutionists, [1788–1805]*), Cooper studied the impact of slavery in the French colony of Saint Domingue (now Haiti) on the development of the French Revolution.

Cooper's first and most important book, *A Voice from the South,* was published in 1892. A collection of her lectures and speeches, this book contained Cooper's thoughts both on the role of women in the African American community and on the importance of education in uplifting the black race. One of the book's essays was an address she had delivered before a gathering of black Episcopal clergy in 1886. In that speech she praised the "quiet, chaste dignity and decorous solemnity" of the Episcopal Church, which had a distinct appeal to many "thinking colored men." Despite this advantage, the Episcopal Church had failed to gain many African American adherents because its white leadership consistently insulted and mistreated the black priests who led its parishes. Cooper understood the situation faced by black clergy extremely well, for she was an active member of St. Luke's Church in Washington, D.C., where Alexander Crummell* served faithfully as rector for many years.

Cooper was active in numerous organizations throughout her long life. She was the only woman elected to the American Negro Academy, and she was a featured speaker at the historic Pan-African Congress in London in 1900. She was also prominently involved in the black women's club movement, in the Colored Young Women's Christian Association, and in the National Association for the Advancement of Colored People. Although she retired from teaching high school in 1930, she continued to serve as an educator at Frelinghuysen University, an institution organized to provide educational opportunities for working adults in Washington's black community. Surviving to the age of 105, Cooper died peacefully at home in February 1964.

Bibliography

A. Papers at the Moorland-Spingarn Research Center at Howard University; *A Voice from the South* (Xenia, Ohio, 1892); *Slavery and the French Revolutionists (1788–1805),* ed. Frances Richardson Keller (Lewiston, N.Y., 1988); *The Voice of Anna Julia Cooper: Including A Voice from the South and Other Important Essays, Papers, and Letters,* ed. Charles Lemert and Esme Bhan (Lanham, Md., 1998).
B. *ANB* 5, 432–33; *DANB,* 128–29; *FD,* 110–18; *NAW* 4, 163–65; *Washington Post,* 29 February 1964; Sharon Harley, "Anna J. Cooper: A Voice for Black Women," in *The Afro-American Woman: Struggles and Images,* ed. Sharon Harley and Rosalyn Terborg-Penn (Port Washington, N.Y., 1978); Ann Allen Shockley, *Afro-American*

Women Writers, 1746–1933 (New York, 1988): 204–8; Louise Daniel Hutchinson, *Anna J. Cooper: A Voice from the South* (Washington, D.C., 1981); Leona C. Gabel, *From Slavery to the Sorbonne and Beyond: The Life and Writings of Anna J. Cooper* (Northampton, Mass., 1982); Karen Baker-Fletcher, *A Singing Something: Womanist Reflections on Anna Julia Cooper* (New York, 1994).

CRAM, RALPH ADAMS (16 December 1863, Hampton Falls, N.H.–22 September 1942, Boston). *Education:* Graduated from high school in Exeter, N.H., 1880. *Career:* Architect in Boston, 1881–86, 1889–1942; professor of architecture, Massachusetts Institute of Technology, 1914–21.

An acclaimed church architect and Episcopal layman, Ralph Adams Cram was born in New Hampshire in 1863. Lacking sufficient funds for college, he turned to the study of architecture after completing high school in 1880. In 1881 he went to Boston, where he found employment in the office of architects Arthur Rotch and George T. Tilden. Although he quit architecture for a time and became the art critic of the *Boston Evening Transcript,* a quarrel with the editor quickly put a halt to his career in journalism. Traveling in Europe in 1888–89 as the tutor of a friend's stepson, Cram not only gained a new sense of his vocation as an architect while touring Italian cities but also was captivated by the beauty and richness of the Catholic liturgical tradition. When he returned to Boston in 1890, he formed an architectural partnership with Charles Francis Wentworth.

Although he had been raised a Unitarian, Cram found a spiritual home within the Anglo-Catholic movement in the Episcopal Church. Anglo-Catholicism and its institutions provided a significant religious and aesthetic alternative for Cram and other artistic Bostonians who were not comfortable with the "muscular Christianity" often touted by evangelicals during the Victorian era. After receiving instruction from members of the Society of St. John the Evangelist, the monastic order for men in Boston, Cram was baptized and confirmed as an Episcopalian. He maintained a very close relationship with the society for the remainder of his life.

Following this turn toward Anglo-Catholicism, Cram adopted as his guiding norm a highly idealized view of church life in pre-Reformation England, and he became the leading American authority on the English and French Gothic styles of architecture. He believed that Gothic was the architectural form best suited to reinforce and enhance a believer's experience of worship. Gothic had been "the perfect expression of Northern and Western Christianity for five centuries," Cram said; although it "had been most untimely cut off" during the reign of Henry VIII, he wished to take it up again and develop "the style England had made her own" during the Middle Ages. As a result, throughout a period of urban expansion and construction in the early twentieth century, Cram did more than anyone else to popularize the use of Gothic architecture not only in churches and cathedrals but also in many institutions of higher learning in the United States.

Cram was soon joined in this effort by the promising young architect Bertram

Grosvenor Goodhue, with whom he developed a warm friendship. The firm became Cram, Wentworth, and Goodhue in 1890, and when Frank W. Ferguson joined the firm after Wentworth's death in 1899, it became Cram, Goodhue, and Ferguson. This partnership was responsible for the rebuilding of the United States Military Academy at West Point and for the design of St. Thomas' Church on Fifth Avenue in New York. In 1907 Cram began 22 years of service as supervising architect of Princeton University. At Princeton he fully worked out his principle of designing Gothic buildings whose spiritual qualities would counter what he thought were the dominant technocratic, individualistic, and capitalistic impulses of the twentieth century. Starting in 1911, he also became the principal architect of the Cathedral of St. John the Divine in New York, which was the largest religious building in the United States.

Despite his lack of formal academic credentials, Cram taught at the Massachusetts Institute of Technology from 1914 to 1921, and he wrote many significant works in the fields of architecture and aesthetics. His social philosophy, propounded in works written during and after the horrors of World War I, emphasized the importance of a sacramental understanding of reality rather than an outlook that accommodated only power and materialism. He received considerable recognition from his contemporaries for his achievements, and he even appeared on the cover of *Time* magazine in December 1926. In addition, he was one of the founders of the influential Roman Catholic journal *Commonweal* and the Mediaeval Academy of America. He died in Boston in 1942.

Bibliography

A. *Church Building* (Boston, 1901); *The Gothic Quest* (New York, 1907); *The Ministry of Art* (Boston, 1914); *The Substance of Gothic* (Boston, 1917); *The Nemesis of Mediocrity* (Boston, 1917); *The Catholic Church and Art* (New York, 1930); *Convictions and Controversies* (Boston, 1935); *My Life in Architecture* (Boston, 1936); *The End of Democracy* (Boston, 1937).
B. *ANB* 5, 660–62; *DAB* Supp. 3, 194–97; *EDC,* 128; *NCE* 4, 412; M. Schuyler, "Works of Cram, Goodhue and Ferguson," *Architectural Record* 29 (1911): 1–44; Peter W. Williams, "The Iconography of the American City," *CH* 68 (June 1999): 373–97; Peter W. Williams, "A Mirror for Unitarians: Catholicism and Culture in Nineteenth-Century New England" (Ph.D. diss., Yale University, 1970); Robert Muccigrosso, *American Gothic: The Mind and Art of Ralph Adams Cram* (Washington, D.C., 1980); T.J. Jackson Lears, *No Place of Grace: Antimodernism and the Transformation of American Culture, 1880–1920* (New York, 1981); Douglass Shand-Tucci, *Boston Bohemia, 1881–1900,* vol. 1 of *Ralph Adams Cram: Life and Architecture* (Amherst, Mass., 1995); Douglass Shand-Tucci, *Built in Boston: City and Suburb, 1800–2000,* rev. ed. (Amherst, Mass., 1999), chap. 7.

CRUMMELL, ALEXANDER (3 March 1819, New York–10 September 1898, Red Bank, N.J.). *Education:* Studied at Oneida Institute, Whitesboro, N.Y., 1836–39; B.A., Queen's College, Cambridge University, 1853. *Career:* Missionary in

West Africa, 1853–72; founding rector, St. Luke's Church, Washington, D.C., 1879–94.

Alexander Crummell, Episcopal priest and missionary, was a noted scholar and an early leader of the Pan-African movement. Born in New York City in 1819, he began his education at the parish school of St. Philip's Church, a black congregation in Manhattan. He later attended a small boarding school founded by abolitionists in Canaan, New Hampshire, and the Oneida Institute in Whitesboro, New York. Inspired by the example of Peter Williams Jr.,* the rector of St. Philip's Church, Crummell sought ordination in the diocese of New York. Although his academic credentials at first led the General Theological Seminary administration to encourage him to apply, they backed away from accepting him because they feared the loss of a substantial contribution from the diocese of South Carolina. When the seminary finally did offer to admit him—with the stipulation that he would not reside at the school, eat in its refectory, or sit in its lecture halls—Crummell balked, and he commenced a private course of study instead. Ordained to the diaconate in 1842 and to the priesthood in 1844, he engaged in intermittent mission work in small black congregations in New Haven, Providence, Philadelphia, and New York but failed to secure a regular parish position.

In January 1848 Crummell journeyed to England, where he raised funds for black missions in the United States and lectured on behalf of the American abolitionist movement. Anglican friends sponsored his studies at Queen's College, Cambridge, which awarded him a degree in 1853. In June of that year, Crummell and his family departed for Liberia, where he served as a missionary of the Episcopal Church for nearly two decades. He believed that it was the duty of the American black elite to lift up Africans, whom he believed to be uncivilized, "from the rudeness of barbarism." Crummell was hopeful about the future of Africa, not only because of his fundamental belief in providence and progress but also because Africans possessed a "strong vital power" that would enable them to stretch forth their hands to embrace Christianity and civilization.

In 1872 Crummell returned permanently to the United States, becoming rector of St. Mary's Church in Washington, D.C. His health in Africa had not been good, and he was frustrated by both the lack of funds and the slow pace of immigration to Liberia. In 1879 he became rector of St. Luke's Church, Washington, D.C., where he served until 1894. During this period, he rose to prominence as a champion of the rights of African Americans in the Episcopal Church, particularly through his work with the Conference of Church Workers among Colored People, which he helped organize in 1883. Crummell was also one of the founders of the American Negro Academy in 1897. The academy, an exclusive body limited to 40 members, was dedicated to supporting the work of the black intelligentsia in science, economics, political affairs, education, religion, and the arts. Crummell believed that racial uplift depended upon self-discipline and the elevation of the moral life. African Americans, he thought, should unite and work together to increase racial pride. These emphases on celebrating the race and promoting self-help strongly influenced the ideas of such African American leaders as Marcus Garvey and W. E. B. Du Bois in the early twentieth century.

Crummell died in September 1898 while on vacation with his wife in Red Bank, New Jersey.

Bibliography

A. *The Future of Africa* (New York, 1862); *The Greatness of Christ and Other Sermons* (New York, 1882); *Civilization the Primal Need of the Race* (Washington, D.C., 1898); *Destiny and Race: Selected Writings, 1840–1898,* ed. Wilson Jeremiah Moses (Amherst, Mass., 1992); *Civilization and Black Progress: Selected Writings of Alexander Crummell on the South,* ed. J. R. Oldfield (Charlottesville, Va., 1995).

B. *ANB* 5, 820–22; *BB,* 82–83; *DARB,* 132–33; *DANB,* 145–47; *DCA,* 330; *EAAR,* 216–17; *EARH,* 180–81; *EDC,* 131–32; *MCTA,* 260–62; *NCAB* 5, 553; W. E. B. Du Bois, "Of Alexander Crummell," in *The Souls of Black Folk* (Chicago, 1903), 215–27; Wilson J. Moses, "Civilizing Missionary: A Study of Alexander Crummell," *Journal of Negro History* 60 (1975): 229–51; M. B. Akpan, "Alexander Crummell and His African 'Race-Work': An Assessment of His Contributions in Liberia to Africa's 'Redemption,' 1854–1873," *HMPEC* 45 (1976): 177–99; Gregory U. Rigsby, *Alexander Crummell: Pioneer in Nineteenth-Century Pan-African Thought* (New York, 1987); Wilson Jeremiah Moses, *Alexander Crummell: A Study of Civilization and Discontent* (Amherst, Mass., 1992); John R. Oldfield, *Alexander Crummell (1819–1898) and the Creation of an African-American Church in Liberia* (Lewiston, N.Y., 1990).

CUMMINS, GEORGE DAVID (11 December 1822, Smyrna, Del.–26 June 1876, Lutherville, Md.). *Education:* B.A., Dickinson College, 1841; studied for theology under Alfred Lee, 1845. *Career:* Methodist circuit rider, 1842–45; assistant rector, Christ Episcopal Church, Baltimore, 1845–47; rector, Christ Church, Norfolk, Va., 1847–53; rector, St. James's Church, Richmond, Va., 1853–54; rector, Trinity Church, Washington, D.C., 1855–58; rector, St. Peter's Church, Baltimore, 1858–63; rector, Trinity Church, Chicago, 1863–66; assistant bishop, diocese of Kentucky, 1866–73; presiding bishop of the Reformed Episcopal Church, 1873–76.

George David Cummins, a bishop and principal founder of the Reformed Episcopal Church, was born near Smyrna, Delaware, in 1822. Although his family had long been associated with the Episcopal Church, the death of his father and his mother's remarriage brought him under the influence of the Methodists. He officially joined the Methodist Church when he was a college student, and he served for three years as a rider on the Bladensburg circuit in Maryland. A growing preference for more formal worship, however, encouraged him to return to the Episcopal fold. After studying briefly under the direction of Alfred Lee, the bishop of Delaware, he was ordained a deacon in 1845. Over the next 20 years, Cummins served successfully as a priest in parishes in several different dioceses.

He was elected assistant bishop of the diocese of Kentucky in June 1866 and consecrated five months later in Louisville. Since Benjamin Bosworth Smith, the diocesan bishop, was quite elderly at that time, Cummins assumed oversight of most of the ecclesiastical affairs in the diocese.

A committed member of the evangelical party in the Episcopal Church, Cummins became increasingly alarmed at the advances made by the Anglo-Catholic wing of his denomination during the mid-nineteenth century. He was especially offended by the ritualism of the Oxford movement, for he considered Anglo-Catholic liturgical practices to represent a fundamental betrayal of Anglicanism's Protestant principles. Joining with other evangelical Episcopalians, he pressed for a revision of the 1789 *Book of Common Prayer*—a new prayer book from which all offensive phrases and ideas (e.g., the use of "regeneration" in the baptismal service and references to ministers as "priests") would be removed. In 1873 Cummins finally concluded that he could no longer remain an Episcopalian. He made this decision after being roundly denounced by Anglo-Catholics for participating in a joint communion service with other Protestant clergy at a meeting of the Evangelical Alliance in New York City. Exasperated by this response to his well-meaning ecumenical initiative, he resigned from his episcopate on November 10, 1873, and five days later issued a call to organize a new, unapologetically evangelical Episcopal denomination. Although only a small number of evangelical Episcopalians ultimately chose to follow his lead, Cummins presided over the formation of the Reformed Episcopal Church in December 1873.

Cummins served as the presiding bishop of the Reformed Episcopal Church from 1873 until his death. After settling his affairs in Kentucky, he moved to Lutherville, Maryland, a suburb of Baltimore, to be closer to the geographical center of Reformed Episcopal strength. The responsibilities of his office, however, proved to be more than his health could bear. After suffering a series of heart attacks in mid-June 1876, he died.

Bibliography

A. *A Sketch of the Life of the Rev. William M. Jackson* (Washington, D.C., 1855); *The Life of Mrs. Virginia Hale Hoffman* (Philadelphia, 1859); *Primitive Episcopacy: A Return to the "Old Paths" of Scripture and the Early Church* (New York, 1874).

B. *ANB* 5, 855–56; *DAB* 4, 599–600; *DARB*, 134–35; *DCA*, 332; *EDC*, 132–33; *MM*, 410–24; *NCAB* 7, 57–58; *SH* 3, 321; *WWWA* Historical vol. 1607–1896, 130; *NYT*, 29 June 1876; Alexandrine M. Cummins, *Memoir of George David Cummins, D.D., First Bishop of the Reformed Episcopal Church* (Philadelphia, 1878); Allen C. Guelzo, *For the Union of Evangelical Christendom: The Irony of the Reformed Episcopalians* (University Park, Pa., 1994).

CUTLER, TIMOTHY (31 May 1684, Charlestown, Mass.–17 August 1765, Boston, Mass.). *Education:* B.A., Harvard College, 1701. *Career:* Congregational minister, Stratford, Conn., 1710–19; rector (i.e., president), Yale College, 1719–22; rector, Christ Church, Boston, Mass., 1723–65.

Timothy Cutler, an Anglican clergyman and famous convert from Congregationalism, was born in Charlestown, Massachusetts, and graduated from Harvard
College in 1701. He served as a Congregational minister at Stratford, Connecticut,
from 1710 until 1719, when he was chosen to lead Yale College. As the head of
Yale, he read books by a wide range of thinkers, including several seventeenth-
century Anglican divines, about the theological foundations of both presbyterian
ordination and congregational polity. After studying these texts, Cutler became
convinced that his ministerial orders were invalid and that it was necessary to
seek ordination by a bishop in apostolic succession.

On September 13, 1722, Cutler and several other Congregational ministers who
were on the Yale faculty met with the trustees of the college and informed them
of their doubts regarding the validity of their orders. This announcement became
known in Congregationalism as "the Yale apostasy" or the "Dark Day" of 1722.
After being relieved from his duties by the Yale trustees, Cutler and two colleagues, Samuel Johnson* and Daniel Brown, journeyed to Great Britain to seek
episcopal ordination. Ordained in London in March 1723, Cutler returned to
America as a missionary of the Society for the Propagation of the Gospel in
Foreign Parts (SPG). Yale acted to prevent future defections by requiring all
prospective rectors and tutors to subscribe to the Saybrook Platform, which denounced "Arminian and prelatical corruptions."

For more than 40 years Cutler served as rector of Christ Church (the Old North
Church) in Boston. Throughout this period he clung to his high views of episcopal
polity, and he petitioned the bishop of London for a resident bishop in the American colonies. In politics he was a Tory and a strong supporter of royal authority.
He was also intolerant of religious dissent and harshly critical of revivalism. Thus,
he had little sympathy for the Great Awakening, and when George Whitefield
came to Boston in 1740, Cutler complained to SPG officials about the "Infidel
and Libertine Principles" aroused by the great revivalist's preaching.

Having established himself as one of the leading Anglican clergymen of New
England, Cutler remained in Boston until his death in 1765.

Bibliography

A. Papers at the archives of the Society for the Propagation of the Gospel in Foreign Parts
    in London.
B. *AAP* 5, 50–52; *ANB* 5, 935–37; *DAB* 5, 14–15; *DARB,* 136–37; *DCA,* 334; *EDC,* 133–
    34; *NCAB* 1, 165; *SPCK,* 109; Robert E. Daggy, "Education, Church, and State:
    Timothy Cutler and the Yale Apostasy of 1722," *Journal of Church and State* 13
    (1971): 23–42; Douglas C. Stenerson, "An Anglican Critique of the Early Phase
    of the Great Awakening in New England: A Letter by Timothy Cutler," *WMQ,* 3rd
    ser., 30 (1973): 475–88; Donald L. Huber, "Timothy Cutler: The Convert as Con-
    troversialist," *HMPEC* 44 (1975): 489–96.

D

DANIELS, JONATHAN MYRICK (20 March 1939, Keene, N.H.–20 August 1965, Hayneville, Ala.). *Education:* B.S., Virginia Military Institute, 1961; graduate student, Harvard University, 1961–62; seminarian, Episcopal Theological School, 1963–65. *Career:* Office assistant and hospital orderly, Keene, N.H., 1962–63; civil rights worker in Alabama, 1965.

Jonathan Daniels, a seminarian killed while working in the civil rights movement in Alabama, was born in Keene, New Hampshire, in March 1939. After graduating from high school, he attended the Virginia Military Institute in Lexington, Virginia. Although he entered graduate study in English literature at Harvard University in the fall of 1961, he realized that he was not interested in an academic career and chose to leave Harvard after completing just one year. During that period in Cambridge, however, he attended the Church of the Advent, an Anglo-Catholic parish in Boston. Drawn to that parish's music and liturgy, he underwent a profound conversion experience and began to consider the idea of entering the ordained ministry. He spent the next few months working at home in Keene but returned to Cambridge in the fall of 1963 as a seminarian at the Episcopal Theological School (ETS).

In March 1965 the great civil rights leader Martin Luther King Jr. issued a call to Christians throughout the United States to come to Selma, Alabama, and assist the campaign for the voting rights of African Americans. King's appeal persuaded Daniels and several other ETS students to join the civil rights movement in Alabama. After they arrived in Selma, the ETS students participated with several thousand other volunteers in the march from Selma to Montgomery, the state capital. After the march, Daniels and his fellow seminarian Judith Upham decided to remain in Alabama and participate in efforts to desegregate worship at St. Paul's Church, the all-white Episcopal parish in Selma. After negotiating with T. Frank

Mathews, the rector of St. Paul's, and Charles C.J. Carpenter, the Episcopal bishop of Alabama, they were eventually able to attend communion at the church with a small group of African Americans.

Although Daniels went back to Cambridge in May 1965 to complete his academic course work, he decided to return to Alabama as a civil rights worker during the summer. A representative of the Episcopal Society for Cultural and Racial Unity (ESCRU), he was involved in a drive to register black voters in rural Lowndes county, southeast of Selma. Although he understood the risks involved in this activity, his religious faith inspired him to overlook the dangers. As he observed in a letter to a friend, "I am beginning to feel that ultimately the revolution to which I am committed is the way of the Cross." Daniels and other civil rights workers were arrested on August 14, 1965, while participating in a protest demonstration. Imprisoned in Hayneville, Alabama, they were released six days later. Walking with a white Roman Catholic priest and two female African American teenagers toward a small store in the town, Daniels and his three companions were accosted by a white man holding a shotgun. The man cursed at them and then pulled the trigger on his gun. Pulling down Ruby Sales, the young woman who stood between him and the gunman, Daniels received the shotgun blast in his chest and died instantly. His body was returned to Keene, New Hampshire, where he was buried on August 24.

Twenty-six years later, in July 1991, John B. Morris, the former executive director of ESCRU, led a successful movement to have Daniels's name added to the calendar of the Episcopal Church as a martyr in the cause of racial justice.

Bibliography

A. Papers at the Episcopal Divinity School in Cambridge, Mass.; letters and papers in *American Martyr: The Jon Daniels Story,* William J. Schneider, [ed.] (1967; reprint, Harrisburg, Pa., 1992).
B. *EDC,* 136–37; Charles W. Eagles, *Outside Agitator: Jon Daniels and the Civil Rights Movement in Alabama* (Chapel Hill, N.C., 1993).

DEKOVEN, JAMES (19 September 1831, Middletown, Conn.–19 March 1879, Racine, Wis.). *Education:* Graduated from Columbia College, 1851; graduated from General Theological Seminary, 1854. *Career:* Tutor, Nashotah House, 1854–59; rector, Church of St. John Chrysostom, Delafield, Wis., 1855–59; founder and headmaster, St. John's Hall, Delafield, Wis., 1858–59; warden (i.e., president), Racine College, 1859–79.

James DeKoven, a nineteenth-century Anglo-Catholic leader, was born in Middletown, Connecticut, in 1831. After graduating from Columbia College and General Theological Seminary, he began his career in the home missions field in Wisconsin. He was ordained to the priesthood by Jackson Kemper,* who was then missionary bishop of the Northwest. DeKoven's early years included service as a tutor at Nashotah House seminary, as the rector of a church in nearby De-lafield, and as the headmaster of St. John's Hall, a preparatory school in Delafield. In 1859 he was made warden of Racine College, which grew steadily in size and reputation under his leadership. Always intent on fostering an academic environ-ment that nurtured faith, DeKoven instituted a rich eucharistic ceremonial at the college.

DeKoven represented his diocese at each General Convention that met between 1868 and 1877. During these years, when dissension over ritual was most severe, he was recognized as the most able and widely admired spokesperson of the Anglo-Catholic party. At the 1871 General Convention, for example, he con-vinced the deputies to exercise restraint in responding to legislation that would have curtailed the use of eucharistic rituals favored by Anglo-Catholics. He denied that candles on the holy table, the use of incense, or genuflections in worship reflected belief in the Roman Catholic doctrine of transubstantiation. What those observances did affirm, he insisted, was a recognition of the real, spiritual pres-ence of Christ in the elements of bread and wine. DeKoven made an even more impassioned and effective speech at the General Convention of 1874. In a care-fully prepared address, he not only explained the ritualists' viewpoint but also offered a plea on behalf of doctrinal comprehensiveness, arguing that both evan-gelicals and Anglo-Catholics had an important role to play within the Anglican tradition.

Although DeKoven's attitudes on ritual and Anglican comprehensiveness later were widely accepted in the church, they kept him from being elected a bishop. During the 1870s, he was nominated for bishop in three separate dioceses—Wisconsin, Massachusetts, and Fond du Lac (in Wisconsin)—but failed to win sufficient votes in each election. In September 1875 he actually was elected bishop of Illinois, but when a majority of diocesan standing committees refused to con-firm his election, he withdrew his name from consideration. The strain caused by this party conflict coupled with the ongoing burden of teaching and administrative worries soon took their toll on DeKoven's health. He died suddenly when he was just 48 years old, and his body was laid to rest in eucharistic vestments with a crucifix placed over his heart.

Bibliography

A. E. Clowes Chorley, ed., "The Journal of the Reverend Doctor DeKoven," *HMPEC* 2 (1933): 205–10; *The Canon on Ritual, and the Holy Eucharist: A Speech Delivered in the General Convention, October 26th, 1874* (New York, 1874); *Sermons Preached on Various Occasions* (New York, 1880).
B. *ANB* 6, 358–59; *DAB* 5, 205–206; *DCA,* 347–48; *EDC,* 143; *MM,* 322–34; *NCAB* 11, 199; *SPCK,* 109–10; *WWWA* Historical vol. 1607–1896, 143; *NYT,* 20 March 1879; Thomas F. Gailor, "The Rev. James DeKoven," *American Church Monthly* 29 (1931): 426–29; Frederick Cook Morehouse, *Some American Churchmen* (Mil-waukee, 1892); William Cox Pope, *Life of the Reverend James DeKoven, D.D.,*

Sometime Warden of Racine College (New York, 1899); *James DeKoven: Anglican Saint,* ed. Thomas C. Reeves (Racine, Wis., 1978).

DELANY, HENRY BEARD (5 February 1858, St. Mary's, Ga.–14 April 1928, Raleigh, N.C.). *Education:* Graduated from St. Augustine's College, Raleigh, N.C., 1885. *Career:* Teacher, later vice-principal, St. Augustine's College, 1885–1918; assistant minister, St. Augustine's Chapel, Raleigh, and priest-in-charge, All Saints' Mission, Warrenton, N.C., 1889–1904; archdeacon for Work among Colored People, diocese of North Carolina, 1908–18; suffragan bishop for Colored Work, diocese of North Carolina, 1918–28.

Henry Beard Delany, the second African American to serve as an Episcopal bishop in the United States, was born in slavery in Georgia, near the Florida border, in 1858. After their emancipation in 1865, his family moved to Fernandina Beach, Florida, where Delany spent the rest of his childhood. Following his graduation from St. Augustine's College in Raleigh, North Carolina, in 1885, he served as a teacher and later as the vice-principal of the school. After deciding to enter the ordained ministry, he was ordained to the diaconate in 1889 and to the priesthood three years later. In 1908 he became the archdeacon for "colored work" in the diocese of North Carolina. He was serving in this position when white Episcopalians in North Carolina chose him for the new position of suffragan bishop, to whom the supervision of all African American clergy and parishes in their diocese was assigned. He was consecrated on November 21, 1918, only two months after the consecration of Edward T. Demby,* the first black Episcopal bishop in the United States. In accordance with an agreement signed by the bishops of North Carolina, East Carolina (i.e., coastal North Carolina), Asheville (later Western North Carolina), and South Carolina, Delany exercised authority over four dioceses—a large geographical area covering two states and containing over 60 African American parishes.

   Delany's episcopal duties eventually took a toll on his physical strength and forced him to give up an active schedule of parish visitation. Having worked effectively, if not always comfortably, within the racially segregated system of the South, he died in 1928 at St. Augustine's, where he had continued to live after his consecration. He had 10 children; one of his sons, Hubert, became a prominent judge in New York, and two of his daughters, Sadie and Bessie, published their memoirs, *Having Our Say* (1993), when they were more than one hundred years old.

Bibliography

B. *EAAR,* 231; *EDC,* 143; George F. Bragg, *History of the Afro-American Group in the Episcopal Church* (Baltimore, 1922); Lawrence Foushee London, "The Diocese in the First Decades of the Twentieth Century, 1901–1922," in *The Episcopal Church in North Carolina, 1701–1959,* ed. Lawrence Foushee London and Sarah McCulloh Lemmon (Raleigh, N.C., 1987), 309–28; Sarah L. and A. Elizabeth Delany, *Having Our Say: The Delany Sisters' First 100 Years* (New York, 1993).

DEMBY, EDWARD THOMAS (13 February 1869, Wilmington, Del.–14 October 1957, Cleveland, Ohio). *Education:* Attended but did not graduate from Lincoln University, Centenary Biblical Institute, and Howard University; B.D., Payne Theological Seminary, Wilberforce University, 1893; S.T.D., National University (now the University of Chicago), 1894; graduate, St. Matthew's Hall, Denver, Colo., 1896. *Career:* Dean, Paul Quinn College, Waco, Tex., 1894–96; in charge of three small African American institutions in the diocese of Tennessee, 1896–1900; rector, St. Paul's Church, Kansas City, Mo., 1900–1903; vicar, St. Michael's Church, Cairo, Ill., 1903–4; rector, St. Peter's Church, Key West, Fla., 1904–7; rector, Emmanuel Church, Memphis, Tenn., 1907–15; archdeacon, Colored Convocation of the diocese of Tennessee, 1912–17; suffragan bishop for Work among Colored People, diocese of Arkansas, 1918–39.

Edward T. Demby, the first African American to serve as a bishop in the United States, was born in Wilmington, Delaware, in February 1869. After briefly attending colleges in Pennsylvania, Maryland, and Washington, D.C., he graduated from Payne Theological Seminary of Wilberforce University in 1893. Raised in the African Methodist Episcopal (AME) Church, he entered the ordained ministry of that denomination after his graduation from Payne Seminary. While serving as the dean of Paul Quinn College, an AME institution in Waco, Texas, he was attracted to the Anglo-Catholic movement within the Episcopal Church, and he chose to be confirmed as an Episcopalian in 1895. Trained at the diocesan seminary in Denver, Colorado, he was ordained to the Episcopal diaconate by Thomas F. Gailor,* the bishop of Tennessee, in 1898; Gailor also ordained him a priest one year later. Demby served pastorally in a series of African American parishes in Tennessee, Missouri, and Florida. One of those parishes, St. Peter's Church in Key West, Florida, which contained over eleven hundred baptized members in 1906, was the second largest black parish in the Episcopal Church at that time.

In 1912 Demby became the archdeacon for "colored work" in the diocese of Tennessee. In the early twentieth century, the Episcopal Church in Tennessee, like many other white-controlled organizations in the South, was in the process of segregating its membership by barring the clergy and lay representatives of black parishes from participation in the annual diocesan convention. As part of this effort, the diocese of Tennessee created a Colored Convocation in 1910, assigning to it the six hundred black Episcopalians in the state. As archdeacon, Demby served as the liaison between Bishop Gailor and the church's African American members. His duties included the distribution of funds to mission churches and the recruitment and placement of African American clergy.

Demby served as archdeacon in Tennessee for five years. After the diocese of Arkansas created the new position of suffragan bishop for colored work in that state, Demby was chosen for the post. He was consecrated bishop on September 29, 1918. Although many leading black Episcopalians opposed the "colored suffragan" plan and were displeased by Demby's decision to accept that position, he became the first African American ordained to the episcopate for service within the United States. (Two months later, the African American priest Henry B. De-lany* was consecrated for a similar ministry in the diocese of North Carolina.) Demby exercised authority not only in the five African American congregations in Arkansas but also in 15 other parishes spread throughout the eight dioceses (covering five states—Arkansas, Kansas, Missouri, Oklahoma, and Texas) that composed the province of the Southwest. Although Demby acquitted himself very well, his position was a highly ambiguous one given the racism that existed in the segregated Episcopal Church. After Henry Delany's death in 1928, he was the only black bishop in the denomination, and he was treated with little respect by many of his fellow bishops. One of his most rewarding experiences, however, was his service on the church's Joint Commission on Negro Work, which spear-headed the campaign to select a black priest as the national church officer in charge of evangelism among African Americans in the United States.

Demby retired in 1939 at the age of 70 and moved to Cleveland, Ohio, where he resided for the rest of his life. Surviving well into his eighties, he lived long enough to see the beginning of the overthrow of racial segregation both in the churches and in society as a whole. He died in Cleveland in October 1957.

Bibliography

A. Papers at AEC, at the General Theological Seminary in New York, and at the Schomberg
    Center for Research in Black Culture in New York; *A Bird's Eye View of Exegetical
    Studies: The Writings of St. Paul and St. James* (Waco, Tex., 1895); *The Mission
    of the Episcopal Church among the Negroes of the Diocese of Arkansas* (n.p.,
    1921).
B. *EAAR,* 232–33; *EDC,* 144; George F. Bragg, *History of the Afro-American Group in
    the Episcopal Church* (Baltimore, 1922); Harold T. Lewis, "Archon Edward T.
    Demby, Pioneer of Social Justice," *Boulé Journal,* fall 1992, 8–9; and Michael J.
    Beary, *Black Bishop: Edward T. Demby and the Struggle for Racial Equality in
    the Episcopal Church* (Urbana, Ill., 2001).

DUBOSE, WILLIAM PORCHER (11 April 1836, Winnsboro, S.C.–18 August 1918, Sewanee, Tenn.). *Education:* Graduated from the Military College of South Carolina (The Citadel), 1855; M.A., University of Virginia, 1859; studied at di-ocesan seminary, Camden, S.C., 1859–61. *Career:* Officer and chaplain, Confed-erate army, 1861–65; rector, St. John's Church, Fairfield, S.C., 1865–67; rector, Trinity Church, Abbeville, S.C., 1868–71; chaplain (1871–83), theology profes-sor (1871–1908), dean of the School of Theology (1894–1901), dean and pro-fessor emeritus (1908–18), University of the South, 1871–1918.

William Porcher DuBose, a priest and arguably the most creative theologian in the history of the Episcopal Church, was a descendent of Huguenots and the product of the slaveholding South. He studied at the Citadel, the University of Virginia, and the theological seminary of the diocese of South Carolina in the decade before the Civil War. During the Civil War, he served as an officer in the

Confederate army. Wounded in battle in August 1862, he was captured and held for two months as a prisoner of war. After his release, he was ordained a deacon in 1863 and began his ministry as a chaplain in Kershaw's Brigade. He spent the rest of the war ministering to (what he later called) "the most brilliant congregation of major-generals down to privates that I have ever had to address." He was ordained to the priesthood in September 1866 at St. John's Church in Fairfield, South Carolina, where he served briefly as rector.

In July 1871 DuBose began his lengthy tenure as an academic and spiritual leader at the University of the South in Sewanee, Tennessee. He was the faculty member most instrumental in the founding of the theological school at Sewanee. His first book was published when he was 56 years old, and it was followed over the next 19 years by five other major theological studies. His most important contribution to scholarship was *The Soteriology of the New Testament* (1892), in which he argued that Jesus Christ was the representative of all human beings. DuBose believed that while Christ is the particular incarnation of God, all human beings participate in and reflect the divine reality: incarnation, therefore, is generically present in humanity. Divinity, moreover, is manifested in and through humanity, for "the incarnation of God in man is still going on in the world." As he wrote in *The Gospel according to St. Paul* (1907), "God was in Christ" manifesting himself as a human being so that men and women might realize their humanity in Christ.

Although DuBose was influenced at an early age by southern evangelicalism, he was essentially a liberal Catholic. While his theology retained its evangelical roots in the New Testament, he also exhibited a high, catholic view of the church and the sacraments. He developed no systematic theology but attempted to address the challenge that the scientific and historical studies of the late nineteenth century posed to traditional belief. Strongly influenced by evolutionary theory, he sought to accommodate those ideas to traditional Christian orthodoxy. Thus, he repeatedly linked the idea of evolution to the claim that "the Word became flesh and dwelt among us." He wrote that "the natural is God's way. The natural is the rational and divine. There is no real break between the natural and the supernatural." By this reasoning he concluded that the theory of evolution did not contravene "the great primal truth of God creating."

DuBose served at the University of the South for 47 years. When he was 75 years old, he gave a series of autobiographical talks, published as *Turning Points in My Life* (1912), at a reunion of his friends and former students in 1911. In those talks, he described the process of his spiritual development over several decades. The Sewanee trustees later wrote that he held "firmly to the old truths," bringing out from them "new faith to meet new doubts—new truths to meet new needs." In this effort, DuBose bore a close resemblance to other late nineteenth-century liberal (or, in the Episcopal context, "broad church") theologians. He died at Sewanee in August 1918.

Bibliography

A. *The Soteriology of the New Testament* (New York, 1892); *The Ecumenical Councils* (New York, 1897); *The Gospel in the Gospels* (New York, 1906); *The Gospel according to St. Paul* (New York, 1907); *High Priesthood and Sacrifice: An Exposition of the Epistle to the Hebrews* (New York, 1908); *The Reason of Life* (New York, 1911); *Turning Points in My Life* (New York, 1912); *Unity in the Faith,* ed. W. Norman Pittenger (Greenwich, Conn., 1957); *A DuBose Reader: Selections from the Writings of William Porcher DuBose,* ed. Donald S. Armentrout (Sewanee, Tenn., 1984); *William Porcher DuBose: Selected Writings,* ed. Jon Alexander (New York, 1988).

B. *ANB* 6, 952–53; *DAB* 5, 472–73; *DARB,* 152–53; *DCA,* 367; *EDC,* 155; *MCTA,* 315–18; *NCAB* 18, 43; *SH* 4, 16; *SPCK,* 115–18; *NYT,* 22 August 1918; John Macquarrie, "William Porcher DuBose and Modern Thought," *St. Luke's Journal of Theology* 31 (1987): 15–24; Donald S. Armentrout, "William Porcher DuBose and the Quest for the Informed Priest," *St. Luke's Journal of Theology* 31 (1988): 255–74; Dan Edwards, "Deification and the Anglican Doctrine of Human Nature: A Reassessment of the Historical Significance of William Porcher DuBose," *AEH* 58 (1989): 196–212; J.O.F. Murray, *DuBose as a Prophet of Unity* (London, 1924); Theodore DuBose Bratton, *An Apostle of Reality: The Life and Thought of the Reverend William Porcher DuBose* (New York, 1936); Ralph E. Luker, *A Southern Tradition in Theology and Social Criticism, 1830–1930: The Religious Liberalism and Social Conservatism of James Warley Miles, William Porcher DuBose, and Edgar Gardner Murphy* (New York, 1984); Robert Boak Slocum, *The Theology of William Porcher DuBose: Life, Movement, and Being* (Columbia, S.C., 2000).

E

ELY, RICHARD THEODORE (13 April 1854, Ripley, N.Y.–4 October 1943, Old Lyme, Conn.). *Education:* Studied at Dartmouth College, 1872–73; B.A., Columbia University, 1876; Ph.D., Heidelberg University, 1879. *Career:* Lecturer and associate professor of political economy, Johns Hopkins University, 1881–92; director, School of Economy, Political Science, and History, University of Wisconsin, 1892–1925; director, Institute for Research in Land Economy and Public Utilities, Northwestern University, 1925–32; president, Institute for Economic Research and School of Land Economy, Columbia University, 1937–43.

A leading economist and proponent of the social gospel, Richard T. Ely was born in Ripley, New York, in 1854. Although his parents were Presbyterians, he later rejected their denomination in favor of the theologically more broad-minded Episcopal Church. Shaped by his years of study at the Universities of Halle and Heidelberg, he was a scholar whose ideas about economic change were rooted in the German school of historical economics, which emphasized the sociocultural and governmental influences on economic systems. Rejecting a natural-law school of thought in favor of a dynamic understanding of economic forces, he opposed laissez-faire competition and unrestrained individualism. As a consequence of these views, he favored state support for higher wages, shorter working hours, immigration restrictions, the education of children (rather than child labor), and the elimination of slums.

Ely developed positions that were influenced by his Christian faith, specifically the social gospel's emphasis on human brotherhood. A founder of the American Economic Association, Ely also joined fellow social gospel advocate William D. P. Bliss* in organizing the Christian Social Union. Christians, Ely believed, have a duty to work to improve relations among the various classes of society, to overcome labor strife, and to be faithful stewards of the earth. A pioneering scholar and promoter of social reform, Ely influenced not only his students and other economists but also large numbers of Christian clergy and laypeople who read his books, especially *Social Aspects of Christianity* (1889) and the autobiographical *Ground under Our Feet* (1938). He founded and served as the first president (1906–8) of the American Association for Labor Legislation, whose work helped to bring about a pathbreaking piece of New Deal legislation, the Social Security Act of 1937.

Director of a research institute at Columbia University when he was in his eighties, Ely died in Old Lyme, Connecticut, in October 1943.

Bibliography

A. *The Past and Present of Political Economy* (Baltimore, 1884); *The Labor Movement in America* (New York, 1886); *The Social Aspects of Christianity and Other Essays* (New York, 1889); *Outlines of Economics* (New York, 1893); *The Social Law of Service* (New York, 1896); *Ground under Our Feet: An Autobiography* (New York, 1938).

B. *ANB* 7, 475–76; *DAB* supp. 3, 248–51; *DARB*, 167–68; *DCA*, 387–88; *EDC*, 166; *NCAB* 9, 200; *NYT*, 5 October 1943; John Rutherford Everett, *Religion in Economics: A Study of John Bates Clark, Richard T. Ely [and] Simon N. Patten* (Morningside Heights, N.Y., 1946); Benjamin G. Radar, *The Academic Mind and Reform: The Influences of Richard T. Ely in American Life* (Lexington, Ky., 1966); Mary O. Furner, *Advocacy and Objectivity: A Crisis in the Professionalization of American Social Science, 1865–1905* (Lexington, Ky., 1975); Dorothy Ross, *The Origins of American Social Science* (Cambridge, 1991).

EMERY, JULIA CHESTER (24 September 1852, Dorchester, Mass.–9 January 1922, Scarsdale, N.Y.). *Education:* Studied at Dorchester High School. *Career:* General Secretary, Woman's Auxiliary to the Board of Missions, 1876–1916.

Julia Chester Emery, an early leader of women's ministry in the Episcopal Church, was born and raised in Dorchester, Massachusetts (now part of Boston). She was the daughter of Charles Emery, a New England sea captain, and his devout and well-educated wife, Susan Hilton Emery. Her older sister Mary Abbot Emery served as general secretary of the Woman's Auxiliary to the Board of Missions of the Episcopal Church between 1872 and 1876. Julia moved to New York City in 1874 to edit *The Young Christian Soldier,* the denomination's missionary magazine for children. After Mary resigned from her position when she married A. T. Twing in 1876, Julia was hired by the Board of Missions to replace her as head of the Woman's Auxiliary—a post in which she ably served for the next 40 years.

The Woman's Auxiliary, which supported missions and missionaries through educational programs and the provision of money and supplies, grew to healthy maturity under Julia Emery's leadership. Throughout her tenure as general secretary, she was aided by the efforts of various family members. Her younger sister

Margaret Theresa edited *The Young Christian Soldier* and managed the program that sent "mission boxes" to missionaries in the field. Another sister, Helen Winthrop, assisted with the entertaining of missionaries who visited the Emery home on East 24th Street in New York. Mary Abbot Twing accompanied her husband in promoting domestic missions, and, after he died in 1882, she was appointed "honorary secretary" of the Woman's Auxiliary. In this unpaid position, she aided the cause by directing women's attention to vocational opportunities in the church and by helping those who were already employed. Two brothers who were clergymen also lent assistance to the auxiliary in their own parishes and dioceses.

Julia Emery was thoroughly committed to the cause of worldwide evangelism, and by the time she retired, she had not only visited every diocese and missionary district in the United States but also traveled to the church's overseas mission stations in Europe and Asia. On a trip to England in 1908, she attended the first Pan-Anglican Congress as a representative of the diocese of New York and the fifth meeting of the Lambeth conference. During these journeys, she gave speeches and sought to inspire the women in local auxiliaries, who bore most of the responsibility for mission education and for the recruitment of female workers. As she remarked in 1921, "There can hardly be more privileged opportunities presented to the women of the Church in the future than those which officers of the Auxiliary of the past have already enjoyed."

Shortly before her death, Emery published *A Century of Endeavor* (1921), which was a centennial history of the Domestic and Foreign Missionary Society of the Episcopal Church. Although her own rhetoric was largely self-effacing, her work resulted in the significant widening of opportunities for women in various areas of ministry in the church. She died in Scarsdale, New York, in 1922.

Bibliography

A. "Fifty-fifth Annual Report of the Woman's Auxiliary to the Board of Missions, 1915–1916," in *DW*, 429–33; *A Century of Endeavor, 1821–1921* (New York, 1921).
B. *ANB* 7, 498–99; *DC*, chapter 6; *EDC*, 167; *FD*, 96–102; *NYT*, 11 January 1922; Grace Lindley, "Miss Emery in Office," *Spirit of Missions* 87 (1922): 83–84; Abby R. Loring, "Our Dear Miss Emery," *Spirit of Missions* 87 (1922): 82–83; Margaret A. Tomes, *Julia Chester Emery: Being the Story of Her Life and Work* (New York, 1924); Pamela W. Darling, *New Wine: The Story of Women Transforming Leadership in the Episcopal Church* (Cambridge, Mass., 1994), chapter 2.

G

GAILOR, THOMAS FRANK (17 September 1856, Jackson, Miss.–3 October 1935, Sewanee, Tenn.). *Education:* B.A., Racine College, 1876; S.T.B., General Theological Seminary, 1879. *Career:* Rector, Church of the Messiah, Pulaski, Tenn., 1879–82; professor of ecclesiastical history, School of Theology of the University of the South, 1882–90; chaplain, University of the South, 1883–93; vice-chancellor, University of the South, 1890–93; chancellor, 1908–35; bishop coadjutor, diocese of Tennessee, 1893–98; bishop, diocese of Tennessee, 1898–1935; chairman, House of Bishops, 1916–22; president, National Council of the Episcopal Church, 1919–25.

A bishop and influential educator in the post–Civil War South, Thomas Gailor was born in Jackson, Mississippi, in 1856, but he was raised in Memphis, Tennessee. As a boy he witnessed the devastation caused by the war, and his father, who was an officer in a Tennessee regiment, was killed in battle in 1862. A high church Episcopalian, Gailor was educated at Racine College in Wisconsin and at General Theological Seminary in New York. Ordained a deacon in 1879 and a priest in 1880, he began his ministry at a parish in Pulaski, Tennessee—the town in which the Ku Klux Klan was first organized. In 1882 Gailor began his long association with the University of the South in Sewanee, Tennessee. Serving at "Sewanee" for 53 years, he was the only person in the history of the school to have been professor, chaplain, vice-chancellor (president), and chancellor (chairman of the board). His influence with such northern capitalists as J.P. Morgan* and Andrew Carnegie also enabled him to secure important financial contributions for the school, and under his distinguished leadership the university became a center for the education of white Episcopal clergy in the southern states.

Possessing a fine voice, an imposing physique, a good sense of humor, and a warm manner, Gailor was a popular church leader who was in great demand as a preacher both in the United States and in Great Britain. In Chattanooga, four thousand people turned out to hear him discuss Near East relief; in New York City, five thousand heard him speak at a chamber of commerce convention. Indeed, he was recognized as one of the greatest Episcopal preachers of his day. Following the restructuring of the Episcopal Church in 1919, Gailor also became the first president of the National Council, which functioned as the executive committee of the General Convention and oversaw such important areas of the church's work as education, social service, missions, and finance.

Gailor did not shy away from controversial issues. A resident of temperance-minded Tennessee, he was nonetheless a vigorous critic of Prohibition. Widely traveled, he visited not only Great Britain but also the Middle East, China, and Japan, and he consistently opposed communism, fascism, isolationism, and anti-Semitism. His support of the League of Nations and the New Deal was appreciated by Presidents Woodrow Wilson and Franklin Roosevelt, and in 1922 he convened and presided over the first national meeting of Episcopal social workers. Although primarily a progressive, Gailor also believed in many of the traditional virtues of the white South. The commandant of the Nathan Bedford Forrest Camp of the United Sons of Confederate Veterans, he actively promoted the cult of the Lost Cause. To him the "ringing cheers of the gray battalions" and their "splendid heroic sacrifice" in defense of slavery always remained "fresh in memory."

He died at Sewanee in 1935.

Bibliography

A. "A Church University, August 1, 1897," in *DW,* 366–68; Thomas Frank Gailor, "James Hervey Otey, First Bishop of Tennessee," *HMPEC* 4 (1935): 53–56; *A Manual of Devotion* (New York, 1889); *The Christian Church and Education* (New York, 1910); *Some Memories* (Kingsport, Tenn., 1937).
B. *ANB* 8, 615–16; *DAB* 21, 329; *DCA,* 471; *EDC,* 211; *ERS,* 281; *SH* 4, 418; Charles Reagan Wilson, "Bishop Thomas Frank Gailor: Celebrant of Southern Tradition," *Tennessee Historical Quarterly* 38 (1979): 322–31; Don S. Armentrout, *The Quest for the Informed Priest: A History of the School of Theology* (Sewanee, Tenn., 1979); Moultrie Guerry, Arthur Chitty, and Elizabeth Chitty, *Men Who Made Sewanee,* 3rd ed. (Sewanee, Tenn., 1981).

GALLAUDET, THOMAS (3 June 1822, Hartford, Conn.–27 Aug. 1902, New York). *Education:* B.A., Washington College (later Trinity College), Hartford, Conn., 1842. *Career:* Teacher in the public schools of Glastonbury and Meriden, Conn., 1842–43; teacher, New York Institution of the Deaf and Dumb (later New York Institute for the Deaf), 1843–58; assistant rector, St. Stephen's Church, New York, 1850–51; priest-in-charge, St. Paul's Chapel, Morrisania, N.Y., 1851–52; organized St. Ann's Church for Deaf-Mutes, New York, 1852; rector, St. Ann's Church, 1852–92; founded Gallaudet Home for the Aged and Infirm Deaf, Poughkeepsie, N.Y., 1885.

A pathbreaking minister to the hearing-impaired, Thomas Gallaudet was the oldest child of Sophia Fowler Gallaudet and Thomas Hopkins Gallaudet, a Congregational clergyman who founded the first free school for the deaf in the United States. Young Thomas learned to communicate with the hearing-impaired through interaction both with his mother, who was deaf, and with playmates who attended his father's school. As a student at Washington College, an Episcopal institution in Hartford, Connecticut, he became interested in entering the ordained ministry. Having doubts about the validity of Congregational orders, however, he chose not to follow in his father's footsteps but sought ordination as an Episcopalian instead. He was eventually ordained to the diaconate in 1850 and to the priesthood in 1851.

Gallaudet's work as a missionary to the deaf began in the early 1850s when he ministered to a hearing-impaired student, Cornelia Lathrop, who was slowly dying of tuberculosis. This experience prompted him to consider how much more churches could do in that pastoral area. Because of its fixed liturgy, Gallaudet believed that his denomination was particularly well suited for ministry with the hearing-impaired community. Thus, in 1852 he established the first Episcopal mission devoted to the hearing-impaired: St. Ann's Church for Deaf-Mutes in New York City—a parish with which he was associated for the rest of his life. Over the next 40 years he also served as a traveling missionary, establishing congregations for the deaf in Baltimore, Philadelphia, Boston, Washington, D.C., and Albany, N.Y. In 1885 he founded the Gallaudet Home for the Aged and Infirm Deaf in Poughkeepsie, N.Y.

Gallaudet played a leading role in awaking Episcopalians to the importance of ministry among the hearing-impaired. Through his efforts, the Episcopal Church became a major participant in this work, especially in the provision of sign-language worship. Believing that the leadership of signing congregations should stem largely from the deaf themselves, Gallaudet had a significant impact on the life and career of Henry Winter Syle (1846–90). A hearing-impaired man who had been active at St. Ann's Church, Syle was encouraged by Gallaudet to prepare for the ordained ministry. After his ordination, Syle led the way in the construction of the first Episcopal church built specifically for the hearing-impaired: All Souls' Church for the Deaf, established in Philadelphia in 1888. Gallaudet's younger brother, Edward Miner Gallaudet, also opened a school for deaf-mutes in Washington, D.C., the upper branch of which became Gallaudet University. By 1930 this institution had graduated 21 of the 24 hearing-impaired men who had been ordained as Episcopal clergy.

Gallaudet died in New York City in 1902.

Bibliography

A. "A Sketch of My Life," unpublished autobiographical manuscript in the archives of Gallaudet University, Washington, D.C.

B. *ANB* 8, 644–45; *BB,* 86–88; *DAB* 7, 110–11; *EDC,* 509; *HEC,* 182–83; Amos G. Draper,

"Thomas Gallaudet," *American Annals of the Deaf* 47 (Nov. 1902): 393–403; John H. Kent, "Rev. Thomas Gallaudet," *American Annals of the Deaf* 67 (Sept. 1922): 326–33; Otto Benjamin Berg, *A Missionary Chronicle: Being a History of the Ministry to the Deaf in the Episcopal Church, 1850–1980* (Hollywood, Md., 1984); Otto Benjamin Berg and Henry L. Buzzard, *Thomas Gallaudet: Apostle to the Deaf* (New York, 1989).

GARDINER, ROBERT HALLOWELL III (9 September 1855, Fort Tejon, Calif.–15 June 1924, Boston). *Education:* A.B., Harvard College, 1876; studied at Harvard Law School, 1878–79. *Career:* French teacher, Roxbury Latin School, 1877; lawyer, Boston, 1880–1924.

Robert Gardiner, an active Episcopal layman and leading contributor to the early stages of the ecumenical movement, was born in California in 1855. He was educated at Harvard University and became a successful Boston lawyer at the end of the nineteenth century. Committed to the cause of social reform, he served as a trustee of the Christian Social Union and of the Episcopal City Mission in Boston. He was also a delegate to numerous General Conventions, and at the 1916 convention he espoused the idea of electing women as deputies. Following the World Missionary Conference in Edinburgh in 1910, he was appointed by the Episcopal Church to help in the planning of a world conference on faith and order. Gardiner's preparation for this event, which eventually took place in 1927 in Lausanne, Switzerland, was thorough and effective. He assumed the burden of carrying out the negotiations and writing the letters necessary to pave the way for this remarkable international Christian gathering—an organizing effort to which he gave the last 14 years of his life.

Gardiner's stress on Christian unity derived from his understanding of the church as the corporate body of Christ. He especially believed in the Johannine Christ who is one with the Father and with his followers (John 17:20–21). As he wrote in an article in *The Churchman* magazine, he looked forward to "the time when the Church, visibly the one Body, shall proclaim, with irresistible power, the Gospel of the Incarnation." Gardiner's thoughtful and well-informed approach to the Christian faith also led him to emphasize the church's responsibilities in the world. He urged Christians "to fight personally against the sin around us, especially the great sin of the unjust conditions of society."

Although Gardiner died in Boston in 1924, he was honored posthumously at the Lausanne conference in 1927.

Bibliography

A. Papers at the headquarters of the World Council of Churches in Geneva, Switzerland, and at General Theological Seminary in New York; "A Lawyer's View of the Function of the Church," *Publications of the Christian Social Union,* no. 37 (15 May 1897): 1–20; "The Church and the Federal Council," *TLC,* 28 December 1912, 290–93; "Creed, Life, and Unity," *Christian Union Quarterly* 3 (April 1914): 111–

18; "The American Council for Organic Union," *Churchman,* 21 February 1920, 12.

B. *ANB* 8, 699–700; *ECUS,* 374; *WWWA* 1, 439.

GRAFTON, CHARLES CHAPMAN (12 April 1830, Boston–30 August 1912, Fond du Lac, Wis.). *Education:* LL.B., Harvard Law School, 1853; studied theology under William R. Whittingham, Baltimore, 1853–55. *Career:* Curate, St. Paul's Church, Baltimore, 1859–64; in England, 1865–72; rector, Church of the Advent, Boston, 1872–88; bishop, diocese of Fond du Lac, 1889–1912.

Charles C. Grafton, a bishop and prominent Anglo-Catholic leader, was born in Boston in 1830. Influenced as a youth by William Croswell, the founding rector of the Church of the Advent in Boston, Grafton decided after completing law school that he would pursue a career in the ordained ministry of the Episcopal Church. He went to Baltimore, where he read theology under the direction of William R. Whittingham,* the renowned high church bishop of Maryland. Following his ordination, Grafton served briefly as chaplain to a house of deaconesses in Maryland and then became a curate at St. Paul's Church, Baltimore. Attracted by the idea of the religious life, he journeyed to England in 1865 to learn more about monasticism. While in England he served as chaplain of a hospital for cholera patients, worked as a priest in London's impoverished East End, and helped organize a successful preaching mission. After being introduced by Edward B. Pusey, the Oxford movement leader, to the English priest R. M. Benson, he and Benson joined an Eton College tutor, S. W. O'Neill, to make their profession to the religious life. This event, which took place at Cowley, near Oxford, on December 27, 1866, marked the beginning of the Society of St. John the Evangelist (also known as the Cowley Fathers), the first permanent monastic order for men in the Episcopal Church.

The vestry of the Church of the Advent in Boston invited the Cowley Fathers to take charge of their parish, and in 1872 Grafton became rector of the parish he had known since boyhood. During his tenure, he increased the church's membership and oversaw the construction of its present Gothic revival edifice. In 1888 he left the Church of the Advent, intending to preach missions, conduct retreats, and build up the Sisters of the Holy Nativity, the women's religious order he had founded in Providence, Rhode Island. Later that year, however, he was elected bishop of the diocese of Fond du Lac in Wisconsin. After some delay caused by concerns about his extreme Anglo-Catholic views, he was ordained bishop in April 1889. As bishop, Grafton began with 20 vacant parishes and missions and only 18 clergy. He not only significantly increased the number of parishes and priests in his diocese but also improved diocesan finances, started schools, and raised money for Nashotah House, the Anglo-Catholic seminary in Wisconsin. In addition, he was eager to pursue ties with Orthodox Christianity, and he became the first Episcopal bishop to travel to Russia to meet with Orthodox church leaders.

The central concern of Grafton's episcopate was the strengthening of Anglo-Catholic principles and ritual throughout his diocese. He believed that Catholic ceremonial practices added a sense of holiness to the liturgy and helped keep the attention of worshipers focused on the divine presence in their midst. In his diocese he established what he called the "six points of ritual": eucharistic vestments, the mixed chalice (water mixed with the communion wine), unleavened communion wafers (rather than ordinary bread), the eastward-facing position of priests, candles on the altar, and incense. Grafton's extreme Catholic piety, in fact, became infamous among low church Episcopalians, especially after a controversy in 1900. In November of that year, at the consecration of his coadjutor, Reginald Heber Weller, there were 10 bishops, including prelates of the Russian Orthodox and the Polish National (Old) Catholic churches. In a photograph published in *The Living Church* magazine, all the officiating bishops were depicted wearing copes and miters, which was unusual garb for Episcopal bishops at that time. The photograph of the bishops vested in their regalia caused such consternation among Episcopalians that it came to be referred to, irreverently, as the "the Fond du Lac Circus."

In his later years, when he was unable to travel around his diocese, Grafton devoted himself to writing. One of his most popular works was *Pusey and the Church Revival* (1902), in which he reminisced about his association with the great leader of the Catholic revival in the Church of England. Grafton died in Fond du Lac in August 1912.

Bibliography

A. *Plain Suggestions for a Reverent Celebration of the Holy Communion* (Cambridge, Mass., 1884); *Vocation; or, Call of the Divine Master to a Sister's Life* (New York, 1889); *Pusey and the Church Revival* (Milwaukee, 1902); *Christian and Catholic* (New York, 1905); *A Catholic Atlas; or, Digest of Catholic Theology* (New York, 1908); *A Journey Godward* (New York, 1910); *The Works of the Rt. Rev. Charles C. Grafton* (New York, 1914).
B. *ANB* 9, 372–74; *DAB* 7, 470–71; *EDC*, 225; *HPEC*, 319–20; *MM*, 342–49; *SH* 5, 44; *WWWA* 1, 475; Ernest C. Miller, "Bishop Grafton of Fond du Lac and the Orthodox Church," *Sobernost* 4 (1982): 38–48; Glenn Johnson, "Battling Bishop," *TLC*, 23 April 1989, 8–9; George E. DeMille, *The Catholic Movement in the American Episcopal Church*, 2nd ed. (Philadelphia, 1950).

GRISWOLD, ALEXANDER VIETS (22 April 1766, Simsbury, Conn.–15 February 1843, Boston). *Education:* Private study of law and theology. *Career:* Minister, missions in Plymouth, Harwinton, Litchfield, Waterbury, and Reading, Conn., 1795–1804; rector, St. Michael's Church, Bristol, R.I., 1804–30; rector, St. Peter's Church, Salem, Mass., 1830–35; bishop, Eastern diocese, 1811–43; presiding bishop of the Episcopal Church, 1836–43.

A bishop and one of the early leaders of the evangelical party in the Episcopal Church, Alexander Griswold was raised in Simsbury, Connecticut. He was educated privately by his uncle, Roger Viets, the rector of the Episcopal parish in his hometown. Having been persuaded by friends that his character and skills were well suited for the ministry, he studied theology privately and was ordained in 1795. At first, Griswold not only served as a priest in five small Connecticut towns but also supplemented his income by working as a farmer in the summer and as a schoolteacher in the winter. In 1804, he was called to be the rector of St. Michael's Church in Bristol, Rhode Island. In May 1810, under Griswold's leadership, representatives from churches in New Hampshire, Vermont, Rhode Island, and Massachusetts (then including Maine) met in Boston and organized the "Eastern diocese"—a jurisdiction that contained relatively few churches but included all of New England except Connecticut. Griswold was elected the bishop of the diocese in 1810, and he was consecrated in May 1811.

Griswold's life changed dramatically after he became a bishop. During the period he had ministered in Connecticut, his sermons had emphasized the importance of morality rather than sin, salvation, and forgiveness. As he began to think in earnest about the nature of his calling, however, his preaching became more heartfelt and evangelical. A new warmth and zeal enlivened his discourse, giving him a new level of authority. Following a religious revival at St. Michael's, Bristol, at the beginning of his episcopate, he began to conduct informal evening meetings in parishioners' homes. He would usually sit at a small table, read from the Bible and prayer book, preach a biblically based sermon, and then allow time for personal prayer. These gatherings became so well attended that a private home could no longer accommodate them, and they soon inspired other parishes in the diocese to hold their own weekly prayer meetings.

Toward the end of his tenure as bishop, Griswold confronted the challenge of the Oxford movement. Refusing to turn back to what he called "the dark ages of Christianity," he saw no value in using medieval liturgical practices in Episcopal worship. Thus, he rejected adopting the eastward position in prayer because he believed it suggested belief in the Roman Catholic doctrine of transubstantiation. Christ, Griswold argued, is among the people who are worshiping; he is no more present in the consecrated bread and wine of communion than he is in any other place in the church. For similar reasons, Griswold opposed calling the holy table an "altar," and he disapproved of the use of candles, flowers, and pictures, speaking of such customs as "superstitious mummeries and idolatrous practices."

Griswold was so successful in rebuilding the Episcopal Church in New England that at his death the Eastern diocese was able to be divided into five independent dioceses. The bishop's enthusiasm and strenuous efforts also resulted in a dramatic increase in the number of Episcopal parishes, from 24 in 1810 to more than 100 congregations 30 years later. Emphasizing the missionary nature of the church, he encouraged the establishment of Sunday schools, and he confirmed over 11,000 persons during his tenure as bishop. In 1836, by seniority of consecration, Griswold succeeded William White* of Pennsylvania as presiding bishop. He served in that post until his death in Boston in 1843.

Bibliography

A. *Convention Addresses* (Middlebury, Vt., 1827); *Discourses on the Most Important Doctrines and Duties of the Christian Religion* (Philadelphia, 1830); *The Reformation: A Brief Exposition of Some of the Errors and Corruptions of the Church of Rome* (Boston, 1843); *Remarks on Social Prayer-Meetings* (Boston, 1858).
B. *AAP* 5, 415–25; *ANB* 9, 639–40; *DAB* 8, 7–8; *DARB*, 220–21; *DCA*, 500–1; *EDC*, 231; *MM*, 36–38, 101–4; *NCAB* 4, 78–79; W. W. Manross, "Alexander Viets Griswold and the Eastern Diocese," *HMPEC* 4 (1935): 13–25; John S. Stone, *Memoir of the Life of the Rt. Rev. Alexander Viets Griswold* (Philadelphia, 1844); John Nicholas Norton, *The Life of Bishop Griswold,* 2nd ed. (New York, 1857).

H

HALE, SARAH JOSEPHA BUELL (24 October 1788, Newport, N.H.–30 April 1879, Philadelphia). *Education:* Educated at home by family members. *Career:* Schoolteacher, 1806–13; writer, 1823–77; editor, *Ladies' Magazine* (later *American Ladies' Magazine*), 1828–37; editor, *Godey's Lady's Book,* 1837–77.

A magazine editor, writer, and social reformer, Sarah Hale was born in Newport, New Hampshire, the daughter of Gordon Buell and Martha Whittlesey, who were farmers. She was educated at home by her mother and by her older brother. After teaching school for five years, she married David Hale, a lawyer, in 1813. Following her husband's death in 1822, Hale began writing in order to support her family of five children. In 1827 she published a successful novel, *Northwood,* that portrayed domestic habits during the postcolonial period. It was also one of the first American novels to deal with the issue of slavery, which she described as a "stain on our national character." Besides writing numerous other books during her career, Hale composed poetry. Her most famous poem, "Mary Had a Little Lamb," first appeared in 1830 in her book *Poems for Our Children.*

Hale's popularity as a writer convinced a publishing house in Boston to hire her as editor of the first American periodical directed exclusively at women. In the inaugural issue of *Ladies' Magazine,* which appeared in January 1828, Hale stated that the publication would print material that aided "female improvement." In 1837 she accepted an offer to become the literary editor of *Godey's Lady's Book,* into which *Ladies' Magazine* was then incorporated. Although she remained in Boston until her sons graduated from college, in 1841 Hale moved to Philadelphia, where *Godey's* was based. After converting to the Episcopal Church, she became an active member of Philadelphia's prestigious Holy Trinity Church.

During the nearly 50 years she worked as an editor, Hale supported numerous public causes. For example, she campaigned for funds to complete the Bunker Hill monument in Boston, and she sought to restore Mount Vernon plantation for preservation as a national shrine. In the 1860s she also led the campaign to have Thanksgiving Day declared a national holiday. Her principal interests, however, concerned organizations that aided the advancement of women in American society. Thus, she was a strong advocate of women's education, and she urged the establishment of state normal schools for the training of women as teachers. In the ecclesiastical sphere, Hale supported the deaconess movement then being introduced into the Episcopal Church from German Lutheranism, and she encouraged religiously committed women to serve in the foreign mission field. Her most ambitious work, *Woman's Record* (1853), was a biographical encyclopedia that contained short sketches of over 2,500 notable women.

Hale retired from her position at *Godey's* in 1877, and she died in Philadelphia two years later.

Bibliography

A. Papers at the Houghton Library of Harvard University, at the Schlesinger Library of Radcliffe College, and at the Pierpont Morgan Library in New York; autobiographical sketches in *Godey's Lady's Book,* December 1850, and *Godey's Lady's Book,* December 1877; *The Genius of Oblivion* (Concord, N.H., 1823); *Northwood* (Boston, 1827); *Poems for Our Children* (Boston, 1830); *Flora's Interpreters* (Boston, 1832); *Traits of American Life* (Philadelphia, 1835); *The Ladies' Wreath* (Boston, 1837); *Woman's Record; or, Sketches of All Distinguished Women* (New York, 1853); *Manners* (Boston, 1867).

B. *ANB* 9, 836–37; *DAB* 8, 111–12; *DCA,* 505; *EDC,* 234; *NAW* 2, 110–14; *WWWA* Historical vol. 1607–1896, 226; Ruth E. Finley, *The Lady of Godey's: Sarah Josepha Hale* (Philadelphia, 1931); Isabelle Webb Entrikin, *Sarah Josepha Hale and "Godey's Lady's Book"* (Philadelphia, 1946); Sherbrooke Rogers, *Sarah Josepha Hale: A New England Pioneer* (Grantham, N.H., 1985); Patricia Okker, *Our Sister Editors: Sarah J. Hale and the Tradition of Nineteenth-Century American Women Editors* (Athens, Ga., 1995).

HARE, WILLIAM HOBART (17 May 1838, Princeton, N.J.–23 October 1909, Atlantic City, N.J.). *Education:* Studied at the University of Pennsylvania; studied for the ordained ministry on his own. *Career:* Served several churches in the Philadelphia area, 1861–71; secretary and general agent, Foreign Committee of the Board of Missions, 1871–73; bishop, missionary district of Niobrara, 1873–83; bishop, diocese of South Dakota, 1883–1909.

William Hobart Hare, a bishop and missionary to American Indians, was born in Princeton, New Jersey, in May 1838. He was the son of an Episcopal priest (the first dean of the Philadelphia Divinity School) and the grandson (on his mother's side) of John Henry Hobart,* the first bishop of the diocese of New York. Hare was ordained to the diaconate in 1859 and served for the next two years as assistant to the rector of St. Luke's Church, Philadelphia. He became rector of St. Paul's Church, Chestnut Hill, near Philadelphia, in May 1861, and a year later he was ordained to the priesthood by Alonzo Potter, the bishop of

Pennsylvania. His wife's failing health prompted Hare to resign from his parish and move to Minnesota, hoping that the state's bracing climate would prove restorative to her. It was there, in 1863, that he first became acquainted with American Indians and witnessed how little the church was doing on their behalf. Returning to Philadelphia, he served again at St. Luke's and then, in 1867, soon after his wife's death, he became rector of the Church of the Ascension. In 1871, upon being appointed secretary and general agent of the Foreign Committee of the Board of Missions, he moved to New York City.

In October 1871 the House of Bishops created the missionary district of Niobrara in Dakota Territory, and in November 1872 Hare was elected its bishop. Niobrara was the vast region, largely unknown to whites, north of the Niobrara River (which marked the border between Nebraska and Dakota) and west of the Missouri River. This land was inhabited by the Ponca and Lakota/Dakota Indians, and the Oneidas in Wisconsin and the Santee in Nebraska were also transferred to the oversight of the newly elected bishop. Hare was consecrated in January 1873, at the age of 34. Over the next 37 years, he endured great physical hardship while establishing chapels, boarding schools, and missionary residences and supervising the training and deployment of clergy, catechists, and other church workers. During this period, the number of native clergy, candidates for the ministry, and catechists grew significantly, as did the number of children in the four Indian boarding schools Hare founded. His Indian work eventually included 90 congregations, with 57 church buildings and 3,200 communicants. In 1883 the House of Bishops changed the boundaries of Hare's jurisdiction almost exactly to those of the present state of South Dakota and substituted the name "South Dakota" for "Niobrara."

By the 1880s large numbers of white immigrants were streaming into the Dakotas, and Hare's ministry began to include more and more of them as well. In September 1885 he established All Saints School in Sioux Falls to educate the daughters of these newcomers as well as of his own missionaries. He maintained a residence for himself on the grounds of the school, which became a place of welcome rest after long and exhausting missionary journeys. By the late 1890s, heart trouble had reduced Hare's former vigor, and after 1903 a facial cancer made it very difficult for him to carry on his work. The election of a coadjutor, Frederick Foote Johnson, helped lighten the burden of his duties in 1905. In 1907 Hare underwent disfiguring surgery for a malignant growth on his face.

By the time of his death, half the 25,000 Indians in South Dakota were baptized members of the Episcopal Church, and Hare himself had confirmed over 7,000 of them. The annual gatherings of the Niobrara deanery, which included all the Indian missions in South Dakota, attracted several thousand Native Americans for worship and fellowship on the Great Plains. In 1891 the daughter of the Lakota war chief Gall, victor against Custer at the battle of the Little Bighorn in 1876, presented to Hare an offering of eight hundred dollars on behalf of the Niobrara (i.e., the American Indian) branch of the Woman's Auxiliary. On the next fourth of July, Chief Gall himself was baptized in the Episcopal Church.

While on a visit to Atlantic City, New Jersey, for medical treatment—Hare suffered from heart disease as well as cancer—the bishop died. His body was returned to Sioux Falls, South Dakota, where it was buried on the grounds of All Saints School.

Bibliography

A. *Reminiscences* (Philadelphia, 1888).

B. *ANB* 10, 76–77; *DAB* 8, 264–65; *ECUS,* chap. 18; *EDC,* 235–36; *NCAB* 3, 468; *WWWA* 1, 519; *NYT,* 24 October 1909; M. A. DeWolfe Howe, *The Life and Labors of Bishop Hare* (New York, 1911); Virginia Driving Hawk Sneve, *That They May Have Life: The Episcopal Church in South Dakota, 1859–1976* (New York, 1977); Owanah Anderson, *400 Years: Anglican/Episcopal Mission among American Indians* (Cincinnati, 1997), chapter 4.

HINES, JOHN ELBRIDGE (3 October 1910, Seneca, S.C.—19 July 1997, Austin, Tex.). *Education:* B.A., University of the South, 1930; B.D., Virginia Theological Seminary, 1933. *Career:* Curate, Church of St. Michael and St. George, St. Louis, Mo., 1933–35; rector, Trinity Church, Hannibal, Mo., 1935–37; rector, St. Paul's Church, Augusta, Ga., 1937–41; rector, Christ Church, Houston, Tex., 1941–45; bishop coadjutor, diocese of Texas, 1945–55; bishop, diocese of Texas, 1955–64; presiding bishop of the Episcopal Church, 1965–74.

John E. Hines, the 22nd presiding bishop of the Episcopal Church, was born in Seneca, South Carolina, in 1910. After graduating from the University of the South and Virginia Theological Seminary, he was ordained a deacon in August 1933 and a priest the following year. He began his ministry in the diocese of Missouri, where he prospered under the leadership of William Scarlett,* the diocesan bishop and one of the most prominent advocates of the social gospel in the Episcopal Church. Next serving as rector of a parish in Augusta, Georgia, Hines began to question and confront the South's racial segregation laws. In 1941 he became rector of Christ Church, Houston, the second largest parish in the diocese of Texas. After a brief but highly successful tenure there, he was elected bishop coadjutor of his diocese in May 1945. He was only 35 years old at the time of his consecration later that year.

Over the next decade, Hines established a reputation as a builder of ecclesiastical institutions. He encouraged the founding of a seminary (the Episcopal Theological Seminary of the Southwest in Austin), a secondary school (St. Stephen's in Austin), and 41 new congregations in his rapidly expanding diocese. When Clinton Quin retired from his position as bishop of Texas, Hines succeeded him in December 1955. Although he often faced opposition from white Episcopalians in his diocese, Hines consistently struggled against racial intolerance both in the church and in society. Eventually, in 1963, St. Stephen's School became the first fully desegregated coeducational boarding school in the South. His extraordinary leadership abilities were further recognized in 1964 when the House of Bishops of the Episcopal Church elected him as the presiding bishop of the denomination. Preaching at his installation in January 1965, Hines called Episcopalians to meet the challenges of the modern day. A liberal evangelical, he emphasized the need not only to have "a real and saving encounter with Jesus Christ as Savior" but also to become involved in the process of social change during the "most unpredictable, exciting and frightening era in recorded history."

Between 1965 and 1974, Hines encouraged important changes both in the church's internal structure and in its outward focus. During this period, he supported the civil rights movement, liturgical renewal, ecumenical participation, the ordination of women, and other progressive causes. His commitment to social change was most evident in his response to the crisis in American cities in the late 1960s. In his opening address to the 1967 General Convention, Hines summoned the members of his church to reorder their priorities by making a substantial commitment to the economic empowerment of African Americans and other poor people in the United States. The convention quickly approved Hines's ambitious proposal and committed $9 million over three years to what became known as the General Convention Special Program (GCSP). The operations of GCSP began in 1968. Despite the program's many accomplishments, however, it soon provoked a bitter controversy within the Episcopal Church. Faced with a strong backlash by conservatives against the social ministry of their denomination, the church's national leadership first curtailed the work of GCSP in 1970 and then terminated the program entirely in 1973. During that same period, Hines himself was subjected to continual abuse, and he eventually chose to cut short his term as presiding bishop. When he retired prematurely in the spring of 1974, the editors of *Christian Century* remarked that he had ridden "the bucking bronco of a polarized church during one of the most controversial decades in American history."

After his retirement, Hines moved to western North Carolina, where he lived for nearly 20 years. In poor health, he remained in semi-reclusion, preaching or serving as a guest lecturer on only a few occasions. In 1993 he returned to the diocese of Texas and settled in Austin, where he died in 1997.

Bibliography

A. Papers at AEC; "Sermon, 1967," in *DW,* 508–10; *Christ Church Sermons* (Houston, Tex., 1946); *Focus on the Cross: Twelve Sermons* (Atlanta, 1967); *Thy Kingdom Come* (New York, 1967); *The Prophetic Vision of John E. Hines* (Cincinnati, 1993).
B. *EDC,* 243; *ERS,* 324–25; *NYT,* 22 July 1997; Kenneth Kesselus, *John E. Hines: Granite on Fire* (Austin, Tex., 1995).

HINMAN, SAMUEL DUTTON (1839, Pittsburgh, Pa.–24 March 1890, Birch Coulee, Minn.). *Education:* Studied at Cheshire Academy, Connecticut; graduated from Seabury Divinity School, Faribault, Minn., 1860. *Career:* Missionary to the Dakota Indians in Minnesota, Nebraska, and South Dakota, 1860–90.

Samuel Hinman, a missionary to the Dakota Indians, was born in Pittsburgh in 1839. Orphaned at an early age, he moved west and eventually studied under

James Lloyd Breck* at the Seabury Divinity School. After his ordination to the diaconate in 1860, he journeyed to Redwood County, Minnesota, where, at the Lower Sioux Agency, he established a mission to the Dakotas. His two years' work at Redwood began slowly, handicapped by a shortage of funds and by his own lack of familiarity with the language and customs of the Dakota people. Gradually, his steady efforts on behalf of the poor and sick began to earn him respect, and some Indians began attending his school. Hinman was assisted by Emily J. West, who had served with Breck among the Ojibwas and who had also had the care of the Indian children at the mission house in Faribault. By 1862 Hinman had learned the Dakota language well enough to employ it in preaching, and he began a translation of the *Book of Common Prayer,* which he completed and published three years later.

Disgusted by the treachery of the federal government and driven by hunger, the Dakotas broke out of their Minnesota Valley reservation in August 1862. This bloody uprising caused an immediate termination of mission work at Redwood and forced Hinman to flee to Fort Ridgely. In the spring of 1863, the Dakotas, having suffered expulsion from Minnesota, were compelled to live on a new reservation—Crow Creek—on the upper Missouri River in Dakota Territory. Hinman also established an Episcopal presence there. As he remarked to Henry Whipple,* the bishop of Minnesota, "I entered on this work when all looked well; I cannot desert it. I shall go with my people, if it be to the Rocky mountains." In 1866 he traveled with the Dakotas once more, when they were moved to the mouth of the Niobrara River in Nebraska. Lacking financial support from the church's Board of Missions, Hinman relied mainly on donations from sympathetic Episcopalians in the East to sustain his work. Serving as archdeacon of the Nebraska and Dakota Indian work until the arrival of William Hobart Hare* as missionary bishop of Niobrara in 1873, Hinman trained native catechists and built a chapel, school, and mission house at the Santee Agency. He also worked as a government interpreter for the 1868 treaty commission and as a member of the 1876 treaty commission that eventually ceded the Black Hills to the federal government.

After Hare's arrival in the Dakotas, he began to hear rumors that Hinman had misused funds and had even consorted with an Indian prostitute. Concerned about the damage that such reports were causing the church's evangelistic work, Hare removed Hinman from the Santee mission in March 1878 and suspended him from the exercise of his priesthood. Stung both by the ignominy of this dismissal and by Hare's failure to respect his lengthy service in the region, Hinman demanded a trial in a church court. The court, however, found him guilty of "gross immorality . . . and the dishonest . . . use of money entrusted to him for the work of the mission," and it endorsed his expulsion from the reservation. Hinman continued to battle Hare for several more years until, in 1887, they signed an agreement allowing Hinman to resume functioning as a priest. Hinman undoubtedly possessed a difficult temperament, but part of the conflict stemmed from his comparatively tolerant approach to evangelization. He had allowed Indians to continue some of their traditional practices, such as placing food on the graves of their dead and attending native dances. Hare's approach, on the other hand, was far more conservative, and he did not tolerate religious syncretism.

During the period that Hinman was fighting with his bishop, he worked for the Bureau of Indian Affairs as a census enumerator and investigator of hostilities. In the spring of 1886, he took up residence at the Birch Coulee mission in the area that later became the town of Morton, Minnesota. The following year, when his suspension was lifted, Henry Whipple officially received him back into the diocese of Minnesota, and at Birch Coulee, Hinman ministered to Dakotas who had returned to the region. He died and was buried at that mission in March 1890.

Bibliography

A. *Journal of the Rev. S.D. Hinman, Missionary to the Santee Sioux Indians* (Philadelphia, 1869); *A Statement of Samuel D. Hinman, Presbyter and First Missionary to the Dakotas* (Yankton, S.D., 1879).
B. *EDC,* 243; Arlene Hirschfelder and Paulette Molin, *Encyclopedia of Native American Religions* (New York, 1992), 120; Henry Benjamin Whipple, *Lights and Shadows of a Long Episcopate* (New York, 1899); George Clinton Tanner, *Fifty Years of Church Work in the Diocese of Minnesota, 1857–1907* (n.p., 1909); Donald Dean Parker, *Founding the Church in South Dakota* (Brookings, S.D., 1962); Roy W. Meyer, *History of the Santee Sioux: United States Indian Policy on Trial* (Lincoln, Neb., 1967); Virginia Driving Hawk Sneve, *That They May Have Life: The Episcopal Church in South Dakota, 1859–1976* (New York, 1977); Robert H. Keller Jr., *American Protestantism and United States Indian Policy, 1869–82* (Lincoln, Neb., 1983); Owanah Anderson, *400 Years: Anglican / Episcopal Mission among American Indians* (Cincinnati, 1997), chap. 3–4.

HOBART, JOHN HENRY (14 September 1775, Philadelphia–12 September 1830, Auburn, N.Y.). *Education:* Studied at Episcopal Academy, Philadelphia; studied at College and Academy of Philadelphia (now the University of Pennsylvania), 1788–91; B.A., College of New Jersey (now Princeton University), 1793; A.M., College of New Jersey, 1796; studied theology under William White, Philadelphia, 1796–98. *Career:* Curate, Oxford and Perkiomen, Pa., 1798–99; curate, New Brunswick, N.J., 1799–1800; curate, Hempstead, N.Y., 1800–1801; assistant minister, Trinity Church, N.Y., 1801–11; assistant bishop, diocese of New York, 1811–16; bishop, diocese of New York, 1816–30; professor of pastoral theology and pulpit eloquence, General Theological Seminary, 1821–30.

John Henry Hobart, a bishop and influential high church leader, was born in Philadelphia in 1775. Baptized and confirmed by William White,* Hobart attended the College of New Jersey, where debates with Calvinist friends tested and strengthened his high church Anglican convictions. After studying theology under White's tutelage, he was ordained a deacon in 1798 and a priest in 1801. He served briefly in parishes in Pennsylvania, New Jersey, and Long Island before coming to Trinity Church, New York, in 1801. He was elected assistant bishop of New York 10 years later, and because the diocesan bishop, Benjamin Moore, was in very poor health, he essentially ran the diocese from the moment of his consecration. He later became the bishop of New York after Moore's death in 1816.

A powerful preacher as well as an activist bishop, Hobart declared in 1807 that "evangelical truth, apostolic order" were his watchwords. As a vigorous advocate of high church beliefs, he identified the Episcopal Church with the primitive church of the first centuries, a church that held fast to the faith of the apostles in the midst of a hostile population. He also viewed the church and its sacraments as the channels of God's grace by which salvation is mediated to and appropriated by Christians. Because of his stress both on the importance of apostolic succession and on the superiority of the Episcopal Church to other denominations, he strongly opposed ecumenical endeavors with Protestants, who in his view lacked an apostolic ministry and valid sacraments. Although Hobart consistently highlighted the importance of "apostolic order" in his controversial writings, he balanced this emphasis by stressing "evangelical truth" in his pastoral work. He rejected the "comfortless" rationalism of liberal theology, which in his estimation reflected a fundamental indifference to the gospel. In an era when many Episcopal clergy employed a formal mode of sermon delivery, Hobart's impassioned preaching style caused some who heard him early in his ministry to wonder if he had Methodist leanings.

Not content merely to ordain clergy and to preside at church conventions, Hobart redefined the role of bishop through a ministry that included regular parish visitations, pastoral letters to his diocese, and numerous publications. He launched the first diocesan newspaper, *The Churchman's Journal,* and produced the first Episcopal devotional manual, *Companion for the Altar,* which contained meditations preparing the individual to receive communion. A highly effective organizer, Hobart also helped establish the New York Bible and Common Prayer Book Society (1809), the Protestant Episcopal Tract Society (1810), the New York Sunday School Society (1817), and the Protestant Episcopal Press (1817). Finally, his interest in the need for a more formal system of educating clergy led to the founding of General Theological Seminary in New York in 1817. This institution, which he continued to support and advise as a professor and trustee, soon became the principal center of Hobartian high churchmanship in the United States.

Bishop of an area that comprised 46,000 square miles (including New Jersey until 1815), Hobart traveled by horse, stagecoach, and canal boat to reach people throughout his diocese. During his 19-year episcopate, the diocese grew from 25 clergy to 133, from 2 missionaries among the Indians and white settlers of western New York to 50, from 40 parishes to 165, and from 2,300 communicants to 6,700. Having attracted many to the Episcopal Church through the strength of his personal witness, Hobart is now recognized as one of the key figures in the rebuilding of the denomination after the devastating years of the American Revolution. He died in Auburn, New York, in September 1830 while visiting parishes in his diocese.

Bibliography

A. *A Companion for the Altar* (New York, 1804); *An Apology for Apostolic Order and Its Advocates* (New York, 1807); *The Churchman* (New York, 1819); *Sermons on the Principal Events and Truths of Redemption,* 2 vols. (New York, 1824); *The Correspondence of John Henry Hobart,* ed. Arthur Lowndes, 6 vols. (New York, 1911–12).

B. *AAP* 5, 440–53; *ANB* 10, 894–95; *DAB* 9, 93–94; *DARB,* 244–45; *DCA,* 535–36; *EARH,* 312–13; *EDC,* 246; *MM,* 140–56; *NCAB* 1, 514–15; *NCE* 7, 42; *SH* 5, 302; John McVickar, *The Early Life and Professional Years of Bishop Hobart* (Oxford, 1838); John N. Norton, *Life of the Rt. Rev. John Henry Hobart* (New York, 1857); R. W. Wertz, "John Henry Hobart, 1775–1830: Pillar of the Episcopal Church" (Ph.D. diss., Harvard University, 1967); Robert Bruce Mullin, *Episcopal Vision / American Reality: High Church Theology and Social Thought in Evangelical America* (New Haven, 1986).

HODGES, GEORGE (6 October 1856, Rome, N.Y.—27 May 1919, Holderness, N.H.). *Education:* A.B., Hamilton College, 1877; graduated from Berkeley Divinity School, Middletown, Conn., 1881. *Career:* Assistant minister, Calvary Church, Pittsburgh, and priest-in-charge, St. Stephen's Church, 1881–89; rector, Calvary Church, Pittsburgh, 1889–94; dean and professor of homiletics and pastoral theology, Episcopal Theological School, 1894–1919.

George Hodges, a progressive clergyman concerned about the practical application of Christianity to the conditions of modern existence, was born in Rome, New York, in 1856. After graduating from Hamilton College and Berkeley Divinity School, he was ordained to the diaconate in June 1881 and to the priesthood almost exactly one year later. He served pastorally at Calvary Church in Pittsburgh between 1881 and 1894. As rector of Calvary, he led the parish in supporting political and social reform in Pittsburgh and in launching a settlement house. Named Kingsley House, this institution reflected Hodges's ecumenical spirit; it was begun in 1893 with the help of Unitarians, Roman Catholics, and others. Declining election as bishop coadjutor of the diocese of Oregon, he accepted an invitation to become dean of the Episcopal Theological School (ETS) in Cambridge, Massachusetts, where he became one of the leading theological educators of his day.

Influenced by the writings of the English priests Charles Kingsley and Frederick Denison Maurice, Hodges was a strong advocate of the social gospel. In *The Administration of an Institutional Church* (1906), he urged attention to the social, economic, and recreational requirements of parish members as well as to their spiritual needs. He also believed the church needed to confront such issues as universal education, decent housing, and fair wages for workers. As dean at ETS, Hodges introduced courses in sociology into the curriculum. His conviction that seminarians needed training both in theology and in sociology was part of his larger intellectual view that Christians should recognize truth wherever it existed. In embracing this position, he helped Episcopalians reckon with many of the social and intellectual challenges that faced Christians at the turn of the twentieth century.

The author of numerous books and journal articles on theology, scripture, and Christian sociology, Hodges looked favorably upon new critical approaches to the Bible and the history of Christianity. He was particularly successful as a popularizer of church history; his *Three Hundred Years of the Episcopal Church in America* (1906), for example, sold 24,444 copies during its first year of publication. In addition, his historical writing exhibited his sense of humor, and he was much in demand as a guest preacher and lecturer. In a lecture on the Episcopal Church later published in *The Religious History of New England* (1917), he mentioned how Manton Eastburn, the bishop of Massachusetts, disapproved of the use of a cross and altar candles at the Church of the Advent in Boston. Hodges dryly remarked: "The bishop refused to visit the parish for confirmation till the offensive ornaments were removed, and the rector and vestry refused to remove them. Each side exhibited that perseverance of the saints which in sinners is called obstinacy."

Hodges suffered a physical collapse in 1915, and despite remaining as dean, he struggled with poor health for the rest of his life. He died while vacationing at his summer home in Holderness, New Hampshire, in May 1919.

Bibliography

A. "The Episcopalians," in *The Religious History of New England* (Cambridge, Mass., 1917); *Christianity between Sundays* (New York, 1892); *The Heresy of Cain* (New York, 1894); *In This Present World* (New York, 1896); *Faith and Social Service* (New York, 1896); *The Battles of Peace,* 2nd ed. (New York, 1899); *The Administration of an Institutional Church* (New York, 1906); *Three Hundred Years of the Episcopal Church in America* (Philadelphia, 1906); *The Training of Children in Religion* (New York, 1910); *Everyman's Religion* (New York, 1910); *Henry Codman Potter, Seventh Bishop of New York* (New York, 1915); *Religion in a World at War* (New York, 1917).

B. *ANB* 10, 917; *DAB* 9, 100–101; *EDC,* 246–47; *WWWA* 1, 572; obituary, *Proceedings of the Massachusetts Historical Society* 53 (1919–20): 131–39; James Arthur Muller, "George Hodges: Popularizer of Church History," *HMPEC* 9 (1940): 78–89; Julia Shelley Hodges, *George Hodges: A Biography* (New York, 1926); James Arthur Muller, *The Episcopal Theological School, 1867–1943* (New York, 1943).

HOLLY, JAMES THEODORE (30 October 1829, Washington, D.C.–13 March 1911, Port au Prince, Haiti). *Education:* No formal education. *Career:* Shoemaker, Brooklyn, N.Y., and Burlington, Vt., 1843–51; newspaper editor, Windsor, Ont., Canada, 1851–53; public school principal, Buffalo, N.Y., 1854; representative, National Emigration Board and Episcopal Board of Missions, 1855; rector, St. Luke's Church, New Haven, Conn., 1856–61; missionary in Haiti, 1861–74; missionary bishop of Haiti, 1874–1911.

James T. Holly, the first African American bishop of the Episcopal Church, was born in Washington, D.C., in 1829. He was the son of James Overton Holly, a free man and shoemaker, and his wife, Jane. When he was 14 years old, Holly's family moved to Brooklyn, New York, and he worked for the next eight years in the shoemaking business. In 1848 he became involved with the antislavery movement, and during debates over the emigration of freed blacks to Liberia, he strongly supported the emigrationist position. Between 1851 and 1853, he also helped edit Henry Bibb's *Voice of the Fugitive* newspaper in Windsor, Ontario.

Although raised a Roman Catholic, Holly joined the Episcopal Church as an adult. He was ordained a deacon in June 1855 and a priest a few months later. In 1855, while working as a representative of both the National Emigration Board and the Episcopal Board of Missions, he traveled to Haiti in an effort to locate a site where a church mission might be established. During this period, he became increasingly active in promoting the idea of emigration among black Americans. His lecture *Vindication of the Capacity of the Negro Race for Self Government, and Civilized Progress,* which was published in 1857, urged emigration to Haiti, a place of "far more security for the personal liberty and general welfare of the governed" than the United States. Holly helped found the Episcopal Society for Promoting the Extension of the Work among Colored People, and he served as rector of St. Luke's Church in New Haven, Connecticut, between 1856 and 1861.

Holly was eventually able to convince the Board of Missions to support him as a missionary in Haiti. Moving to the island in 1861, he was committed to the idea of replacing Haiti's dominant Roman Catholic faith with a national Episcopal Church. In 1874 the House of Bishops of the Episcopal Church reached an agreement on this plan with the Orthodox Apostolic Church of Haiti. As a result, in 1874 Holly was consecrated a missionary bishop—the first African American to become a bishop in the Episcopal Church. Recognizing that education and good health were important concerns of the church, he sought to establish schools and medical institutions in Haiti. Despite his high hopes and energetic ministry, he received only minimal financial backing from his denomination, and various natural and political calamities continually hampered his work. At the time of Holly's death in 1911, his denomination numbered only a few thousand members in Haiti.

Bibliography

A. Papers at AEC; *Vindication of the Capacity of the Negro Race for Self Government, and Civilized Progress* (New Haven, 1857).
B. *ANB* 11, 72–73; *DAB* 9, 156–57; *DANB,* 319–20; *EAAR,* 353–54; *EDC,* 248; *WWWA* 1, 580; Floyd J. Miller, *The Search for a Black Nationality: Black Emigration and Colonization, 1787–1863* (Urbana, Ill., 1975); David M. Dean, *Defender of the Race: James Theodore Holly, Black Nationalist and Bishop* (Boston, 1979).

HOPKINS, JOHN HENRY (30 January 1792, Dublin, Ireland–9 January 1868, Rock Point, Vt.). *Education:* Attended boarding schools in Trenton and Bordentown, N.J.; read for the law with a Pittsburgh attorney. *Career:* Lawyer, Pittsburgh, 1818–23; rector, Trinity Church, Pittsburgh, 1823–31; assistant minister, Trinity Church, Boston, 1831–32; bishop, diocese of Vermont, 1832–68; rector of St. Paul's Church, Burlington, Vt., 1832–65; presiding bishop of the Episcopal Church, 1865–68.

A bishop, high church leader, and notable proslavery advocate, John Henry Hopkins was born in Dublin, Ireland, in 1792. When he was eight years old, he emigrated with his family to the United States, settling near Philadelphia. He later moved to Pittsburgh as a young man and worked for several years in the iron industry. Finding little success in that field, he took up the practice of law, but after the accidental death of his wife's brother, he began to reexamine both his life and his professional commitments. During this period, the vestry of Trinity Church, Pittsburgh (where he served as organist) asked him to be rector. Although Hopkins lacked a formal theological education and had not yet been ordained, he accepted the vestry's call. Within nine months he completed the course of study prescribed by the bishop of Pennsylvania, and he was ordained both a deacon (December 1823) and a priest (May 1824).

Hopkins's eight years at Trinity were active and successful. An able evangelist, he saw the number of communicants in his parish increase almost tenfold, and he established seven other churches in the Pittsburgh area. In 1831 he went to Boston to be the assistant minister at Trinity Church. He remained in Boston only a short time, for in 1832 he accepted election as the first bishop of the diocese of Vermont, which had recently split off from the Eastern diocese. Since the new diocese, which consisted of only 13 parishes and missions, could not afford to pay him an adequate salary, he supplemented his income by serving as the rector of St. Paul's Church, Burlington.

A powerful controversialist and prolific writer, Hopkins's theological guides were the Bible and the testimony of the early Christian church. Like most Episcopalians of his day, he was very antagonistic toward Roman Catholicism, and by 1844 he had also come out strongly against the Oxford movement, scoring the Tractarians' theological "novelties." Hopkins was careful, however, to distinguish between ecclesiastical practice and church doctrine, between ritualism and "popery." Consequently, in *The Law of Ritualism* (1866), he supported the use of eucharistic vestments, incense, and stone altars without subscribing to the Roman Catholic beliefs (e.g., transubstantiation) that many Episcopalians assumed those practices signified. Hopkins accurately predicted that many liturgical innovations seen by his peers as exceptional and disturbing would one day be accepted as normal within the Episcopal Church. His published works (more than 50 books, sermons, and pamphlets) included the first book on Gothic architecture by an American, and he was also an able artist and lithographer. In addition, his 1851 letter to the archbishop of Canterbury helped lead to the calling of the first Lambeth conference of Anglican bishops in 1867.

Hopkins's most crucial and disturbing writings concerned American slavery.

Indeed, he was one of the leading slavery defenders in his denomination. In 1851 he delivered a lecture in Buffalo, New York, with three major points: (1) slavery was not a sin because it was not forbidden in the Bible or in the teaching of the early church; (2) slavery was nonetheless a moral evil that should be eliminated; and (3) the abolition of slavery should be accomplished by purchasing slaves and by transporting them to Liberia. This plan, he emphasized, could only be effected with the consent of slaveholders in the southern states. Hopkins returned to these ideas on several occasions over the next decade. By the late 1850s, he became concerned that abolitionists in the North were pushing the southern states toward secession. To prevent disunion, he expressed his sympathy for slavery as it existed in the South, arguing that it was not cruel or immoral except in a few special cases. These comments led Alonzo Potter, the bishop of Pennsylvania, to comment that Hopkins's defense of slavery was "unworthy of any servant of Jesus Christ."

During the Civil War, Hopkins was loyal to the Union, but he had strong personal and professional ties to the South. At the General Convention of 1862, he tried to block efforts to censure southerners for seceding from the Union. He also strongly opposed the adoption of a pastoral letter supporting the Union cause because he believed the church should not take sides in the national conflict. Determined to prevent the dissension and bitterness that had earlier torn apart the Presbyterian, Methodist, and Baptist denominations, he had the names of his absent southern colleagues read at every vote taken in the House of Bishops. Hopkins became the presiding bishop of the church in January 1865. When the war ended a few months later, he was successful in reconciling the northern and southern dioceses without mentioning the moral and political issues over which the American people had been bitterly fighting. At the 1865 General Convention, southern bishops and deputies were officially welcomed to take their accustomed seats, and by 1866 all of the southern dioceses had returned to the Episcopal Church.

Hopkins died in Rock Point, Vermont, in January 1868.

Bibliography

A. *Christianity Vindicated* (Burlington, Vt., 1833); *The Primitive Creed* (Burlington, Vt., 1834); *The Primitive Church* (Burlington, Vt., 1835); *Essay on Gothic Architecture* (Burlington, Vt., 1836); *History of the Confessional* (New York, 1850); *A Scriptural, Ecclesiastical and Historical View of Slavery* (New York, 1864); *The Law of Ritualism* (New York, 1866).

B. *ANB* 11, 176; *BB,* 98–99; *DAB* 9, 212–13; *DCA,* 553; *EDC,* 254; *MM,* 373–76; John Henry Hopkins III, "John Henry Hopkins, First Bishop of Vermont," *HMPEC* 6 (1937): 187–206; DuBose Murphy, "The Spirit of Primitive Fellowship: The Reunion of the Church," *HMPEC* 17 (1948): 435–48; Ronald Levy, "Bishop Hopkins and the Dilemma of Slavery," *Pennsylvania Magazine of History and Biography* 91 (1967): 56–71; Robert Bruce Mullin, "Ritualism, Anti-Romanism, and the Law in John Henry Hopkins," *HMPEC* 50 (1981): 377–90; John Henry Hopkins Jr., *The Life of the Late Right Reverend John Henry Hopkins* (New York, 1873);

Charles F. Sweet, *A Champion of the Cross, Being the Life of John Henry Hopkins* (New York, 1894).

HUNTINGTON, FREDERIC DAN (28 May 1819, Hadley, Mass.–11 July 1904, Hadley, Mass.). *Education:* B.A., Amherst College, 1839; B.D., Harvard Divinity School, 1842. *Career:* Minister, South Congregational Church (Unitarian), Boston, 1842–55; editor, *Monthly Religious Magazine,* 1845–59; chaplain and professor of Christian morals, Harvard College, 1855–60; rector, Emmanuel Episcopal Church, Boston, 1861–69; bishop, diocese of Central New York, 1869–1904.

A bishop and important convert from Unitarianism, Frederic D. Huntington was born in western Massachusetts in 1819. After graduating from Amherst College and Harvard Divinity School, he entered the Unitarian ministry in 1842. He served as the minister at the South Congregational Society in Boston from 1842 until 1855, when he went to Harvard as preacher to the college and Plummer professor of Christian morals. He also edited the Unitarian *Monthly Religious Magazine* between 1845 and 1859.

During his relatively brief tenure at Harvard, Huntington struggled with his Unitarian faith and eventually decided to become an Episcopalian. His conversion was the result of several factors. On the one hand, he was troubled by the extent to which Unitarianism, then influenced by the transcendentalist movement, was giving short shrift to the Bible as a source of revelation. On the other hand, he was attracted by the prayer book liturgy and by the historic polity of the Episcopal Church, and he had come to believe in the doctrine of the Trinity and in the divinity of Christ. Huntington was confirmed in March 1860, and within a year he had been ordained both to the diaconate and to the priesthood. In 1861 he organized Emmanuel Church in Boston, where he served as rector until his consecration as bishop of the diocese of Central New York in April 1869. He was also father of James O.S. Huntington,* the founder of the Order of the Holy Cross.

As an Episcopal clergyman, Huntington became well known for his devotion to missionary work and to social betterment—a social conscience that was nurtured in part by his earlier involvement in urban institutions, especially prisons, while at Harvard. As the first bishop of Central New York, a post he held for 35 years, he attempted to bring Christian principles to bear on politics and business. In harmony with the social gospel movement, he looked for Christian answers to the problems of labor, criticizing an economic system in which wage earners were subject to the capricious control of their employers. He also urged other clergy to join him in efforts to resolve labor-management disputes, and for 17 years he served as the president of the Church Association for the Advancement of the Interests of Labor. He was attracted by Henry George's single-tax idea, supported women's suffrage, and opposed the acquisition of the Philippines after the Spanish-American War. In addition, he demonstrated a special regard for American Indians, working with the Onondagas, a tribe of the Iroquois Confederacy in upstate New York.

Throughout his ecclesiastical career, Huntington sought to benefit individuals and society at large without stressing religious affiliation, party allegiance, or extremes in ritual observances—a broad, ecumenical outlook derived in part from his own experience. He died in Hadley, Massachusetts, in July 1904.

Bibliography

A. Papers at the archives of Harvard University and at General Theological Seminary; *Sermons for the People* (Boston, 1856); *Divine Aspects of Human Society* (Boston, 1858); *Human Society: Its Providential Structure, Relations, and Offices* (New York, 1859); *Christian Believing and Living: Sermons by F. D. Huntington* (New York, 1860); *Helps to a Holy Lent* (New York, 1872); *Christ and the World* (New York, 1874); *The Fitness of Christianity to Men* (New York, 1878); *Christ in the Christian Year and in the Life of Man*, 2 vols. (New York, 1878–81); *Forty Days with the Master* (New York, 1891).

B. *ANB* 11, 539–40; *DAB* 9, 413–14; *DCA,* 562; *EDC,* 256; *NCAB* 3, 363; *SH* 5, 412; *WWWA* 1, 610; *NYT,* 12 July 1904; A. L. Byron-Curtiss, "Bishop Frederic Dan Huntington as I Knew Him," *HMPEC* 25 (1956): 378–90; Douglas C. Stange, "The Conversion of Frederic Dan Huntington (1859): A Failure of Liberalism?" *HMPEC* 37 (1968): 287–98; Arria S. Huntington, *Memoir and Letters of Frederic Dan Huntington* (Boston, 1906); George C. Richmond, *Frederic Dan Huntington* (Rochester, N.Y., 1908).

HUNTINGTON, JAMES OTIS SARGENT (23 July 1854, Boston–29 June 1935, West Park, N.Y.). *Education:* Studied at Boston Latin School; St. John's School, Manlius, N.Y.; B.A., Harvard College, 1875; studied at St. Andrew's Divinity School, 1876–79. *Career:* Assistant, Calvary Mission, Syracuse, N.Y., 1875–81; Holy Cross Mission, New York, 1881–89; professed, Order of the Holy Cross, 1884; superior, Order of the Holy Cross, 1884–88, 1897–1907, 1915–18, 1921–30.

James O.S. Huntington, the founder of the Order of the Holy Cross (OHC), was born in Boston in July 1854. He was the son of Frederic Dan Huntington,* then a Unitarian minister, and Hannah Dane Sargent Huntington. After studying at Harvard College and St. Andrew's Divinity School in Syracuse, New York, Huntington was ordained an Episcopal deacon in September 1878 and a priest in May 1880. He served for several years as an assistant at Calvary Mission in Syracuse but experienced a call to the monastic life while attending a retreat in Philadelphia in 1880. In response to this call, he associated himself with the Holy Cross Mission in New York City, where he and two other young priests, Robert S. Dod and James G. Cameron, ministered to the poor in the slums of the lower East Side. In 1881 Dod, Cameron, and Huntington adopted a simple habit and common rule in order to test their vocations. Dod and Cameron later withdrew, but Huntington persevered, and on November 25, 1884, he made his profession as the first member of the OHC before Henry Codman Potter,* assistant bishop of New York.

Huntington, an Anglo-Catholic, was as theologically conservative as he was socially liberal. He taught that the sacramental life was the motivating force behind the reconciliation of all races and classes. He also embraced monasticism in large part because of his commitment to the world beyond the monastery walls. Only through rigorous self-denial and total devotion of self, he believed, could one truly serve the poor and work to ameliorate the problems of society. During the summer of 1889, he worked as a common laborer among farmworkers in western New York to understand their condition more fully. Huntington's reading tastes were wide-ranging; he read not only theology and church history but also the latest work of socialist and progressive writers. He campaigned for better wages and conditions for working men and women, and he longed to see the church become, in his words, "the great Anti-Poverty Society." The church must be on the side of the poor, he said, "if she is going to live at all."

In 1887 Huntington played a leading role in founding the Church Association for the Advancement of the Interests of Labor (CAIL). Huntington's father was the president of CAIL for 17 years, and 47 bishops served as honorary vice-presidents. The organization helped secure the passage of pioneer legislation abolishing child labor in New York State. In addition, it investigated conditions in tenements and sweatshops, arbitrated strikes, and instituted the observance of Labor Sunday (the Sunday before Labor Day) in the Episcopal Church. With chapters in a number of cities, especially in the East, CAIL became known to unions as a friend of labor in the late nineteenth and early twentieth centuries.

In 1892 Lucretia Van Bibber offered, and Huntington accepted, the gift of a house in Westminster, Maryland. He moved there with two other priests to seek a deeper devotional life and to build a stronger community. The Holy Cross fathers lived in Westminster until 1904, when they moved to their present headquarters at West Park, New York, on the Hudson River. Over the years, Huntington became a well-known and beloved confessor, and the work of the OHC increasingly consisted of preaching missions, retreats, and spiritual direction. Possessing an extraordinary capacity to work and to love, Huntington was a gracious host at his monastery, a priest of great dignity and silence. At the time of his death in West Park in 1935, the OHC numbered 21 professed members and 2 novices.

Bibliography

A. "Beginnings of the Religious Life for Men in the American Church," *HMPEC* 2 (March 1933): 35–36; *Bargainers and Beggars: A Study of the Parable of the Laborers in the Vineyard* (West Park, N.Y., 1919); *The Work of Prayer,* 2nd ed. (West Park, N.Y., 1923); *The School of the Eternal* (West Park, N.Y., 1933).

B. *EDC,* 256; *WWWA* 1, 610; *NYT,* 30 June 1935; Robert William Adamson, "Father Huntington's Formative Years (1854–1892): Monasticism and Social Christianity" (Ph.D. diss., Columbia University, 1971); Vida Dutton Scudder, *Father Huntington, Founder of the Order of the Holy Cross* (New York, 1940).

HUNTINGTON, WILLIAM REED (20 September 1838, Lowell, Mass.–26 July 1909, Nahant, Mass.). *Education:* B.A., Harvard College, 1859; studied theology with Frederic D. Huntington, Boston, 1859–62. *Career:* Instructor in chemistry, Harvard College, 1859–60; curate, Emmanuel Church, Boston, 1861–62; rector, All Saints' Church, Worcester, Mass., 1862–83; rector, Grace Episcopal Church, New York, 1883–1909.

A liturgical reformer and early proponent of ecumenism, William Reed Huntington was born in Lowell, Massachusetts, in September 1838. After graduating from Harvard College in 1859, he studied theology under the tutelage of his distant cousin Frederic Dan Huntington.* He was ordained a deacon in October 1861 and a priest 14 months later. He served briefly as a curate at Emmanuel Church in Boston, where his cousin was rector; he then served for two lengthy periods as the rector of prominent parishes in Worcester, Massachusetts, and New York City.

Throughout his distinguished career, Huntington was committed to furthering the cause of church unity. In 1870 he published a widely remarked book on the subject, *The Church-Idea.* Writing in the period after the Civil War, Huntington was extremely concerned about national as well as church unity. Who spoke for Christians in the United States? he asked. If the Episcopal Church did not, then at least it held to principles that might one day form a basis for overcoming divisions among American ecclesiastical bodies. Huntington named four essentials for an ecumenical "Church of the Reconciliation": the Holy Scriptures as the Word of God; the primitive creeds (Apostles' and Nicene) as the rule of faith; Baptism and Eucharist as the two sacraments ordained by Jesus Christ; and the episcopate as the keystone of the church's polity. This four-sided platform came to be known as Huntington's "quadrilateral," and his idea was later adopted both by the House of Bishops of the Episcopal Church (in 1886) and by the bishops of the Anglican Communion (in 1888).

Huntington also attempted to modify the liturgy of the Episcopal Church through a revision of the 1789 *Book of Common Prayer.* An advocate of using contemporary language in worship, he sought to effect reforms that would make Episcopal church services more accessible to ordinary Americans. Although the prayer book that he and his colleagues proposed failed to gain acceptance at the 1886 General Convention, the one that was eventually adopted six years later, the 1892 *Book of Common Prayer,* contained many petitions composed by Huntington.

A leading figure in the broad church party, Huntington was sometimes called "the first presbyter" of the Episcopal Church. Long interested in ecclesiastical art and architecture, he contributed ideas for the design of the Cathedral of St. John the Divine in New York, where he served for 22 years as a trustee. With Mary Abbot Emery, he was also a prime mover behind the establishment of the order of deaconesses in 1889. Huntington died while on vacation in Nahant, Massachusetts, in July 1909.

Bibliography

A. Papers at AEC, at the Episcopal Divinity School in Cambridge, Massachusetts, and in
the archives of Grace Church, New York; *The Church-Idea: An Essay toward Unity*
(New York, 1870); *Conditional Immortality* (New York, 1878); *Materia Ritualis*
(Worcester, Mass., 1882); *The Book Annexed: Its Critics and Its Prospects* (New
York, 1886); *The Causes of the Soul* (New York, 1891); *The Spiritual House* (New
York, 1895); *A National Church* (New York, 1898); *Psyche: A Study of the Soul*
(New York, 1899); *Four Key Words of Religion* (New York, 1899); *Theology's
Eminent Domain, and Other Papers* (New York, 1902); *A Good Shepherd and
Other Sermons* (New York, 1906).

B. *ANB* 11, 547–48; *BB*, 107–9; *DAB* 9, 420–21; *DARB*, 260–61; *DCA*, 562; *EDC*, 256–
57; *HEC*, 188–91; *NCAB* 38, 131–32; *SH* 5, 412–13; *SPCK*, 146–52; *NYT*, 27 July
1909; Charles J. Minifie, "William Reed Huntington and Church Unity," *HMPEC*
35 (1966): 155–66; John F. Woolverton, "W.R. Huntington: Liturgical Renewal
and Church Unity in the 1880s," *ATR* 48 (1966): 175–99; John F. Woolverton,
"Huntington's Quadrilateral: A Critical Study," *CH* 39 (1970): 198–211; John F.
Woolverton, "Stirring the Religious Pot at Harvard on the Eve of the Civil War:
Two Huntingtons and a Cooke," *AEH* 58 (1989): 37–49; John W. Suter, *Life and
Letters of William Reed Huntington: A Champion of Unity* (New York, 1925).

I

INGLIS, CHARLES (1734, Glencolumbkille, Donegal, Ireland–24 February 1816, "Clermont" [summer home], near the Parish Church of Aylesford, Nova Scotia, Canada). *Education:* Largely self-educated. *Career:* Assistant master, the Free School (for German immigrants), Lancaster, Pa., 1755–58; missionary of the Society for the Propagation of the Gospel in Foreign Parts, Dover, Del., 1759–65; assistant rector, Trinity Church, New York, 1765–77; rector, Trinity Parish, New York, 1777–83; in England, 1784–87; bishop, diocese of Nova Scotia, 1787–1816.

An Anglican missionary to North America and later the first bishop appointed to a colony by the Church of England, Charles Inglis emigrated from Ireland to Pennsylvania in 1754. After teaching German immigrants for three years in a school in Lancaster, Pennsylvania, he was ordained and became a missionary in Dover, Delaware, with responsibility for all of Kent County. There he performed creditably, gaining a reputation as an outstanding preacher and a devoted minister of the gospel. He served as assistant rector of Trinity Church in New York between 1765 and 1777 and as rector of the parish between 1777 and 1783.

Like his friend and colleague Thomas B. Chandler,* Inglis was a high churchman and supported efforts to have a bishop for the colonies. A loyalist during the American Revolution, he wrote pamphlets attacking Congress, countering Thomas Paine's *Common Sense,* criticizing George Washington, and arguing against the substitution of an untried form of government (democracy) for a sound and stable monarchy. He continued to pray for the king of England even when George Washington and armed patriots were present in his congregation. He also served as a British army chaplain in New York. Attainted for high treason by the state of New York in 1779, he was one of the last loyalist clergy to flee the colonies, leaving New York when the British forces abandoned the city in November 1783.

In 1787 Inglis was appointed the first colonial bishop of Nova Scotia, which included jurisdiction over not only the Maritime provinces but also much of eastern Canada and Bermuda. Serving in Nova Scotia until his death in 1816, Inglis ministered to thousands of American loyalists in exile and (with his clerical assistants) founded 44 churches in that diocese.

Bibliography

A. *The True Interest of America Impartially Stated* (Philadelphia, 1776); *The Christian Soldier's Duty Briefly Delineated* (New York, 1777); *The Duty of Honoring the King, Explained and Recommended* (New York, 1780); *Dr. Inglis's Defence of His Character* (London, 1784).

B. *AAP* 5, 186–91; *ANB* 11, 657–58; *DAB* 9, 476; *DCA*, 576; *EDC*, 264; *HEC*, 56, 76–77, 86, 91; Morgan Dix, ed., *A History of the Parish of Trinity Church in the City of New York*, 7 vols. (New York, 1898); Reginald V. Harris, *Charles Inglis: Missionary, Loyalist, Bishop (1734–1816)* (Toronto, 1937); Brian Cuthbertson, *The First Bishop: A Biography of Charles Inglis* (Halifax, 1987).

IVES, LEVI SILLIMAN (16 September 1797, Meriden, Conn.–13 October 1867, Manhattanville, N.Y.). *Education:* Studied at Hamilton College, 1816; studied theology with John Henry Hobart, New York, and at General Theological Seminary, 1819–22. *Career:* Deacon, St. James' Church, Batavia, N.Y., 1822–23; rector, Trinity Church, Philadelphia, 1823–26; co-rector, St. James' Church, Lancaster, Pa., 1826–27; assistant minister, Christ Church, New York, 1827–28; rector, St. Luke's Church, New York, 1828–31; bishop, diocese of North Carolina, 1831–52; lecturer in rhetoric, St. Joseph's Seminary and St. John's College, and agent for Roman Catholic charities, New York, 1854–67.

An Episcopal bishop and prominent convert to Roman Catholicism during the Oxford movement controversy, Levi Silliman Ives was raised by Presbyterian parents in Connecticut. Although as a young man he thought about pursuing a career as a Presbyterian minister, he changed his mind after becoming convinced of the importance both of apostolic succession and of a liturgy that followed primitive Christian forms. This conviction led him to join the Episcopal Church in 1819. He studied theology under John Henry Hobart,* the bishop of New York (and later his father-in-law). After his ordination, Ives served in several parishes in New York and Pennsylvania before being elected the second bishop of North Carolina in 1831.

During his episcopate, Ives recruited clergy, established missions, and encouraged the evangelization of African American slaves. A strong supporter of schools for the young people of his diocese, he established academic institutions that emphasized Christian nurture in the doctrine, discipline, and worship of his church. Raleigh's Episcopal School of North Carolina for boys and St. Mary's School for girls opened in 1834 and 1842, respectively. Ives also founded a mission in Watauga County with the intention of using it as a base from which to evangelize the financially impoverished people of the mountainous western region of his state. Calling his mission Valle Crucis ("Valley of the Cross"), he hoped to train young men as teachers, catechists, and priests. This mission was to include an agricultural school and model farm, which were meant to provide instruction in modern methods of agriculture.

Ives became one of the best-known high church bishops of the first half of the nineteenth century. Strongly influenced by the Oxford movement, he founded a semi-monastic order, the Brotherhood of the Holy Cross, at Valle Crucis in 1847. Observers grew worried, however, that Ives had started to move away from the teachings of the Episcopal Church and was embracing practices borrowed from Roman Catholicism, including private confession to a priest and prayers to the Virgin Mary and the saints. In response to these concerns, he suppressed his brotherhood in 1848. That year, his diocesan convention held a hearing on Ives's theological positions, and he was forced to provide a written pledge that he would prohibit any liturgical practice not authorized by the Episcopal Church in the *Book of Common Prayer.* Despite this concession, Ives's own theological convictions continued to evolve until he was no longer able to accept that his denomination was a branch of the true catholic church. Obtaining a six-month leave of absence, he left for Europe with his wife in 1852, and on Christmas Day he was formally received by Pope Pius IX into the Roman Catholic Church. The following October, the House of Bishops formally deposed him from his episcopal office.

As a lay Roman Catholic, whose marriage barred him from the priesthood, Ives returned to New York City, where he served as a lecturer in rhetoric at St. Joseph's Seminary and St. John's College. Over the succeeding years his most important contributions were on behalf of Roman Catholic charities, especially the New York Catholic Protectory, which he founded in 1863 and served as president. He died in Manhattanville, New York, in 1867.

Bibliography

A. *Humility: A Ministerial Qualification* (New York, 1840); *The Apostles' Doctrine and Fellowship: Five Sermons* (New York, 1844); *The Obedience of Faith* (New York, 1849); *The Trials of a Mind in Its Progress to Catholicism: A Letter to His Old Friends* (Boston, 1854).

B. *ANB* 11, 723–24; *DAB* 9, 521–22; *DARB,* 266–67; *DCA,* 583–84; *EDC,* 270; *MM,* 228–34; *NCAB* 5, 409; *NCE* 7, 776–77; *SH* 6, 71; *NYT,* 14 October 1867; Michael T. Malone, "The Gentle Ives and the Unruly Prescott: Changes in the Church," *ATR* 69 (1987): 363–74; Richard Rankin, "Bishop Levi S. Ives and High Church Reform in North Carolina: Tractarianism as an Instrument to Elevate Clerical and Lay Piety," *AEH* 57 (1988): 298–319; Michael T. Malone, "Levi Silliman Ives: Priest, Bishop, Tractarian, and Roman Catholic" (Ph.D. diss., Duke University, 1970); Marshall D. Haywood, *Lives of the Bishops of North Carolina* (Raleigh, N.C., 1910); John O'Grady, *Levi Silliman Ives: Pioneer Leader in Catholic Charities* (New York, 1933); Blackwell P. Robinson, "The Episcopate of Levi Silliman Ives," in *The Episcopal Church in North Carolina, 1701–1959,* ed. Lawrence F. London and Sarah McCulloh Lemmon (Raleigh, N.C., 1987), 171–219.

J

JARRATT, DEVEREUX (17 January 1733, New Kent County, Va.–29 January 1801, Dinwiddie County, Va.). *Education:* Attended a local school until 1744–45; continued study on his own. *Career:* Rector, Bath Parish, Dinwiddie County, Va., 1763–1801.

One of the best known and most effective of the eighteenth-century Anglican clergy in the South, Devereux Jarratt was born in New Kent County, Virginia, the youngest of six children. Raised a nominal Anglican, he was far more interested as a young man in training racehorses and preparing gamecocks for competition than in Christianity. However, the influence of a family of "New Light" Presbyterians with whom he lived, together with spiritual reading and the advice of friends, eventually encouraged his conversion to a vital evangelical faith. Believing that he would have the greatest opportunity for Christian service as a priest in the Church of England, he sailed for London in October 1762 to be ordained. Returning to Virginia the following summer, he began 38 years of ministry at Bath Parish in Dinwiddie County, Virginia.

Traveling tirelessly through nearly 30 counties in Virginia and North Carolina, Jarratt played a major role in the southern phase of the Great Awakening. Between 1764 and 1772, he led religious revivals, undertook lengthy evangelistic tours (often preaching five days in the week), and organized religious societies designed to foster spiritual growth. He was very critical of other Anglican clergy, whom he accused of holding only lukewarm religious convictions. A forceful preacher himself, Jarratt begged his congregations to seek refuge in Jesus Christ, and, having done so, to "enter more and more into the Spirit of the gospel, and the depths of holiness."

In the early 1770s Jarratt joined forces with the Methodists and welcomed their work in reviving the spiritual life of southern Anglicanism. He became a close friend of Wesleyan leader Francis Asbury and cooperated with the Methodist itinerants who were sent into Virginia during that period. However, when the Methodists separated from the Church of England and organized the Methodist Episcopal Church in 1784, Jarratt reacted bitterly. He felt betrayed by his erstwhile colleagues who seemed to value independence over loyalty to ecclesiastical tradition. Toward the end of his career, when so much had changed in the churches as a result of the American Revolution, his effectiveness waned. He shunned not only the Methodists but also many of his fellow Episcopalians, who considered him to be merely a religious fanatic. During the last seven years of his life, Jarratt suffered from a painful and malignant tumor on the side of his face, which eventually caused his death in 1801.

Bibliography

A. *Sermons on Various and Important Subjects,* 3 vols. (Philadelphia, 1793–94); *Thoughts on Some Important Subjects in Divinity* (Baltimore, 1806); *The Life of the Reverend Devereux Jarratt* (1806; reprint, Cleveland, 1995).
B. *AAP* 5, 214–22; *ANB* 11, 870–71; *DAB* 9, 616–17; *DARB,* 270–71; *DCA,* 588–89; *EARH,* 352–53; *EDC,* 271–72; *ERS,* 346; *MM,* 1–25; *NCAB* 10, 118; Douglass Adair, "The Autobiography of Devereux Jarratt, 1732–1763," *WMQ,* 3d ser., 9 (1952): 346–93; Harry G. Rabe, "The Reverend Devereux Jarratt and the Virginia Social Order," *HMPEC* 33 (1964): 299–336; David L. Holmes, "Devereux Jarratt: A Letter and a Reevaluation," *HMPEC* 47 (1978): 37–49.

JOHNSON, SAMUEL (14 October 1696, Guilford, Conn.–6 January 1772, Stratford, Conn.). *Education:* Graduated from Collegiate School (later Yale College), 1714. *Career:* Schoolteacher, Guilford, Conn., 1714–16; tutor, Yale College, 1716–19; Congregational minister, West Haven, Conn., 1720–22; rector, Stratford, Conn., 1723–54, 1764–72; president, King's College, New York, 1754–63.

Samuel Johnson, who became a noted leader of the Anglican church in colonial New England, began his career as a Congregationalist minister in Connecticut. Between 1716 and 1722, his employment, first as a tutor at Yale College and then as the pastor of a nearby Congregational church, afforded him the opportunity to read widely in theology and church history. As a result of this reading, he adopted views of grace and free will that were much closer to Anglicanism than to Congregationalism. He warmly appreciated the *Book of Common Prayer* and became convinced of the necessity of episcopacy, believing that valid ministerial orders required a tangible connection with the church of apostolic times. In 1722 Johnson joined his classmate Daniel Brown, Yale's only tutor, and Timothy Cutler,* Yale's rector, in renouncing his Congregational orders—an event that became infamous in Congregational circles as the "Yale Apostasy."

Along with Brown and Cutler, Johnson sailed to England, where he was soon ordained an Anglican priest. He returned to America in 1723 as a missionary of the Society for the Propagation of the Gospel in Foreign Parts (SPG), and on Christmas Day in 1724, he opened the first Anglican church building in Connecticut, at Stratford. Over the years, Johnson became a leader among the SPG missionaries serving congregations in Connecticut, and he was a consistent advocate of an American episcopate.

He also became an intellectual disciple of the Irish philosopher George Berkeley, with whom he maintained a correspondence. Although he was not a particularly original thinker, Johnson did help to introduce in the colonies new themes in European thought, and his *Elementa Philosophica* (1752) was the first philosophy textbook published in America. Unlike the great Congregational theologian Jonathan Edwards, he defended belief in the freedom of the will and rejected the Calvinist doctrine of predestination as incompatible with true human freedom and morality.

In 1749 Johnson turned down an invitation to become president of the College of Philadelphia. In 1754, however, he reluctantly accepted a request to become the first president of King's College (now Columbia University) in New York. His nine years there were marred not only by institutional problems but also by personal tragedy, as epidemics of smallpox led to the deaths of two wives, a son, and a stepdaughter. Johnson returned to Stratford as rector in 1764, and he served there until his death in 1772.

Bibliography

A. *Elementa Philosophica* (Philadelphia, 1752); *Samuel Johnson, President of King's College: His Career and Writings,* ed. Herbert Schneider and Carol Schneider, 4 vols. (New York, 1929).

B. *AAP* 5, 52–61; *ANB* 12, 125–26; *DAB* 10, 118–19; *DCA,* 598; *MCTA,* 64–66; *NCAB* 6, 341; *SPCK,* 153–56; *WWWA* Historical vol. 1607–1896, 281; Don R. Gerlach, "Champions of an American Episcopate: Thomas Secker of Canterbury and Samuel Johnson of Connecticut," *HMPEC* 41 (1972): 381–414; George E. DeMille and Don R. Gerlach, "Samuel Johnson and the 'Dark Day' at Yale, 1772," *Connecticut History* 19 (1977): 38–63; Donald Francis Marc Gerardi, "Samuel Johnson and the Yale 'Apostasy' of 1722: The Challenge of Anglican Sacramentalism to the New England Way," *HMPEC* 47 (1978): 153–75; Donald Francis Marc Gerardi, "The American Doctor Johnson: Anglican Piety and the Eighteenth Century Mind" (Ph.D. diss., Columbia University, 1973); Eben Edwards Beardsley, *The Life and Correspondence of Samuel Johnson* (New York, 1874); Joseph John-Michael Ellis III, *The New England Mind in Transition: Samuel Johnson of Connecticut, 1696–1772* (New Haven, 1973); Peter N. Carroll, *The Other Samuel Johnson: A Psychohistory of Early New England* (Rutherford, N.J., 1978).

JONES, ABSALOM (6 November 1746, Sussex, Del.–13 February 1818, Philadelphia). *Education:* Self-taught. *Career:* Store clerk, Philadelphia, 1762–94; lay minister, later deacon and priest, St. Thomas African Episcopal Church, Philadelphia, 1794–1818.

The first African American to be ordained an Episcopal priest, Absalom Jones was born in slavery in Delaware in 1746. He was brought to Philadelphia by his master in 1762. Working as a clerk in his master's store, he gradually taught himself how to read and write, and in 1766 he began attending a night school operated by Quakers for the education of African Americans in the city. When he was 24, Jones married a slave woman named Mary, whose freedom he purchased in 1778. He was eventually able to purchase his own freedom as well in 1784.

Along with many other free blacks in Philadelphia, Jones attended St. George's Methodist Church. Thanks to the preaching skills of Richard Allen (who later became the founder of the African Methodist Episcopal Church), St. George's became increasingly popular among African Americans. This caused considerable friction with white church members, who resented having to share seating space with blacks. One Sunday morning in 1786, Jones was pulled from his knees while at prayer and told to move to another place in the building. This affront prompted the wholesale exodus of black parishioners from St. George's. Meeting in April 1787, this group, then under the leadership of Jones and Allen, formally organized the Free African Society. Although initially intended to be merely a benevolent society, the Free African Society evolved into a separate parish church. When an election was held in 1794 to determine the denomination with which the society would unite, the majority of parishioners voted in favor of the Episcopal Church. Thus, St. Thomas African Episcopal Church of Philadelphia became the first Episcopal parish organized and governed by African Americans.

After being licensed as a lay reader by William White,* the bishop of Pennsylvania, Jones was officially placed in charge of St. Thomas in October 1794. At its gathering in 1795, however, the Pennsylvania diocesan convention ruled that neither Jones nor the elected lay representatives of his parish were entitled to participate in its meetings—a discriminatory prohibition that remained in effect until the early 1860s. Jones was ordained a deacon in August 1795 and a priest in September 1804. From 1794 until his death, he not only served as a conscientious pastor at his church, but also was active in the formation of voluntary associations that pressed for the rights of African Americans and strengthened the black community in Philadelphia. He died at his home in 1818.

Bibliography

A. Papers at AEC; *A Narrative of the Proceedings of the Black People . . . in Philadelphia* (Philadelphia, 1794); "A Thanksgiving Sermon," in *Black Gospel / White Church,* ed. John M. Burgess (New York, 1982).

B. *ANB* 12, 176–77; *BB,* 53–54; *EAAR,* 404–5; *EARH,* 358–59; *DANB,* 363–64; Ann C. Lammers, "The Rev. Absalom Jones and the Episcopal Church: Christian Theology and Black Consciousness in a New Alliance," *HMPEC* 51 (1982): 159–84; George F. Bragg, *History of the Afro-American Group of the Episcopal Church* (Baltimore, 1922); George F. Bragg, *Heroes of the Eastern Shore: Absalom Jones, the First of the Blacks* (Baltimore, 1939).

K

KEMPER, JACKSON (24 December 1789, Pleasant Valley, Dutchess County, N.Y.–24 May 1870, Delafield, Wis.). *Education:* Graduated from Columbia College, 1809; studied theology with Benjamin Moore and John Henry Hobart, New York. *Career:* Assistant minister, United Parishes of Christ Church, St. Peter's, and St. James', Philadelphia, 1811–31; rector, St. Paul's Church, Norwalk, Conn., 1831–35; missionary bishop of Indiana and Missouri, 1835–38; missionary bishop of the Northwest, 1838–59; bishop, diocese of Wisconsin, 1854–70.

Jackson Kemper, the first missionary bishop of the Episcopal Church, was born in Pleasant Valley, New York, in 1789. After graduating from Columbia College in New York City, he studied for the ordained ministry under Benjamin Moore and the influential high church leader John Henry Hobart.* Ordained a deacon in 1811 and a priest in 1814, he served for 20 years as the parish assistant of Bishop William White* in Philadelphia. Vitally interested in missions, Kemper was the principal leader of the Society for the Advancement of Christianity in Pennsylvania, a diocesan organization that supported missionaries in the more remote corners of the state. He made missionary tours of western Pennsylvania in 1812 and again in 1814, when he also ventured into Ohio, and he accompanied White on a visit to the western portion of his diocese in 1826.

In 1835, the Episcopal Church decided to make evangelism a churchwide responsibility and to create missionary districts to which bishops would be sent. Immediately after that decision was made, Kemper was elected to oversee and develop a jurisdiction that eventually included the present-day states of Indiana, Iowa, Kansas, Minnesota, Missouri, Nebraska, and Wisconsin—a vast region in which Episcopal membership lagged far behind that of other denominations. Influenced by Kemper's high church beliefs, a strong Catholic ethos soon developed among the clergy and laity of the Episcopal Church in that area. Facing a chronic shortage of clergy, Kemper traveled back East not only to recruit priests but also to raise funds to support a school that would train men for ordained ministry in his missionary district. Addressing the students of General Theological Seminary in May 1840, he spoke honestly and effectively about the challenges of mission work. James Lloyd Breck,* a second-year student at the seminary, heard Kemper's call for "self-denying" associates. Leaving for Wisconsin with two other young men after their graduation in 1841, Breck helped organize the community that became Nashotah House seminary.

Although he was elected bishop of Maryland in 1838, Kemper chose at that time to remain at his post. However, in 1854 he accepted election as the bishop of Wisconsin, which had just been organized as an independent diocese; five years later he resigned from his position as missionary bishop. Often called the "apostle of the Northwest," Kemper's accomplishments were prodigious: he founded Racine College in Wisconsin, consecrated one hundred church buildings, ordained two hundred men, and confirmed ten thousand people during the course of his episcopate. He died at his home in Delafield, Wisconsin, in 1870 and was buried on the grounds of Nashotah House.

Bibliography

A. Papers at the Wisconsin State Historical Society; James Arthur Muller, ed., "Two Letters from Bishop Kemper," *HMPEC* 14 (1945): 302–6; "The Duty of the Church with Respect to Missions, 1841" in *DW,* 120–26.
B. *ACAB* 3, 512; *ANB* 12, 548–49; *BB,* 80–81; *BHEC,* 62–65; *DAB* 10, 321; *ECUS,* 140–44; *EDC,* 285; *HAEC,* 257–60; *HPEC,* 217–24; *NCAB* 7, 57–58; *SBAE,* 117–19; Edward R. Hardy, "Kemper's Missionary Episcopate, 1835–1859," *HMPEC* 4 (1935): 195–218; E. Clowes Chorley, "The Missionary March of the Episcopal Church: Jackson Kemper and the Northwest," *HMPEC* 17 (1948): 3–17; Jack Richardson, "Kemper College of Missouri," *HMPEC* 30 (1961): 111–26; Greenough White, *An Apostle of the Western Church: Memoir of Jackson Kemper* (New York, 1900); George C. Tanner, *Fifty Years of Church Work in the Diocese of Minnesota, 1857–1907* (St. Paul, Minn., 1909); *Beyond the Horizon: Frontiers for Mission,* ed. Charles R. Henery (Cincinnati, 1986).

L

LAWRENCE, WILLIAM (30 May 1850, Boston–6 November 1941, Milton, Mass.) *Education:* B.A., Harvard College, 1871; studied at Andover Theological Seminary and the Philadelphia Divinity School, 1872–75; B.D., Episcopal Theological School, 1875. *Career:* Assistant, Grace Church, Lawrence, Mass., 1876–77; rector, Grace Church, Lawrence, Mass., 1877–83; professor of homiletics and pastoral care, Episcopal Theological School, 1884–88; vice-dean, Episcopal Theological School, 1888–89; dean, Episcopal Theological School, 1889–93; bishop, diocese of Massachusetts, 1893–1927.

William Lawrence, a bishop and seminary dean, was born in Boston in May 1850. He was the son of Amos Adams Lawrence, an important New England merchant and businessman, and Sarah Elizabeth Appleton. Raised in an environment of wealth and privilege, William graduated from Harvard College in 1871 and from the Episcopal Theological School (ETS) in Cambridge in 1875. He was ordained a deacon in June 1875 and a priest 12 months later. While at Harvard, he came under the influence of the great broad church leader Phillips Brooks,* who had recently become rector of Trinity Church in Boston. Brooks helped nurture in Lawrence a tolerant and liberal religious faith.

Lawrence began his ministry in 1876 as the assistant to George Packard, the rector of Grace Church in Lawrence, Massachusetts. A city north of Boston, Lawrence contained large numbers of working-class people, many of whom were employed in mills owned and operated by William Lawrence's relatives. Although Lawrence confessed that he "knew only the point of view of the capitalist" when he began his work in 1876, over the next few months he was able to gain some knowledge of the everyday lives of the city's millworkers. After Packard's death, Lawrence was chosen to succeed him as rector. He remained in that position until 1883. In January 1884, he became professor of homiletics and pastoral care at

ETS. After serving as the school's vice-dean for a year, he became the fourth dean of ETS in 1889. Lawrence stayed there for only four years, but many believe that he led the seminary during its "flowering period." After the death of Phillips Brooks, then serving as the bishop of Massachusetts, Lawrence was elected as his successor. The first ETS graduate to become a bishop, he was consecrated in October 1893.

Lawrence's lengthy episcopate was a remarkable period of growth and transformation both in the diocese of Massachusetts and in the Episcopal Church as a whole. First, Lawrence oversaw the division of his diocese into two parts. Because of the size of the Episcopal population in Massachusetts, it was difficult for the bishop to visit regularly every parish in the state. The diocese was cut in two in 1901, therefore, and a new diocese was created, Western Massachusetts, which comprised the central and western portions of the state. Second, to achieve greater unity among the parishes that remained under his care, Lawrence emphasized the need for "a visible expression" of the episcopal nature of their organization. At a time when the idea of a separate cathedral still seemed novel, Lawrence chose St. Paul's Church, a parish in Boston, and set it apart as the "Cathedral of St. Paul" in October 1912. Third, Lawrence worried that the average Episcopal clergyman was unable to accumulate sufficient funds for his retirement. Hoping to improve this situation, he introduced a resolution at the 1910 General Convention calling for a study of clerical support. This effort eventually resulted in the creation of a mandatory national pension plan for Episcopal clergy in 1916. Having led the movement to establish what became known as the Church Pension Fund, Lawrence helped raise over $8 million so that the plan could begin its operations.

Lawrence retired in 1927 but remained active in church life for many more years. He continued to serve as a member of the National Council and as president of the Church Pension Fund. In addition, he was given oversight of the small group of Episcopal churches that were located in Europe. At the time of his death in 1941, he was the oldest living bishop of the Episcopal Church.

Bibliography

A. Papers at the archives of the diocese of Massachusetts in Boston and at the archives of the Episcopal Divinity School in Cambridge, Massachusetts; *Phillips Brooks, a Study* (Boston, 1903); *Fifty Years* (Boston, 1923); *Memories of a Happy Life* (Boston, 1926); *Life of Phillips Brooks* (New York, 1930).
B. *ANB* 13, 290–91; *DAB* supp. 3, 446–48; *EDC,* 295; *WWWA* 1, 710; obituary, *TLC,* 19 November 1941; Henry K. Sherrill, *William Lawrence: Later Years of a Happy Life* (Cambridge, Mass., 1943); James Arthur Muller, *The Episcopal Theological School, 1867–1943* (Cambridge, Mass., 1943); Dudley Tyng, *Massachusetts Episcopalians, 1607–1957* (Boston, 1960); Harold C. Martin, *"Outlasting Marble and Glass": The History of the Church Pension Fund* (New York, 1986).

LEE, ROBERT EDWARD (19 January 1807, "Stratford," Westmoreland County, Va.–12 October 1870, Lexington, Va.) *Education:* Graduated from the U.S. Military Academy at West Point, 1829. *Career:* Brevet second lieutenant to colonel, U.S. army, 1829–61; superintendent, U.S. Military Academy at West Point, 1852–56; general, Confederate army, 1861–65; president, Washington College (later renamed Washington and Lee University), Lexington, Va., 1865–70.

The premier Confederate general in the Civil War as well as an active Episcopal layman, Robert E. Lee was born at his family's plantation on the Potomac River in Virginia in 1807. He was the son of a devout mother, Ann Carter Lee, from whom he received his early religious training, and of a famous but unstable father, Revolutionary War cavalry officer and former Virginia governor "Light Horse Harry" Lee. Robert grew up admiring George Washington above all, and at age 24 he married Mary Ann Randolph Custis, the pious daughter of George Washington Parke Custis, grandson of Martha Washington.

After graduating from West Point in 1829, Lee began a distinguished army career that included service in the Mexican War (1846–48) and a term as superintendent of the Military Academy. The secession crisis of 1861 confronted him with the question of whether to continue his service in the U.S. army or to join the Confederate cause. Although he revered the Union and had doubts about the merits of secession, in the end he decided that his first allegiance lay with his native state of Virginia. In June 1862 he received command of the Confederate army of Northern Virginia, a position he held until the end of the Civil War. After surrendering his army at Appomattox, Virginia, in April 1865, Lee applied for a pardon and urged other ex-Confederates to obey the civil authorities. Southerners, he believed, should accept the outcome of the conflict and focus on the future. With this goal in mind, he assumed the presidency of Washington College, a small, struggling institution of higher learning in Lexington, Virginia, and improved it both academically and financially.

Lee was a lifelong Episcopalian. Before he could read, he learned the catechism from William Meade,* the rector of Christ Church, Alexandria, and later bishop of Virginia. Although a thoughtful and sincere Christian, Lee never underwent a dramatic conversion experience. In fact, he was not confirmed until 1853, on the same day that two of his daughters were confirmed. During his more than 35 years in the army, he kept the Sabbath, served on vestries, and made substantial contributions to parishes and other church institutions. When he was commanding a cavalry regiment in Texas during the 1850s, he presided at the burials of soldiers and, on one occasion at the parents' request, read the funeral service for a small boy who had died in camp. During the Civil War, he periodically called for days of corporate prayer, either to give thanks to God for a victory or to repent of the personal moral failings that had contributed to defeat in battle. When a religious revival swept through the Confederate military forces in 1863, Lee also frequently attended prayer meetings with his soldiers.

Almost immediately after his arrival in Lexington in September 1865, Lee was elected to the vestry of Grace Church, where William Nelson Pendleton, the former chief of artillery in his army, served as rector. Lee played a very active role in the parish, and his last public act was on behalf of the church. At a meeting of the Grace Church vestry, the final budget item to be reviewed was Pendleton's salary. When it became apparent that pledged funds fell short of the amount necessary to increase the rector's pay, Lee said, "I will give that sum." Within the hour, however, he suffered a stroke, and, after lingering for two weeks, he died. In his honor, the parish was renamed the R. E. Lee Memorial Church, making it one of the few Episcopal churches to be named after an American.

With the death of Lee the man in 1870, a second, mythical figure was born. Lee's legend, which remained strong well into the twentieth century, was rooted in the image of him as the archetypal Christian gentleman. After the Civil War, he was not only revered as a Christian knight throughout white southern society but compared to Christ. As Jesus had suffered at Calvary, they reasoned, Lee had undergone humbling at Appomattox. The subject of countless biographies, pictures, monuments, and memorial addresses, the mythical Lee had a major impact on the development of popular religion in the South in the late nineteenth and early twentieth centuries.

Bibliography:

A. J. William Jones, *Personal Reminiscences, Anecdotes, and Letters of Gen. Robert E. Lee* (New York, 1875); Robert E. Lee [Jr.], *Recollections and Letters of General Robert E. Lee* (Garden City, N.Y., 1904); J. William Jones, *Life and Letters of Robert Edward Lee: Soldier and Man* (New York, 1906).

B. *ANB* 13, 392–97; *DAB* 6, 120–29; *DCA,* 640–41; *EDC,* 299; Marshall W. Fishwick, "Robert E. Lee, Churchman," *HMPEC* 30 (1961): 251–65; Emory M. Thomas, "God and General Lee," *AEH* 60 (1991): 15–24; Gamaliel Bradford, *Lee the American* (Boston, 1912); Douglas Southall Freeman, *R. E. Lee: A Biography,* 4 vols. (New York, 1934–35); Thomas L. Connelly, *The Marble Man: Robert E. Lee and His Image in American Society* (New York, 1977); Charles Bracelen Flood, *Lee: The Last Years* (Boston, 1981); Emory M. Thomas, *Robert E. Lee: A Biography* (New York, 1995); Robert R. Brown, *"And One Was a Soldier": The Spiritual Pilgrimage of Robert E. Lee* (Shippensburg, Pa., 1998); Michael Fellman, *The Making of Robert E. Lee* (New York, 2000).

LE JAU, FRANCIS (1665, Angers, France–15 September 1717, Goose Creek, S.C.). *Education:* M.A., Trinity College, Dublin, 1693. *Career:* Canon, St. Paul's Cathedral, London, 1696–1700; missionary in the West Indies, 1700–1706; rector, St. James Church, Goose Creek, S.C., 1706–17; Anglican commissary and rector, St. Philip's Church, Charleston, 1717.

An Anglican clergyman and missionary in colonial South Carolina, Francis Le Jau was born in France. Although little is known of his early life, his parents were Huguenots, and he moved to England in 1685, presumably to escape the persecution of French Protestants that followed the revocation of the Edict of Nantes. Like many Huguenots, he converted to Anglicanism after reaching England. Ordained a priest of the Church of England, he served for four years at St. Paul's Cathedral in London before being sent to Antigua in the West Indies as a missionary of the Society for the Propagation of the Gospel in Foreign Parts (SPG). In 1706 the SPG appointed him to be a missionary in South Carolina, and soon after his arrival in that colony, he was elected rector of St. James Church in Goose Creek (located in the low country outside of Charleston).

Le Jau took an exceptionally active interest in the evangelization of both American Indians and enslaved Africans in his parish. Although he never challenged the institution of slavery, he braved the opposition of many planters who objected to the religious instruction he offered to their slaves. To calm the fears of slaveholders about the liberating implications of the Christian gospel, he required any slave whom he converted to take an oath prior to his or her baptism. When enslaved Africans were baptized, they swore in the presence of their masters that they did not believe that the sacrament freed them from their civil status as slaves. They also agreed neither to practice polygamy nor to take part in the "feasts, dances, and merry meetings" (i.e., the remnants of traditional African religious customs) in which other slaves often participated on Sundays and holidays. Despite this heavy-handed requirement, most slaveholders in Le Jau's parish still continued to resist his evangelistic efforts.

In July 1717 the bishop of London not only made Le Jau his commissary in South Carolina but also appointed him rector of St. Philip's Church in Charleston. However, he became ill and died in Goose Creek before he was able to assume that new position.

Bibliography

A. *The Carolina Chronicle of Dr. Francis Le Jau, 1706–1717,* ed. Frank J. Klingberg (Berkeley, 1956).

B. *ANB* 13, 460–61; *DAB* 11, 158; *EDC,* 299; *WWWA* Historical vol. 1607–1896, 311; Arthur Henry Hirsch, "Reverend Francis Le Jau, First Rector of St. James Church, Goose Creek, S.C.," *Transactions of the Huguenot Society of South Carolina* 34 (1929): 25–47; Frank J. Klingberg, "The Indian Frontier in South Carolina as Seen by the S.P.G. Missionary," *Journal of Southern History* 5 (1939): 479–500; S. C. Bolton, "South Carolina and the Reverend Francis Le Jau: Southern Society and the Conscience of an Anglican Missionary," *HMPEC* 40 (1971): 63–80; Robert S. Matteson, "Francis Le Jau in Ireland," *South Carolina Historical Magazine* 78 (1977): 83–91; Annette Laing, " 'Heathens and Infidels'? African Christianization and Anglicanism in the South Carolina Low Country, 1700–1750," *Religion and American Culture* 12 (2002): 197–228; Edgar Legare Pennington, *The Reverend Francis Le Jau's Work among Indians and Negro Slaves* (Baton Rouge, La., 1935).

M

MANNING, WILLIAM THOMAS (12 May 1866, Northampton, England–18 November 1949, New York). *Education:* B.D., School of Theology of the University of the South, 1894. *Career:* Curate, Calvary Church, Memphis, Tenn., 1889–91; rector, Trinity Church, Redlands, Calif., 1891–93; professor of systematic divinity, School of Theology of the University of the South, 1893–95; priest-in-charge, Trinity Mission, Cincinnati, 1895–96; rector, Church of St. John the Evangelist, Lansdowne, Pa., 1896–98; rector, Christ Church, Nashville, Tenn., 1898–1903; vicar, St. Agnes' Chapel of Trinity Parish, New York, 1903–4; assistant rector, Trinity Church, New York, 1904–8; rector, Trinity Church, New York, 1908–21; bishop, diocese of New York, 1921–46.

William T. Manning, an influential high church bishop in the early twentieth century, was born in May 1866 in Northampton, England. Little is known about his childhood, but when he was 16 years of age, he emigrated to the United States with his family. The Mannings settled first in Nebraska and later in San Diego, California, where William became active in St. Paul's Church. The most crucial event in his early spiritual development was his decision to enter the School of Theology of the University of the South in Sewanee, Tennessee. At Sewanee he studied with the theologian William Porcher DuBose* and assisted him in the writing and publication of *The Soteriology of the New Testament* (1892). DuBose helped Manning to see that the church's teachings on the Incarnation and the sacraments were consistent with scientific and historical thought. Manning was also encouraged by DuBose to define his faith broadly and to nurture a piety that was experiential and evangelical.

Manning was ordained to the diaconate in December 1889 and to the priesthood two years later. Between 1889 and 1903, he served as a parish minister in Tennessee, California, Ohio, and Pennsylvania and as a professor at Sewanee. In

1903 Morgan Dix, the rector of Trinity Church in New York City, invited Manning to become vicar of St. Agnes' Chapel, a small congregation supported by Trinity parish. Manning accepted the invitation and moved to New York. He served at St. Agnes' for a year and then became the assistant rector at Trinity. When Dix died in 1908, the parish vestry chose Manning as their new rector. Leading one of the most prominent and wealthy parishes in the Episcopal Church, Manning quickly gained recognition throughout his denomination. He served on the Board of Missions, represented his diocese at the General Conventions of 1910 and 1913, and joined with Charles Henry Brent* and others in calling for an ecumenical conference on faith and order. At Trinity Church, he improved the condition of the tenement houses the parish owned, cancelled mortgages Trinity held on other churches, and sponsored the construction of the Chapel of the Intercession.

In 1921 Manning accepted election as bishop of New York after previously declining similar offers from the diocesan conventions of Harrisburg and Western New York. During his tenure as bishop, he started a building campaign that resulted in further construction on the Cathedral of St. John the Divine in Morningside Heights. Started in 1892 but still unfinished in 1921, the cathedral was designed to be the largest Gothic cathedral in the world. The great nave was completed in 1939, and the whole length of the cathedral was opened in 1941. Manning was also an advocate of human rights, and in 1933 he spoke out against the persecution of Jews in both Germany and the Soviet Union. An Anglophile as well as an opponent of Nazism, he strongly urged American support for Great Britain and the Allied cause in 1940.

Manning, an Anglo-Catholic, said that he decided to enter the ministry because of the example of his father, a layman who had been strongly influenced by the Oxford movement. Embodying a Catholic emphasis on the necessity of the historic episcopate for a valid ministry, Manning opposed the participation of the Episcopal Church in the 1914 Panama Conference, which supported cooperative Protestant missions in Latin America. For the same reason he fought against proposals for union with the Presbyterians during the 1930s and 1940s. Since the Presbyterian Church lacked the apostolic succession through the historical episcopate, Manning did not think Episcopalians had anything to gain from ecumenical discussions with that denomination. He did, however, support ecumenical efforts that included the Roman Catholic and Eastern Orthodox traditions.

Taking part in the modernist-fundamentalist dispute in the 1920s, Manning drafted the House of Bishops' letter on modernism and the Virgin Birth in 1923. In it he distinguished between assent to facts and personal surrender to God, and he stated his belief that Episcopalians could use the methods of modern historical science as long as they maintained this deeper evangelical faith. Because of his Anglo-Catholic background, he did not believe in biblical inerrancy, but he thought it was the church's task to protect the truth of the gospel. In this context he often quoted his mentor W. P. DuBose, who emphasized that the creeds were "not true because the Church says so, but . . . the Church says so because they are true."

Suffering from cancer, Manning retired as bishop in December 1946. He died in New York City three years later, and his body was enshrined in a tomb in the Cathedral of St. John the Divine.

Bibliography

A. Papers at the General Theological Seminary and the archives of the diocese of New York; *The Call to Unity* (New York, 1920); *Neither Fundamentalism nor Modernism* (New York, 1923); *Be Strong in the Lord* (New York, 1947).
B. *ANB* 14, 445–46; *DAB* supp. 4, 546–48; *EDC,* 318; *SPCK,* 169–70; John H. Seabrook, "William Thomas Manning: A Study of Christian Unity," *HMPEC* 34 (1965): 147–70; John H. Seabrook, "Bishop Manning and World War I," *HMPEC* 36 (1967): 301–22; Charles Thorley Bridgeman, *A History of the Parish of Trinity Church in the City of New York* (New York, 1962); W.D.F. Hughes, *Prudently with Power: William Thomas Manning, Tenth Bishop of New York* (West Park, N.Y., 1964); James Elliott Lindsley, *This Planted Vine: A Narrative History of the Episcopal Diocese of New York* (New York, 1984), chapter 13; William H. Katerberg, *Modernity and the Dilemma of North American Anglican Identities, 1880–1950* (Montreal, 2001), chapter 6.

MCGUIRE, GEORGE ALEXANDER (26 March 1866, Sweets, Antigua, B.W.I.–10 November 1934, New York). *Education:* Graduated from Mico College, Antigua, B.W.I., 1886; graduated from Moravian Theological Seminary, Nisky, St. Thomas, Danish W.I., 1888; studied for the Episcopal ministry under Henry L. Phillips, Philadelphia, 1894–96; M.D., Boston College of Physicians and Surgeons, 1910. *Career:* Pastor, Moravian church, Frederiksted, St. Croix, 1888–94; priest, St. Andrew's Church, Cincinnati, 1897–99; priest, St. Philip's Church, Richmond, Va., 1899–1901; rector, St. Thomas African Episcopal Church, Philadelphia, 1901–5; archdeacon for Colored Work, diocese of Arkansas, 1905–9; rector, St. Bartholomew's Church, Cambridge, Mass., 1909–11; field secretary, American Church Institute for Negroes, 1911–13; rector, St. Paul's Church, Falmouth, Antigua, B.W.I., 1913–18; rector, (Independent Episcopal) Church of the Good Shepherd, New York, 1919–20; chaplain-general, Universal Negro Improvement Association, 1920–21; bishop (later archbishop and patriarch), African Orthodox Church, 1921–34.

George Alexander McGuire, an Episcopal priest and founder of the African Orthodox Church, was born in the British West Indies in 1866. The son of an Anglican father and a Moravian mother, he was baptized in his father's church but educated in his mother's tradition. After graduating in 1888 from the Moravian seminary at Nisky, St. Thomas, he served as pastor of a Moravian congregation in Frederiksted, St. Croix. In 1894 he emigrated to the United States, and a year later he was confirmed in the Episcopal Church. Deciding to seek ordination as an Episcopalian, he studied for the ministry under the tutelage of Henry

L. Phillips, a West Indian priest who led the Church of the Crucifixion in Philadelphia. McGuire was ordained a deacon in 1896 and a priest in 1897. Holding
a succession of church-related positions over the next two decades, he sought to
strengthen and improve the tenuous position of blacks within the Episcopal
Church.

In 1913 McGuire returned to the West Indies to serve as rector of St. Paul's
Church, Falmouth, in his native Antigua. During this period, he learned about the
black nationalist ideas of Marcus Garvey, whose emphasis on racial independence
rather than on assimilation with whites had a major effect on McGuire's thinking.
Convinced that whites were incapable of treating black Anglicans as their equals,
McGuire submitted his resignation to the bishop of Antigua in 1918 and traveled
back to the United States. He settled in New York City in Harlem, where he
became involved in Garvey's Universal Negro Improvement Association and was
soon elected chaplain-general of the organization. Seeking to create a separate
denomination that would especially appeal to black Anglo-Catholics from the
West Indies, McGuire organized the Independent Episcopal Church, later renamed
the African Orthodox Church (AOC), in September 1921. The AOC adopted a
constitution and declaration of faith that affirmed traditional Catholic doctrines
and liturgical practices, and McGuire was chosen as its first bishop. After unsuccessful attempts to obtain ordination from Episcopal, Roman Catholic, and Russian Orthodox bishops, McGuire was eventually consecrated by Joseph René
Vilatte, a bishop of the Old Catholic Church of America.

By the mid-1920s, the AOC had gained approximately 12,000 adherents, with
congregations mainly in the northeastern United States and in the Caribbean.
McGuire, who in 1927 was raised to the rank of patriarch in his denomination,
also founded a theological seminary and a journal, *The Negro Churchman*. He
died in New York City in November 1934.

Bibliography

A. "What Is in Thine Hand," in Randall K. Burkett, *Black Redemption: Churchmen Speak
    for the Garvey Movement* (Philadelphia, 1978); *The Universal Negro Ritual* ([New
    York], 1921).
B. *ANB* 15, 76–78; *DANB*, 416–17; *DCA*, 689; *EAAR*, 474–75; *EDC*, 326–27; *WWWA* 1,
    813; Gavin White, "Patriarch McGuire and the Episcopal Church," *HMPEC* 39
    (1969): 109–41; Byron Rushing, "A Note on the Origin of the African Orthodox
    Church," *Journal of Negro History* 57 (1972): 37–39; Arthur Cornelius Terry-
    Thompson, *The History of the African Orthodox Church* (n.p., 1956); Randall
    Burkett, *Garveyism as a Religious Movement: The Institutionalization of Black
    Civil Religion* (Metuchen, N.J., 1978); Elias Farajajé-Jones, *In Search of Zion: The
    Spiritual Significance of Africa in Black Religious Movements* (Bern, 1990); Harold
    T. Lewis, *Yet with a Steady Beat: The African American Struggle for Recognition
    in the Episcopal Church* (Valley Forge, Pa., 1996), 100–106.

MCILVAINE, CHARLES PETTIT (18 January 1799, Burlington, N.J.–13
March 1873, Florence, Italy). *Education:* Graduated from the College of New

Jersey (now Princeton University), 1816; private theological study, 1816–17, 1819–20; studied at Princeton Theological Seminary, 1817–19. *Career:* Rector, Christ Church, Georgetown, D.C., 1820–24; chaplain and professor of geography, history, and ethics, U.S. Military Academy at West Point, 1825–27; rector, St. Ann's Church, Brooklyn, N.Y., 1827–32; bishop, diocese of Ohio, 1832–73.

A bishop and leading figure in the evangelical party of the mid-nineteenth century, Charles Pettit McIlvaine was the son of a prominent lawyer (later U.S. senator) in New Jersey. After graduating from the College of New Jersey in 1816, he studied theology at Princeton Theological Seminary, which was strongly Calvinist in its theological orientation. Ordained in 1820, he served as rector of Christ Church in Georgetown from 1820 to 1824 and as chaplain of the Senate for one year during that period. Appointed chaplain and professor at the U.S. Military Academy in 1825, McIlvaine was an outstanding preacher who had a profound influence on the corps of cadets. His call for a personal, heartfelt faith led to a spiritual awakening at West Point; among those converted by his preaching was Cadet Leonidas Polk,* who later became the first bishop of Louisiana and a Confederate general. After serving for six years as rector of St. Ann's, Brooklyn, and for part of that time (1831–32) as professor of Christian evidences at the University of the City of New York, McIlvaine was elected as the second bishop of Ohio, succeeding Philander Chase.*

Consecrated in 1832, McIlvaine quickly rose to prominence as a controversialist in the Episcopal Church. An unbending critic of the Oxford movement, he published a book, *Oxford Divinity* (1841), which was the first sustained assault on Tractarianism by an American evangelical. In it he criticized the Tractarians for leading their followers to Rome (he called their beliefs and practices "thoroughly Popish"), for obscuring the Protestant doctrine of justification by grace through faith, and for failing to adhere to either the Bible or the Thirty-nine Articles of Anglicanism. The title of an 1846 volume clearly indicates his point of view on another disputed subject: *Reasons for Refusing to Consecrate a Church Having an Altar Instead of a Communion Table.* McIlvaine said that he preferred "an honest table with legs" to a stone altar. Critical of ritualism, Roman Catholicism, and religious rationalism, McIlvaine also warned against the excesses of evangelicalism—against what he called "excitement" and "animal feeling." He cautioned the clergy of his diocese about adopting the "new measures" revivalism then enjoying great popularity. Emphasizing the need for a steadfast faith and the gradual development of Christian character through the church, he advocated growth in the "peaceful love of God," promoted by prayer, adherence to truth, and patient attention to the teaching and example of Jesus.

At the outbreak of the Civil War in 1861, at the time of the "Trent Affair," President Abraham Lincoln chose McIlvaine to go to England as his special emissary. To prevent Confederate commissioners from reaching their posts in London and Paris, an American warship had halted a British mail packet, the *Trent,* and forcibly removed the Confederate diplomats. This act provoked a wave of anti-American feeling and indignation in Great Britain. Although McIlvaine had doubts about the propriety of his acting in a quasi-political role, he accepted Lincoln's invitation to aid his country's war effort. He proved to be an adept diplomat, and his mission was successful in keeping Great Britain out of the war. The archbishop of Canterbury later wrote of McIlvaine's mission, "Few men living have done so much to draw England and the United States together."

Never robust, McIlvaine endured considerable difficulties in his constant and arduous travels throughout Ohio. But thanks to his untiring efforts, the diocese grew considerably during his long episcopate: from 40 to 116 parishes, from 900 to approximately 15,000 communicants, and from 17 to 108 clergy. He also helped to strengthen Kenyon College and its theological department, Bexley Hall. McIlvaine died in Florence, Italy, during one of his trips abroad to restore his health. With his death, the evangelical party in the Episcopal Church lost its most respected spokesperson.

Bibliography

A. "Oxford Divinity Compared, 1841" and "Pastoral Letter of the House of Bishops, 1862" in *DW,* 56–58, 158–64; *The Evidences of Christianity* (New York, 1832); *Oxford Divinity: Compared with That of the Romish and Anglican Churches* (London, 1841); *Reasons for Refusing to Consecrate a Church Having an Altar Instead of a Communion Table* (Mt. Vernon, Ohio, 1846); *No Priest, No Sacrifice, No Altar but Christ* (New York, 1850); *Righteousness by Faith* (Philadelphia, 1862).
B. *ACAB* 4, 122–23; *ANB* 15, 84; *BB,* 100–102; *DAB* 12, 64–65; *DCA,* 690; *EDC,* 327; *NCAB* 7, 2–3; *SH* 7, 114–15; *NYT,* 15 March 1873; B.Z. Stambaugh, "The McIlvaine Episcopate," *HMPEC* 6 (1937): 299–307; Mark Heathcote Hall, "Bishop McIlvaine: The Reluctant Frontiersman," *HMPEC* 44 (1975): 81–96; William Carus, ed., *Memorials of the Right Reverend Charles Pettit McIlvaine* (New York, 1882); Diana H. Butler, *Standing against the Whirlwind: Evangelical Episcopalians in Nineteenth-Century America* (New York, 1995).

MEADE, WILLIAM (11 November 1789, Frederick County, Va.–14 March 1862, Alexandria, Va.). *Education:* Graduated from the College of New Jersey (now Princeton University), 1808; studied for the ordained ministry under Walter Dulaney Addison, St. John's Parish, Md. *Career:* Rector, Christ Church, Alexandria, Va., 1811–14; minister, Frederick County, Va., 1814–21; rector, Christ Church, Winchester, Va., 1821–29; assistant bishop, diocese of Virginia, 1829–41; bishop, diocese of Virginia, 1841–62; presiding bishop of the Protestant Episcopal Church in the Confederate States of America, 1861–62.

William Meade, a bishop and early leader of the evangelical party, was born in Frederick County, Virginia, in 1789. After graduating from the College of New Jersey in 1808, he studied privately under the tutelage of Walter Addison, rector of St. John's Parish, Maryland, who inspired in him an interest in evangelical doctrine. Ordained a deacon by James Madison, the bishop of Virginia, in February 1811, he served for three years as the rector of Christ Church in Alexandria. Meade began his ministerial career at the lowest point in the Episcopal Church's history in Virginia. On the day of his ordination at the woefully dilapidated Bruton Parish Church in Williamsburg, the congregation consisted of no more than 20 people, most of whom were either his friends or his relatives. Ordained to the priesthood three years later, Meade next served as the minister for Frederick County (1814–21) and as the rector of Christ Church, Winchester (1821–29). In 1829 he was chosen to be the assistant bishop of Virginia, and when Richard Channing Moore, the diocesan bishop, died in 1841, Meade succeeded him as the third bishop of Virginia.

More than anyone else in his diocese, Meade was responsible for restoring the fortunes of the church in Virginia over the next 50 years. Along with Bishop Moore and William Holland Wilmer, he helped establish the Virginia Theological Seminary in Alexandria in 1823. This school, the second seminary founded in the Episcopal Church, soon became the most important center of evangelical principles in the denomination. Meade also helped found the Protestant Episcopal Society for the Promotion of Evangelical Knowledge. He was deeply concerned about the need for people to experience personal conversion. He emphasized that the Christian who had been baptized as an infant should make a conscious renewal of faith as an adult. Like evangelicals in other Protestant denominations, Meade believed that the Bible was "the infallible word of God . . . our only rule of faith and great instrument of conversion and sanctification." He taught that the preacher's primary task was to preach the gospel, thereby convincing members of his congregation that they were sinners who needed to turn to Jesus Christ for salvation.

Meade's episcopate took place during the heyday of slavery in the southern states. Although he never challenged slavery directly, he was an early supporter of the American Colonization Society, which beginning in 1816 pressed both for the emancipation of slaves and for their emigration to Liberia. During the political crisis of 1860, Meade opposed secession, but after Virginia left the Union, he insisted that Christians had a duty to bear arms to defend their homeland. The formation of the Confederacy also compelled Episcopalians in the South to organize a new denomination. As the senior bishop in the southern dioceses, Meade presided at the meeting that drew up the constitution of the Protestant Episcopal Church in the Confederate States of America in 1861. On March 6, 1862, he was the chief consecrator of Richard Hooker Wilmer as bishop of Alabama, the only Episcopal bishop consecrated in the Confederacy during the Civil War. Meade died eight days later in Alexandria, and he was buried at Virginia Seminary.

Bibliography

A. Papers at the archives of Virginia Theological Seminary in Alexandria; "Documentary History of the American Church: The Autobiography of William Meade," *HMPEC* 31 (1962): 379–94; *Companion to the Font and the Pulpit* (Washington, D.C., 1846); *Lectures on the Pastoral Office* (New York, 1849); *Reasons for Loving the*

Episcopal Church (New York, 1851); *The True Churchman* (Charlottesville, Va., 1851); *Old Churches, Ministers, and Families of Virginia,* 2 vols. (Philadelphia, 1857); *The Bible and the Classics* (New York, 1861).

B. *ACAB* 4, 282–83; *ANB* 15, 219–20; *BB,* 71–73, 84–85; *DAB* 12, 480–81; *DCA,* 721–22; *EDC,* 327; *ERS,* 465; *NCAB* 7, 216; *SPCK,* 172–73; *WWWA* Historical vol. 1607–1896, 352; David L. Holmes Jr., "William Meade and the Church of Virginia, 1789–1829" (Ph.D. diss., Princeton University, 1971); John Johns, *A Memoir of the Life of the Right Rev. William Meade* (Baltimore, 1867); Philip Slaughter, *Memoir of the Life of the Rt. Rev. William Meade* (Cambridge, 1881).

MILES, JAMES WARLEY (24 November 1818, Orangeburg district, S.C.–14 September 1875, Charleston, S.C.). *Education:* Studied at Waddel's Academy, Willington, S.C., 1834–35; South Carolina College (now the University of South Carolina), 1835–37; studied law, 1837–38; graduated from General Theological Seminary, 1841. *Career:* Served several small missions in the diocese of South Carolina, 1841–43; missionary in the Near East, 1843–47; interim parish priest, Charleston, S.C., 1847–50; professor, College of Charleston, 1850–54, 1866–71; librarian, College of Charleston, 1856–63; interim parish priest, diocese of South Carolina, 1871–75.

James Warley Miles, an Episcopal priest and theologian, was the son of James Sanders Miles, a South Carolina planter, and Sarah Bond Warley. Although he studied for two years at South Carolina College in Columbia, he was expelled when school authorities learned of his plans to fight a duel with another student. After briefly studying law, he entered General Theological Seminary, from which he graduated in 1841. Although he considered a plan to join James Lloyd Breck* and other seminarians in missionary work in Wisconsin, Miles eventually returned to his home diocese, where he served as a deacon in several small parishes. This work did not satisfy him, however, and after being ordained to the priesthood in 1843, he received permission from his bishop to become a foreign missionary in Constantinople. Upon his return to South Carolina four years later, he held interim parish appointments until February 1850, when he was elected to a newly created professorship in the history of philosophy and Greek literature at the College of Charleston. Troubled by poor health, he resigned from the college in 1854 and sailed to Europe for a period of travel and rest.

Miles's real interests lay in the study of languages and philosophy. In the late 1840s, he began publishing articles on those subjects in the *Southern Quarterly Review.* At this time, he also put together a series of sermons he had preached while serving as an assistant at St. Michael's Church, Charleston, and published them under the title *Philosophic Theology* (1849). After friends enticed him to come back to the United States in 1856, Miles assumed responsibilities as the librarian of the College of Charleston. Often withdrawn and self-pitying, he enjoyed that position because it allowed him to be among books and to pursue his intellectual pursuits without appreciable interruption. He remained at the college until 1863, when Union attacks against Charleston during the Civil War forced many civilians to evacuate the city. He spent the next two years living with relatives in Anderson, South Carolina.

Unlike many of his contemporaries, Miles was a theological modernist who emphasized God's progressive self-revelation in history. Because he thought that the human ability to understand divine truths was independent of scripture, he also believed that the Bible was part of the historical process and thus could be judged by the standards of human reason. Unfortunately, in the antebellum South, Miles's theological liberalism was used to promote not human freedom and enlightenment but rather proslavery ideology and rigid social conservatism. In his writings on race, for example, Miles rejected the literal interpretation of the creation accounts in the book of Genesis. Rather than following the biblical narrative, which posited a single creation of humankind, Miles considered that polygenesis—the notion that each race was an entirely distinct species—better described the relationship among the peoples of the world. Moreover, because of the original diversity of humankind, an immutable "ethnological law" not only controlled the development of the races but also placed blacks in a position of subordination to whites. "The negro is a totally different man from the white man," he wrote in 1864, and "left to himself he is a savage." Thus, slavery simply reflected the "Law of Nature," which it was the "great destiny" of the Confederate states to defend.

Bitterly disappointed by the defeat of the Confederacy, Miles returned to Charleston after the war and served again on the faculty of the college from 1866 to 1871. Pleading poor health, he resigned and spent the final years of his life engaged in various academic and ministerial pursuits. He died in Charleston in 1875.

Bibliography

A. Papers at Duke University, at the College of Charleston, and at the South Carolina Historical Society in Charleston; *Philosophic Theology; or, Ultimate Ground of All Religious Belief Based on Reason* (Charleston, 1849); *The Discourse on the Occasion of the Funeral of the Hon. John C. Calhoun* (Charleston, 1850); *Discourse, Delivered before the Graduating Class of the College of Charleston* (Charleston, 1851); *The Student of Philology: Annual Oration Delivered before the Literary Societies of the South-Carolina College . . . December 7th, 1852* (Charleston, 1853); *The Relation between the Races at the South* (Charleston, 1861); *God in History: A Discourse Delivered before the Graduating Class of the College of Charleston . . . March 19, 1863* (Charleston, 1863); *Annual Oration Delivered at the Commencement of the Chrestomathic Society, College of Charleston, February 27, 1874* (Charleston, 1874).

B. *ANB* 15, 443–44; *EDC,* 332; *ERS,* 477; Ralph E. Luker, "God, Man and the World of James Warley Miles, Charleston's Transcendentalist," *HMPEC* 39 (1970): 101–36; George W. Williams, *The Reverend James Warley Miles* (Charleston, 1954); Ralph E. Luker, *A Southern Tradition in Theology and Social Criticism, 1830–1930: The Religious Liberalism and Social Conservatism of James Warley Miles, William Porcher DuBose, and Edgar Gardner Murphy* (New York, 1984).

MORGAN, EMILY MALBONE (10 December 1862, Hartford, Conn.–27 February 1937, Boston). *Education:* Tutored privately at home. *Career:* Organizer and leader, Society of the Companions of the Holy Cross, 1884–1937.

Emily M. Morgan, a social reform advocate and founder of the Society of the Companions of the Holy Cross (SCHC), was born in Hartford, Connecticut, in December 1862. The youngest child and only daughter of a wealthy merchant family, she grew up with a strong desire to help working women. The Morgans attended Trinity Church in Hartford. Like her mother, Emily was a committed Anglo-Catholic, and she experienced her first monastic retreat with the Sisters of St. Margaret in Boston when she was 21 years old. She admired Anglo-Catholicism because of its historical inclusiveness and use of visible symbolism, which presented a far more appealing face to outsiders, especially the downtrodden, than the cold rationalism of low church worship. Committed to a life of personal holiness, she poured most of her financial resources into the purchase and maintenance of hospitality houses for female workers.

Along with Harriet Hastings, Morgan formed the SCHC in 1884. The society had its origins in a small group of young Hartford women who regularly joined Morgan and her invalid friend Adelyn Howard for prayer and spiritual support. As an organization of Episcopal laywomen who emphasized the importance of intercessory prayer, the SCHC was neither a typical church-based women's organization nor a traditional monastic order. Morgan believed in the need for a devotional structure flexible enough to accommodate women whose vocations were lived in the secular world. Members of the society pledged themselves to six ideals: the Way of the Cross, the Life of Intercession, Social Justice, Christian Unity, Simplicity of Life, and Thanksgiving. They were dedicated to spiritual combat with the modern, secular industrial world, and they consistently aligned themselves with movements of social change and reform. "We felt the wrongs of the world very keenly," Morgan reported in 1921, "and expressed our feelings strongly."

The SCHC purchased property in Byfield, Massachusetts, in 1913, and by January 1915 the society had constructed and dedicated a meeting place, called Adelynrood, where members came together on retreat every summer. Although all of the original Companions were from New England, the society gradually spread throughout the United States and overseas; by 1908 there were more than 250 members worldwide. In the early 1930s Morgan said that when she "looked down the table at Adelynrood [she] saw people from some thirty dioceses in the east, south, and west." The SCHC, she thought, was "like a feminine fragment of a General Convention without a House of Bishops." Both through the commitment they made as individuals and through their corporate activities, Morgan and other Companions such as the prominent educator Vida Scudder* significantly increased the social conscience of the Episcopal Church in the early twentieth century.

Morgan died in Boston in February 1937.

Bibliography

A. Papers at the archives of the Society of the Companions of the Holy Cross in Byfield, Mass.; *Letters to Her Companions,* ed. Vida Scudder (Byfield, Mass., 1944).

B. *DC,* 148–54, 159; *EDC,* 343; *FD,* 144–51; Joanna Bowen Gillespie, "Emily M. Morgan's 'Religious Order': The Society of the Companions of the Holy Cross, 1884," *Journal of the Canadian Church Historical Society* 44 (2002): 83–105; Miriam U. Chrisman, *To Bind Together: A Brief History of the Society of the Companions of the Holy Cross* (Byfield, Mass., 1984).

MORGAN, JOHN PIERPONT (17 April 1837, Hartford, Conn.–31 March 1913, Rome, Italy). *Education:* Graduated from English High School, Boston, 1854; two years of mathematics study, University of Göttingen, Germany. *Career:* Junior accountant, firm of Duncan, Sherman and Co., New York, 1857–60; New York agent for his father's London-based Junius Morgan and Co., 1860–64; partner, Dabney, Morgan and Co., investment securities, 1864–71; partner, Drexel, Morgan and Co. (after 1895, J.P. Morgan and Co.), 1871–1913.

J.P. Morgan, a philanthropist, financier, and prominent Episcopal layman, was born in Hartford, Connecticut, in 1837. In 1857, he began his banking career in New York. He rose to prominence during the 1870s, when his firm emerged from the financial panic of 1873 as the dominant player in the field of government financing. His stature further increased in the 1880s as he became successfully engaged in the reorganization of major railway companies in the United States. Morgan found ways to eliminate wasteful competition, to reduce managerial inefficiency, and to centralize financial control, thus making the railroads more secure and profitable. In the 1890s he also began consolidating industrial corporations. His investment banking firm organized General Electric, American Telephone and Telegraph, International Harvester, and, in 1901, United States Steel, the first billion-dollar corporation. By 1909, many Americans viewed him as the most powerful man in the country—the personification of individual financial power.

Morgan also made many significant contributions to the life of the Episcopal Church. As senior warden of St. George's Church in New York, he helped revitalize a moribund congregation in 1883 by extending a call to William S. Rainsford.* The dynamic new rector transformed the church and made it a center of outstanding preaching and vigorous social service. Rainsford and Morgan had breakfast together every Monday morning. Despite grumbling a bit about Rainsford's fervor for social democracy, he admired his priest's drive and conviction. On one memorable occasion, Morgan tried to resist Rainsford's effort to make the St. George's vestry more representative of his socially diverse congregation by increasing the size of its membership. Ultimately accepting the worthiness of Rainsford's plan, Morgan had wanted to limit the vestry to, as he put it, "a body of gentlemen whom I can ask to meet in my study." After Morgan's death, Rainsford said that "without Pierpont Morgan I certainly could not have made the success I did." A dedicated low church Episcopalian, Morgan even began his will with a statement affirming his belief in the doctrine of the atonement.

Unreflective and even inarticulate, Morgan was generally a man of action rather than of ideas. His support of the ecumenical movement was demonstrated in his gift of $100,000 to begin preparations for a world conference on faith and order, and he was a major benefactor of the Cathedral of St. John the Divine. Some of his other benefactions included a trade school for the boys of St. George's Church, a new parish house and rectory for the church, a department of natural history at Trinity College in Hartford, and a complete electrical plant for St. Paul's Cathedral in London. He also served as a deputy to the General Convention, where he dutifully sat and listened to the often tedious ecclesiastical proceedings.

Morgan died in Italy in March 1913. He was so well known in the Episcopal Church that the bishops of Massachusetts, Connecticut, and New York all participated in his funeral at St. George's Church.

Bibliography

B. *ANB* 15, 833–39; *DAB* 13, 175–80; *NCAB* 14, 66–68; *WWWA* 1, 865; Zachary Leader, "800 Napkins, 47 Finger Bowls," *London Review of Books,* 16 March 2000, 18–20; Frederick L. Allen, *The Great Pierpont Morgan* (New York, 1949); William S. Rainsford, *The Story of a Varied Life: An Autobiography* (Garden City, N.Y., 1922); Vincent P. Carosso, *The Morgans: Private International Bankers, 1854–1913* (Cambridge, Mass., 1987); Ron Chernow, *The House of Morgan: An American Banking Dynasty and the Rise of Modern Finance* (New York, 1990); Jean Strouse, *Morgan: American Financier* (New York, 1999).

MUHLENBERG, WILLIAM AUGUSTUS (16 September 1796, Philadelphia– 8 April 1877, New York.). *Education:* B.A., University of Pennsylvania, 1815; studied theology under William White, Philadelphia, 1815–18. *Career:* Curate, Christ Church, Philadelphia, 1817–20; rector, St. James's Church, Lancaster, Pa., 1820–26; supply rector, St. George's Church, Flushing, N.Y., 1826–28; founder and headmaster, Flushing Institute, 1828–46; professor, St. Paul's College, College Point, N.Y., 1838–46; rector, Church of the Holy Communion, New York, 1846–58; pastor-superintendent, St. Luke's Hospital, New York, 1858–77.

William Augustus Muhlenberg, arguably the most influential Episcopal priest of the mid-nineteenth century, was born in Philadelphia in 1796. He was the great-grandson of the eighteenth-century Lutheran leader Henry Melchior Muhlenberg. Baptized in a Lutheran church, he first became acquainted with the Episcopal liturgy at the age of five, when his family began attending services at Christ Church in Philadelphia. After studying theology under the direction of William White,* the bishop of Pennsylvania, Muhlenberg was ordained a deacon in 1817 and a priest in 1820. Although he served briefly in parishes in Pennsylvania and New York, he was chiefly interested in the development of social service institutions. One of his most important experiments began in the spring of 1828, when he opened the Flushing Institute on Long Island, New York. Despite its relatively short life (it closed in 1848), the Flushing Institute provided the model for a later generation of church-related boarding schools.

Between 1844 and 1846, Muhlenberg was involved in the organization of the Church of the Holy Communion in New York City, a parish that was to become a forerunner of the "institutional church" and one of the first American churches to be sustained by voluntary offerings rather than by pew rents. Muhlenberg introduced a number of liturgical innovations in the parish, including daily offices, a weekly Eucharist, antiphonal chanting, lighted candles, and the first vested boys' choir in the city. A man of action rather than a systematic theologian, he described himself as an "evangelical catholic." The evangelical Muhlenberg stressed the importance of a personal experience of saving grace, but, attuned as well to the emphases of the Tractarian movement, he tried to develop and channel this experience through the sacraments of the church. Under his direction, the parish became not only, in his phrase, "a house of unceasing Prayer" but also the center of a successful ministry among the poor. At the laying of the cornerstone for the church in 1844, Muhlenberg said there would be no place for social distinctions in the new parish, just as there were none at the altar rail: "Here let there be a sanctuary consecrated especially to fellowship in Christ, and to the great ordinance of His love"—a dedication and practice that would "rebuke all the distinctions of pride and wealth."

One of his biographers, E. R. Hardy Jr., called Muhlenberg "the founder of social Christianity" in the Episcopal Church. From 1851 to 1853, he published a monthly magazine, *The Evangelical Catholic,* which discussed the need for Christian service to the poor. Besides his work at the Church of the Holy Communion, he began a hospital for residents of the New York slums, who had suffered grievously during the cholera epidemic of 1849. This ministry expanded into the founding of St. Luke's Hospital in 1858. Much of the nursing work at Muhlenberg's parish was performed by a group of religious sisters who were just beginning to come together as an order. While on vacation in England in 1843, Muhlenberg had learned about the reestablishment of the female diaconate in the Lutheran church in Kaiserswerth, Germany. Seeing the potential of having nursing sisters serving in his church-sponsored hospital, he professed Anne Ayres* as the first member of this order, the Sisterhood of the Holy Communion.

A bridge builder throughout his life, Muhlenberg hoped for the eventual implementation of what he called "the church idea." This principle looked forward to the growth of a single church body that would include all Christians. To implement this goal, he introduced a "memorial" to the House of Bishops of the Episcopal Church in 1853. He asked the bishops to support a movement that would both relax the liturgical rigidity of Episcopal services and allow episcopal ordination to be extended to the clergy of other Protestant denominations. Muhlenberg's proposal, while ultimately unsuccessful, prompted Episcopalians to begin to consider critical issues regarding the prayer book and Christian unity.

In 1870 Muhlenberg developed a charitable organization, St. Johnland, on a large tract of land on Long Island, about 45 miles from New York City. There he attempted not only to build a cooperative industrial community but also to practice forms of Christian socialism. He hoped to move poor people out of the city, settling them in inexpensive but comfortable homes in a place where they could learn trades, be self-supporting, and sustain a healthy family life. In addition, the community was meant to give young men an education that would prepare them for the ordained ministry. St. Johnland included a home for old men, a home for crippled and destitute children, a schoolhouse, a library, a village hall, shops, and a chapel. Unfortunately, the experiment never proved appealing to the workers whom it was intended to attract, and it became Muhlenberg's least successful institution.

Muhlenberg died in poverty at St. Luke's Hospital, having spent all his money on projects aimed at human betterment. A visionary and a risk taker, he pushed the Episcopal Church in directions that future leaders would follow.

Bibliography

A. *Christian Education* (Flushing, N.Y., 1840); *St. Johnland: Ideal and Actual* (New York, 1867); *Evangelical Catholic Papers,* ed. Anne Ayres, 2 vols. (New York, 1875–77).

B. *ANB* 16, 62–63; *BB,* 67–68, 78–79, 89–91; *DAB* 13, 313–14; *DARB,* 381–82; *DCA,* 782–83; *EDC,* 345–46; *HEC,* 150–52; *NCAB* 9, 199; *SH* 8, 51; *NYT,* 9 April 1877; E.R. Hardy Jr., "Evangelical Catholicism: W.A. Muhlenberg and the Memorial Movement," *HMPEC* 13 (1944): 155–92; Richard G. Becker, "The Social Thought of William Augustus Muhlenberg," *HMPEC* 27 (1958): 307–23; John Frederick Woolverton, "William Augustus Muhlenberg and the Founding of St. Paul's College," *HMPEC* 29 (1960): 192–218; Anne Ayres, *Life and Work of William Augustus Muhlenberg* (New York, 1880); William Wilberforce Newton, *Dr. Muhlenberg* (New York, 1891); Alvin W. Skardon, *Church Leader in the Cities: William Augustus Muhlenberg* (Philadelphia, 1971).

MURPHY, EDGAR GARDNER (31 August 1869, near Fort Smith, Ark.–23 June 1913, New York). *Education:* Graduated from the University of the South, 1889; studied at General Theological Seminary, 1889–90. *Career:* Assistant, St. Mark's Church, San Antonio, Tex., 1890–93; minister-in-charge, Christ Church, Laredo, Tex., 1893; rector, St. Paul's Church, Chillicothe, Ohio, 1894–97; rector, St. John's Church, Kingston, N.Y., 1897–98; rector, St. John's Church, Montgomery, Ala., 1898–1901; executive secretary, Southern Education Board, 1901–8.

Edgar Gardner Murphy, a priest and conservative social reformer, was born near Fort Smith, Arkansas, in 1869. Befriended by the priest Walter Richardson when he was growing up in San Antonio, Texas, Murphy decided to prepare for the ordained ministry by entering the University of the South at Sewanee, Tennessee. While at Sewanee, he was deeply influenced by the theologian William Porcher DuBose.* After graduating from college in 1889, he studied for a year in New York at General Theological Seminary but did not receive a degree. Ordained a deacon in 1890, he returned to Texas to assist Richardson at St. Mark's

Church. In 1893 he accepted the call to be rector of Christ Church in Laredo, Texas, where he was ordained a priest the following September. When an African American man was lynched in Laredo for allegedly raping and murdering a white girl, Murphy organized a protest against the lynching. Health reasons forced Murphy to leave Christ Church at the end of 1893, and between 1894 and 1898 he served briefly in parishes in Ohio and in New York State.

In 1898, Murphy was accorded the opportunity to return to the South when he received a call from the vestry of St. John's Church in Montgomery, Alabama. St. John's was one of the leading parishes in the diocese of Alabama, and Murphy welcomed the chance to apply his developing ideas about the social gospel to race relations in the South. Soon after his arrival in Montgomery, he created a new parish, the Church of the Good Shepherd, for African Americans who wished to belong to the Episcopal Church. In January 1900 he persuaded a group of prominent white citizens to work with him in organizing the Southern Society for the Promotion of the Study of Race Relations and Problems in the South. Under his direction, the first (and only) annual conference of that society was held in Montgomery in May 1900. At that gathering, whites offered ideas about how they might aid the advance of African Americans without seriously challenging traditional racial mores in the South. While serving at St. John's, Murphy was also involved with the problem of child labor, and he helped organize both the Alabama Child Labor Committee and the National Child Labor Committee.

Murphy resigned from his position as rector of St. John's in 1901. Having been hired as the executive secretary of the Southern Education Board, he wanted to be able to throw himself fully into the movement for educational reform. As he told the St. John's vestry when he resigned, it was his "best response to God's will, and to the needs of our church and our country." Fifteen months after leaving St. John's, he decided to renounce his clerical orders as well. In the letter he wrote to his bishop, Murphy explained that he had made this decision because he had encountered too many awkward questions about his ministerial role while performing secular tasks; he did not want his priesthood to interfere with his involvement in social reform.

Although the southern education movement thrived under Murphy's leadership, it failed to address the wide disparity between the opportunities available for whites and those available for African Americans. Murphy examined this issue in his two most significant books, *Problems of the Present South* (1904) and *The Basis of Ascendancy* (1909). As one historian has suggested, Murphy was arguably "the white South's most sophisticated spokesman for racial segregation." Addressing southern race relations from the perspective of a white paternalist motivated by a sense of *noblesse oblige,* Murphy insisted that it was in the best interests of African Americans if they were kept as separate as possible from whites. "It is just because I profoundly believe in the Negro's destiny that I beg him to follow, not those who would turn him into a white man," Murphy asserted, "but those who would turn him into the worthier and finer possibilities of his own nature."

Having suffered from a heart condition for nearly 20 years, Murphy grew increasingly ill during his tenure at the Southern Education Board. He eventually announced his resignation in 1908 and retired a few months later. He continued to battle with poor health during retirement and died of heart failure in New York in 1913.

Bibliography

A. Papers at the Southern Historical Collection, University of North Carolina at Chapel Hill; "The Task of the Leader," *Sewanee Review* 15 (1907): 25–27; *Words for the Church* (New York, 1897); *The Larger Life: Sermons and an Essay* (New York, 1897); *Problems of the Present South: A Discussion of Certain of the Educational, Industrial, and Political Issues in the Southern States* (New York, 1904); *The Basis of Ascendancy: A Discussion of Certain Principles of Public Policy Involved in the Development of the Southern States* (New York, 1909).

B. *ANB* 16, 127–28; *DAB* 13, 348–49; *DCA*, 784; *EDC*, 346–47; *ERS*, 516–17; *WWWA* 1, 882; Allen J. Going, "The Reverend Edgar Gardner Murphy: His Ideas and Influence," *HMPEC* 25 (1956): 391–402; Daniel Levine, "Edgar Gardner Murphy: Conservative Reformer," *Alabama Review* 15 (1962): 100–16; Ronald C. White Jr., "Beyond the Sacred: Edgar Gardner Murphy and a Ministry of Social Reform," *HMPEC* 49 (1980): 51–70; Stephen C. Compton, "Edgar Gardner Murphy and the Child Labor Movement," *HMPEC* 52 (1983): 181–214; Maud King Murphy, *Edgar Gardner Murphy, from Records and Memories* (New York, 1943); Hugh C. Bailey, *Edgar Gardner Murphy: Gentle Progressive* (Coral Gables, Fla., 1968); Ralph E. Luker, *A Southern Tradition in Theology and Social Criticism, 1830–1930: The Religious Liberalism and Social Conservatism of James Warley Miles, William Porcher DuBose, and Edgar Gardner Murphy* (New York, 1984).

MURRAY, PAULI (20 November 1910, Baltimore–1 July 1985, Pittsburgh). *Education:* B.A., Hunter College, 1933; L.L.B., Howard University, 1944; L.L.M., University of California, Berkeley, 1945; J.S.D., Yale University Law School, 1965; M.Div., General Theological Seminary, 1976. *Career:* Field representative, *Opportunity* magazine, 1933–34; remedial reading teacher, Works Progress Administration (WPA), 1935–36; staff member, WPA Worker's Education Project, 1936–39; administrative committee member, Workers Defense League, 1940–42; private law practice in New York, 1946–56; lawyer, firm of Paul, Weiss, Rifkind, Wharton, and Garrison, New York, 1956–60; teacher at the Ghana Law School in Accra, 1960–61; vice president, Benedict College, Columbia, S.C., 1967–68; visiting professor, later Louis Stulberg professor of law and politics, Brandeis University, 1968–73; priest-in-charge, Church of the Atonement, Washington, D.C., 1977–82; priest associate, Church of the Holy Nativity, Baltimore, 1982–85.

Pauli Murray, an activist lawyer and priest, was born in Baltimore in November 1910. Although she was given the name Anna Pauline at birth, she changed it to Pauli when she was an adult. Her father, William Henry Murray, was a public school teacher, and her mother, Agnes Fitzgerald, was a nurse. They both died when Murray was a child, and she was raised in Durham, North Carolina, by her mother's oldest sister, Pauline Fitzgerald Dame, a teacher. Murray moved to New York City in 1927 and graduated from Hunter College in 1933. After working at many different jobs between 1933 and 1941, she entered Howard University to study for a law degree.

Beginning in 1938, Murray became an active crusader for civil rights. In that year she applied for admission to the graduate school of the University of North Carolina but was rejected because she was an African American. Her decision to enter Howard University was related to her "single-minded intention of destroying Jim Crow." While a Howard student, she participated in sit-in demonstrations that challenged racial segregation in drugstores and cafeterias in the city of Washington. In 1942, moreover, Murray served as a delegate to the national conference of A. Philip Randolph's March on Washington movement. During this period she also met and developed a friendship with Eleanor Roosevelt, the president's wife, bringing her to an awareness of the injustices suffered by black Americans because of segregation laws. As Murray wrote in an article published near the end of World War II, "the prophecy that all men are created equal" would not be realized until southern blacks were freed from the onerous burden of racial discrimination.

After graduating from Howard and then from the University of California at Berkeley, Murray held several jobs before moving to New York City in 1946 and establishing a law practice. Thanks to the Women's Division of Christian Service of the Methodist Church, Murray was able to make a significant contribution to the civil rights movement in the early 1950s. Staff members of the Women's Division hired her in 1948 to work with them in compiling information about segregation laws in the South. Since many states outside of the South had enacted laws that opposed racial discrimination and protected the rights of African Americans, Murray decided to include all legislation relating to race in the United States in her research. Published in 1951, this book, *States' Laws on Race and Color,* was so informative that it was used by Thurgood Marshall of the National Association for the Advancement of Colored People as a key document in the legal strategy that ultimately resulted in the decisive *Brown* Supreme Court decision of 1954.

Murray worked as a lawyer in New York through 1960. After teaching for a year in a law school in Ghana, she returned to the United States and entered Yale University Law School, from which she earned a doctorate in 1965. By the mid-1960s, she had become aware of the close relationship between "the evil of racism (Jim Crow)" and "the evil of antifeminism (Jane Crow)." She served on the President's Commission on the Status of Women in 1962–63, and she lobbied on behalf of the inclusion of the word "sex" in Title VII, the Equal Employment Opportunities section, of the 1964 Civil Rights Act. With the assistance of a colleague, Murray published a law review article in 1965 in which she asserted that "the rights of women and the rights of Negroes are only different phases of the fundamental and indivisible issue of human rights." She became acquainted with Betty Friedan in the fall of 1965. One year later, Friedan, Murray, and others founded the National Organization for Women.

After completing her studies at Yale, Murray served briefly as vice president at Benedict College, a black school in South Carolina, before accepting a teaching position at Brandeis University. Although she taught at Brandeis for five years and achieved a tenured faculty position, she felt increasingly called to the ordained ministry. She had been a member of the Episcopal Church all her life, beginning with her baptism by the famed black priest George Freeman Bragg* in Baltimore. In the 1960s, she belonged to St. Mark's Church in the Bowery in New York, but she felt increasingly troubled by "the submerged position of women" in her denomination. Pursuing her call, she was eventually accepted as a candidate for ordination in the diocese of Massachusetts, and leaving her position at Brandeis, she entered General Theological Seminary in 1973. Murray graduated in 1976, a few months before the General Convention of the Episcopal Church officially approved the right of women to be ordained to the priesthood. She was ordained a deacon in June 1976, and on January 8, 1977, she was ordained a priest in the Washington National Cathedral. She was, therefore, not only one of the first women priests of the Episcopal Church but also the first African American woman to be ordained in that denomination.

Murray served in parishes in Washington, D.C., and Baltimore between 1977 and 1985. Although her health was poor, she continued to write until her death in 1985. Her autobiography, *Song in a Weary Throat,* was published posthumously in 1987 and reissued two years later under the title *Pauli Murray: The Autobiography of a Black Activist, Feminist, Lawyer, Priest, and Poet.*

Bibliography

A. Papers at the Schlesinger Library of Radcliffe College; "Negroes Are Fed Up," *Common Sense,* August 1943, 274–76; "An American Credo," *Common Ground,* winter 1945, 22–24; *States' Laws on Race and Color* (1951; reprint, Athens, Ga., 1997); *Proud Shoes: The Story of an American Family* (1956; reprint, New York, 1978); *The Constitution and Government of Ghana* (London, 1961); *Human Rights U.S.A.* (Cincinnati, 1967); *Dark Testament and Other Poems* (Norwalk, Conn., 1970); *Pauli Murray: The Autobiography of a Black Activist, Feminist, Lawyer, Priest, and Poet* (1987; reprint, Knoxville, Tenn., 1989).
B. *ANB* 16, 167–68; *EAAR,* 517–20; *EDC,* 347; *FD,* 272–79; Harriet Jackson Scarupa, "The Extraordinary Faith of Pauli Murray," *Essence,* December 1977, 91, 107–10; Michelle Burgen, "Lifestyle: Rev. Dr. Pauli Murray," *Ebony,* September 1979, 107–12; Casey Miller and Kate Swift, "Pauli Murray," *Ms.,* March 1980, 60–64.

N

NEAL, EMILY GARDINER (22 October 1910, New York–23 September 1989, Glendale, Ohio). *Education:* Attended Brearly School and David Mannes College of Music. *Career:* Freelance journalist and writer; staff member, St. Thomas Episcopal Church, Terrace Park, Ohio, 1976–86; ordained deacon, diocese of Pittsburgh, 1978; founding president, Episcopal Healing Ministry Foundation, 1987.

Emily Gardiner, a deacon and leader of the healing ministry in the Episcopal Church, was born in New York City in October 1910. She was the daughter of John deBarth Gardiner and Rebekah McLean, neither of whom were Christian believers, and she grew up as a religious skeptic. Educated at Brearly School and David Mannes College of Music, she was originally trained as a concert violinist. She married Alvin W. Neal in 1930, and they had two daughters. While Alvin worked as an executive of the Gulf Oil Corporation, Emily had a successful career as a freelance journalist, publishing over 50 articles in popular magazines such as *Look* and *Redbook*.

Emily's life was changed dramatically after attending a healing service—an event that she described in her first book, *A Reporter Finds God through Spiritual Healing* (1956). From that point on, she became a lecturer and counselor on the subject of spiritual healing in the church. In 1961 she was appointed to the Joint Commission on the Ministry of Healing, and she wrote the commission's report to the 1964 General Convention. She always resisted the label of "healer" in reference to her work and preferred to say that she was simply an "enabler of healing" or "an instrument that is used for *God's* healing." She joined the staff of St. Thomas Episcopal Church in Terrace Park, Ohio, in 1976, and in January 1978, after 20 years of lay ministry, she was ordained a deacon at Trinity Cathedral in the diocese of Pittsburgh. The Episcopal Healing Ministry Foundation was founded in her honor in 1987, and she was its first president.

Neal was the author of numerous works about Christian healing, including a posthumous work, *Celebration of Healing,* compiled by her friend Anne Cassel and published in 1992. Her husband died in 1961, and during the later years of her life she lived at the Convent of the Transfiguration in Glendale, Ohio. An associate of the community, she was active as a spiritual counselor and led a healing service every week. She died in Glendale in 1989.

Bibliography

A. Papers at the Marion B. Wade collection, Wheaton College, Wheaton, Ill.; *A Reporter Finds God through Spiritual Healing* (New York, 1956); *God Can Heal You Now* (Englewood Cliffs, N.J., 1958); *The Lord Is Our Healer* (Englewood Cliffs, N.J., 1961); *Father Bob and His Boys* (Indianapolis, 1963); *Where There's Smoke: The Mystery of Christian Healing* (New York, 1967); *The Healing Power of Christ* (New York, 1972); *The Healing Ministry: A Personal Journey* (New York, 1982); *Celebration of Healing* (Boston, 1992); *The Reluctant Healer: One Woman's Journey of Faith,* ed. Anne Cassel (Colorado Springs, Colo., 2000).

B. *EDC,* 354; *FD,* 263–71.

NEWTON, RICHARD HEBER (31 October 1840, Philadelphia–19 December 1914, East Hampton, N.Y.). *Education:* A.B., University of Pennsylvania, 1861; studied at the Philadelphia Divinity School, 1862–63. *Career:* Assistant minister, Church of the Epiphany, Philadelphia, 1863–64; minister-in-charge, Trinity Church, Sharon Springs, N.Y., 1864–66; rector, St. Paul's Church, Philadelphia, 1866–69; rector, All Souls' Church, New York, 1869–1902.

R. Heber Newton, a priest and author who sought to commend biblical criticism to a broad lay audience, was born in Philadelphia in 1840. After studying at the University of Pennsylvania and the Philadelphia Divinity School, he was ordained to the diaconate in January 1862 and to the priesthood in July 1866. He served briefly in parishes in Philadelphia and in Sharon Springs, New York, between 1863 and 1869. His most significant ministry, however, was as rector of All Souls' Church in New York City, where he served for over 30 years during the period of great intellectual and social ferment at the end of the nineteenth century.

Throughout his lengthy tenure at All Souls', Newton was known as a social gospel reformer who emphasized the relevance of Jesus' message not only to individuals but also to society at large. He argued for the application of Christian ethical principles to business practices, and he believed that the government should intervene to mitigate harms caused by unbridled laissez-faire capitalism. Favoring cooperation over competition, he saw a role for the Episcopal Church as the conscience within American society, and he became a leader in the Society of Christian Socialists. A broad churchman, Newton was also an active contributor to the Church congress movement, which was composed of Episcopalians who stressed the need for liturgical openness, ecumenical unity, and the open examination of troubling social and theological questions.

In 1883 Newton attracted widespread attention as a result of the publication of a series of his sermons that advocated the higher criticism of the Bible. Although two priests in his diocese attempted to bring him to trial for his supposedly heterodox views, Henry C. Potter,* the bishop of New York, was able to deflect their complaint. The outcome of this controversy gave comfort to those who hoped the Episcopal Church would be able to tolerate honest intellectual inquiry even when other American denominations were becoming seriously divided over the question of biblical criticism.

Newton died on Long Island at East Hampton in December 1914. According to the author of a letter to *The Churchman* published shortly after his death, Newton had transformed All Souls' Church into "a Mecca for thousands who had become acquainted with [his] fearless, illuminative thought." He treated "science or metaphysic in a way to make [his parishioners] feel that religion was the ally and not the foe of any truth," and he successfully "stirred the spark of devotion in not a few who had become indifferent to or . . . cynical about religion."

Bibliography

A. *The Morals of Trade* (New York, 1876); *Womanhood: Lectures on a Woman's Work in the World* (New York, 1881); *The Right and Wrong Uses of the Bible* (New York, 1883); *The Book of the Beginnings: A Study of Genesis with an Introduction to the Pentateuch* (New York, 1884); *Philistinism: Plain Words concerning Certain Forms of Modern Skepticism* (New York, 1885); *Social Studies* (New York, 1887); *Church and Creed* (New York, 1891); *Christian Science: The Truths of Spiritual Healing and Their Contribution to the Growth of Orthodoxy* (New York, 1899); *Parsifal: An Ethical and Spiritual Interpretation* (Oscawana-on-Hudson, N.Y., 1904); *The Mysticism of Music* (New York, 1915); *Catholicity: A Treatise on the Unity of Religion* (New York, 1918).

B. *ANB* 16, 364–65; *DAB* 13, 474–75; *EDC,* 360; *SH* 8, 155; *NYT,* 20 December 1914; R. M. W. Black, letter ("The Rev. Heber Newton"), *Churchman,* 23 January 1915.

O

OAKERHATER, DAVID PENDLETON (ca. 1846, Cheyenne reservation in western Oklahoma–31 August 1931, Oklahoma). *Education:* Studied for the ministry under John B. Wicks, Paris, N.Y., 1878–80. *Career:* Missionary deacon among the Cheyenne in the Indian Territory (present-day Oklahoma), 1881–1931.

Oakerhater ("O-kuh-ha-tah," literally, "Making Medicine"), a deacon and missionary, was born on the Cheyenne reservation in western Oklahoma in the mid-1840s. When he was in his late twenties, he became one of 28 Cheyenne Indians confined at Fort Marion, a military prison in St. Augustine, Florida, for his role in the battle of Adobe Walls in Texas in June 1874. These confined Indian men were a popular tourist attraction in St. Augustine, and in the winter of 1875 Oakerhater and three other prisoners were introduced to two prominent vacationers from Cincinnati: Alice Pendleton, daughter of Francis Scott Key, and her husband, George Hunt Pendleton, a railroad president and politician. After talking about the Christian faith with Alice Pendleton, the four men decided not only to be baptized but also to seek ordination in the Episcopal Church. With the assistance of Mary Douglass Burnham, a deaconess from the diocese of Central New York, Pendleton obtained their release from prison, and in the spring of 1878 they journeyed to Burnham's diocese. There, they studied theology under the direction of John B. Wicks, rector of St. Paul's Episcopal Church in Paris, New York.
Oakerhater was baptized in October 1878 in Grace Church, Syracuse. Like many nineteenth-century Episcopal Indians, he took an English name at the time of his baptism—David Pendleton, in honor of his benefactors. In 1881, after his ordination to the diaconate, he returned to the Indian Territory with Wicks. Wicks built a mission house near Fay, where Oakerhater assisted him and acted as his interpreter. Both men also conducted services in Indian camps and taught children and their families. Among the early converts to the Episcopal Church were Whirl-

wind, chief of the Cheyennes and son of the famous chief Black Kettle, and Wah-Nach, Oakerhater's mother. After poor health forced Wicks to leave the mission two years later, Oakerhater remained. He served as the sole representative of the Episcopal Church in the Indian Territory between 1884, when Wicks departed, and 1893, when Francis Key Brooke took office as the district's first missionary bishop.

Never advanced to the priesthood and often given little or no support, Oakerhater served the Episcopal Church faithfully for 36 years of full-time ministry. During another 15 years of active retirement, he continued to preach, to offer advice, to prepare candidates for confirmation, to train lay readers, and to conduct baptismal and burial services among his people. He died in Oklahoma in 1931.

Bibliography

B. *BB,* 103–4; *EDC,* 367; *HEC,* 163–64; Sam L. Botkin, "Indian Missions of the Episcopal Church in Oklahoma," *Chronicles of Oklahoma* 36 (1958): 40–47; *Oakerhater* (Oklahoma City, 1982); Lois Clark, *God's Warrior: David Pendleton Oakerhater* (Oklahoma City, 1985); Owanah Anderson, *400 Years: Anglican / Episcopal Mission among American Indians* (Cincinnati, 1997), chapter 6.

ONDERDONK, BENJAMIN TREDWELL (15 July 1791, New York–30 April 1861, New York). *Education:* Graduated from Columbia College, 1809; studied theology under John Henry Hobart. *Career:* Assistant minister, Trinity Church, New York, 1814–35; professor of ecclesiastical history, General Theological Seminary, 1821–22; professor of ecclesiastical polity and law, General Theological Seminary, 1821–61; bishop, diocese of New York, 1830–45.

A controversial bishop and high church leader, Benjamin T. Onderdonk, the younger brother of Henry Ustick Onderdonk,* was born and educated in New York. After graduating from Columbia College, he studied theology under John Henry Hobart,* from whom he learned his high church principles. Ordained to the diaconate in 1812 and to the priesthood in 1815, he began his career as an assistant at Trinity Church in Manhattan, the parish where he had been baptized and where his father had served faithfully on the vestry. Beginning in 1821, he also became a professor at General Theological Seminary. Upon Hobart's sudden death in 1830, Onderdonk was elected to succeed him as the fourth bishop of New York. A hard worker, he doubled the number of Episcopal communicants in his diocese during the 15 years of his episcopate. And thanks to his efforts to reach every part of the state, the diocese of Western New York was created in 1838—the first division of a diocese in the history of the Episcopal Church.

Despite these evangelistic successes, Onderdonk came under scrutiny from his many detractors in the church, and he was eventually suspended from his office. He ruled the diocese with an iron hand, accomplishing results but at a cost. As an advocate of his denomination's Catholic heritage, and as a particularly tenacious defender of the Oxford movement, Onderdonk infuriated most low church

Episcopalians. He exacerbated already existing tensions in 1843 by ordaining the brilliant, ultra-pious Arthur Carey, a graduate of General Seminary whom evangelicals suspected of having Roman Catholic tendencies. Unfortunately, Onderdonk's own misbehavior provided additional ammunition for his opponents, and they began to gather evidence of his alleged sexual harassment of women while under the influence of alcohol. Eventually, after four women agreed to testify against him, the General Convention of 1844 determined to try the bishop for "immorality and impurity."

Onderdonk's trial was the first held under the canons of the Episcopal Church. It began in November 1844 in New York, and the court of 17 bishops heard testimony regarding improper acts committed between 1837 and 1842. Although *The Churchman,* a high church newspaper, thought the accusations were completely unjustified, it is likely that some witnesses were telling the truth. In any case, Onderdonk was found guilty in January 1845 and suspended "from the office of a Bishop . . . and from all the functions of the sacred ministry." Although his supporters viewed this sentence as a lesser sanction than deposition, it nonetheless had a similar effect, for no time period was stipulated for its duration, and no mechanism existed for lifting it.

Onderdonk was never restored to his office and stayed close to home for the rest of his life. Although the General Seminary trustees expressed their loyalty by declining to remove him from his professorship, he no longer taught at the school because there were fears that his presence might raise unnecessary suspicions about the institution. He died in New York City in April 1861.

Bibliography

A. Papers at AEC, at the General Theological Seminary in New York, and at the Maryland Diocesan Archives in Baltimore.

B. *ACAB* 4, 580–81; *ANB* 16, 721–22; *DAB* 14, 38–39; *DCA,* 845; *EDC,* 373–74; *NCAB* 1, 515; *SBAE,* 100–101; E. Clowes Chorley, "A Tragedy of the Last Century," *American Church Monthly* 34 (1933): 211–19; E. Clowes Chorley, "Benjamin Tredwell Onderdonk: Fourth Bishop of New York," *HMPEC* 9 (1940): 1–51; Walter H. Stowe, "The Election of Benjamin T. Onderdonk as Fourth Bishop of New York," *HMPEC* 23 (1954): 65–68; James Elliott Lindsley, *This Planted Vine: A Narrative History of the Episcopal Diocese of New York* (New York, 1984); Robert Bruce Mullin, *Episcopal Vision / American Reality: High Church Theology and Social Thought in Evangelical America* (New Haven, 1986), 101–3, 161–65.

ONDERDONK, HENRY USTICK (16 March 1789, New York–6 December 1858, Philadelphia). *Education:* Graduated from Columbia College, 1805; M.D., University of Edinburgh, 1811; studied theology under John Henry Hobart, 1814–15; S.T.D., Columbia College, 1827. *Career:* Associate editor, *New York Medical Journal,* 1814–15; missionary, Canandaigua, N.Y., 1815–20; rector, St. Ann's Church, Brooklyn, N.Y., 1820–27; assistant bishop, diocese of Pennsylvania, 1827–36; bishop, diocese of Pennsylvania, 1836–44.

Henry U. Onderdonk, a theologically astute but controversial bishop, was born in New York City, the son of a physician and the elder brother of Benjamin T. Onderdonk,* who also was an Episcopal bishop. After graduating from Columbia College in 1805, he studied medicine in Edinburgh and London, eventually receiving an M.D. from the University of Edinburgh. Returning to the United States in 1811, he briefly practiced medicine but then decided to pursue a career in the ordained ministry of the Episcopal Church instead. He received theological instruction from John Henry Hobart,* the bishop of New York, and consequently he strongly identified with the high church party of his denomination. Ordained a deacon in 1815 and a priest in 1816, Onderdonk served as a missionary in Canandaigua in western New York from 1815 to 1820 and as the rector of St. Ann's Church, Brooklyn, from 1820 to 1827. In a hotly contested election between the high church and evangelical factions in the church, he was elected assistant bishop of Pennsylvania in 1827. He became the bishop of the diocese when William White* died in 1836, but the unpleasantness produced by his election was still present.

Onderdonk was known as one of the outstanding ecclesiastical scholars of his day. Beginning in 1818 with the publication of his *An Appeal to the Religious Public,* he ably defended Episcopal theology and practice against the conversion-oriented piety of American evangelicalism. In the late 1820s, he engaged in a debate over the qualifications of Charles Pettit McIlvaine,* who succeeded him as rector of St. Ann's in Brooklyn. Onderdonk charged that McIlvaine was a "promoter of schemes that would blend us with the Presbyterians," meaning that he was not sufficiently committed to the theological uniqueness of the Episcopal Church. In other books, Onderdonk articulated high church ideas about baptismal regeneration—*An Essay on Regeneration* (1835)—and examined the biblical origins of the office of bishop—*Episcopacy Tested by Scripture* (1831) and *Episcopacy Examined and Re-examined* (1835). He also wrote poetry, composing a number of hymns that were popular during the nineteenth century.

Onderdonk's high church sympathies led him to support the Oxford movement in the early 1840s, but that stance further exacerbated the partisan tensions already existing in his diocese. Unfortunately, because he was subject to chronic intestinal problems, he had become addicted to the brandy that had been medically prescribed to relieve his pain. This situation created such a scandal that he was forced to write to his fellow bishops in 1844 and confess his addiction. Because the majority of his evangelical critics were also temperance advocates, the issues of alcoholism and churchmanship were closely related as they considered Onderdonk's character. Whatever the exact reason for his troubles in Pennsylvania, the House of Bishops chose to suspend him indefinitely from his office as diocesan bishop. This sentence stayed in effect until 1856. However, despite being allowed to function again in a ministerial capacity, Onderdonk was never restored to the position of episcopal leadership. He continued to reside in Philadelphia until his death in 1858.

Bibliography

A. *An Appeal to the Religious Public* (Canandaigua, N.Y., 1818); *Episcopacy Tested by Scripture* (New York, 1831); *An Essay on Regeneration* (Philadelphia, 1835); *Episcopacy Examined and Re-examined* (New York, 1835); *Sermons and Episcopal Charges,* 2 vols. (Philadelphia, 1851).
B. *ACAB* 4, 580; *ANB* 16, 722–23; *DAB* 14, 40–41; *DCA,* 845; *EDC,* 374; *NCAB* 3, 470; *WWWA* Historical vol. 1607–1896, 387; William Stevens Perry, *The Bishops of the American Church* (New York, 1897); Elmer Onderdonk, *Genealogy of the Onderdonk Family in America* (New York, 1910); J. Wesley Twelves, *A History of the Diocese of Pennsylvania of the Protestant Episcopal Church* (Philadelphia, 1969).

OTEY, JAMES HERVEY (27 January 1800, Bedford County, Va.–23 April 1863, Memphis, Tenn.). *Education:* B. Belle-lettres, University of North Carolina, 1820; studied for ordination under William Mercer Green and John Stark Ravenscroft. *Career:* Tutor, University of North Carolina, 1820–21; principal, Harpeth Academy, Maury County, Tenn., 1821–23; principal, Warrenton Academy, Warrenton, N.C., 1823–25; rector, St. Paul's Church, Franklin, Tenn., 1827–34; bishop, diocese of Tennessee, 1834–63; missionary bishop, various jurisdictions, 1834–59; chancellor, University of the South, 1857–61.

James Hervey Otey, the first bishop of Tennessee, was born in Bedford County, Virginia, in 1800. After graduating from the University of North Carolina in 1820, he worked as a teacher and school principal for the next five years. Although not raised as a member of any denomination, he found himself increasingly drawn to the Episcopal Church during this period in his life. He received religious instruction from two prominent Episcopal clergymen: William Mercer Green, the chaplain of the University of North Carolina, who baptized him; and John Stark Ravenscroft,* the bishop of North Carolina, who both confirmed and ordained him. Otey served as rector of St. Paul's Church in Franklin, Tennessee, between 1827 and 1834. He helped organize the diocese of Tennessee in 1829, and he was elected its bishop four years later. He not only exercised jurisdiction over the state of Tennessee but also provided pastoral oversight to Episcopalians in Alabama, Arkansas, Florida, the Indian Territory, Kentucky, Louisiana, Mississippi, and Texas at various times during his episcopate.

Otey's initiative in the early development of the University of the South was undoubtedly his most notable achievement. Always concerned about higher education, he had visited several English and European universities in 1851. Along with Leonidas Polk,* the bishop of Louisiana, and Stephen Elliott, the bishop of Georgia, he envisioned the establishment of a major university, equal to the best in Europe, that would educate young men in the social and cultural ideals of the antebellum South. The first meeting of the trustees of the proposed school was held on Lookout Mountain, near Chattanooga, Tennessee, in July 1857. Otey was elected chairman of that meeting, and as the senior bishop in the 10 southern dioceses that supported the school, he later received the title of chancellor. Although a cornerstone was laid in 1860, the Civil War prevented any further construction of the university. When the school finally opened at Sewanee, Tennessee, in 1868—five years after Otey's death—its first academic building was named in his honor.

In the years before the outbreak of the Civil War, Otey was adamantly opposed to secession. As the threat to national unity grew stronger, he wrote to his fellow southern bishops, imploring them to support the Union. In 1861 he even contacted William Seward, Abraham Lincoln's secretary of state, in an effort to avoid a war. When the war did begin, Otey loyally supported the Confederacy, but he refused to participate in the creation of a new Episcopal denomination in the South. His wife's death in 1861, the shock of the war, and his extensive travels all took a tremendous toll on his health. He died in Memphis in April 1863.

Bibliography

A. Papers at AEC, at the archives of the University of the South, at the Southern Historical Collection of the University of North Carolina at Chapel Hill, and at the library of General Theological Seminary in New York; *An Address to the Members and Friends of the Protestant Episcopal Church in the Southern and South-western States* (Philadelphia, 1856); *Christian Education* (Richmond, 1859); *The Christian Ministry: A Sermon* (New York, 1860); *The Doctrine, Discipline, and Worship of the American Branch of the Catholic Church: Explained and Defended in Three Sermons* (New York, 1870).

B. *ACAB* 4, 604; *ANB* 16, 824–25; *BB,* 74–75; *DAB* 14, 90–91; *DCA,* 854; *EDC,* 380; *ERS,* 572; *NCAB* 5, 486–87; *WWWA* Historical vol. 1607–1896, 389; W. H. Odenheimer, "The Rt. Rev. James Hervey Otey, . . . the Late Bishop of Tennessee," *Church Review* 15 (1863–64): 455–90; Arthur H. Noll, "Bishop Otey as Provisional Bishop of Mississippi," *Publications of the Mississippi Historical Society* 3 (1900): 139–45; Hiram K. Douglass, "The First Bishop of Tennessee," *American Church Monthly* 20 (1927): 454–62; Thomas Frank Gailor, "James Hervey Otey, First Bishop of Tennessee," *HMPEC* 4 (1935): 53–56; Fred C. Wolf Jr., ed., "Documentary History: The Right Reverend James Hervey Otey and His Early Views on Tennessee and the West," *HMPEC* 32 (1963): 139–70; Frank M. McClain, "The Theology of Bishops Ravenscroft, Otey, and Green Concerning the Church, the Ministry, and the Sacraments," *HMPEC* 33 (1964): 103–36; William Mercer Green, *Memoir of Rt. Rev. James Hervey Otey* (New York, 1885); Donald Smith Armentrout, *James Hervey Otey, First Episcopal Bishop of Tennessee* (Knoxville, 1984).

P

PERKINS, FRANCES (10 April 1880, Boston–14 May 1965, New York). *Education:* B.A., Mount Holyoke College, 1902; studied at the University of Pennsylvania, 1907–9; M.A., Columbia University, 1910. *Career:* Teacher, Monson Academy, Worcester, Mass., 1902–4; teacher, Ferry Hall, Lake Forest, Ill., 1904–7; general secretary, Philadelphia Research and Protective Association, 1907–9; executive secretary, New York City Consumers' League, 1910–12; lecturer in sociology, Adelphi College, 1911; executive secretary, Committee on Safety of the City of New York, 1912–13; volunteer social worker in New York, 1913–18; member, New York State Industrial Commission (later Industrial Board), 1919–21, 1923–26; chairman, 1926–29; executive secretary, Council on Immigrant Education, New York, 1921–23; Industrial Commission of the State of New York, 1929–33; Secretary of Labor, 1933–45; member, U.S. Civil Service Commission, 1945–52; visiting lecturer at the University of Illinois, in Salzburg, Austria, and at Cornell University, 1953–57; visiting professor, School of Industrial and Labor Relations, Cornell University, 1957–65.

Frances Perkins, an Episcopal laywoman and public official, was born Fannie Coralie Perkins in Boston in 1880. After graduating from Mount Holyoke College, she worked as a teacher for five years. While teaching in Lake Forest, Illinois, she was attracted to the liturgy of the Episcopal Church and was confirmed at the Church of the Holy Spirit in June 1905, when she changed her name to Frances C. Perkins. While living in Illinois, she began to spend her free time at various Chicago settlement houses, including Hull House, where she was exposed for the first time to the conditions of the working poor. Believing that social work offered her greater personal and spiritual satisfaction than teaching, Perkins moved to Philadelphia, where she served as general secretary of the Philadelphia Research and Protective Association, a group that helped immigrant girls and

African Americans who had migrated from the South. In 1911, while working at the New York City Consumers' League, she witnessed the Triangle Shirtwaist Factory fire, which claimed the lives of 146 workers, mainly women and children. In the aftermath of that terrible event, she became the executive secretary of the Committee on Safety of the City of New York, and she worked as a lobbyist on behalf of labor organizations at the New York State legislature.

Perkins married Paul Wilson, an economist, in 1913, but she insisted on retaining her maiden name. For the first years of her marriage, she worked mainly as a volunteer social worker, but as her husband became increasingly susceptible to prolonged depressions, she sought full-time work. In 1919, Al Smith, the governor of New York, named Perkins to the state's Industrial Commission. Remaining involved both in labor issues and in the affairs of the Democratic party in New York, she became acquainted with Franklin D. Roosevelt, who chose her to chair the same commission (then called the Industrial Board) during his two terms as governor of the state. After Roosevelt was elected president of the United States in 1932, he appointed Perkins to the post of Secretary of Labor, making her the first woman cabinet member in the nation's history. She served in that position for virtually all of Roosevelt's years as president, and she was instrumental in drafting and implementing much of the New Deal legislation, including the creation of the Civilian Conservation Corps and the Social Security Act.

After Roosevelt's death in 1945, President Harry Truman appointed Perkins to the Civil Service Commission, and she continued in that capacity until the beginning of the administration of Dwight D. Eisenhower. Following the death of her husband in December 1952, Perkins was free to travel for long periods of time, and she served as a visiting lecturer in the field of labor and industrial relations. This work eventually led to the offer of a professorship at Cornell University. Accepting that position, she taught at Cornell from 1957 to 1965.

Perkins was an associate of the All Saints' Sisters of the Poor in Catonsville, Maryland, where she was a regular retreatant. She insisted that her religious faith was central to her work as a government official. In 1948, she presented the St. Bede lectures at St. Thomas Church in New York City. In those lectures, she articulated her incarnational theological views, emphasizing that God's becoming human in Jesus gave human beings the capacity to cooperate with God in the creation of a Christian social order. She also spoke of "the special vocation of the laity to conduct and carry on the worldly and secular affairs of modern society . . . in order that all men may be maintained in health and decency." Perkins worked actively until just before a series of strokes led to her death in May 1965.

Bibliography

A. Papers at Columbia University, at the Schlesinger Library of Radcliffe College, at the Franklin D. Roosevelt Presidential Library in Hyde Park, N.Y., and at the National Archives in Washington, D.C.; numerous articles in periodicals, including "Do Women in Industry Need Special Protection?" *Survey,* 15 February 1925, 529–31; "Eight Years as Madame Secretary," *Fortune,* September 1941, 76–79; and "The People Mattered," *Survey,* February 1946, 38–39; "Full Employment," in *Chris-*

tianity Takes a Stand: An Approach to the Issues of Today, ed. William Scarlett
(New York, 1946), 94–109; *The Roosevelt I Knew* (New York, 1946); *Al Smith,
Hero of the Cities: A Political Portrait Drawing on the Papers of Frances Perkins,*
ed. Matthew and Hannah Josephson (Boston, 1969).

B. *ANB* 17, 339–41; *DAB* supp. 7, 607–10; *EDC*, 396–97; *FD*, 159–64; *NAW* 4, 535–39;
WWWA 4, 744; *NYT*, 15 May 1965; Augustus W. Hinshaw, "The Story of Frances
Perkins," *Century*, September 1927, 596–605; Inis W. Jones, "Frances Perkins,
Industrial Crusader," *World's Work*, April 1930, 64–67; Russell Lord, "Madame
Secretary: A Profile," *New Yorker*, 2 and 9 September 1933; Marguerite Young,
"Frances Perkins, Liberal Politician," *American Mercury*, August 1934, 398–407;
Irving Bernstein, *Turbulent Years: A History of the American Worker, 1933–1941*
(Boston, 1970); George Martin, *Madame Secretary, Frances Perkins* (Boston,
1976).

PIKE, JAMES ALBERT (14 February 1913, Oklahoma City, Okla.–?3–7 Sep-
tember 1969, Israel). *Education:* Studied at the University of Santa Clara, 1930–
32; B.A., University of California at Los Angeles, 1934; LL.B., 1936; J.S.D.,
Yale University, 1938; studied at the Virginia Theological Seminary, 1945–46;
studied at General Theological Seminary, 1946–47; B.D., Union Theological
Seminary, New York, 1951. *Career:* Attorney, U.S. Securities and Exchange
Commission, Washington, D.C., 1938–42; officer, U.S. Navy, 1942–45; curate,
St. John's Church, Washington, D.C., 1944–46; fellow and tutor, General Theological Seminary, 1946–47; rector, Christ Church, Poughkeepsie, N.Y., 1947–49;
chaplain, Columbia University, 1949–52; dean, Cathedral of St. John the Divine,
New York, 1952–58; bishop, diocese of California, 1958–66; theologian-in-
residence, Center for the Study of Democratic Institutions, Santa Barbara, Calif.,
1966–69.

James A. Pike, a bishop and controversial theologian, was born in Oklahoma
City in 1913. Although he was raised a Roman Catholic and entered college with
the intention of entering the priesthood, he rebelled against the church and became
an agnostic. He joined the Episcopal Church, however, during his brief but suc-
cessful law career in Washington, D.C., and after serving in the U.S. Navy during
World War II, he decided to enter the ordained ministry. Ordained to the diaconate
in December 1944, he served for two years as a curate at St. John's Church in
Washington, D.C. He next served as the rector of Christ Church in Poughkeepsie,
New York, where he also held the Episcopal chaplain's position at Vassar College.
In 1949 he became chaplain and head of the religion department at Columbia
University. While he was at Columbia, he published *The Faith of the Church*
(1951), which he wrote with W. Norman Pittenger of General Theological Seminary. This book was the third volume in the *Church's Teaching* series. As Pike
and Pittenger emphasized, the Episcopal Church was rightly characterized as
" 'the roomiest Church in Christendom' . . . not because it does not care about
what people believe, but because it knows that the truth of the Christian Gospel

is so wonderfully rich and so infinitely great that no single human expression can exhaust all its truth and splendor."

Pike became the dean of the Cathedral of St. John the Divine in New York City in 1952. He began to be known as a highly controversial figure who was passionately concerned about the church's stance on public issues. In the winter of 1953, he was chosen by the trustees of the University of the South at Sewanee, Tennessee, to receive an honorary degree. Because those same trustees were then embroiled in a bitter dispute over their refusal to desegregate Sewanee's School of Theology, Pike declined their offer and immediately issued a press release articulating his reasons for refusing the school's "doctorate in . . . white divinity." In the late 1950s, he also hosted "The Dean Pike Show," a weekly religious program on the ABC television network. Having risen to prominence in the Episcopal Church, Pike was elected bishop of the diocese of California in 1958. One of his most constructive acts as bishop was to join Eugene Carson Blake, the stated clerk of the United Presbyterian Church, in proposing the unification of the major Protestant denominations in the United States. Although no new denomination was actually formed, this proposal resulted in the creation of an ecumenical organization, the Consultation on Church Union, in 1962.

Pike was a prolific writer who published numerous books and magazine articles. While a bishop, he began to be not only more outspoken in his political opinions but also increasingly heterodox in his theological views. He supported a wide assortment of liberal and radical causes: civil rights, peace, birth control, abortion, the ordination of women, and gay rights. In addition, he questioned the veracity of the Bible itself, dismissing it for being filled with "superstition, sheer evil, and flat contradiction." He also rejected traditional church doctrines such as the Trinity, the Virgin Birth, and the divinity of Jesus, all of which he labeled as "excess baggage" that modern Christians had no reason to believe. These radical ideas quickly caused an uproar within the Episcopal Church, and in 1966 a group of his fellow bishops brought formal charges of heresy against him. A few months later, the House of Bishops censured him for offering religious interpretations that were "marred by caricatures of treasured symbols and . . . by cheap vulgarizations of great expressions of the faith."

When Pike's oldest son committed suicide in 1966, his search for religious meaning turned in another direction, and he became obsessed with forms of parapsychology, especially communication with the dead. He resigned as bishop that year in order to devote more time to this new interest. His attempts to contact the spirit of his son were recorded in *The Other Side* (1968), which he wrote with Diane Kennedy, the woman who in December 1968 became his second wife. A few months after they were married, the Pikes traveled to Israel to study the Dead Sea scrolls. Inadequately equipped, they drove into the Judean wilderness on September 3, 1969. When their car broke down in the desert, they went searching for help. Although Diane was eventually rescued, Pike died of thirst and exposure during the time they were separated.

Even in death, Pike attained a certain notoriety. As the essayist Joan Didion observed when reflecting on the meaning of his life, Pike was made for the 1960s, "those years when no one at all seemed to have any memory or mooring." Commenting more sympathetically, John Krumm, an Episcopal priest, praised Pike for his insatiable intellectual curiosity. Pike's questioning of the articles of the faith had inspired others to think more about them, Krumm concluded: "It's been a long time since the doctrine of the Trinity was cocktail party conversation, but now it is."

Bibliography

A. *The Faith of the Church* (New York, 1951); *Beyond Anxiety* (New York, 1953); *If You Marry Outside Your Faith* (New York, 1954); *The Church, Politics and Society* (New York, 1955); *Doing the Truth: A Summary of Christian Ethics* (Garden City, N.Y., 1955); *A Time for Christian Candor* (New York, 1964); *Teenagers and Sex* (Englewood Cliffs, N.J., 1965); *You and the New Morality* (New York, 1967); *If This Be Heresy* (New York, 1967); *The Other Side: An Account of My Experiences with Psychic Phenomena* (Garden City, N.Y., 1968).

B. *DARB,* 434–35; *DCA,* 907–8; *EDC,* 401–2; *NCAB* 56, 147–49; *WWWA* 5, 571; *Contemporary Authors: New Revisions Series,* vol. 4 (Detroit, 1981), 482–84; *NYT,* 8 September 1969; Joan Didion, "James Pike, American," in *The White Album* (New York, 1979), 51–58; Edwin Gould Wappler, "Four Anglican Situationists and Their Tradition: A Study in Fletcher, Pike, Robinson, and Rhymes" (Ph.D. diss., Duke University, 1972); Frederick M. Morris, *Bishop Pike: Ham, Heretic, or Hero* (Grand Rapids, Mich., 1967); William Stringfellow and Anthony Towne, *The Bishop Pike Affair: Scandals of Conscience and Heresy, Relevance and Solemnity in the Contemporary Church* (New York, 1967); Diane K. Pike, *Search: The Personal Story of a Wilderness Journey* (Garden City, N.Y., 1970); Allen Spraggett, *The Bishop Pike Story* (New York, 1970); William Stringfellow and Anthony Towne, *The Death and Life of Bishop Pike* (Garden City, N.Y., 1976); Robert S. Ellwood, *The Sixties Spiritual Awakening: American Religion Moving from Modern to Postmodern* (New Brunswick, N.J., 1994), 127–29.

POLK, LEONIDAS (10 April 1806, Raleigh, N.C.–14 June 1864, Pine Mountain, near Marietta, Ga.). *Education:* Attended the University of North Carolina, 1821–23; graduated from the U.S. Military Academy at West Point, 1827; graduated from the Virginia Theological Seminary, 1830. *Career:* Assistant minister, Monumental Church, Richmond, Va., 1830–31; traveled in Europe, 1831–33; plantation owner, west Tennessee, 1833–38; rector, St. Peter's Church, Columbia, Tenn., 1834–38; missionary bishop of the Southwest, 1838–41; bishop, diocese of Louisiana, 1841–64; major general, Confederate army, 1861–64; chancellor, University of the South, 1863–64.

A bishop and a general in the Confederate army, Leonidas Polk was born in North Carolina in 1806. He was the son of Sarah Hawkins and William Polk, a revolutionary war veteran and prosperous planter. After studying for two years at the University of North Carolina, he entered the U.S. Military Academy in 1823. As a result of the preaching of Charles P. McIlvaine,* the chaplain at West Point,

Polk experienced a religious conversion, and shortly after his graduation in 1827, he resigned his military commission and entered Virginia Theological Seminary. Ordained a deacon in April 1830 and a priest 13 months later, he served briefly as the assistant minister at the Monumental Church in Richmond, Virginia. When poor health forced him to resign in 1831, he traveled in Europe for two years before settling on a plantation in west Tennessee. Between 1833 and 1838, he worked both as a plantation owner and as rector of the Episcopal parish in Columbia, Tennessee. In 1838 he was appointed missionary bishop of the Southwest and placed in charge of the evangelistic efforts of the Episcopal Church in Alabama, Arkansas, Louisiana, and Mississippi. In October 1841 he was elected as the first bishop of the newly organized diocese of Louisiana.

Following his consecration, Polk took charge of a large sugar plantation in Louisiana. Although not a talented plantation manager or spiritual leader, he was a sociable man who had many influential and important friends. With the assistance of James Hervey Otey,* the bishop of Tennessee, and Stephen Elliott, the bishop of Georgia, he conceived the idea of creating a University of the South for the education of the sons of slaveholders. Polk helped raise funds for the establishment of that institution, and in October 1860 he laid the school's cornerstone at Sewanee, Tennessee. He also served as the second chancellor of the University of the South from April 1863 until his death.

After Louisiana seceded from the Union, Polk quickly took the lead in urging Episcopalians in the South to "follow our Nationality" and organize a new denomination—a proposal that eventually culminated in the formation of the Protestant Episcopal Church in the Confederate States of America. With the outbreak of hostilities in the spring of 1861, Polk also came to the aid of the Confederacy. Having been a friend of Confederate president Jefferson Davis when they were cadets together at West Point, Polk volunteered to assist him in military matters. This offer led Davis to appoint Polk a major general and to place him in charge of the Confederacy's defenses in the Mississippi valley at the beginning of the Civil War. Although Polk was not a very successful general, he served as a corps commander in the Army of Tennessee during several major campaigns in 1862 and 1863. Throughout the war, he remained the bishop of Louisiana, but army responsibilities prevented him from ministering actively in his diocese. He was killed in battle at Pine Mountain, outside of Atlanta, in June 1864.

Bibliography

A. Papers at the Southern Historical Collection, University of North Carolina at Chapel Hill; "Pastoral Letter of Bishop Leonidas Polk, January 30, 1861," *HMPEC* 31 (1962): 296–98.
B. *ACAB* 5, 57; *ANB* 17, 626–27; *DAB* 15, 39–40; *DARB,* 436–37; *DCA,* 916–17; *EDC,* 406; *ERS,* 591–92; *NCAB* 11, 341–42; *WWWA* Historical vol. 1607–1896, 416–17; William M. Polk, *Leonidas Polk: Bishop and General,* 2 vols. (New York, 1893); Joseph H. Parks, *General Leonidas Polk, C.S.A., the Fighting Bishop* (Baton Rouge, La., 1962).

POTTER, HENRY CODMAN (25 May 1835, Schenectady, N.Y.–21 July 1908, Cooperstown, N.Y.). *Education:* Graduated from the Virginia Theological Seminary, 1857. *Career:* Minister-in-charge, Christ Church, Greensburg, Pa., 1857–59; rector, St. John's Church, Troy, N.Y., 1859–66; assistant minister, Trinity Church, Boston, 1866–68; rector, Grace Church, New York, 1868–83; assistant bishop, diocese of New York, 1883–87; bishop, diocese of New York, 1887–1908.

Henry Codman Potter, a bishop and social gospel advocate, was born in Schenectady, New York, in May 1835. His father, Alonzo Potter, was then a professor at Union College and later became the third bishop of Pennsylvania. Henry studied at Virginia Theological Seminary, and he was ordained a deacon in 1857 and a priest in 1858. After serving briefly in three different parishes, he became the rector of Grace Church, New York, in 1868. In that position he helped transform his parish into an early example of an "institutional church." He erected Grace Chapel in 1876 as a free church (i.e., a church that was not supported by pew rents), and the following year he built Grace House as a headquarters for missionary work among Germans living in the neighborhood. Grace House included a reading room for working men and women as well as a day nursery for their children. It was widely recognized as a center of service to the people of the city, and its active social programs were further developed under the rectorship of Potter's successor, William Reed Huntington.*

Potter was consecrated as the assistant bishop of New York in 1883 and as the diocesan bishop four year later. As bishop, he became a leader of the Church Association for the Advancement of the Interests of Labor, which was founded in New York City in 1887. In a pastoral letter he argued against treating labor as a mere market commodity, and he supported arbitration in labor disputes while opposing sweatshops. A promoter of social reform, he sought better living and working conditions for laborers and fought against police corruption. In addition to these activities, Potter was a broad church Episcopalian who sought to overcome petty divisions over party issues in his denomination. He dealt skillfully with three particularly troublesome conflicts during his episcopate: the ordination of the outspoken biblical critic Charles A. Briggs,* the controversial lectures on biblical criticism given by R. Heber Newton,* and the extreme ritualist practices adopted by Arthur Ritchie, the Anglo-Catholic rector of the Church of St. Ignatius. Employing a mixture of tact, humility, and good sense, Potter adroitly handled problems with an eye to the long-term good of the Episcopal Church as a whole.

Energetic on behalf of the spiritual welfare of New York Episcopalians, Potter instituted the Advent Mission, an Episcopal form of revival, in 1885, and he began spiritual retreats for clergy and ordinands. A champion of cathedrals as spiritual centers for dioceses, he presided at the laying of the cornerstone of the Cathedral of St. John the Divine in New York City in 1892. A supporter of religious orders for men and women, he was among the first Episcopalians to proclaim the value of sisterhoods and deaconesses in his denomination, and he heard the profession of James O.S. Huntington* as a monk in the Order of the Holy Cross.

Potter died in Cooperstown, New York, in July 1908.

Bibliography

A. Papers at AEC and at General Theological Seminary, New York; *Sisterhoods and Deaconesses at Home and Abroad* (New York, 1871); *The Gates of the East: A Winter in Egypt and Syria* (New York, 1877); *Sermons of the City* (New York, 1881); *Waymarks* (New York, 1892); *The Scholar and the State* (New York, 1897); *Addresses to Women Engaged in Church Work* (New York, 1898); *The East of Today and Tomorrow* (New York, 1902); *The Citizen in His Relation to the Industrial Situation* (New York, 1902); *Law and Loyalty* (New York, 1903); *The Modern Man and His Fellow Man* (New York, 1903); *Reminiscences of Bishops and Archbishops* (New York, 1906).

B. *ANB* 17, 746–48; *DAB* 15, 127–29; *EDC*, 408; *SH* 9, 144; *NYT*, 22 July 1908; Harriette A. Keyser, *Bishop Potter: The People's Friend* (New York, 1910); George Hodges, *Henry Codman Potter, Seventh Bishop of New York* (New York, 1915); James Sheerin, *Henry Codman Potter: An American Metropolitan* (New York, 1933); James Elliott Lindsley, *This Planted Vine: A Narrative History of the Episcopal Diocese of New York* (New York, 1984), chapter 11.

Q

QUINTARD, CHARLES TODD (22 December 1824, Stamford, Conn.–15 February 1898, Meridian, Ga.). *Education:* Attended Columbia College; M.D., medical college of the University of the City of New York, 1847; studied for ordination under James H. Otey, 1854–55. *Career:* Practiced medicine in New York and in Athens, Ga., 1847–51; professor of physiology and pathological anatomy, Memphis Medical College, 1851–55; rector, Calvary Church, Memphis, Tenn., 1857–58; rector, Church of the Advent, Nashville, Tenn., 1858–61; chaplain and medical surgeon, Confederate army, 1861–65; bishop, diocese of Tennessee, 1865–98; vice-chancellor, University of the South, 1867–72.

Charles Todd Quintard, a bishop and an educator, was born in Stamford, Connecticut, in December 1824. After successfully pursuing a career as a physician, medical researcher, and anatomy professor, he sought ordination in the Episcopal Church. He studied theology under the tutelage of James H. Otey,* the bishop of Tennessee, who ordained him a deacon in January 1855 and a priest one year later. After serving briefly as a rector in parishes in Memphis and Nashville, Quintard enlisted in the First Tennessee regiment in the Confederate army at the outbreak of the Civil War. He served as both chaplain and surgeon of that regiment until the war's end. Bishop Otey died in April 1863, and a few months after the return of peace, Quintard was chosen to be his successor. He was consecrated bishop in October 1865.

Quintard was instrumental in reviving the Episcopal Church in Tennessee after four years of devastating warfare. During the early days of his episcopate, he sought to rebuild church institutions that had been damaged or destroyed during the conflict. A supporter of the Oxford movement, he was especially concerned about the church's educational ministry. He is best known for his rebuilding efforts at the University of the South, which had been founded by three southern bishops—Leonidas Polk* of Louisiana, Stephen Elliott of Georgia, and Otey—in 1857. Quintard successfully raised funds in the North and in England, and thanks to his labors, the university was at last able to open in September 1868. He served as the school's vice-chancellor (president) from 1867 to 1872, and he continued to help it grow and develop in numerous other ways for the remainder of his life.

Quintard believed that his main purpose as bishop was to make the church "a refuge for all—the lame, halt and blind as well as the rich." Consequently, he opposed parish pew rents and fostered a ministry on behalf of the disadvantaged. Worried about the effects of industrialization on workers, he established a refuge for the poor in Memphis in 1869, and in 1873 he presented his diocese with a plan to assist people lacking food, housing, and education. He founded missions to the laborers at the foundries in South Pittsburg (1876) and in Chattanooga (1880). Hoping that the Episcopal Church would also expand its evangelistic work among African Americans, he opposed plans to segregate the black congregations of the denomination, and he assisted in the founding of Hoffman Hall, a seminary for African Americans on the campus of Fisk University in Nashville.

Quintard died in February 1898 in Meridian, Georgia, while staying there in an effort to improve his health.

Bibliography

A. Papers at the archives of the University of the South, at the archives of Duke University, and at the archives of the diocese of Tennessee in Nashville; Arthur Howard Noll, ed., *Doctor Quintard, Chaplain C.S.A. and Second Bishop of Tennessee, Being His Story of the War (1861–1865)* (Sewanee, Tenn., 1905).
B. *ANB* 18, 46–47; *DAB* 15, 313–14; *DCA,* 968; *EDC,* 429; *ERS,* 630–31; Hiram K. Douglass, "Charles Todd Quintard," *American Church Monthly* 27 (1930): 142–47; Richard Neil Greatwood, "Charles Todd Quintard (1824–1898): His Role and Significance in the Development of the Protestant Episcopal Church in the Diocese of Tennessee and in the South" (Ph.D. diss., Vanderbilt University, 1977); Moultrie Guerry, "Charles Todd Quintard," in *Men Who Made Sewanee* (Sewanee, Tenn., 1905).

R

RAINSFORD, WILLIAM STEPHEN (30 October 1850, near Dublin, Ireland–17 December 1933, New York). *Education:* A.B., Cambridge University, 1874. *Career:* Curate, St. Giles's Church, Norwich, England, 1873–76; traveling missionary in Canada and the United States, 1876–78; assistant rector, St. James' Cathedral, Toronto, 1878–82; rector, St. George's Church, New York, 1883–1906; travels in Africa, 1906–10; renounced his Episcopal orders, 1912.

William S. Rainsford, a priest and social gospel advocate, was born near Dublin, Ireland, in 1850. The son of an Anglo-Irish vicar, he was educated in England. Ordained a deacon in 1873 and a priest one year later, he began his ministry at St. Giles's Church in Norwich. He came to North America in 1876. Although he served for several years as a priest in Canada, he rose to fame after becoming rector of St. George's Church in New York City. Although St. George's was moribund when Rainsford arrived in 1883, he soon transformed it into a thriving "institutional church" that offered parishioners not only worship and Christian education but also a varied social service program.

A broad church Episcopalian, Rainsford had become highly critical of the otherworldliness of evangelicalism while serving in England, and he was determined to reach out in concrete ways to poor people in St. George's neighborhood. After gaining the support of the prominent businessman J. Pierpont Morgan,* his senior warden, Rainsford was able to accomplish so much at St. George's that he significantly altered American Protestants' beliefs about the purposes of church life. His controversial decision to abolish pew rents was one of the keys to his eventual success. The various social services that St. George's provided, together with Rainsford's own focus on political reform, helped broaden the appeal of the Episcopal Church, especially among the urban working class. Thanks to these efforts, his parish grew to four thousand communicants and became a model for other urban parishes in the United States.

Liberal in theology, Rainsford stressed the divine presence in this world and shunned traditional Trinitarian dogma. After poor health forced his resignation from St. George's in 1906, his religious views grew increasingly more humanistic and less orthodox. Developing a religious philosophy utterly devoid of supernatural elements, he eventually abandoned Christianity altogether and renounced his priestly orders. Although he spent the last years of his life in retirement at Ridgefield, Connecticut, he died while being treated at a hospital in New York in 1933.

Bibliography

A. *Sermons Preached in St. George's Church* (New York, 1887); *The Church's Opportunity in the City Today* (New York, 1895); *Good Friday Meditation* (New York, 1901); *The Reasonableness of Faith, and Other Addresses* (New York, 1902); *A Preacher's Story of His Work* (New York, 1904); *The Land of the Lion* (New York, 1909); *The Reasonableness of the Religion of Jesus* (New York, 1913); *The Story of a Varied Life: An Autobiography* (Garden City, N.Y., 1922).

B. *ANB* 18, 83–84; *DAB* 21, 618–19; *EDC,* 430; *SH* 9, 385; *WWWA* 1, 1006; *NYT,* 18 December 1933; Henry Anstice, *History of St. George's Church in the City of New York* (New York, 1911); Elizabeth Moulton, *St. George's Church, New York* (New York, 1964); Paul T. Phillips, *A Kingdom on Earth: Anglo-American Social Christianity, 1880–1940* (University Park, Pa., 1996).

RAMSAY, MARTHA LAURENS (3 November 1759, Charleston, S.C.–10 June 1811, Charleston, S.C.). *Education:* Privately tutored. *Career:* Wife and mother, 1787–1811.

A lay Anglican and the author of a notable spiritual diary, Martha Laurens Ramsay was born in Charleston, South Carolina, in 1759. She was the member of a prominent South Carolina family. Her father, Henry Laurens, served as the president of the Continental Congress and as a diplomat during the American Revolution; her mother, Eleanor Ball, was the daughter of a prosperous Charleston planter. Following her mother's death in 1770, she spent much of her late adolescence in England and France, where she nursed ailing family members and founded a school in the village of Vigan (in southern France). Between 1782 and 1784, when her father was involved in the peace negotiations with Great Britain, she enjoyed a public role as his hostess and secretary. Returning to Charleston in 1785 after her sojourn in Europe, she assumed responsibility for the management of her family's household. During that period, she became acquainted with David Ramsay, her father's physician, whom she married in January 1787.

The Laurens family belonged to St. Philip's Church, Charleston, where Martha was confirmed when she was 12 years old. In the midst of a family crisis in 1773, she entered into a "solemn covenant with God," in which she dedicated herself to a life of moral and religious seriousness. This covenant remained a secret for most of her life, but shortly before she died, Martha disclosed to her husband that she had kept a spiritual diary covering the years 1791 through 1808. David Ramsay edited and published a posthumous version of this diary as well as some of his wife's letters and meditations. The largest portion of the printed diary concerned the year 1795, when Martha suffered a severe emotional depression. The literary outpouring of that period reveals an articulate person attempting to regain her psychic equilibrium using the language and ideas of evangelical Protestantism. "I am in straits, trials, and perplexities of soul and of body," she wrote. "My outward affairs can only be helped by thy providence; my spiritual troubles by thy grace."

Martha Ramsay suffered from an unnamed but debilitating illness during the last three years of her life. A highly respected figure at the time of her death in Charleston in 1811, her passing was noted as far away as Boston. David Ramsay decided to publish his wife's *Memoirs* because he believed they exemplified the civic and spiritual virtues that all Americans needed to uphold. He was correct in this assessment. Martha's spiritual struggles were cited favorably throughout the nineteenth century, and her *Memoirs* were repeatedly reprinted until the 1890s.

Bibliography

A. Papers at the South Caroliniana Library in Columbia and at the South Carolina Historical Society in Charleston; *Memoirs of the Life of Martha Laurens Ramsay,* ed. David Ramsay (Charleston, S.C., 1811).

B. *ANB* 18, 95–96; *FD,* 1–5; *NAW* 3, 111–13; Joanna Bowen Gillespie, "1795: Martha Laurens Ramsay's 'Dark Night of the Soul,' " *WMQ* , 3rd ser., 48 (1991): 68–92; Joanna Bowen Gillespie, *The Life and Times of Martha Laurens Ramsay, 1759–1811* (Columbia, S.C., 2001).

RAVENSCROFT, JOHN STARK (17 May 1772, Prince George County, Va.– 5 March 1830, Raleigh, N.C.). *Education:* Studied law at the College of William and Mary. *Career:* Planter, 1793–1817; rector, St. James Church, Mecklenburg County, Va., 1817–23; bishop, diocese of North Carolina, 1823–30; rector, Christ Church, Raleigh, N.C., 1823–28; rector, St. John's Church, Williamsboro, N.C., 1828–30.

John Stark Ravenscroft, a bishop and early high church leader, was born in Virginia in 1772. Although his family moved to the south of Scotland soon after his birth, Ravenscroft returned to Virginia when he was 16 years old. He studied law at the College of William and Mary but never practiced that profession. In 1792 he purchased a large estate in Lunenburg County, Virginia, where he lived as a slaveholding plantation owner for the next 18 years. After experiencing a religious conversion in 1810, Ravenscroft joined the Republican Methodists and became a lay preacher. He later left that denomination and joined the Episcopal Church instead. Ordained in 1817 by Richard Channing Moore, the bishop of Virginia, he served as rector of St. James Church in Mecklenburg County until 1823, when he was elected as the first bishop of the diocese of North Carolina. Organized in 1817, the diocese of North Carolina was quite weak at the time of

Ravenscroft's arrival, having only eight clergy and about four hundred members. Because the diocese could not afford to pay him a full-time salary, Ravenscroft served simultaneously as the rector of Christ Church in Raleigh.

Ravenscroft was a high church Episcopalian in the tradition of his fellow bishop John Henry Hobart* of New York. Although Ravenscroft believed in the value of religious experience in salvation, he also stressed the apostolic character of the Episcopal Church and the importance of the historic succession of bishops. As a result, he discouraged cooperation between Episcopalians and other Protestants in his state. These high church ideas continued to influence the diocese of North Carolina for many years after Ravenscroft's death. Although the diocese was still small in 1830, the number of communicants had doubled to approximately eight hundred by then, and most of the clergy were committed to their bishop's views about the uniqueness of the Episcopal Church.

Exhausted by the travel required of a bishop, Ravenscroft decided in 1828 that he could no longer serve as rector of Christ Church, Raleigh. He moved to Williamsboro, where he took over Saint John's Church, a smaller parish. Further weakened by a trip to Philadelphia to attend the 1829 General Convention, his health continued to decline. He eventually died in Raleigh in March 1830.

Bibliography

A. Papers at AEC; *The Works of the Right Reverend John Stark Ravenscroft*, 2 vols. (New York, 1830).

B. *AAP* 5, 617–25; *ACAB* 5, 187–88; *ANB* 18, 193–93; *DAB* 15, 397–98; *DCA*, 975–76; *EDC*, 431; *ERS*, 636–37; *MM*, 159–66; *NCAB* 6, 52; *WWWA* Historical vol. 1607–1896, 433; William Mercer Green, "Bishop Ravenscroft," *American Quarterly Church Review* 22 (1870–1871): 526–53; Frank M. McClain, "The Theology of Bishops Ravenscroft, Otey, and Green Concerning the Church, the Ministry, and the Sacraments," *HMPEC* 33 (1964): 103–36; John N. Norton, *The Life of Bishop Ravenscroft* (New York, 1858); Marshall DeLancey Haywood, *Lives of the Bishops of North Carolina* (Raleigh, N.C., 1910); Henry S. Lewis, "The Formation of the Diocese of North Carolina, 1817–1830," in *The Episcopal Church in North Carolina, 1701–1959*, ed. Lawrence Foushee London and Sarah McCulloh Lemmon (Raleigh, N.C., 1987), 94–170.

RUSSELL, JAMES SOLOMON (20 December 1857, near Palmer Springs, Va.–28 March 1935, Lawrenceville, Va.). *Education:* Studied at Hampton Institute, 1874–75, 1877–78; studied at St. Stephen's Normal and Theological Institute (later Bishop Payne Divinity School), Petersburg, Va., 1878–82. *Career:* Missionary, Brunswick County, Va., 1882–88; founding principal and chaplain, Saint Paul's Normal and Industrial School (later St. Paul's College), Lawrenceville, Va., 1888–1929; archdeacon for Colored Work, diocese of Southern Virginia, 1898–1935.

James Solomon Russell, a priest and educator, was born in slavery on the Hendrick Estate in Mecklenburg County near Palmer Springs, Virginia. Despite being raised in poverty during the Reconstruction period in the South, Russell was able to attain a meager education, and he eventually studied for two academic years at Hampton Institute. As a boy, he attended Zion Union Apostolic Church, an African American denomination organized in southern Virginia after the Civil War. At age 10 he dedicated himself to becoming a preacher of the gospel. Thanks to the efforts of a white benefactor, Russell not only converted to the Episcopal Church but also was introduced to Francis M. Whittle, the bishop of Virginia. Although the diocese of Virginia had never had a black candidate for the ordained ministry, Whittle helped organize a seminary for African Americans at St. Stephen's Church in Petersburg, Virginia. In 1878 Russell became the first student at the school, which later became Bishop Payne Divinity School.

After being ordained a deacon in March 1882, Russell was dispatched by his bishop to serve as a missionary among African Americans in Brunswick County, Virginia. He was ordained a priest five years later. Religion and education were closely related in Russell's mind, and with the aid of his wife, Virginia Morgan, he opened a school (now St. Paul's College) in 1888. St. Paul's offered black youth in Brunswick and surrounding counties virtually their only opportunity to achieve an education at that time. Known as "Pa Jim," Russell served as the school's principal and chaplain for several decades. He required students to attend chapel twice a day and made religion a mandatory subject. Following the organization of a new diocese (Southern Virginia) in 1892, Russell continued to serve as a missionary at Lawrenceville. Later named archdeacon for Colored Work in Southern Virginia, he eventually supervised 11 clergymen, 28 churches, and over 2,000 communicants. He was the most prominent African American priest in the South in the early twentieth century, and he was the first person elected to serve as suffragan bishop for Work among Colored People in the diocese of Arkansas. Russell decided to decline that election, however, and Edward T. Demby* was chosen instead as the first black Episcopal bishop in the United States.

Influenced by the philosophy of the great African American educator Booker T. Washington, Russell always advised his students to own land, to keep out of debt, and—when whites allowed it—to vote. Under Russell's dedicated leadership, Saint Paul's became the largest business in Brunswick County, and he attracted both the attention and financial support of a number of important white philanthropists in the North. In 1917 he also became the first African American to receive an honorary degree from the Virginia Theological Seminary in Alexandria. Russell died in Lawrenceville in March 1935, and approximately three thousand people attended his funeral on the St. Paul's campus.

Bibliography

A. Papers at Saint Paul's College in Lawrenceville, Virginia, and at AEC; *Adventure in Faith: An Autobiographic Story of St. Paul Normal and Industrial School, Lawrenceville, Virginia* (New York, 1936).
B. *ANB* 19, 103 4; *DAB* supp. 1, 645; *WWWA* 1, 1068; *NYT,* 29 March 1935; J. Carleton

Hayden, "James Solomon Russell (1857–1935): Missionary and Founder of St. Paul's College," *Linkage* 7 (March 1987): 10–11; Frances Ashton Thurman, "History of Saint Paul's College" (Ph.D. diss., Howard University, 1978); Roberta Arnold, *A Man and His Work: The Life Story of Archdeacon James Solomon Russell* (Lawrenceville, Va., 1938).

S

SCARLETT, WILLIAM (3 October 1883, Columbus, Ohio–28 March 1973, Castine, Me.). *Education:* A.B., Harvard College, 1905; B.D., Episcopal Theological School, 1909. *Career:* Assistant, St. George's Church, New York, 1909–11; dean, Trinity Cathedral, Phoenix, 1911–22; dean, Christ Church Cathedral, St. Louis, 1922–30; bishop coadjutor, diocese of Missouri, 1930–33; bishop, diocese of Missouri, 1933–53.

A bishop and advocate of the social gospel, William Scarlett was born in Columbus, Ohio, in 1883. After graduating from Harvard College, he could not decide whether to become a doctor or an Episcopal priest. He spent a year working on a ranch in western Nebraska and eventually decided to study for the ordained ministry. In 1906, he entered the Episcopal Theological School. In his early life he had been influenced by two great social gospel leaders: Washington Gladden, the minister of the Congregational church in Columbus, and Walter Rauschenbusch, a theologian who taught at Rochester Theological Seminary. While he was studying at the theological school, Scarlett also attended classes at Harvard in the new field of Christian ethics. Following his graduation and ordination in the spring of 1909, he served for two years as an assistant at St. George's Church in New York City—an Episcopal parish renowned for its social outreach ministry.

In 1911 Scarlett was called to be dean of Trinity Cathedral in Phoenix. While serving there, he began to establish a reputation as a preacher and pastor who was willing to assist workers in disputes with management. He next accepted a call in 1922 to become the dean of Christ Church Cathedral in St. Louis, a downtown church and the oldest Episcopal parish west of the Mississippi. Along with the rabbi of a local Jewish congregation, Scarlett created the Social Justice Commission in St. Louis. This organization offered mediation in various labor-related conflicts in the city. When Frederick Foote Johnson, the bishop of Missouri, became ill, he called for the election of a bishop coadjutor to assist him with his duties. Scarlett easily won that election, and in May 1930 he was consecrated bishop. Three year later, he succeeded Johnson as the diocesan bishop.

According to Reinhold Niebuhr, his friend and political ally, Scarlett was often called "the conscience of the community," for throughout his 20 years as bishop of Missouri he sought to bring a sense of Christian compassion to numerous social issues. For example, he served for many years as a member of the Commission on Marriage and Divorce of General Convention. In that capacity he lobbied for the liberalization of the church's position on marriage after divorce. During World War II, he also encouraged communication with a commission of the Church of England that was considering plans for the postwar reconstruction of Europe. When the 1943 General Convention created a Joint Commission on Social Reconstruction to deliberate on this matter, Scarlett was appointed its chairman. In 1946 the commission published a book, entitled *Christianity Takes a Stand,* with chapters on subjects such as "the moral meaning of the atomic bomb" and "the Negro problem." As Scarlett emphasized in his introduction, "Christianity is not something irrelevant to life, not something that touches only the fringes of life. . . . Rather, we believe that Christianity is the truth about . . . man's relation to God and God's relation to the world, and about man's relation to his fellow men."

A low church Episcopalian, sometimes known as the "red tie" bishop because he did not wear a clerical collar, Scarlett was committed to ecumenical relations with other Protestants. He encouraged interdenominational celebrations of the Eucharist at Christ Church Cathedral at a time when such services were frowned on by many Anglo-Catholics. He not only overlooked those objections but also strongly supported efforts to establish intercommunion with the Presbyterians during the 1940s. Having heard, moreover, that Presbyterians in St. Louis were interested in establishing a hospital, he encouraged them to cooperate instead in the operation of St. Luke's Episcopal Hospital. The result was St. Luke's Episcopal-Presbyterian Hospital, a collaborative effort that inspired similar health and welfare projects in the St. Louis metropolitan area.

Scarlett retired from his diocesan post in November 1952. However, he continued to receive honors from many groups and organizations in the state of Missouri, and even in retirement he remained extremely active as a writer and preacher. He eventually moved to Castine, Maine, where he died in March 1973.

Bibliography

A. Papers at AEC and at the archives of the diocese of Missouri in St. Louis; *Toward a Better World for All People* (Philadelphia, 1946); *Christianity Takes a Stand* (New York, 1946); *To Will One Thing* (St. Louis, 1948); *Christian Demands for Social Justice* (New York, 1949); *Phillips Brooks—Selected Sermons* (New York, 1949).
B. *ANB* 19, 347–49; *WWWA* 5, 637; *NYT,* 29 March 1973; Charles F. Rehkopf, "The Episcopate of William Scarlett," *Bulletin of the Missouri Historical Society* 20 (1964): 193–217.

SCHERESCHEWSKY, SAMUEL ISAAC JOSEPH (6 May 1831, Tauroggen, Russian Lithuania–15 October 1906, Tokyo). *Education:* Studied at the University of Breslau in Germany, 1852–54; at Western Theological Seminary (Presbyterian) in Allegheny, Pa., 1855–58; and at General Theological Seminary, 1858–59. *Career:* Missionary in Shanghai, 1860–63, and in Beijing, 1863–75; traveled in the United States, 1875–78; missionary bishop of Shanghai, 1877–83; lived in China, 1895–97, and in Japan, 1897–1906.

Samuel Schereschewsky, a missionary bishop and translator of Christian writings, was born in Lithuania in 1831. The son of Jewish parents, he became interested in Christianity as a result of contact with missionaries and through his study of a Hebrew translation of the New Testament. Having emigrated to the United States in 1854, he decided to enter the ordained ministry of the Presbyterian Church and studied for three years at Western Theological Seminary in Pennsylvania. He was attracted, however, by Anglican theology and polity and left Presbyterianism to join the Episcopal Church. He then studied briefly at General Theological Seminary and in October 1860 was ordained to the priesthood by William Jones Boone, the first missionary bishop of China.

Influenced by Boone, Schereschewsky became a missionary to China. He focused his efforts on translating the Bible and the *Book of Common Prayer* into Mandarin. His translations of the New Testament and the prayer book were published in 1872, and his translation of the Hebrew Bible appeared two years later. The House of Bishops elected him "Missionary Bishop of Shanghai, having Episcopal jurisdiction in China," and following his consecration in October 1877, he undertook the establishment of a college for the training of indigenous leaders for the Chinese church. "We want an institution in which to train youth for the service of Christ," he declared. "I believe the true apostles of Christ must be natives." The cornerstone of what later became St. John's University was laid in 1879.

In 1881 Schereschewsky nearly died after being afflicted with a high fever. The physical disability that resulted from his illness forced him to resign his see in 1883. He was mentally unimpaired, however, and with the invaluable assistance of his wife, Susan, who served as a missionary with him, he continued his translation work. In 1881 his translation of the *Book of Common Prayer* into Easy Wenli appeared, and in 1908 the American Bible Society published his Mandarin Reference Bible. He lived in China and Japan for the remainder of his life, eventually dying in Tokyo in 1906.

Bibliography

A. Papers at AEC and at the archives of the American Bible Society in New York; "Appeal for Funds to Establish a Missionary College in China, 1877," in *DW*, 137–39.
B. *ANB* 19, 371–72; *DAB* 16, 428–29; *ECUS,* 240–41; *EDC,* 469; *SH* 10, 236; *WWWA* 1, 1087; Arthur R. Gray and Arthur M. Sherman, *The Story of the Church in China*

(New York, 1913); Kenneth S. Latourette, *A History of Christian Missions in China* (New York, 1929); *James Arthur Muller, Apostle of China: Samuel Isaac Joseph Schereschewsky, 1831–1906* (New York, 1937).

SCUDDER, VIDA DUTTON (15 December 1861, Madura, India–9 October 1954, Wellesley, Mass.). *Education:* B.A., Smith College, 1884; studied at Oxford University, 1884–85; M.A., Smith College, 1889. *Career:* Instructor, then professor of English literature, Wellesley College, 1887–1928; writer and social critic, 1928–54.

Vida Scudder, an educator and social reformer, was born in Madura, India, in December 1861. She was the daughter of David Coit Scudder, a Congregational missionary, and Harriet Dutton. Following the drowning death of her husband, Harriet returned to the Dutton family home in Auburndale, Massachusetts, where Vida grew up. Both Harriet and Vida were confirmed as Episcopalians at Trinity Church in Boston in the 1870s. Vida was educated at the Girls' Latin School in Boston, and she earned her B.A. from Smith College in 1884. Following her graduation from Smith, she studied for a year at Oxford University. During that period, she was encouraged to think critically about social class and the stratification of society—an experience that radicalized her and prompted her to dedicate herself to reform. After returning to Boston and earning an M.A. from Smith College, she accepted a position teaching English literature at Wellesley College in 1887. In 1910 she became a full professor at Wellesley, where she remained until her retirement.

Scudder helped organize the College Settlements Association (CSA) in 1890. According to the settlement idea, which originated in England, educated middle-class workers moved into working-class neighborhoods, where they offered cultural and educational programs to members of the local community. The reforming impulse of this movement very much appealed to Scudder, and she met with a group of fellow Smith graduates to discuss the establishment of a settlement house in the United States. These women eventually opened the first successful American settlement house, located on Rivington Street in New York City, in September 1889. This effort led to the CSA's founding a year later. Membership in the organization grew quickly, and by 1898 it had more than two thousand adherents throughout the United States. By 1892 the CSA had also opened two more houses: Denison House in Boston and the College Settlement in Philadelphia.

After an emotional breakdown in 1901, Scudder lived for two years in Italy, where she recuperated by immersing herself in medieval literature. When she returned to Massachusetts, she became even more active both in the church and in socialist activities. In 1911 she helped found the Episcopal Church Socialist League and joined the Socialist Party, and in 1913 she was appointed to her denomination's new Joint Commission on Social Service. She offered such strong support to striking textile workers in Lawrence, Massachusetts, in 1912 that she came under severe attack from members of the Wellesley College community. This criticism led her to resign from the CSA lest her affiliation with socialism damage the reputation of that organization. Although she initially supported the American entry into World War I, she joined the Fellowship of Reconciliation in 1923 and by 1930 she had become an absolute pacifist.

Scudder grounded her socialist beliefs in the Christian faith, especially in the doctrine of the incarnation, and she used the sacramental emphases of Anglo-Catholicism as the basis for an assault on Protestant individualism. She published numerous books on the Catholic tradition, including several popularized biographies of medieval saints. The art, architecture, and religious beliefs of the Middle Ages, she thought, pointed toward "a life . . . sweetly ordered through the acceptance of supernatural verities." Thus, in one of her most important books, *Socialism and Character* (1912), she asserted the spiritual and political union between Marxism and Catholicism. Scudder's commitment to a disciplined religious life also led her to join the Society of the Companions of the Holy Cross, a women's organization practicing regular intercessory prayer, in 1889. She served as companion-in-charge of probationers between 1909 and 1942, and she remained active in the Companions until her death. As she wrote in 1934, "there is one sure . . . way of directly helping on the Kingdom of God. That way is prayer. Social intercession may be the mightiest force in the world."

Scudder retired from Wellesley College in 1928, and she spent the rest of her life writing. She published the first volume of her autobiography, *On Journey,* in 1937, and she later wrote a second volume, *My Quest for Reality* (1952). Among her many other publications was a hagiographic biography of James O.S. Huntington,* the founder of the Order of the Holy Cross. Scudder died at her home in Wellesley, Massachusetts, in October 1954.

Bibliography

A. Papers at the Wellesley College Archives, at the archives of the Society of the Companions of the Holy Cross in Byfield, Mass., and at the Sophia Smith Collection of the Smith College Library; "Social Problems Facing the Church in 1934," in *DW,* 357–61; "Democracy and the Church," *Atlantic Monthly* 90 (October 1902): 521–27; *The Witness of Denial* (New York, 1895); *The Life of the Spirit in Modern English Poets* (Boston, 1895); *Social Ideals in English Letters* (Boston, 1898); *Introduction to the Study of English Literature* (New York, 1901); *A Listener in Babel* (Boston, 1903); *Saint Catherine of Siena as Seen in Her Letters* (New York, 1905); *Socialism and Character* (Boston, 1912); *The Church and the Hour: Reflections of a Socialist Churchwoman* (New York, 1917); *Social Teachings of the Christian Year* (New York, 1921); *The Franciscan Adventure: A Study in the First Hundred Years of the Order of St. Francis* (London, 1931); *On Journey* (New York, 1937); *The Privilege of Age: Essays Secular and Spiritual* (New York, 1939); *Father Huntington, Founder of the Order of the Holy Cross* (New York, 1940); *My Quest for Reality* (Wellesley, Mass., 1952).

B. *ANB* 19, 544–45; *DARB,* 481–82; *EDC,* 471; *FD,* 119–27; *NAW* 4, 636–38; *NCAB* 4, 468–69; *WWWA* 3, 769; *NYT,* 11 October 1954; Elizabeth Palmer Hutcheson Carrell, "Reflections in a Mirror: The Progressive Woman and the Settlement Experience" (Ph.D. diss., University of Texas at Austin, 1981); T.J. Jackson Lears, *No Place of Grace: Antimodernism and the Transformation of American Culture, 1880–1920* (New York, 1981), 209–15; Theresa Corcoran, *Vida Dutton Scudder* (Boston, 1982); Patricia Ann Palmieri, *In Adamless Eden: The Community of Women Faculty at Wellesley* (1995).

SEABURY, SAMUEL (30 November 1729, Groton, Conn.–25 February 1796, New London, Conn.). *Education:* B.A., Yale College, 1748; studied medicine at the University of Edinburgh, 1752–53. *Career:* Missionary for the Society for the Propagation of the Gospel in Foreign Parts (SPG) in N.J., 1754–57; rector, Jamaica, N.Y., 1757–66; rector, St. Peter's Church, Westchester, N.Y., 1766–76; private physician and chaplain to British troops, Staten Island and New York, 1776–83; bishop, diocese of Connecticut, 1784–96; presiding bishop of the Episcopal Church, 1789–92; bishop, diocese of Rhode Island, 1790–96.

The first Anglican clergyman to be ordained a bishop for the Episcopal Church, Samuel Seabury was raised in Connecticut and graduated from Yale College in 1748. After briefly studying medicine in Scotland, he was ordained a deacon and priest of the Church of England in 1753. He returned to America in 1754 and began his clerical career as an SPG missionary in New Jersey. In the late 1760s and 1770s, while serving as rector of a parish in Westchester, New York, he was one of several high church leaders who sought to secure a bishop for the American colonies.

Conservative by nature and mindful of having sworn an oath of loyalty to the British sovereign, Seabury remained a steadfast subject of the king throughout the revolutionary period. Employing the pseudonym A.W. Farmer, he wrote pamphlets opposing American independence and urging obedience to the crown. At the beginning of the war, he was seized by patriot militiamen and held prisoner for over a month in New Haven. He later served as chaplain to a regiment of American loyalist troops fighting in the British army.

Seabury's most important contribution was securing the episcopate for the Episcopal Church. After the war, the clergy of Connecticut, wishing to have a diocesan in the apostolic succession, chose Seabury to be their bishop. Accordingly, he traveled to England in 1783 to seek consecration, but the archbishop of Canterbury refused to comply with his request. Concerned both about the lack of participation by Connecticut laity in Seabury's election and about his inability as an American to swear the necessary oath of allegiance to George III, the English bishops doubted whether they had the authority to make him a bishop. Consequently, in 1784 Seabury journeyed to Aberdeen, Scotland, where three nonjuring bishops of the Episcopal Church of Scotland consecrated him instead. Seabury also signed a concordat with the Scottish bishops in which he recognized the legitimacy of their church and promised to incorporate many of its high church principles within the new institutional structures of Anglicanism in the United States.

Returning to Connecticut in June 1785, Seabury labored to rebuild the church in southern New England. Opposed to lay participation in ecclesiastical councils and to any diminution of what he deemed to be episcopal prerogatives, he refused to attend the initial meetings of the General Convention of the recently organized Episcopal Church. The validity of his consecration was also questioned by a number of Episcopal leaders because it had been performed by schismatic bishops rather than by bishops of the Church of England. Seabury eventually attended the second session of the 1789 General Convention after its first session made several concessions in his favor (including the creation of a separate House of Bishops) and recognized his episcopal orders. Serving as bishop of Connecticut until his death in 1796, he also concurrently held the positions of presiding bishop of the Episcopal Church (1789–92) and bishop of Rhode Island (1790–96).

Bibliography

A. *Discourses on Several Subjects,* 2 vols. (New York, 1793); *An Earnest Persuasive to Frequent Communion* (New Haven, 1789); *Discourses on Several Important Subjects* (New York, 1798); *Letters of a Westchester Farmer,* ed. Clarence H. Vance (White Plains, N.Y., 1930).
B. *AAP* 5, 149–54; *ANB* 19, 549–50; *DAB* 16, 528–30; *DARB,* 482–83; *DCA,* 1066; *EARH,* 660–61; *EDC,* 472; *HEC,* 87–91, 94–97; *MM,* 137–39, 175–78; *NCAB* 3, 475; *NCE* 13, 13; *SH* 10, 315–16; Eben E. Beardsley, *Life and Correspondence of the Right Reverend Samuel Seabury* (Boston, 1881); William J. Seabury, *Memoir of Bishop Seabury* (New York, 1908); Herbert Thomas, *Samuel Seabury: Priest and Physician, Bishop of Connecticut* (Hamden, Conn., 1962); Bruce E. Steiner, *Samuel Seabury, 1729–1796: A Study in the High Church Tradition* (Athens, Ohio, 1971); Anne W. Rowthorn, *Samuel Seabury: A Bicentennial Biography* (New York, 1983).

SHERRILL, HENRY KNOX (8 November 1890, Brooklyn, N.Y.–11 May 1980, Boxford, Mass.). *Education:* B.A., Yale College, 1911; B.D., Episcopal Theological School, 1914. *Career:* Assistant minister, Trinity Church, Boston, 1914–17; hospital chaplain, U.S. Army, 1917–19; rector, Church of Our Saviour, Brookline, Mass., 1919–23; rector, Trinity Church, Boston, 1923–30; bishop, diocese of Massachusetts, 1930–47; presiding bishop of the Episcopal Church, 1947–58; president, National Council of Churches, 1950–52; president, World Council of Churches, 1954–61.

Henry Knox Sherrill, a presiding bishop and ecumenical leader, was born in Brooklyn, New York, in November 1890. While a student at Yale College, he attended St. Paul's Church in New Haven, where he taught Sunday school and experienced a call to the ordained ministry. After graduating from Yale in 1911, he entered the Episcopal Theological School, from which he received his B.D. in 1914. He was ordained to the diaconate in June 1914 and to the priesthood in May 1915. Sherrill began his ministry as an assistant at Trinity Church in Boston. He remained there until 1917, when he entered the army as a hospital chaplain and served in France during World War I. Discharged from the army in 1919, he became rector, first, of the Church of Our Saviour in Brookline, Massachusetts, and four years later, of Trinity Church in Boston. While he was at Trinity Church, he was active in a number of civic and religious organizations, including the Greater Boston Council of Churches—a position that introduced him to the possibilities of the ecumenical movement.

In 1930 Sherrill was elected the ninth bishop of the diocese of Massachusetts. Under Sherrill's leadership, the diocese grew considerably, and Sherrill became widely known for being a capable manager of one of the Episcopal Church's largest dioceses. At the 1946 General Convention, the House of Bishops elected him presiding bishop. A canon had been passed at the 1943 convention that required a presiding bishop to resign from his previous jurisdiction before assuming office, and Sherrill was the first presiding bishop chosen after the passage of this canon. As a result, he resigned as bishop of Massachusetts in June 1947.

During Sherrill's tenure as presiding bishop, one of the greatest periods of religious growth in U.S. history occurred. Both the membership and the bureaucratic apparatus of the Episcopal Church increased dramatically in size. Sherrill helped organize the Episcopal Church Foundation, which operated a large fund lending money to dioceses for the construction of church buildings. He also participated in the establishment of Seabury Press, which became the official publishing firm of the denomination in 1952, and he created the Presiding Bishop's Fund for World Relief, the primary relief agency of the Episcopal Church. Sherrill was strongly interested in the church's work on behalf of social justice, especially in relationship to the burgeoning civil rights movement. He made a critical decision in the spring of 1954, when a number of leaders in the church expressed concern about the meeting site of the 1955 General Convention. Although the convention was scheduled to assemble in Houston, Texas, the continuing existence of segregation laws in that city promised to cause severe embarrassment for black Episcopalians wishing to use housing and transportation facilities there. After carefully studying the situation and listening to advice from African Americans, Sherrill decided to move the convention to Honolulu, Hawaii. Although criticized by white southerners and segregationists, he believed that the Episcopal Church needed to make an unequivocal statement about the need for racial integration.

While serving as presiding bishop, Sherrill greatly improved ecumenical relations. Church unity, he believed, was the key to the renewal of human society. How could there be true international cooperation, he asked in the aftermath of World War II, unless the churches presented "a united Christian approach to world problems"? Sherrill helped form the World Council of the Churches at Amsterdam in 1948, and he was one of its six presidents from 1954 until 1961. He had already served as the first president of the National Council of Churches in Cleveland, Ohio.

Sherrill retired from his post as presiding bishop in 1958, but he remained active, traveling and lecturing for the next 20 years. He died in Boxford, Massachusetts, in May 1980.

Bibliography

A. Papers at the archives of the diocese of Massachusetts in Boston and at AEC; *William Lawrence: Later Years of a Happy Life* (Cambridge, Mass., 1943); *The Church's Ministry in Our Time* (New York, 1949); *Among Friends* (Boston, 1962).
B. *ANB* 19, 823–24; *EDC,* 482; *NYT,* 13 May 1980.

SHOEMAKER, SAMUEL MOOR (27 December 1893, Baltimore–31 January 1963, Baltimore). *Education:* B.A., Princeton University, 1916; further study at General Theological Seminary and at Union Theological Seminary (N.Y.), 1920–22. *Career:* YMCA worker in China, 1917–19; independent evangelist, 1919–20, 1922–25; assistant, Grace Church, New York, 1921–22; rector, Calvary Church, New York, 1925–52; rector, Calvary Church, Pittsburgh, 1952–62.

Samuel Shoemaker, a priest and one of the founders of Alcoholic Anonymous (AA), was born in Baltimore in December 1893. In the summers of 1911 and 1912, he attended conferences at Northfield, Massachusetts, where he heard evangelical Protestant leaders such as John R. Mott, Robert E. Speer, and Sherwood Eddy speaking about the need for overseas evangelistic work. After graduating from Princeton University in 1916, Shoemaker answered this call by serving as a missionary with the YMCA in China. In Peking in 1918 he first came to know the controversial American evangelist Frank Buchman, who in 1921 became the founder and director of the Oxford Group, later renamed Moral Re-Armament.

During the late 1910s, Shoemaker, an evangelical Episcopalian, was regularly invited to speak on personal evangelism at schools and universities in the Northeast. In June 1920 he was ordained deacon at his home parish, Emmanuel Church, in Baltimore, and a year later, in the same church, he was ordained to the priesthood. In 1921 he began a brief term as assistant at Grace Church in New York City, where he threw himself vigorously into parish work. In the winter of 1924–25 he toured Europe and the Middle East with three other young men and Frank Buchman, attempting to bring spiritual refreshment to workers in schools and mission hospitals.

Shoemaker's successful evangelistic efforts attracted the attention of the vestry of Calvary Church, New York. He accepted their call and in 1925 began a lengthy tenure as their rector. He posted advertisements in the city's trolley cars, promising "straight preaching, a friendly atmosphere, personal religion, and good music" at Calvary Church. In the summer of 1927, he also started holding outdoor services in nearby Madison Square. Signs carried around the square by young men of the church read: "The Church has come to you. Will you come to the Church?" The eight-story Calvary House, which opened next door to Calvary Church in 1928, was a residence for church workers, a training center for religious leaders, a gathering spot for hundreds of young people, and the hub of an extensive ministry to the urban poor. This "spiritual powerhouse" attracted visitors from all over the world who wanted to learn more about making the Christian experience available to others.

Shoemaker, who was exposed to the problems of alcoholism throughout his work at Calvary, helped give AA its religious foundation. According to Bill Wilson, cofounder of the organization, Shoemaker contributed most of the principles contained in the Twelve Steps. This philosophy was shaped in part by Shoemaker's reading of William James's *The Varieties of Religious Experience* (1902), with its discussion of self-surrender to a "higher power." The development of AA was also influenced by the moral reformism of the Oxford Group, which featured personal transformation both by self-help and by divine agency through participation in small group meetings. Shoemaker himself spoke of "the crucible of laymen working it out among themselves, sharing experiences with one another." Especially after Shoemaker's renewed involvement with AA in the 1950s, the Episcopal Church came to be looked upon by many recovering alcoholics as a place where they could find acceptance and refuge. Indeed, by 1955 Shoemaker was emphasizing how much organized Christianity could learn from AA, which had a fellowship that was closer and more demanding than that of the church.

In 1952 Shoemaker assumed the rectorship of Calvary Church, Pittsburgh, where he reached out especially to young married couples and to local executives. He immediately sought ways to get the steel industry, as he put it, "down on its knees in prayer." His highly effective "Pittsburgh experiment" entailed going after those he referred to as the "golf club crowd." Begun in 1955, the experiment brought laypeople (usually businessmen) together in small groups for discussion, fellowship, and prayer. These informal "cells" were an important evangelistic tool, helping both to nurture new Christians and to deepen their spiritual lives. Shoemaker succeeded among America's social elite because he was an evangelist who packaged his message in a manner that appealed to them. The *Princeton Alumni Weekly* described him as "no tub-thumping Billy Sunday or hypocritical Elmer Gantry, but a ruggedly handsome, stocky minister with a soft and cultivated Baltimore accent and a long Princeton background."

Shoemaker was the founder of *Faith at Work* magazine, and he wrote 23 brief, nontechnical books about Christian faith and life. Although he sometimes ministered to the down-and-out, he never embraced the social gospel. Instead, his conservative economic views and anti-Communism were often revealed in his contributions to *Christian Economics,* a right-wing, anti–New Deal publication. Throughout his ministry, Shoemaker continued to work on college campuses, usually at schools that reflected his own cultural background: wealthy Episcopal boarding schools and topnotch eastern universities and colleges. As Shoemaker once told *Fortune* magazine, "The Lord loves snobs as well as other people."

At the end of his life, Shoemaker focused less on self-surrender to a personal Christ and more on the work of the Holy Spirit. He thereby provided a bridge to the charismatic revival that emerged in the Episcopal Church in the 1970s. He was also the husband of Helen Smith Shoemaker, who had been active in the Moral Re-Armament movement in the 1920s and who was a cofounder of the

Anglican Fellowship of Prayer. Samuel Shoemaker died in Baltimore in January 1963.

Bibliography

A. *Realizing Religion* (New York, 1921); *Calvary Church Yesterday and Today* (New York, 1936); *How You Can Find Happiness* (New York, 1947); *Revive Thy Church, Beginning with Me* (New York, 1948); *By the Power of God* (New York, 1954); *With the Holy Spirit and with Fire* (New York, 1960); *Beginning Your Ministry* (New York, 1963); *Extraordinary Living for Ordinary Men: Excerpts Selected from the Writings of Sam Shoemaker,* ed. Helen Shoemaker Rea (Grand Rapids, Mich., 1965).

B. *DCA,* 1084–85; *EDC,* 483; *WWWA* 4, 859; "Princeton Miniatures: Dr. Samuel M. Shoemaker '16," *Princeton Alumni Weekly,* 11 May 1956, 13; John F. Woolverton, "Evangelical Protestantism and Alcoholism, 1933–1962: Episcopalian Samuel Shoemaker," *HMPEC* 52 (1983): 53–65; Daniel Sack, "Reaching the 'Up-and-Outers': Sam Shoemaker and Modern Evangelicalism," *AEH* 64 (1995): 37–57; Helen Smith Shoemaker, *I Stand by the Door: The Life of Sam Shoemaker* (New York, 1967); Irving Harris, *The Breeze of the Spirit: Sam Shoemaker and the Story of Faith at Work* (New York, 1978).

SMITH, WILLIAM (7 September 1727, Aberdeen, Scotland–14 May 1803, Philadelphia). *Education:* M.A., University of Aberdeen, 1743–47. *Career:* Private tutor, Long Island, N.Y., 1751–53; instructor, the Academy of Philadelphia, 1754–56; provost, the College of Philadelphia, 1756–79, 1789–91; rector, Trinity Church, Oxford, Pa., 1766–77; rector, Chester Parish, Chestertown, Md., and head of the Kent School (later, Washington College), 1779–89.

An Anglican clergyman and educator who played a key role in the organization of the Episcopal Church, William Smith was born in Scotland and educated at the University of Aberdeen. He came to New York in 1751 as a tutor to a family on Long Island. While serving in that position, he wrote and published *A General Idea of the College of Mirania* (1753), an essay articulating his vision of an ideal institution of higher education. Although he returned briefly to England to be ordained in December 1753, Smith's educational ideas attracted the attention of Benjamin Franklin, who secured an appointment for him as a teacher at the Academy of Philadelphia. In 1756 Franklin approved Smith's plan to reorganize the school as the College of Philadelphia, where Smith served as provost for the next 23 years. During his tenure there, Smith not only raised the school to collegiate status but also gave the officially nondenominational institution a distinctly Anglican ethos.

By the mid-1770s, Smith's attempts to walk a fine line between loyalty to the British sovereign and sympathy toward colonial grievances and his appeals for caution amid cries for independence branded him a Tory in the eyes of many American patriots. His political stance at the beginning of the American Revolution influenced the decision of the Pennsylvania legislature to dissolve the charter of the College of Philadelphia in 1779. Although the school later was reorganized as the University of Pennsylvania, Smith left Philadelphia in 1779 and moved to Chestertown, Maryland. While serving as the rector of Chester Parish in Kent County on Maryland's Eastern Shore, he helped transform Kent School into Washington College in 1782. To support and maintain the college, he secured funds from wealthy planters and instituted a solid academic curriculum.

Along with his former student William White,* Smith was extremely active both in the formation of the Episcopal Church and in the adaptation of the *Book of Common Prayer* for use in the United States. Starting in 1780 he presided over state conventions that organized the church in Maryland and chose the name "Protestant Episcopal Church" to replace the no longer acceptable "Church of England." A low churchman, Smith favored a democratic approach to church government, disagreeing with those who touted the authority of bishops over that of priests and laity. Although a Maryland convention elected him bishop in 1783, rumors of public drunkenness undermined his position in the church, and the General Convention never approved his consecration. In many ways an able man, he was also an exceedingly complex figure who was often said to be irritable, overbearing, slovenly, avaricious, and intoxicated. One of the most enigmatic figures in the history of the Episcopal Church, Smith died in Philadelphia in 1803.

Bibliography

A. *The Works of William Smith,* 2 vols. (Philadelphia, 1803); Horace W. Smith, ed., *Life and Correspondence of the Rev. William Smith,* 2 vols. (1879–80; reprint, New York, 1972).
B. *AAP* 5, 158–63; *ANB* 20, 305–6; *DAB* 17, 353–57; *DARB,* 500–501; *DCA,* 1100; *EDC,* 488–89; *NCAB* 1, 340–41; 33–42; Ralph Ketcham, "Benjamin Franklin and William Smith," *Pennsylvania Magazine of History and Biography* 88 (1964): William D. Andrews, "William Smith and the Rising Glory of America," *Early American Literature* 8 (1973): 142–63; James Warnock, "Thomas Bradbury Chandler and William Smith: Diversity within Colonial Anglicanism," *AEH* 57 (1988): 272–97; Albert F. Gegenheimer, *William Smith: Educator and Churchman, 1727–1803* (Philadelphia, 1943); Thomas Firth Jones, *A Pair of Lawn Sleeves: A Biography of William Smith (1727–1803)* (Philadelphia, 1972).

STANTON, ELIZABETH CADY (12 November 1815, Johnstown, N.Y.–26 October 1902, New York). *Education:* Graduated from Johnstown Academy, 1830; graduated from Troy Female Seminary, 1832. *Career:* Co-editor, *Revolution* magazine, 1868–70; president, National Woman Suffrage Association, 1868–90; writer and public speaker, 1881–1902; president, National American Woman Suffrage Association, 1890–92.

Elizabeth Cady Stanton, a women's rights leader, was born in Johnstown, New York, in November 1815. She was the daughter of Margaret Livingston and Daniel Cady, who was a lawyer and prominent politician. Educated at the all-male

Johnstown Academy and at Emma Willard's Troy Female Seminary, she sought to practice law, but as a woman she was denied a legal career. In 1840 she married Henry Stanton, an abolitionist and social reformer. The couple removed the word "obey" from their wedding service, and after the ceremony, they sailed to England to attend the World's Anti-Slavery Convention. The decision by that convention to bar Lucretia Mott and other American women from taking their seats as delegates eventually led to the creation of the British and American women's rights movements. After their return to the United States, the Stantons lived in various places during the first years of their marriage. Despite remaining at home to raise her children, Elizabeth became friends with many of the leading women in the antislavery movement at that time.

In 1847 the Stantons moved to Seneca Falls, New York, and a year later Elizabeth initiated the call for a women's rights convention. At that meeting, which was held on July 19–20, 1848, she read her famous Declaration of Sentiments, which was modeled after the Declaration of Independence. When women in other locales learned about the Seneca Falls convention, petitions both for property rights and for suffrage began to circulate, and conventions of women's rights advocates soon became commonplace. Elizabeth met Susan B. Anthony in 1851, and they were soon working together as leaders in the cause of women's rights. Although they were often denounced and ridiculed for their views, Stanton and Anthony kept up the pressure. Thus, when the Republicans gained control of the New York legislature in 1861, the two women won significant revisions in the state's laws governing the status of married women.

During the Civil War, Stanton brought women's rights meetings to a halt because she thought women could play an even more important role in the political mobilization of the North. In 1863 she helped organize the Women's Loyal National League and strongly supported efforts to abolish slavery by constitutional amendment—a movement that eventually culminated in the ratification of the Thirteenth Amendment in 1865. During Reconstruction, however, the alliance between abolitionists and women's rights advocates fell apart. When Republican leaders pressing for universal manhood suffrage refused to support suffrage for women, Stanton gave her backing to Democratic politicians, who declared that no black man should be allowed to vote until white women had first gained that right. Stanton herself lectured against the Fifteenth Amendment, and she insinuated that the enfranchisement of black men would endanger the safety of white women. Although she never repudiated these openly racist attacks on African Americans, she later mounted a vigorous suffrage campaign on behalf of "National Protection for National Citizens," arguing that the voting rights of *all* Americans should be guaranteed by an amendment to the federal constitution.

Although Stanton had been raised a conservative Presbyterian, she attended Trinity Episcopal Church while living in Seneca Falls. In the 1880s, however, she increasingly turned against the churches, which she believed needed to be held accountable for perpetuating the oppression of women. "The only religious sect . . . that has recognized the equality of woman," she observed, "is the Spiritualists." After the 1881 release of the Revised Version of the Bible, published without the consultation of even one woman scholar, Stanton organized her own exegetical committee and solicited commentaries on biblical passages that were commonly used to degrade women. She was also the principal author of *The Woman's Bible,* published in two volumes in 1895 and 1898. As she emphasized in the introduction of that work, "the Scriptures, the creeds and codes and church discipline of the leading religions bear the impress of fallible men, and not of our ideal great first cause, 'the Spirit of all Good,' that set the universe of matter and mind in motion." For that reason, the traditional text of the Bible had always been used to enslave rather than liberate women, she said.

Between 1881 (when she officially retired from the lecture circuit) and 1902, Stanton published five books and hundreds of articles. By her eightieth birthday, however, her health had begun to fail, and by 1899 she had lost her eyesight. She continued, nevertheless, to dictate articles and to revise her speeches orally. She died at her home in New York City in October 1902. Because of her association with the Episcopal Church, Stanton is commemorated in the calendar of the Episcopal Church on July 20—the anniversary of the Seneca Falls convention.

Bibliography

A. *Papers of Elizabeth Cady Stanton and Susan B. Anthony* [microfilm], ed. Patricia G. Holland and Ann D. Gordon (n.p., 1831–1906); *History of Woman Suffrage,* 3 vols. (New York, 1881–87); *The Woman's Bible,* 2 vols. (New York, 1895 and 1898); *Eighty Years and More: Reminiscences, 1815–1897* (New York, 1898); *Elizabeth Cady Stanton, as Revealed in Her Letters, Diary and Reminiscences,* ed. Theodore Stanton and Harriot Stanton Blatch, 2 vols. (New York, 1922); Ellen Carol DuBois, ed., *The Elizabeth Cady Stanton—Susan B. Anthony Reader: Correspondence, Writings, Speeches,* rev. ed. (Boston, 1992).
B. *ANB* 20, 562–65; *DAB* 17, 521–23; *DARB,* 511–12; *DCA,* 1129; *EARH,* 707–8, 799; *EDC,* 501–2; *FD,* 50–58; *NAW* 3, 342–47; *NCAB* 3, 84–85; *WWWA* 1, 1171; *NYT,* 27 October 1902; Alma Lutz, *Created Equal: A Biography of Elizabeth Cady Stanton, 1815–1902* (New York, 1940); Lois Banner, *Elizabeth Cady Stanton: A Radical for Woman's Rights* (Boston, 1980); Elisabeth Griffith, *In Her Own Right: The Life of Elizabeth Cady Stanton* (New York, 1984); Kathi Kern, *Mrs. Stanton's Bible* (Ithaca, N.Y., 2001).

STOWE, HARRIET BEECHER (14 June 1811, Litchfield, Conn.–1 July 1896, Hartford, Conn.). *Education:* Studied at the Litchfield Female Academy, Litchfield, Conn., 1819–24; at the Hartford Female Seminary, Hartford, Conn., 1824–29. *Career:* Teacher, 1829–36; writer, 1833–78.

The renowned American author Harriet Beecher Stowe was born in Litchfield, Connecticut, in June 1811. She was the daughter of Lyman Beecher, the popular Congregational clergyman, and Roxana Foote. Because her mother died when Harriet was five years old, she was raised by a combination of sisters, aunts, and her grandmother Foote, an Episcopalian who introduced her to the *Book of Com-*

mon Prayer. She was educated at the Litchfield Female Academy, a school founded to "vindicate the equality of female intellect," and at her sister Catherine's Hartford Female Seminary, where she later taught composition. After her father accepted the presidency of Lane Theological Seminary in Cincinnati, Harriet moved to Ohio with her family. In 1836 she married Calvin Stowe, a professor at Lane Seminary. To supplement the family's income, she began to write and publish short stories. The Stowes later lived at Bowdoin College in Maine and at Andover Theological Seminary in Massachusetts, where Calvin held teaching posts.

Stowe is best remembered for her antislavery novel, *Uncle Tom's Cabin* (1852), which she wrote to protest the passage of the Fugitive Slave Law of 1850. Originally serialized in the *National Era,* her story about the experiences of the faithful, Christ-like slave Tom gained a tremendous following and sold more than 300,000 copies during its first year of publication in book form. Although the character of Uncle Tom later came under severe criticism as a symbol of black passivity in the face of white oppression, Stowe intended the novel to arouse the conscience of the North about the suffering caused by slavery. The success of *Uncle Tom's Cabin* made Stowe a celebrity in Great Britain and the United States. So great was her novel's impact on the coming of the Civil War that when Stowe visited the White House in 1862, Abraham Lincoln allegedly quipped as he greeted her, "So you're the little woman who wrote the book that started this great war."

Increasingly troubled in middle age by the implications of the Calvinist faith in which she had been raised, Stowe turned to the Episcopal Church for spiritual solace. When her 19-year-old son drowned without having formally joined a church, she struggled with the possibility that, dying "unregenerate," he might have been damned by God. In the novel *The Minister's Wooing* (1859), she attempted to deal with her ambivalent feelings about the orthodox Congregationalism of her youth. After moving to Hartford, Connecticut, in 1864, Stowe bought a pew at St. John's Church, to which the aesthetic sense and theological flexibility of the Episcopal Church had drawn her. After buying a house in Mandarin, on the St. John River in Florida, she also supported an Episcopal missionary project that ministered to the newly freed African Americans in the South.

When her husband retired in 1863, Stowe used her writing skills to support her large family. Although health problems, the deaths of loved ones, and repeated bouts of melancholy took their toll on her, she remained committed to the precept, "Trust in the Lord and do good." Her final book was *Poganuc People* (1878), which contained fictionalized reminiscences of her childhood in Litchfield. She died in Hartford in July 1896.

Bibliography

A. Papers at the Harriet Beecher Stowe Center in Hartford, Conn., at the Schlesinger Library of Radcliffe College, and at the Sterling Library and Beinecke Library of Yale University; *Uncle Tom's Cabin* (Boston, 1852); *Four Ways of Observing the*

Sabbath (Glasgow, 1854); *Dred, A Tale of the Great Dismal Swamp* (Boston, 1856); *The Minister's Wooing* (New York, 1859); *Oldtown Folks* (Boston, 1869); *Lady Byron Vindicated* (Boston, 1870); *Poganuc People: Their Loves and Lives* (New York, 1878); *The Writings of Harriet Beecher Stowe,* 16 vols. (Boston, 1896); *The Oxford Harriet Beecher Stowe Reader* (New York, 1999).

B. *ANB* 20, 906–8; *DAB* 18, 115–20; *DARB,* 524–25; *DCA,* 1137–38; *EARH,* 710–11; *FD,* 39–49; *MCTA,* 149–52; *NAW* 3, 393–402; Charles Edward Stowe, *Life of Harriet Beecher Stowe, Compiled from Her Journals and Letters* (Boston, 1890); Charles Edward Stowe and Lyman Beecher Stowe, *Harriet Beecher Stowe: The Story of Her Life* (Boston, 1911); Forrest Wilson, *Crusader in Crinoline: The Life of Harriet Beecher Stowe* (Philadelphia, 1941); Charles H. Foster, *The Rungless Ladder: Harriet Beecher Stowe and New England Puritanism* (Durham, N.C., 1954); Edward Wagenknecht, *Harriet Beecher Stowe: The Known and the Unknown* (New York, 1965); Joan D. Hedrick, *Harriet Beecher Stowe: A Life* (New York, 1994).

STRINGFELLOW, FRANK WILLIAM (26 April 1928, Johnston, R.I.–2 March 1985, Providence, R.I.). *Education:* B.A., Bates College, 1949; studied at the London School of Economics, 1950; studied at the Episcopal Theological School, 1953; LL.B., Harvard Law School, 1956. *Career:* Sergeant, U.S. Army, 1950–52; legal counsel, East Harlem Protestant Parish, New York, 1956–57; lawyer and writer, New York, 1957–67, Block Island, R.I., 1967–85; cofounder, law firm of Ellis Stringfellow and Patton, New York, 1961.

William Stringfellow, an activist lawyer and theologian, was born in Johnston, Rhode Island, in April 1928. The son of working-class parents, he grew up in Northampton, Massachusetts. After graduating from Bates College in 1949, he won a Rotary International fellowship that enabled him to study political theory at the London School of Economics. He entered the U.S. Army in 1950 and served for two years in Germany. After studying briefly at the Episcopal Theological School in Cambridge, Massachusetts, he entered Harvard Law School in 1953. Following his graduation in 1956, he worked as a legal counsel for the East Harlem Protestant Parish, a pathbreaking inner-city ministry in New York. Although he continued to live in Harlem, Stringfellow angrily resigned from the parish in 1957 because he thought its leadership was "neglecting the Word of God." He later wrote about this experience in one of his first books, *My People Is the Enemy* (1964).

During the 1960s, Stringfellow not only practiced law in New York but also maintained a rigorous schedule of writing and public speaking. He was very active in both the civil rights movement and the antiwar movement, and in 1964 *Time* magazine referred to him as "one of the most persuasive of Christianity's critics-from-within." He consistently defended Episcopalians and other church people who were harassed by either legal or ecclesiastical authorities for their heterodox and radical views. Thus, in 1966 Stringfellow provided counsel to James Pike,* the bishop of California, regarding the heresy charges that had been brought against him. In 1970 Stringfellow was indicted for harboring the fugitive Roman

Catholic priest Daniel Berrigan, who had burned the files of a draft board in Catonsville, Maryland. And he served as an adviser to the first women priests of the Episcopal Church after their irregular service of ordination in Philadelphia in July 1974. Stringfellow believed that Christians needed always to scrutinize American society through the lens of scripture, especially the teachings of the prophets who spoke of God's judgment on an apostate nation. For this reason, the great neo-orthodox theologian Karl Barth once said of Stringfellow: "This is the man America should be listening to."

In 1968 Stringfellow became gravely ill and underwent surgery for the removal of his pancreas. Following that illness, he and his partner, the poet Anthony Towne, left New York and moved permanently to a house on Block Island, off the coast of Rhode Island. The two men not only lived together until Towne's death in 1980 but also collaborated on the writing of three books. In *A Simplicity of Faith* (1982), Stringfellow described his love for Towne and the grief process through which he passed in mourning his death. Despite his own poor health, Stringfellow remained an active, sometimes acerbic social critic for the remainder of his life. Early in 1985 he suffered a diabetic coma, and he died in March of that year while hospitalized in Providence, Rhode Island.

Bibliography

A. Papers at the Cornell University Library; numerous articles in theological and religious periodicals (1947–1985); *A Private and Public Faith* (Grand Rapids, Mich., 1962); *Instead of Death* (New York, 1963); *My People Is the Enemy* (New York, 1964); *Free in Obedience* (New York, 1964); *Dissenter in a Great Society* (New York, 1966); *The Bishop Pike Affair: Scandals of Conscience and Heresy, Relevance and Solemnity in the Contemporary Church* (New York, 1967); *A Second Birthday* (Garden City, N.Y., 1970); *Suspect Tenderness: The Ethics of the Berrigan Witness* (New York, 1971); *An Ethic for Christians and Other Aliens in a Strange Land* (Waco, Tex., 1973); *The Death and Life of Bishop Pike* (Garden City, N.Y., 1976); *A Simplicity of Faith: My Experience in Mourning* (Nashville, 1982); *The Politics of Spirituality* (Louisville, Ky., 1984); *A Keeper of the Word: Selected Writings of William Stringfellow,* ed. Bill Wylie Kellermann (Grand Rapids, Mich., 1994).
B. *ANB* 21, 28–29; *DCA,* 1138–39; *EDC,* 504–5; *SPCK,* 205–7; *NYT,* 3 March 1985; "Episcopalians: Critic from Within," *Time,* 5 June 1964, 72; Walter Wink, "A Mind Full of Surprises," *Sojourners,* December 1985, 25; *Radical Christian and Exemplary Lawyer: Honoring William Stringfellow,* ed. Andrew W. McThenia Jr. (Grand Rapids, Mich., 1995); *Prophet of Justice, Prophet of Life: Essays on William Stringfellow,* ed. Robert Boak Slocum (New York: Church Publishing, 1997).

STUCK, HUDSON (11 November 1863, Paddington, England–11 October 1920, Fort Yukon, Alaska). *Education:* Studied at King's College, London; graduated from the theological department of the University of the South, 1892. *Career:* Schoolteacher, near Junction City and San Angelo, Tex., 1885–89; rector, Grace Church, Cuero, Tex., 1892–94; dean, St. Matthew's Cathedral, Dallas, Tex., 1894–1904; archdeacon of the Yukon, 1904–20.

Hudson Stuck, a priest and missionary to Alaska, was born in Paddington, England, in 1863. After immigrating to the United States in 1885, he worked as a cowboy and as a teacher before studying for the priesthood at the University of the South. An Anglo-Catholic, he had a strong sense of the church's responsibility to the larger society. The church, he said, "should be the neighbor of all the world and love that neighbor and help that neighbor." Ordained in 1892, he served for two years as the rector of Grace Church in Cuero, Texas, and for 10 years as dean of St. Matthew's Cathedral in Dallas. At St. Matthew's he founded a grammar school, a home for children, a home for aged women, and a night school for millworkers. Unafraid to challenge his richest parishioners, he campaigned against child labor, helping to secure passage in 1903 of the first factory law in the state of Texas.

Eager to satisfy both his wanderlust and his keen desire to perform missionary service, Stuck moved to Alaska in 1904, a time when that frontier region was the site of the last great expansion of the Episcopal Church's mission work. Based first in Fairbanks and later in Fort Yukon, he became the archdeacon of the Yukon, ably serving under Peter Trimble Rowe, the first missionary bishop of Alaska. Traveling by dogsled and motorboat, Stuck proved himself an industrious and sensitive missionary to both native peoples and miners. Opposed to the complete assimilation of native peoples, he sought the protection and continuation of traditional ways of living and working. He also favored native clothing and architecture over European-style dress and dwellings. Indeed, he was unusual among white missionaries in his toleration, even admiration, of what was best in the native culture.

An enthusiastic, energetic, adventurous man, Stuck was a bachelor whose vocation and avocation united to form one passion. In 1913 he and three companions made the first complete ascent of Mount McKinley, the tallest mountain in North America. His writings and speeches about that adventure and about other equally bold exploits won him a sizeable audience, and this wide appeal assisted his successful efforts to raise funds for mission work. Among his greatest admirers were progressives and conservationists such as Theodore Roosevelt. His campaign to shut down a salmon cannery at the mouth of the Yukon River that threatened native fishing also helped inspire the later development of even stronger environmental measures in the 1920s.

Stuck died in October 1920 at Fort Yukon after contracting bronchial pneumonia.

Bibliography

A. Papers at AEC and at the archives of the University of Alaska, Fairbanks; *The Ascent of Denali (Mount McKinley)* (New York, 1914); *Ten Thousand Miles with a Dog Sled* (New York, 1914); *Voyages on the Yukon and Its Tributaries* (New York, 1917); *A Winter Circuit of Our Arctic Coast* (New York, 1920).
B. *ANB* 21, 83–84; *DAB* 18, 178–79; *EDC,* 505; *WWWA* 1, 1202; Grafton Burke, "Hudson

Stuck from Texas to Alaska," *Alaska Churchman,* February 1921, 39–48; John W. Wood, "Hudson Stuck: Missionary and Pioneer," *TLC,* 23 October 1920, 857–58; Paul E. Thompson, "Who Was Hudson Stuck?" *Alaska Journal* 10 (1980): 62–65; David M. Dean, *Breaking Trail: Hudson Stuck of Texas and Alaska* (Athens, Ohio, 1988).

T

TUCKER, HENRY ST. GEORGE (16 July 1874, Warsaw, Va.–8 August 1959, Richmond, Va.). *Education:* B.A., M.A., University of Virginia, 1895; B.D., Virginia Theological Seminary, 1899. *Career:* Missionary in Japan, 1899–1923; president, St. Paul's College (now Rikkyo University), Tokyo, 1903–12; missionary bishop of Kyoto, 1912–23; professor of pastoral theology, Virginia Theological Seminary, 1923–26; bishop coadjutor, diocese of Virginia, 1926–27; bishop, diocese of Virginia, 1927–44; presiding bishop of the Episcopal Church, 1938–46; president, Federal Council of Churches, 1942–44.

Henry St. George Tucker, a missionary leader and bishop, was born in Warsaw, Virginia, in July 1874. After a brilliant career as a student at the University of Virginia and the Virginia Theological Seminary, he was ordained a deacon in June 1899 and a priest 13 months later. He began his ordained ministry as a missionary in Japan, where he labored for 24 years. He served the Nippon Sei Ko Kwai (the Holy Catholic Church in Japan), organized in 1887 as a province of the Anglican Communion. Since this church was still controlled by foreigners at the time of Tucker's arrival, one of his central concerns was to develop indigenous leadership, thus enabling it to become autonomous and self-supporting. Soon preaching sermons in fluent Japanese, he emphasized that "Japan as a nation can be won for Christ only by Japanese." In 1903 he also became president of St. Paul's College, now Rikkyo University, in Tokyo.

In 1912 Tucker was named second missionary bishop of Kyoto, a diocese with about 50 churches and mission stations and 2,200 communicants in a district of two million people. In the last year of World War I, at the request of the American Red Cross, he went to Vladivostok to develop plans for dealing with the refugee problem in eastern Siberia. Holding the rank of major in the American Expeditionary Force, he remained in Siberia during the fall of 1918 to supervise relief work among the civilian refugees. By 1923 one of his principal objectives had been achieved when independent, Japanese-led dioceses were established in Osaka and Tokyo. Wanting to provide an opportunity for a Japanese bishop in Kyoto, Tucker resigned his bishopric at that time. He left his diocese confident of its ability to support a Japanese bishop and proud of the large body of Japanese priests he had trained to carry on the work there. Returning to the United States, he became a professor of pastoral theology at Virginia Seminary, where he hoped to share with students his enthusiasm for missionary work.

Tucker's teaching career was interrupted in 1926 when he was elected bishop coadjutor of Virginia. The following year, he succeeded William Cabell Brown as diocesan and was also elected to the denomination's National Council, which looked to him for advice on missions in Asia. In 1937 he was chosen to succeed James DeWolf Perry as presiding bishop of the Episcopal Church.. The House of Bishops made this decision partly because of Tucker's range of experience but largely because of his appealing personal qualities. Although he was an evangelical, he nonetheless displayed an ability to transcend party differences and work effectively with all groups within his denomination. Tucker was especially interested in promoting missionary work and ecumenism, and a major achievement of his presiding episcopate was the development of the church's Reconstruction and Advance Fund. When the pressure of his duties prompted him to resign as bishop of Virginia in 1944, he became the first full-time presiding bishop in the history of the Episcopal Church.

In 1942 Tucker was elected president of the Federal Council of Churches. While holding that office, he spoke out forcefully against Hitler's murderous assault on European Jews and called for efforts to aid Jewish refugees. He and his administrative team also dealt with such domestic issues as race relations, the effects of the Depression and war on the churches, and the challenges posed by a rapidly changing postwar society. He cared deeply for the less fortunate members of society and was a champion of social justice, encouraging people to show loyalty not just to their family or nation but also to the universal community. Appropriately, one of Tucker's last public acts was testifying in 1952 before a committee of the Virginia legislature in favor of a bill to abolish racially segregated seating in public transportation.

He retired as presiding bishop at the end of 1946, and he died in Richmond, Virginia, in August 1959.

Bibliography

A. Papers at the archives of the Virginia Theological Seminary in Alexandria; *Providence and the Atonement* (Richmond, Va., 1934); *The History of the Episcopal Church in Japan* (New York, 1938); *Exploring the Silent Shore of Memory* (Richmond, 1951).

B. *ANB* 21, 895–96; *DAB* supp. 6, 648–49; *DCA*, 1189; *EDC*, 529; *ERS*, 786; *NCAB* 43, 598–99; *Religious Leaders of America*, ed. J. Gordon Melton (Detroit, 1991), 970–71; *WWWA* 3, 864; *NYT*, 9 August 1959; *Newsweek*, 12 August 1946, 88; Charles W. Sheerin, "Profile of a Presiding Bishop," *HMPEC* 15 (1946): 81–89; Virginius

Dabney, "Henry St. George Tucker: Beloved Virginian," *Virginia and the Virginia Record* 77, no. 4 (April 1955): 4–7, 19–24; William L. Sachs, " 'Self-Support': The Episcopal Mission and Nationalism in Japan," *CH* 58 (1989): 489–501; A. Pierce Middleton, *Henry St. George Tucker: Missionary and Bishop* (New York, 1960).

TUTTLE, DANIEL SYLVESTER (26 January 1837, Windham, N.Y.–17 April 1923, St. Louis, Mo.). *Education:* B.A., Columbia University, 1857; B.D., General Theological Seminary, 1862. *Career:* Private tutor, 1857–59; curate and rector, Zion Church, Morris, N.Y., 1862–67; missionary bishop of Montana, 1867–80; bishop, diocese of Utah, 1880–86; bishop, diocese of Missouri, 1886–1923; presiding bishop of the Episcopal Church, 1903–23.

Daniel S. Tuttle, a missionary bishop in the western United States, was born in Windham, New York, in 1837. The son of the village blacksmith, he grew up in a Methodist home but, under the influence of the local Episcopal rector, became interested in the ordained ministry of the Episcopal Church. After graduating from General Theological Seminary, he served a parish in Morris, New York, where, at the age of 29, he learned of his election to the episcopate. Careful to choose healthy young men as missionary leaders because they could more easily endure the hardships of the frontier, the House of Bishops elected Tuttle as the bishop of Montana with jurisdiction in Utah and Idaho.

The territory that the 30-year-old Tuttle ventured into—with a cavalry escort—was vast. In 1867 the 155,000-soul jurisdiction housed neither an Episcopal priest nor any Episcopal congregations. The tremendous size of the area demonstrates one key reason why the Episcopal Church lagged behind other denominations in the West: one bishop could not efficiently oversee a territory of approximately 340,000 square miles. This impediment notwithstanding, Tuttle accomplished a great deal within his domain. Focusing on the region between Salt Lake City, Utah, and Helena, Montana, he preached in mining camps, barrooms, and the rough cabins of pioneer settlers. Concentrating his labors on unchurched white settlers, he did not try to convert either Indians or Mormons. He gradually achieved gains for his denomination, especially among those who had had some contact with Christianity previously. He also built churches and other institutions, including St. Mark's Hospital in Salt Lake City, which was used by people of all denominations.

"Bishop Dan," as many called him, served in this post until 1886, when he accepted election as bishop of Missouri and moved with his family from Salt Lake City to St. Louis. In addition to his duties in Missouri, Tuttle became presiding bishop in 1903. He was the last Episcopalian to assume this role on the basis of seniority rather than election by peers. Generally avoiding controversy throughout his tenure as presiding bishop, he did voice strong opposition to this change in the method of selection, arguing that the choice of presiding bishop should be in the hands of God, not human beings. When he died in 1923 at age

86, Tuttle had been a bishop for 56 years and had been involved in the consecration of 70 bishops.

Bibliography

A. *Reminiscences of a Missionary Bishop* (New York, 1906).
B. *ANB* 22, 890–91; *DAB* 19, 75; *DARB,* 566–67; *ECUS,* 231–34; *EDC,* 530–31; *NCAB*
    6, 58–59; *SH* 12, 44; *NYT,* 18 April 1923; Kenneth L. Holmes, "Bishop Daniel
    Sylvester Tuttle in the West," *HMPEC* 23 (1954): 54–64; James W. Beless Jr.,
    "Daniel S. Tuttle: Missionary Bishop of Utah," *Utah Historical Quarterly* 27
    (1959): 359–78; Charles F. Rehkopf, "The Episcopate of Bishop Tuttle," *Bulletin
    of the Missouri Historical Society* 18 (1962): 207–30; David L. Holmes, "The
    Domestic Missionary Movement in the Episcopal Church in the Nineteenth Cen-
    tury," in *Beyond the Horizon,* ed. Charles R. Henery (Cincinnati, 1985).

TYNG, STEPHEN HIGGINSON (1 March 1800, Newburyport, Mass.–3 Sep-
tember 1885, Irvington-on-Hudson, N.Y.). *Education:* Graduated from Harvard
College, 1817; studied for the ordained ministry under Alexander V. Griswold,
1819–21. *Career:* Worked in business, 1817–19; rector, St. John's Church in
Georgetown, Washington, D.C., 1821–23; rector, Queen Anne's parish, Prince
George's County, Md., 1823–29; rector, St. Paul's Church, Philadelphia, 1829–
34; rector, Church of the Epiphany, Philadelphia, 1834–45; rector, St. George's
Church, New York, 1845–78.

Stephen H. Tyng, a leading evangelical clergyman, was born in Newburyport,
Massachusetts, in 1800. Following his graduation from Harvard College in 1817,
he initially embarked on a commercial career, but after undergoing a religious
conversion, he decided to enter the ordained ministry of the Episcopal Church
instead. He studied under Alexander V. Griswold,* bishop of the Eastern diocese,
who ordained him a deacon in March 1821. He was ordained a priest by James
Kemp, the bishop of Maryland, three years later. Tyng served parishes in Washington, D.C., Maryland, Philadelphia, and New York City during his 57 years of
active ministry.

A major figure in the evangelical party of the Episcopal Church, Tyng emphasized the importance of a conversion experience, personal morality, and cooperation with other Protestants across denominational lines. He was a dedicated
supporter of many of the institutions of the evangelical "Benevolent Empire" of
the mid-nineteenth century: the American Bible Society, the American Tract Society, temperance societies, and the Sunday school movement. At St. George's
Church in New York in the early 1860s, he became involved in an evangelistic
mission to poor people living on the lower east side of the city. He was also
considered to be one of the great preachers of the Episcopal Church. Large congregations flocked to hear his sermons, and when he served at St. Paul's Church
in Philadelphia, it was popularly known as "Tyng's Theatre." He was the editor
of two leading evangelical newspapers—the *Episcopal Recorder* (Philadelphia)
and the *Protestant Churchman* (New York)—and during the period when he

served at St. John's Church in Georgetown, he aided the founding of the Virginia Theological Seminary in Alexandria.

At the beginning of Tyng's ministry, evangelicals were the dominant party in the Episcopal Church, but by the second half of the nineteenth century, both the Tractarian and the broad church movements had begun to supplant them. Standing firmly against this trend, Tyng remained an unbending evangelical who resisted ritualism and theological liberalism with equal fervor. As he remarked at the end of his ministry at St. George's in New York, "I profess myself . . . to be one of these narrow-minded men, holding with unshrinking grasp the inspired word of God; adhering to the old paths and walking in them." Despite such views, Tyng strongly disapproved of the action of George David Cummins* in founding the Reformed Episcopal Church in 1873. He viewed Cummins's enterprise as a sad betrayal of the evangelical party within the Episcopal Church.

Declining health, both physical and mental, prompted Tyng's resignation from St. George's in 1878. He retired to Irvington-on-Hudson, New York, where he died seven years later.

Bibliography

A. *A Memoir of the Rev. Gregory Townsend Bedell* (Philadelphia, 1836); *The Israel of God,* 3rd. ed. (New York, 1845); *Recollections of England* (London, 1847); *Christ Is All* (New York, 1849); *Lectures on the Law and the Gospel* (New York, 1849); *Forty Years' Experience in Sunday-Schools* (New York, 1860); *The Office and Duty of the Christian Pastor* (New York, 1874).

B. *ANB* 22, 86–87; *DAB* 19, 101–2; *DCA,* 1192; *EDC,* 531; *NCAB* 2, 187–88; Charles Rockland Tyng, ed., *Record of the Life and Work of Rev. Stephen Higginson Tyng, D.D.* (New York, 1890); Dudley Tyng, *Stephen Higginson Tyng, 1800–1885, Evangelical, Preacher, Pioneer* (Pascoag, R.I., 1959); Diana Hochstedt Butler, *Standing against the Whirlwind: Evangelical Episcopalians in the Nineteenth Century* (New York, 1995).

W

WASHINGTON, PAUL MATTHEW (26 May 1921, Charleston, S.C.–7 October 2002, Philadelphia). *Education:* B.A., Lincoln University, 1943; Th.B., Philadelphia Divinity School, 1946. *Career:* Assistant minister, Church of the Crucifixion, Philadelphia, 1946–47; missionary, diocese of Liberia, 1948–54; Vicar, St. Cyprian's Church, Philadelphia, 1954–62; rector, Church of the Advocate, Philadelphia, 1962–87; interim rector, Church of the Crucifixion, Philadelphia, 1994–2001.

Paul M. Washington, a priest and social activist, was born in Charleston, South Carolina, in May 1921. Raised a Baptist, he had decided to enter the ordained ministry of that denomination, but he was converted to the Episcopal Church while in college. When he entered the Philadelphia Divinity School in 1943, he was the first African American student to live in the seminary's dormitory. Ordained a deacon in June 1946 and a priest 12 months later, he served briefly as an assistant minister at the Church of the Crucifixion in Philadelphia before traveling to the diocese of Liberia, where he worked as a teacher and priest. Although he enjoyed his ministry in Africa, one of his children contracted malaria, and he decided to return to the United States for the sake of his family's health. He was then appointed vicar of two mission churches in Philadelphia: St. Cyprian's, a black congregation, and St. Titus', a white congregation. However, when the lay leadership at St. Titus' Church objected to having an African American vicar, Oliver Hart, the bishop of Pennsylvania, rescinded that appointment.

Washington served very effectively at St. Cyprian's between 1954 and 1962, but when the church's neighborhood was targeted for demolition, he left to become the rector of the Church of the Advocate in Philadelphia. The congregation of the Advocate was then racially integrated, and the parish had been selected by the national Episcopal Church as the site for a new community outreach program.

Washington ministered at the Advocate for the next 25 years—a tumultuous period in the history of both his city and his denomination. As racial tensions rose in Philadelphia in the mid- and late 1960s, his church building became the scene of numerous community meetings, and he was a leading figure whenever African Americans challenged the continuing symbols of racial segregation and exclusion in the city. People would sometimes ask Washington about the size of his congregation; he would tell them that there were about a hundred worshipers on Sunday morning but over 1,500 present at various social ministry programs during the week. In 1968 the parish hosted one of the first Black Power conferences, and in 1969 Washington provided crucial assistance and support to Muhammed Kenyatta, an community organizer with the Black Economic Development Conference in Philadelphia. At the Special General Convention of the Episcopal Church in 1969, Washington also led a walkout of African American delegates from the convention hall when whites refused to listen to the demands presented by Kenyatta and other Black Power advocates.

Washington's most significant contribution to the institutional life of the Episcopal Church occurred on July 29, 1974. On that date he offered his church as the site for the service at which the first 11 women priests of the Episcopal Church were to be ordained. Because his church building was large enough to hold the huge congregation that gathered to watch the ordinations, and because its location in a poor neighborhood symbolized the marginal status of women in their denomination, the Advocate seemed to be a very appropriate setting for such a historic event. Although Washington himself had a good deal to lose if the bishop of Pennsylvania chose to reprimand him for his actions, he strongly believed that a great Christian ideal—the equality of God's people—would be dramatically affirmed that day.

Washington retired from the Church of the Advocate in 1987, but he remained extremely active in the life of his community. In 1995 he joined the Million Man March in Washington, D.C., but unlike many other black clergy, he opposed the evangelical, politically conservative Promise Keepers movement. He also criticized the black clergy association in Philadelphia when it opposed domestic partnership protection for city workers who were gay. Washington was regarded by his many friends and supporters as "a steadfast acolyte of Christian liberalism" and "the high priest of the progressive movement" in American Christianity. In 1994, he returned to the Church of the Crucifixion, Philadelphia, as the parish's interim rector and helped revitalize a then-declining congregation. After enduring bouts of poor health during the last years of his life, he died in Philadelphia in October 2002.

Bibliography

A. *"Other Sheep I Have": The Autobiography of Father Paul M. Washington,* [ed.] David McI. Gracie (Philadelphia, 1994).
B. *Philadelphia Inquirer,* 9 October 2002; " 'Acolyte of Christian Liberalism' Washington Dies," *Episcopal News Service,* 9 October 2002.

WEDEL, CYNTHIA CLARK (26 August 1908, Dearborn, Mich.–24 August 1986, Alexandria, Va.). *Education:* B.A., Northwestern University, 1929; M.A., 1930; Ph.D., George Washington University, 1957. *Career:* Director of Christian education, St. Luke's Church, Evanston, Ill., 1931–34; fieldworker, then director of youth work, National Council of the Episcopal Church, New York, 1934–39; teacher, National Cathedral School for Girls, Washington, D.C., 1939–49; national executive board, Woman's Auxiliary of the Episcopal Church, 1946–65; presiding officer, Triennial meeting of the Woman's Auxiliary, 1955; president, United Church Women of the National Council of Churches, 1955–58; assistant general secretary, National Council of Churches, 1962–65; associate general secretary for Christian unity, 1965–69; president, 1969–72; associate director, Center for a Voluntary Society, 1969–74; president, World Council of Churches, 1975–83.

Cynthia Clark Wedel, an ecumenical leader and educator, was born in Dearborn, Michigan, in August 1908. She was the daughter of Arthur Pierson Clark, a civil engineer, and Elizabeth Snow Haigh. After receiving degrees from Northwestern University, she became director of the Christian education program at St. Luke's Church in Evanston, Illinois. In 1934 she moved to New York, where she worked at the national headquarters of the Episcopal Church. In 1939 she married Theodore O. Wedel, a priest who was then the general secretary for Episcopal college work. The Wedels left New York soon after their marriage, moving to Washington, D.C., when Theodore was appointed warden of the College of Preachers at the Washington National Cathedral. Cynthia taught religion at the National Cathedral School for Girls between 1939 and 1949, and she earned a Ph.D. in psychology from George Washington University in 1957. During this period, she also became heavily involved as a volunteer in agencies such as the Girl Scouts and the American Red Cross and as a member of the national executive board of the Episcopal Woman's Auxiliary. She also served as the national president of the United Church Women, a department of the National Council of Churches (NCC). In addition, in the early 1960s President John F. Kennedy appointed her to the Commission on the Status of Women.

Wedel's most significant contributions were made as a leader in ecumenical affairs at both the NCC and the World Council of Churches. She was elected president of the NCC—the first woman to hold that position—in December 1969. That election was highly contested because African American delegates nominated Albert B. Cleage Jr., a United Church of Christ minister and author of a recent book on black power, *The Black Messiah* (1968). Although a group of African American church leaders asked Wedel to withdraw from the election in order to further the cause of racial justice, she rejected that request. "I deplore discrimination against black people and have worked hard to eliminate it," she replied, "but women have also been victims of discrimination, and I regard my election as a belated recognition of their importance in the church." Wedel also served as a delegate to the assemblies of the World Council of Churches that met in 1954, 1961, and 1968; and from 1975 until 1983 she was one of the six presidents of that organization. In 1965 she was an official observer at Vatican Council II of the Roman Catholic Church, and in 1978 she became the first woman to speak from the floor at the Lambeth conference of Anglican bishops.

Although Wedel was generally supportive of the social reform movements of the 1960s and 1970s, she also criticized the ordained leadership of the mainline Protestant denominations with whom she was associated through her NCC work. In a 1970 article she wrote for the "How My Mind Has Changed" series in the *Christian Century* magazine, she complained about "a new breed of clergymen," committed to social activism but fundamentally "insensitive to the average man and woman in the pew." She contrasted the tactlessness of those male clergy to the "women in the rank-and-file church membership" who had carried on a number of quiet but effective lay ministries in their parishes over many decades. Wedel consistently supported the cause of women's rights in the church, and with the rise of the movement for women's ordination, she argued that the presence of ordained women would greatly enhance the church's understanding of ministry. Despite this belief, she did not want the question of ordination to overshadow the importance of the ministry of the laity, especially the ministry of laywomen like herself.

Wedel remained active as a public speaker in churches until the last two years of her life, when a painful siege of cancer forced her to curtail her activities. She died in Alexandria, Virginia, in August 1986.

Bibliography

A. Papers at the headquarters of the World Council of Churches in Geneva, Switzerland, and at the archives of the National Council of Churches in New York; "The Church and Social Action," *Christian Century* 87 (1970): 959–62; *Celebrating Thanksgiving* (New York, 1941); *Citizenship, Our Christian Concern* (New York, 1950); *Health and Welfare Needs of the Nation and the Place of the Church Agency* (New York, 1954); *Employed Women and the Church* (New York, 1959); *Faith or Fear and Future Shock* (New York, 1974); *Ecumenical Rivalry and Cooperation* (Cincinnati, 1975); *Reflections on Ministry: Implications of Personhood, Gender and Vocation* (Cincinnati, 1976).
B. *ANB* 22, 878–79; *DARB*, 586–87; *DCA*, 1239–40; *EDC*, 549; *FD*, 255–62; *NCE* 18, 548–49; *NYT*, 28 August 1986; Judy Mathe Foley, "Cynthia Wedel: President-at-Large," *Episcopalian*, May 1972, 11–13, 36; Alan Geyer, "Cynthia Wedel: First Lady of Ecumenism," *Christian Century* 103 (1986): 796–97.

WEEMS, MASON LOCKE (11 October 1759, near Herring Bay, Anne Arundel County, Md.–23 May 1825, Beaufort, S.C.). *Education:* Studied medicine in London and at the University of Edinburgh. *Career:* Rector, All Hallows' Parish, Anne Arundel County, Md., 1784–89; rector, St. Margaret's Parish, Anne Arundel County, Md., 1791–92; book printer, writer, and traveling book agent, 1792–1825.

Mason ("Parson") Weems, a notable Episcopal priest and writer, was born in Maryland in 1759. Little is known about his early life, and despite studying medicine in London and in Edinburgh, he was never a practicing physician. His relatively brief ministerial career, however, represents an important episode in the reorganization of the Episcopal Church after the American Revolution.

Because there was a pressing need for clergy in Maryland, Weems and Edward Gantt Jr. were chosen in 1782 by a convention of clergy and laity, and they were sent to England to seek ordination by an English bishop. Although ongoing hostilities between Britain and America forced Weems to spend several months in France and the Netherlands, he eventually reached England after the peace treaty between the two nations had been signed. In England, he was temporarily stymied by the law that compelled ordinands to swear an oath of allegiance to the king. With the passage of the Enabling Act in August 1784, however, Parliament allowed English bishops to ordain candidates to the diaconate and priesthood without requiring the loyalty oath. As a result, Weems and Gantt were the first two Americans to become Anglican clergy in the postrevolutionary period. They were ordained to the diaconate on September 5, 1784, by the bishop of Chester and to the priesthood a week later by the archbishop of Canterbury.

Weems served as a rector in Maryland for the next eight years, but he quit the parish ministry in 1792 and thereafter devoted himself to the writing, production, and sale of books. His most famous work is a fictionalized biography of George Washington, which first appeared in 1800. By the time of his death in 1825, this biography had gone through 29 editions. In the fifth edition, published in 1806, he also included the memorable but apocryphal story of young George and the cherry tree. Weems wrote several other books, including biographies of Benjamin Franklin, William Penn, and Francis Marion, and he composed a series of pamphlets decrying such contemporary vices as drunkenness, adultery, gambling, and dueling. Designed to edify as well as to instruct, his works were widely read, and they conveyed the idea that the vitality of the young republic depended upon its inhabitants' moral health. Only a virtuous people, capable of self-restraint, Weems suggested, would be able to realize a true and lasting freedom.

Bibliography

A. *The Philanthropist; or, A Good Twelve Cents Worth of Political Love Powder, for the Fair Daughters and Patriotic Sons of Virginia,* 10th ed. (Philadelphia, 1799); *A History of the Life and Death, Virtues and Exploits of General George Washington* (Philadelphia, 1800); *The Drunkard's Looking-Glass: Reflecting a Faithful Likeness of the Drunkard,* 2nd ed. ([Philadelphia], 1813); *Life of General Francis Marion,* 3rd ed. (Baltimore, 1815); *God's Revenge against Adultery,* 3rd ed. (Philadelphia, 1818); *God's Revenge against Dueling,* 2nd ed. (Philadelphia, 1821); *The Bad Wife's Looking Glass,* 2nd ed. (Charleston, S.C., 1823).

B. *ANB* 22, 890–91; *BB,* 49–52, 55–56; *DAB* 19, 604–5; *DCA,* 1240; *EDC,* 550; *HEC,* 83, 88, 108–9; Sydney G. Fisher, "The Legendary and Myth-Making Process in Histories of the American Revolution," *Proceedings of the American Philosophical*

Society 51 (1912): 53–75; Sheldon Sloan, "Parson Weems on Franklin's Death," *Pennsylvania Magazine of History and Biography* 96 (1972): 369–76; Lawrence C. Wroth, *Parson Weems: A Biographical and Critical Study* (Baltimore, 1911); Paul Leicester Ford and Emily Ellsword Ford Skeel, *Mason Locke Weems,* 3 vols. (New York, 1928–29); Lewis G. Leary, *The Book-Peddling Parson* (Chapel Hill, N.C., 1984).

WHIPPLE, HENRY BENJAMIN (15 February 1822, Adams, N.Y.–16 September 1901, Faribault, Minn.). *Education:* Studied at local Presbyterian schools; studied at Oberlin College, 1838–39; studied theology under the Rev. William D. Wilson, Albany, N.Y., 1847–50; *Career:* Rector, Zion Church, Rome, N.Y., 1850–57; rector and missionary, St. Augustine, Fla., 1853–54; rector, Church of the Holy Communion, Chicago, 1857–59; bishop, diocese of Minnesota, 1859–1901.

Henry Benjamin Whipple, a bishop and missionary to American Indians, was brought up in a well-to-do family in upstate New York. Although raised a Presbyterian, he decided to enter the ordained ministry of the Episcopal Church, his grandparents' denomination. Ordained to the diaconate in 1849 and to the priesthood a year later, he served churches in Rome, New York, and St. Augustine, Florida, before accepting a call to organize a new parish for industrial workers on the south side of Chicago. He was elected bishop of Minnesota in 1859, only a decade after being ordained. Thirty-seven years old at the time of his election, Whipple moved to Faribault in 1860. His frontier diocese had been part of the huge seven-state territory over which Jackson Kemper,* the first missionary bishop of the Episcopal Church, had presided.

Facing physical hardship and danger, Whipple traveled extensively throughout his diocese, learning about both the living conditions of its 20,000 Indians and the failures of the federal government in fulfilling its treaty obligations to them. He frequently used his range of personal contacts to appeal to affluent Episcopalians on behalf of the Indians. He sought not only funds but also fair and humane treatment. Recognizing the injustice of the government's policy toward native peoples, he wrote to Abraham Lincoln in March 1862 outlining the flaws in the government's management of Indian affairs and asking for "justice for a wronged and neglected race." In 1871, in response to pleas from Whipple and William Welsh (an Episcopalian who headed the congressional Board of Indian Commissioners), the Episcopal Church formed the Indian Commission under its board of missions to defend the Indians' rights. Whipple received international acclaim as a leading Christian proponent of Indian reform, and his reputation for honesty and plain speaking prompted the Ojibwe to give him the Indian name "Straight Tongue."

These achievements notwithstanding, Whipple was also, like other reformers of his time, an assimilationist who hoped to turn the Indians into, as he put it, "useful Christian citizens." He viewed Native Americans as "heathens" who, though they had been harmed by contact with the worst elements of white culture, were essentially good people who could be "civilized." To this end, he typically recommended moving capable young Indian catechists from the reservation to the church boarding school he had founded in Faribault. In his mind, Christianization invariably required detribalization: cutting family ties, isolating individuals, dividing the Indian community, and undermining tribal political structures.

Although he was a high church Episcopalian, Whipple thought party distinctions were unimportant compared to the duty of preaching "Christ crucified." He was also ecumenically minded, working well with representatives of other denominations. Preaching the opening sermon at the third Lambeth conference in July 1888, he affirmed that "no one branch of the Church is absolutely by itself alone the Catholic Church; all branches need reunion. . . . At a time when every form of error and sin is banded together to oppose the Kingdom of Christ the world needs the witness of a united Church."

In Faribault, Whipple established several important institutions: the Cathedral of Our Merciful Saviour, St. Mary's Hall, Shattuck Military School, and Seabury Divinity School. Having served as the bishop of Minnesota for more than 40 years, he died in September 1901.

Bibliography

A. "The Indian System," *North American Review* 99 (1864): 449–64; Preface, in Helen Hunt Jackson, *A Century of Dishonor* (New York, 1881); *Five Sermons* (New York, 1890); *Lights and Shadows of a Long Episcopate* (New York, 1899).
B. *ANB* 23, 163–64; *BB,* 96–97; *DAB* 20, 68–69; *DARB,* 594–95; *EDC,* 555; *NCAB* 4, 58–59; *SH* 12, 337; *NYT,* 17 September 1901; Everett W. Sterling, "Bishop Henry B. Whipple: Indian Agent Extraordinary," *HMPEC* 26 (1957): 239–47; Martin N. Zanger, " 'Straight Tongue's Heathen Wards': Bishop Whipple and the Episcopal Mission to the Chippewas," in *Churchmen and the Western Indians, 1820–1920,* ed. Clyde A. Milner II and Floyd A. O'Neil (Norman, Okla., 1985), 177–214; George Clinton Tanner, *Fifty Years of Church Work in the Diocese of Minnesota, 1857–1907* (St. Paul, Minn., 1909); Phillips Endecott Osgood, *Straight Tongue: A Story of Henry Benjamin Whipple, First Episcopal Bishop of Minnesota* (Minneapolis, 1958); Francis Paul Prucha, *American Indian Policy in Crisis: Christian Reformers and the Indian, 1865–1900* (Norman, Okla., 1976); Robert H. Keller Jr., *American Protestantism and United States Indian Policy, 1869–82* (Lincoln, Nebr., 1983); Owanah Anderson, *Jamestown Commitment: The Episcopal Church and the American Indian* (Cincinnati, 1988), chapter 5; Owanah Anderson, *400 Years: Anglican / Episcopal Mission among American Indians* (Cincinnati, 1997), chapter 3.

WHITE, WILLIAM (4 April 1748, Philadelphia–17 July 1836, Philadelphia). *Education:* Graduated from the College of Philadelphia (now the University of Pennsylvania), 1765; studied theology under William Smith, Richard Peters, and Jacob Duché in Philadelphia, 1765–70. *Career:* Curate, United Parishes of St. Peter's and Christ Church, Philadelphia, 1772–79; rector, United Parishes of St. Peter's and Christ Church, Philadelphia, 1779–1836; chaplain, Continental and

Federal Congresses, 1777–1800; bishop, diocese of Pennsylvania, 1787–1836; presiding bishop of the Episcopal Church, 1795–1836.

William White, a bishop and one of the chief organizers of the Episcopal Church after the American Revolution, was born into an affluent Philadelphia family in 1748. After graduating from the College of Philadelphia in 1765, he studied theology under the direction of three Anglican clergymen in the city. He was ordained to the priesthood in April 1772 and served for seven years as the assistant to Jacob Duché, rector of Christ Church, Philadelphia. At the outbreak of the Revolution, White was sympathetic to the American cause, and when Duché, a loyalist, fled from Philadelphia in 1779, White became the rector of the United Parishes of St. Peter's and Christ Church. He was also named chaplain of the Continental Congress and became friends with several leading patriots, including George Washington.

In 1782 White published his most important work, *The Case of the Episcopal Churches in the United States Considered.* In that pamphlet, he discussed principles upon which American Anglicans might reorganize their church after their country had won its independence from Great Britain. Wishing to ensure the continuation of Anglican worship and church life in a new nation, he proposed the creation of a presbyterian form of church government until bishops could be obtained from the Church of England—a pragmatic approach that was strongly opposed by Samuel Seabury* and other high church clergy. Despite his views on episcopacy, White was also instrumental in healing divisions that arose in the American church following Seabury's consecration in Scotland in 1784. At the first General Convention of the Episcopal Church, which met in Philadelphia in 1785, White was actively engaged in drafting the constitution of his denomination. He envisioned a republican form of ecclesiastical governance, and he eventually helped fashion a crucial compromise in which Episcopalians agreed to the sharing of power between clergy and laity in the councils of the church.

White was elected bishop of the diocese of Pennsylvania in 1786, and he was consecrated in London a year later. He continued to serve as a parish rector throughout his lengthy episcopate, and he also held the position of presiding bishop from 1795 until his death. He believed in a liberalized version of evangelicalism that eschewed the excesses of Protestant revivalism, and he sought to project an image of theological consensus that would unite the emerging high church and low church parties in his denomination. As presiding bishop, he influenced the development of a number of significant nineteenth-century church leaders, including John Henry Hobart* and William Augustus Muhlenberg.* A public-spirited figure in both religious and civic affairs, White served as president of the Philadelphia Bible Society, and he was a key member of the American Philosophical Society. Remaining active into his eighties, he died in Philadelphia in 1836.

Bibliography

A. Papers at AEC and at Christ Church in Philadelphia; "The Case of the Episcopal Churches in the United States Considered (1782)," in *DW*, 2–14; *Lectures on the Catechism* (Philadelphia, 1813); *Comparative Views of the Controversy between the Calvinists and the Arminians*, 2 vols. (Philadelphia, 1817); *Memoirs of the Protestant Episcopal Church in the United States of America* (Philadelphia, 1820).

B. *AAP* 5, 280–92; *ANB* 23, 248–49; *DAB* 20, 121–22; *DARB*, 599–600; *DCA*, 1250–51; *EDC*, 555–56; *NCAB* 3, 470; *SH* 12, 341; *SPCK*, 232–33; John F. Woolverton, "Philadelphia's William White: Episcopalian Distinctiveness and Accommodation in the Post-Revolutionary Period," *HMPEC* 43 (1974): 279–96; Byrd Wilson, *Memoir of the Life of the Right Reverend William White* (Philadelphia, 1839); Julius Hammond Ward, *The Life and Times of Bishop White* (New York, 1892); Walter H. Stowe, ed., *The Life and Letters of Bishop William White* (New York, 1937); Robert W. Prichard, *The Nature of Salvation: Theological Consensus in the Episcopal Church, 1801–73* (Urbana, Ill., 1997).

WHITEFIELD, GEORGE (27 December 1714, Gloucester, England–30 September 1770, Newburyport, Mass.). *Education:* B.A., Pembroke College, Oxford University, 1736. *Career:* Itinerant preacher in England and the American colonies, 1736–70.

Known as the "Grand Itinerant," George Whitefield was an Anglican clergyman who was a key figure in the Great Awakening of the eighteenth century. During his studies at Oxford University, he befriended the brothers John and Charles Wesley and joined the group that other university students referred to as the "Holy Club" or "Methodists." Persuaded by the Wesleys to travel to Georgia as a missionary, Whitefield arrived in the American colony in the spring of 1738. The following September he sailed back to England to be ordained a priest and to raise money to start an orphanage ("Bethesda") in Savannah.

Shunning the settled existence of a parish vicar, Whitefield devoted his life to evangelistic preaching in England and America, addressing large gatherings several times a week and preaching more than 15,000 sermons during his career. Between 1738 and 1770, he made seven trips to America, where he often attracted huge crowds with his direct, extemporaneous preaching style. Whitefield presented a modified version of John Calvin's doctrine of election. While he rejected the Wesleys' emphasis on the absolute freedom of the human will, he called upon sinners to "choose" salvation by placing their trust entirely in God's grace. Whitefield's phenomenal success as an evangelist, however, made him increasingly unwelcome in Anglican pulpits. Dismissed by many of his fellow clergy as a fanatical "enthusiast," he grew accustomed to preaching in open fields, in barns, in courthouses, in busy markets, and in the meetinghouses of Presbyterians and Congregationalists.

Whitefield's activities in America helped increase the toleration of dissent in a religiously diverse society, and his evangelistic work provided a harbinger of the interdenominational cooperation that became commonplace in the nineteenth century. Downplaying ecclesiastical distinctions, including his own affiliation with the Church of England, he delivered a message that touched thousands of people regardless of church membership or social class. A reawakener of experiential piety, Whitefield was one of the most popular figures in colonial America. He died in Newburyport, Massachusetts, in September 1770 during what proved to be his final American preaching tour.

Bibliography

A. *A Journal* and *A Continuation of the Reverend Mr. Whitefield's Journal,* 7 vols. (London, 1739–43); *The Works of the Reverend George Whitefield, M.A.,* 6 vols. (London, 1771–72); *Memoirs of the Rev. George Whitefield,* ed. John Gillies (London, 1772; reprint, Hartford, 1853); *Fifteen Sermons* (Philadelphia, 1794); *Eighteen Sermons* (Newburyport, Mass., 1797).
B. *AAP* 5, 94–108; *ANB* 23, 255–56; *DAB* 20, 124–29; *DARB,* 600–602; *EARH,* 787–88; *ERS,* 841; *HEC,* 43–59; *NCAB* 5, 384–85; *SH* 12, 341–42; William Howland Kenney III, "George Whitefield: Dissenter Priest of the Great Awakening, 1739–1741," *WMQ,* 3d ser., 26 (1969): 75–93; Luke Tyerman, *The Life of the Rev. George Whitefield,* 2 vols. (New York, 1876–77); Stuart C. Henry, *George Whitefield: Wayfaring Witness* (Nashville, 1954); John Pollock, *George Whitefield and the Great Awakening* (Garden City, N.Y., 1972); Harry S. Stout, *The Divine Dramatist: George Whitefield and the Rise of Modern Evangelism* (Grand Rapids, Mich., 1991); Frank Lambert, *"Pedlar in Divinity": George Whitefield and the Transatlantic Revivals, 1737–1770* (Princeton, 1994).

WHITTINGHAM, WILLIAM ROLLINSON (2 December 1805, New York– 17 October 1879, Orange, N.J.). *Education:* Graduated from the General Theological Seminary, 1825. *Career:* Librarian, General Theological Seminary, 1825– 27; chaplain, Charity School of Trinity Church, New York, 1827–29; rector, St. Mark's Church, Orange, N.J., 1829–30; rector, St. Luke's Church, New York, 1831–35; professor of ecclesiastical history, General Theological Seminary, 1836–40; bishop, diocese of Maryland, 1840–79.

William Rollinson Whittingham, a bishop and influential high church leader, was born in New York City in December 1805. After graduating from General Theological Seminary, he was ordained a deacon in March 1827 and a priest in December 1829. His first major position in the church was at St. Luke's Church in New York, where he served as rector between 1831 and 1835. After poor health required him to resign from St. Luke's, he undertook 15 months of travel abroad, chiefly in the Mediterranean. In 1836 he was appointed professor of ecclesiastical history at General Seminary, then the center of Tractarian high churchmanship in the United States. Whittingham became a popular professor, establishing a reputation for himself as an exceptionally learned and devoted scholar. He also had a marked influence on his students, who took with them the high church values they had learned at General into the parishes where they worked.

Whittingham was elected bishop of Maryland in May 1840, and he was consecrated the following September. Although his diocese, which then encompassed the entire state, including the District of Columbia, was in poor shape, he helped its spiritual life in a number of ways. He played a leading role in founding the College of St. James, near Hagerstown, a successor to William A. Muhlenberg's* Flushing Institute and an important predecessor of St. Paul's School in Concord, New Hampshire. In 1855, with his support, Mary Black and Catherine Minard accepted an offer from Horace Stringfellow, rector of St. Andrew's Church, Baltimore, to become deaconesses. The deaconesses started a nursing ministry in the infirmary attached to the church, and in 1859 they took charge of the Church Home and Infirmary in Baltimore. In 1873 Whittingham welcomed an English religious order, the All Saints Sisters of the Poor, to Maryland; these sisters started a school for African American children at Mount Calvary Church, Baltimore. As a catholic-minded Episcopalian, Whittingham had a vision of the church's responsibilities throughout the world. He provided assistance to missions not only on the American frontier but also in foreign countries, especially Mexico, Cuba, Near Eastern countries, and African countries. Finally, he sought closer ties with Christians abroad, particularly with leaders in the Church of England, the Greek Orthodox church, the Orthodox Church in Russia, and the Old Catholic churches in Europe.

The strife that afflicted Maryland during the Civil War rent Whittingham's diocese as well. He supported the Union at a time when many Episcopal clergy and laypeople were Confederate sympathizers. Like many white Americans in the mid-nineteenth century, he believed that slavery was lawful and abolition a crime, but he opposed allowing the institution to spread beyond the southern states. He understood the South's rebellion to be a grave breach of divine law, not because southerners fought in the defense of slavery but because they disregarded the scriptural principle that "the powers that be are ordained of God" (Romans 13:1). Whittingham thus approved of the effort both to force the seceded states back into the Union and to suppress disloyal sentiment, especially in border states such as Maryland. Erastian in his sympathies, he demanded that the clergy of his diocese continue to pray for the president of the United States when they conducted services, and he regarded the exclusion of those prayers as a mutilation of the liturgy and a violation of their ordination vows. Whenever President Abraham Lincoln proclaimed days of national fasting or thanksgiving, Whittingham issued a pastoral letter in which he set forth the prayers he wanted his clergy to use. He disciplined any man who disobeyed those directives, and he supported a bill introduced in the Maryland House of Delegates that would have required clergy to sign an oath of loyalty to the U.S. government.

An exemplary preacher, Whittingham was concerned that contemporary preaching lacked, in his words, "depth, depth of knowledge, and still more depth of conviction." He had a profound love of the church, demanding everything of himself on its behalf. He even bequeathed his library of 17,000 books to the diocese of Maryland following his death in 1879.

Bibliography

A. Papers at the archives of the diocese of Maryland in Baltimore; *The Voice of the Lord* (Washington, D.C., 1841); *The Priesthood in the Church* (Baltimore, 1842); *The Body of Christ* (Baltimore, 1843); *The Work of Christ by His Ministry* (Baltimore, 1856); *Conformity in Worship* (Baltimore, 1857); *Fifteen Sermons* (New York, 1880).
B. *ACAB* 6, 494–95; *DAB* 20, 176–77; *EDC,* 556; *MM,* 237–45; *NCAB* 6, 225–26; Nelson Waite Rightmyer, "The Church in a Border State—Maryland," *HMPEC* 17 (1948): 411–17; Richard R. Duncan, "Bishop Whittingham, the Maryland Diocese, and the Civil War," *Maryland Historical Magazine* 61 (1967): 329–47; William Francis Brand, *Life of William Rollinson Whittingham,* 2 vols. (New York, 1883); David Hein, ed., *A Student's View of the College of St. James on the Eve of the Civil War: The Letters of W. Wilkins Davis* (Lewiston, N.Y., 1988), chapter 1.

WILLIAMS, CHANNING MOORE (18 July 1829, Richmond, Va.–2 December 1910, Richmond, Va.). *Education:* A.B., College of William and Mary, 1853; graduated from the Virginia Theological Seminary, 1855. *Career:* Missionary in China, 1857–59, and in Japan, 1859–66; missionary bishop of China, with jurisdiction over Japan, 1866–74; missionary bishop of Yedo, Japan, 1874–89; retired bishop in Japan, 1889–1908.

Channing M. Williams, a missionary bishop to China and Japan, was born in Richmond, Virginia, in July 1829. Because his father, a Virginia farmer, died when he was young, Channing grew up in poverty and ill-health. His pious mother, however, strove to strengthen him in body and to nurture him in the Christian faith. After taking some time to earn money for his education, he became a student at the College of William and Mary, obtaining a degree in 1853. Having determined to seek ordination, he entered the Virginia Theological Seminary in Alexandria. At the seminary he was excited to hear reports about the work of the school's graduates in China and Africa, and he decided that such a life was for him as well.

After graduation, Williams journeyed to China, where he served as a missionary priest under William Jones Boone, the missionary bishop. Williams mainly engaged in preaching and handing out books and pamphlets. Believing that the Chinese held books and learning in particularly high regard, he distributed separately bound copies of Genesis, Exodus, the Gospels, and Acts. In 1859 the Board of Missions of the Episcopal Church appointed Williams and a seminary classmate, John Liggins, the first Episcopal missionaries to Japan, a country that had only recently become open to foreigners in residence. Pursuing an indirect approach to evangelism, the two Episcopalians—the first non–Roman Catholic missionaries in the country—sold historical, geographic, and scientific texts that were written in Japanese and contained references to religious themes. Whenever the books stimulated curiosity about Christianity and the Bible, Williams and Liggins encouraged further interest by distributing copies of the New Testament.

In 1865, after the death of Bishop Boone, the House of Bishops chose Williams to be the second missionary bishop of China, with jurisdiction over Japan, and he was consecrated bishop a year later. Until 1871 Williams was the sole Episcopal missionary in Japan, as Liggins had been compelled to leave in 1862 on account of ill health. During this period, Williams prepared books in Japanese and translated the Apostles' Creed, the Lord's Prayer, and the Ten Commandments. In February 1866, seven years after his arrival in the country, he baptized his first Japanese, a samurai of Hiogo. In 1874 the House of Bishops acceded to his request to divide his jurisdiction. As a result, he became the missionary bishop of Yedo (changed to Tokyo after 1893) and relinquished his jurisdiction in China.

Williams built up the church in Japan and had direct charge of several congregations. He also established two dioceses: Tokyo and Kyoto. Among his most notable achievements were his translation of parts of the *Book of Common Prayer* and his founding of a number of schools, including St. Paul's School, which eventually developed into Rikkyo University. Eager to establish a seminary that could train native clergy, Williams and members of the Church of England founded Trinity Divinity School in Tokyo in 1878. This joint effort was undoubtedly facilitated by a meeting in Osaka in 1868, when the idea of uniting the work of the American and English churches in Japan was proposed. Supported by Williams, this proposal eventually achieved concrete expression at the first meeting of the General Synod of the Japanese Church in 1887—a gathering that marked the official beginning of the Nippon Sei Ko Kwai (the Holy Catholic Church of Japan).

In 1889, at the age of 60, Williams retired as bishop but continued to carry out mission work in Japan. In 1895 he went to Kyoto and opened new mission stations in that region. Not until 1908, when he was physically unable to continue his work, did he leave Japan to return to his native land. Two years after coming home, he died in the same city in which he had been born over 80 years before.

Bibliography

A. Papers at AEC and at the archives of Virginia Theological Seminary in Alexandria; "Annual Report of the Missionary Bishop of Yedo, 1889," in *DW,* 148–49.
B. *ANB* 23, 437–38; *DAB* 20, 250–51; *ECUS,* 239–41; *EDC,* 558; *SH* 12, 365; *WWWA* 1, 1350; John C. Ambler, "An Appreciation of 'The Old Bishop,' " *Spirit of Missions* 76 (1911): 307–9; Theodore N. Barth, "The Work of the Seminary in Japan," in *History of the Theological Seminary in Virginia and Its Historical Background,* ed. William A.R. Goodwin (New York, 1924), vol. 2, 326–38; Henry St. George Tucker, *The History of the Episcopal Church in Japan* (New York, 1938); Maria Minor, *Channing Moore Williams: Pioneer Missionary in Japan* (New York, 1959); Hisakazu Kaneto, *A Story of Channing Moore Williams: The Bishop of Yedo* (Tokyo, 1964).

WILLIAMS, PETER JR. (1780?, New Brunswick, N.J.–17 October 1840, New York). *Education:* Studied at the African Free School, New York; tutored privately by Thomas Lyell and John Henry Hobart, New York. *Career:* Lay reader, black congregation associated with Trinity Church, New York, 1812–19; rector, St. Philip's Church, New York, 1819–40.

The second African American ordained to the Episcopal priesthood, Peter Williams Jr. was born in New Brunswick, New Jersey. Although his father (Peter Sr.) was still a slave in 1780, he was able to purchase his freedom in 1796, and he soon became a leading figure in the black community in New York City. Peter Jr. was educated at the African Free School and tutored privately by Thomas Lyell, a white minister of the John Street Methodist Church, where his father worked as a sexton and undertaker. As a teenager, he joined the African American congregation that worshiped on Sunday afternoons in the building of Trinity Church in lower Manhattan. When the lay reader who led Trinity's black congregation died in 1812, Williams was elected to succeed him, and over the next six years, he helped organize the congregation into a separate parish. His people acquired land and constructed a building, which was named "St. Philip's African Church" in 1819. Williams continued to lead the new parish in a lay capacity until his ordination as a deacon in October 1820. Because of racial discrimination, Williams and his parish were not accorded the same privileges as white Episcopalians in the diocese of New York, and he was not ordained a priest until July 1826.

Like his father, Williams was involved in many significant ways in the African American community in his city. In 1808 he published a speech that he delivered in celebration of the end of the American slave trade. Although he eventually denounced the racist efforts and ideas of the American Colonization Society, he once considered the possibility of voluntary black migration out of the United States. He initially favored colonization in the black republic of Haiti, which he visited in 1824, and in 1830 he delivered a speech at St. Philip's on behalf of the recently established African American colony in Wilberforce, Canada. He also was one of the founders of *Freedom's Journal,* the first black newspaper, and he helped found the Phoenix Society, which offered financial support to young African Americans seeking an education. Among the people whom Williams assisted was Alexander Crummell,* who attended St. Philip's Church.

After the founding of the American Antislavery Society (AAS) in 1833, Williams became actively engaged in the abolition movement. However, protests against slavery angered many whites in the city, especially those who feared competition with African Americans for jobs. Thus, in early July 1834 white workers went on a rampage and for several days attacked and terrorized black New Yorkers. Hearing rumors that Williams had performed an interracial marriage, a white mob broke into St. Philip's, burned the church and its rectory, and forced Williams and his family to flee. Instead of denouncing this act of violence against one of his priests, Benjamin T. Onderdonk,* the bishop of New York, reproved Williams and insisted that he resign publicly from the AAS, calling it a threat to "the peace of the community." With great reluctance, Williams acceded to his bishop's demand. Despite this humiliating setback, Williams received the support of most of his parishioners, and he continued to work on behalf of social reform. He remained the rector of St. Philip's until his death in October 1840.

Bibliography

A. "An Oration on the Abolition of the Slave Trade," 1 January 1808, and "A Discourse Delivered in St. Philip's Church for the Benefit of the Colored Community of Wilberforce," 4 July 1830, in *Early Negro Writing, 1760–1837,* ed. Dorothy Porter (Boston, 1971); Williams's response to Benjamin T. Onderdonk is reprinted in *Journal of Negro History* 11 (1926): 181–85.

B. *ANB* 23, 494–95; *DANB,* 660–61; *EAAR,* 841–42; *EDC,* 559; J.B. Wakely, *Lost Chapters Recovered from the Early History of American Methodism* (New York, 1858); B.F. DeCosta, *Three Score and Ten: The Story of St. Philip's Church, New York City* (New York, 1889).

WILMER, RICHARD HOOKER (15 March 1816, Alexandria, Va.–14 June 1900, Mobile, Ala.). *Education:* Graduated from Yale College, 1836; graduated from the Virginia Theological Seminary, 1839. *Career:* Served as a priest in rural parishes in Virginia, 1839–44, 1849–58; rector, St. James Church, Wilmington, N.C., 1844–49; priest, mission in Henrico Country (later Emmanuel Church), Va., 1858–62; bishop, diocese of Alabama, 1862–1900.

Richard Hooker Wilmer, the only bishop consecrated by the Protestant Episcopal Church in the Confederate States of America, was born in Alexandria, Virginia, in 1816. He was the son of the noted evangelical priest William Holland Wilmer, one of the first faculty members of Virginia Theological Seminary. After graduating from that seminary, Richard Wilmer was ordained to the diaconate in March 1839 and to the priesthood a year later. He served in several rural parishes in Virginia in the 1840s and 1850s and as rector of St. James Church in Wilmington, North Carolina, between 1844 and 1849. In 1862, while serving at Emmanuel Church in Henrico County, Virginia, he was elected bishop of the diocese of Alabama. Following the secession of their states and the outbreak of the Civil War, dioceses in the South had organized a new Episcopal Church in the Confederacy. Wilmer thus became a bishop in this denomination at the time of his consecration in 1862.

Wilmer gained considerable notoriety after the conclusion of the Civil War. At the beginning of Reconstruction, when Alabama was under the control of federal military forces, Wilmer instructed his clergy not to use the prayer book collects for the president and those in civil authority when they conducted their services. There was no longer any *civil* authority in the state, he argued, only military rule. George Thomas, the Union general in charge of Alabama, responded to this provocation by closing Episcopal churches and restricting the work of any clergy who complied with the bishop's instructions. Although Thomas's orders were later revoked for being inappropriate, Wilmer soon became a popular figure among conservative whites resisting Reconstruction efforts in the South. In addition, the validity of Wilmer's episcopal orders came under scrutiny from northern Episcopalians because, having been elected in the midst of the Civil War, his conse-cration had not received the approval that was ordinarily required from a majority of dioceses in the United States. The fact that Wilmer's orders were quickly recognized throughout the Episcopal Church was one of the crucial elements in healing the wartime schism among whites in the denomination.

In July 1883 Wilmer was a member of the group of southern clergy and lay leaders who assembled for a conference at the University of the South in Sewanee, Tennessee. This gathering formulated a proposal that was directed to the upcom-ing meeting of the General Convention. The "Sewanee conference" proposed that any Episcopal diocese containing large numbers of African Americans should be allowed to establish a special missionary organization to which black church members could be assigned. This plan represented one of the initial efforts on the part of southern dioceses to segregate the membership of their African American parishes. Wilmer was the only person present at the Sewanee conference to dissent openly from the majority's position. He argued that the proposal was "inconsistent with true Catholicity" and "contrary to the mind of Christ." Although Wilmer's viewpoint was based as much on racial prejudice as on theology—he believed that African Americans were likely to degenerate morally unless they were con-stantly supervised by white church leaders—this reasoning swayed the Episcopal Church as a whole when the General Convention of 1883 vetoed the Sewanee plan.

Serving as bishop from the mid-nineteenth to the very early twentieth century, Wilmer proved to be a transitional figure within the history of the Episcopal Church. He was a low church Episcopalian who condemned both the extreme evangelicals who eventually organized the Reformed Episcopal Church and the extreme Anglo-Catholics who adopted the use of Roman Catholic liturgical prac-tices. In the later years of his episcopate, moreover, Wilmer also refused to offer his assent to the election of Phillips Brooks* as bishop of Massachusetts. He opposed Brooks because he feared the rise of theological liberalism in the emerg-ing broad church wing of his denomination.

Wilmer died in Mobile, Alabama, in June 1900.

Bibliography

A. "Contrary to the Mind of Christ, 1883," in *DW,* 200–202; *The Recent Past from a Southern Standpoint: Reminiscences of a Grandfather* (New York, 1887); *Guide Marks for Young Churchmen* (New York, 1889).
B. *ANB* 23, 551; *DAB* 20, 315; *EDC,* 559–60; *ERS,* 842; *NCAB* 3, 465; *WWWA* Historical vol. 1607–1896, 658; obituary, *Churchman,* 23 June 1900; Gardiner C. Tucker, "Richard Hooker Wilmer, Second Bishop of Alabama," *HMPEC* 7 (1938): 133–53; Walter C. Whitaker, *Richard Hooker Wilmer, Second Bishop of Alabama* (Phila-delphia, 1907).

A CHRONOLOGY OF THE EPISCOPAL CHURCH

1534   British Parliament ends papal authority over English ecclesiastical affairs by declaring Henry VIII "the only supreme head . . . of the Church of England."

1549   First edition of the *Book of Common Prayer* is published.

1593   Theologian Richard Hooker publishes his *Laws of Ecclesiastical Polity,* which summarizes Anglican teaching on the nature of authority in the church.

1607   The English establish a permanent settlement at Jamestown, Virginia.

1619   Dutch traders bring the first enslaved Africans to Virginia.

1662   Anglican parish vestry system is established in Virginia.

1689   James Blair is appointed to serve as the first Anglican commissary in America.

1693   The College of William and Mary opens in Williamsburg, Virginia.

1698   Thomas Bray, Maryland's first commissary, organizes the Society for Promoting Christian Knowledge (SPCK) to provide Bibles and other religious literature for Anglican parishes in the colonies.

1701   Bray and others form the Society for the Propagation of the Gospel in Foreign Parts (SPG), which will send more than three hundred missionaries to plant and nurture Anglican parishes in the colonies.

1722   Seven Congregational ministers in Connecticut, all faculty members at Yale College, convert to the Church of England.

1739   George Whitefield, an Anglican priest, begins his first American preaching tour, one of the major events of the Great Awakening.

1754   King's College (now Columbia University) is founded by Anglicans in New York.

1767   In his *Appeal to the Public in Behalf of the Church of England in America,* Thomas

Bradbury Chandler articulates reasons why an Anglican episcopate should be established in the colonies.

1775   Anglican layman Patrick Henry delivers his "Give me liberty or give me death" speech at St. John's Church in Richmond, Virginia.

1776   The process of Anglican disestablishment in the American colonies begins.

1780   The first use of the name "Protestant Episcopal" occurs at a convention of clergy and laity in Chestertown, Maryland.

1782   William White publishes *The Case of the Episcopal Churches in the United States Considered,* which offers crucial ideas about the reorganization of American Anglicanism.

1784   Samuel Seabury is consecrated to the episcopate by three bishops of the Episcopal Church of Scotland.

1787   Charles Inglis is consecrated bishop of Nova Scotia, thus becoming the first bishop of the Church of England to serve in a British colony.

1789   General Convention meets in Philadelphia and approves a constitution and prayer book for the Episcopal Church.

1792   Thomas Claggett becomes the first Episcopal bishop consecrated on American soil.

1794   St. Thomas African Episcopal Church in Philadelphia becomes not only the first black parish of the Episcopal Church but also the first black congregation of any denomination in the United States.

1804   Absalom Jones is ordained as the first African American priest of the Episcopal Church.

1811   High church leader John Henry Hobart is consecrated as the assistant bishop of New York.

1815   William Holland Wilmer publishes *The Episcopal Manual,* one of the earliest statements of Episcopal evangelical principles.

1820   General Convention creates the Domestic and Foreign Missionary Society of the Episcopal Church.

1835   Jackson Kemper is chosen to be the denomination's first missionary bishop.

1839   The publication of the first American edition of *Tracts for the Times,* the manifesto of Oxford movement principles, causes an outcry of alarm among evangelical Episcopalians.

1845   Anne Ayres, founder of the Sisterhood of the Holy Communion, commits to the religious life.

1852   Levi Silliman Ives, the bishop of North Carolina, announces his conversion to Roman Catholicism.

1853   William Augustus Muhlenberg, concerned about the need for Episcopalians to demonstrate greater sensitivity to the social and religious challenges of mid-nineteenth century America, presents his "memorial" to the House of Bishops.

1859   John Johnson Enmegabowh, a missionary among the Ojibwe people in Minnesota, is ordained to the diaconate.

1861   The short-lived Protestant Episcopal Church in the Confederate States of America is organized at the beginning of the Civil War.

1867   St. Augustine's College is founded by the Protestant Episcopal Freedman's Commission in Raleigh, North Carolina.

1871   The Woman's Auxiliary to the Board of Missions is organized under the leadership of Mary Abbot Emery.

1873   A group of 27 evangelical clergy and laity, including George David Cummins, the assistant bishop of Kentucky, create a new denomination: the Reformed Episcopal Church.

1883   General Convention defeats the "Sewanee plan"—a proposal by white church leaders to create a segregated missionary district for black Episcopalians in the South.

1886   The House of Bishops adopts William Reed Huntington's "quadrilateral" outlining the four essential doctrinal principles of church unity.

1889   General Convention establishes the churchwomen's United Offering (later called the United Thank Offering).

1906   Algernon Sidney Crapsey is convicted of heresy and deposed from the priesthood for questioning belief in the Virgin Birth and the Trinity.

1912   Theologian William Porcher DuBose publishes his important autobiographical work, *Turning Points in My Life.*

1917   Vida Scudder publishes *The Church and the Hour,* in which she argues for the compatibility of Christianity and socialism.

1918   Edward Thomas Demby and Henry Beard Delany become the first two African Americans consecrated as bishops for service in the United States.

1919   A 24-member National Council is created to coordinate the bureaucratic work of the Episcopal Church between meetings of the General Convention.

1927   Charles Henry Brent, the bishop of Western New York, presides at the first session of the World Conference on Faith and Order in Lausanne, Switzerland.

1928   Windham House in New York is opened to provide professional training to women for service in the church.

1933   In the midst of the Depression, the House of Bishops releases a pastoral letter calling Episcopalians to work both for the equitable distribution of wealth and for world peace.

1935   Women are admitted for the first time as elected members of the National Council.

1943   Bravid Harris is appointed the church's new Executive Secretary for Negro Work.

1946   Pressure from Anglo-Catholics leads to the rejection of a proposal for merger with the northern Presbyterians.

1948   The Episcopal Church becomes one of the founding members of the World Council of Churches.

1949   Paul and Jenny Moore, C. Kilmer Myers, and Robert Pegram begin their pioneering urban ministry at Grace Church in Jersey City, New Jersey.

1953   Following a year-long controversy, the School of Theology of the University of the South is officially opened to African American applicants.

1954   Episcopalians J. Waties Waring, Thurgood Marshall, Pauli Murray, and Kenneth and Mamie Clark play crucial roles in the legal campaign leading to the release of the pathbreaking *Brown* Supreme Court decision.

1959   The Episcopal Society for Cultural and Racial Unity is organized both to press for racial integration in the church and to support the civil rights movement.

1960   Dennis Bennett, rector of a church in California, announces that he and other members of his parish have begun to speak in tongues. Presbyterian leader Eugene Carson Blake preaches at Grace Cathedral in San Francisco and proposes a bold scheme for interdenominational unity.

1965   Episcopal seminarian Jonathan Daniels is shot to death while participating in a registration drive for African American voters in rural Alabama.

1966   The number of baptized members of the Episcopal Church peaks at 3.6 million.

1967   General Convention adopts John Hines's proposal for a $9 million fund (later known as the General Convention Special Program) to aid the empowerment of African Americans.

1968   At St. Philip's Church in New York, the Union of Black Clergy and Laity (later renamed the Union of Black Episcopalians) is organized to oppose racial discrimination in the church.

1970   John M. Burgess of Massachusetts becomes the first African American diocesan bishop in the United States. Women are allowed for the first time to be seated as deputies at General Convention.

1971   Harold S. Jones of South Dakota becomes the first American Indian elected to the episcopate.

1974   Eleven women are irregularly ordained to the priesthood at the Church of the Advocate in Philadelphia.

1975   Integrity, an organization for gay and lesbian Episcopalians, holds its first national convention.

1976   The ordination of women to the priesthood is officially approved by General Convention. Charles Radford Lawrence II becomes the first African American to serve as president of the House of Deputies.

1977   Pauli Murray becomes the first African American woman ordained a priest in the Episcopal Church.

1979   General Convention gives final approval to a new edition of the *Book of Common Prayer.*

1989   Barbara C. Harris becomes the first woman consecrated as a bishop in the Anglican Communion.

1991   Pamela P. Chinnis becomes the first woman to be elected as president of the House of Deputies.

2000   General Convention adopts a resolution establishing full communion with the Evangelical Lutheran Church in America.

2003   General Convention gives consent to election of first openly gay bishop, V. Gene Robinson of New Hampshire.

BIBLIOGRAPHIC ESSAY

Readers who wish to delve more deeply into the study of Anglican and Episcopal history should find the following scholarly literature and other resources helpful.

ARCHIVES AND PERIODICALS

The Archives of the Episcopal Church (AEC), located on the campus of the Episcopal Theological Seminary of the Southwest in Austin, Texas, handles the collection and preservation of the denomination's records on the national level. The AEC serves as a repository for all national Episcopal Church bodies, for many affiliated organizations and institutions, and for the papers of prominent lay and clerical leaders in the denomination. Although the AEC is the best single archival source of manuscript materials on the history of the Episcopal Church, each of the more than one hundred individual dioceses of the denomination as well as each Episcopal seminary maintains its own archival collection. For more information about the official records of the denomination and their locations, researchers should consult *The Episcopal Church Annual* (Harrisburg, Pa.: Morehouse, 1882–) or the Episcopal Church's Web site (www.episcopalchurch.org).

There are a number of academic journals where readers may fruitfully begin their research. The most important of these is *Anglican and Episcopal History* (1987–), the quarterly journal of the Historical Society of the Episcopal Church. *AEH* is the continuation of an earlier journal, *Historical Magazine of the Protestant Episcopal Church* (1932–86). *The Historiographer of the National Episcopal Historians and Archivists* (1988–) and *Timelines: The Newsletter of the Episcopal Women's History Project* (1996–) also have many worthwhile and informative articles. In addition to these historical journals, researchers will find occasional articles on Episcopal history in *Anglican Theological Review* (1918–) and *Sewanee Theological Review* (1991–), which continues *Saint Luke's Journal of Theology* (1957–91). *Church History* (1932–), published by the American Society of Church History, and *Religion and American Culture* (1991–) sometimes contain articles on subjects relating to Anglicanism and the Episcopal Church. *Journal of Ecclesiastical History* (1950–), published in London; *Journal of the Canadian Church Historical Society* (1950–), published in Toronto, and *Journal of Religious History* (1960–), published in Sydney,

Australia, are excellent sources for scholarly articles on the Church of England and other churches of the Anglican Communion.

Besides these academic journals, there are a number of more popular magazines that contain not only news and information about the present-day affairs of the Episcopal Church but also occasional articles of a historical nature. *Episcopal Life* (1990–) is the official monthly newspaper of the Episcopal Church. Earlier versions of this periodical were published under the following titles: *The Spirit of Missions* (1836–1939), *Forth* (1940–60), and *The Episcopalian* (1960–90). Press releases of the Episcopal News Service, which is the official news agency of the denomination, are available on the Web (www.episcopalchurch.org/ens). Another essential magazine is *The Living Church* (1942–), a weekly publication that includes numerous op-ed pieces on subjects relevant to the contemporary church. Monthly publications *The Witness* (1917–72, 1974–) and *The Christian Challenge* (1962–) are also useful sources for primary research—the former with a left-wing viewpoint and the latter with a right-wing perspective. Finally, *The Christian Century* (1884–) is a highly respected ecumenical Protestant magazine that often publishes articles about Episcopalians and the Episcopal Church.

GENERAL HISTORICAL BACKGROUND

To understand the larger context in which the Episcopal Church has developed, students of this denominational tradition would do well to consider several fine books that provide an overview of the history of American religion and American religious institutions. Readers interested in church history will find Mark A. Noll, *A History of Christianity in the United States and Canada* (Grand Rapids, Mich.: Eerdmans, 1992), particularly helpful. Noll not only focuses specifically on Christianity but also weaves the history of the churches in Canada into his narrative, thus illuminating important developments within American Anglicanism outside of the United States. Noll's most recent work, *The Old Religion in a New World: The History of North American Christianity* (Grand Rapids, Mich.: Eerdmans, 2002), offers a somewhat briefer but updated introduction to the arrival and expansion of European Christianity in America. Another work that provides copious information about all aspects of American church history is the *Dictionary of Christianity in America,* ed. Daniel G. Reid et al. (Downers Grove, Ill.: InterVarsity, 1990). This book describes the many women and men, events and movements, denominations and organizations, and ideas and practices that have contributed to American Christianity.

Although the Episcopal Church has always been one of the major Christian denominations in the United States, its history cannot be entirely separated from broader trends within all of American religion, non-Christian as well as Christian. The publication of Sydney E. Ahlstrom, *A Religious History of the American People* (New Haven: Yale University Press, 1972), was a significant moment in American religious historiography. Acknowledging that "Christianity is by no means the only current in American religious history" (p. xiii), Ahlstrom chose to explore religious traditions whose history could not be subsumed within the story of so-called mainstream Protestantism. Ahlstrom's effort to highlight the diversity of American religion has now become commonplace within the scholarship on this subject. There are three comprehensive, thoroughly up-to-date studies that offer glimpses into the great complexity and richness of American religious history: Peter W. Williams, *America's Religions: From Their Origins to the Twenty-First Century* (Urbana: University of Illinois Press, 2002); Winthrop S. Hudson and John Corrigan,

Religion in America: An Historical Account of the Development of American Religious Life, 6th ed. (Upper Saddle River, N.J.: Prentice-Hall, 1999); and Edwin S. Gaustad and Leigh E. Schmidt, *The Religious History of America,* rev. ed. (San Francisco: Harper-SanFrancisco, 2002). In addition to his contributions to the aforementioned book, Edwin Gaustad has produced two other works that provide a general introduction to American religious history. His two-volume *A Documentary History of Religion in America,* 2nd ed. (Grand Rapids, Mich.: Eerdmans, 1993), offers a large collection of edited primary sources, in which the development of American Anglicanism in the seventeenth and eighteenth centuries is particularly highlighted. Compiled with the assistance of Philip L. Barlow, Gaustad's *New Historical Atlas of Religion in America* (New York: Oxford University Press, 2000) contains numerous maps and charts that present American religious history in a compelling and vivid manner.

Readers interested in considering future developments in the study of American religion should consult *New Directions in American Religious History,* ed. Harry S. Stout and D. G. Hart (New York: Oxford University Press, 1997). This book contains essays by experts in various aspects of American religious history who summarize both where this academic field is now and where it is likely to move in the next few decades. Another relatively brief but useful reference book that is the work of several scholars, each specializing in one or more subfields of American religion, is Edward L. Queen II, Stephen R. Prothero, and Gardiner H. Shattuck Jr., *Encyclopedia of American Religious History,* rev. ed. (New York: Facts on File, 2001).

Just as the history of the Episcopal Church cannot be understood apart from the larger context of American culture and society, so it is equally important to see the relationship of this denomination to the churches of the Anglican Communion, especially the Church of England. *The Study of Anglicanism,* ed. Stephen Sykes and John Booty (Minneapolis: Fortress, 1988), is an indispensable collection of essays by 31 scholars who are experts in various aspects of Anglican history, theology, ethics, liturgy, and pastoral practice. Another essential book is *The Anglican Tradition: A Handbook of Sources,* ed. G. R. Evans and J. Robert Wright (Minneapolis: Fortress, 1991), which is a compilation of over six hundred documents, arranged chronologically, that together elucidate the unique ethos of Anglicanism. In addition to these two decidedly academic works, readers might also wish to consult the somewhat more accessible volumes published in *The New Church's Teaching Series* (Cambridge, Mass.: Cowley, 1997–2001) of the Episcopal Church. Three books in this series address Anglican and Episcopal history: James E. Griffiss, *The Anglican Vision* (1997); Fredrica Harris Thompsett, *Living with History* (1999); and Harold T. Lewis, *Christian Social Witness* (2001).

Two fine histories of the Episcopal Church have been produced in the past 10 years. The latest and most comprehensive is Robert W. Prichard, *A History of the Episcopal Church,* rev. ed. (Harrisburg, Pa.: Morehouse, 1999), while David L. Holmes, *A Brief History of the Episcopal Church* (Valley Forge, Pa.: Trinity Press International, 1993), offers a sprightly narrative that is particularly attentive to major issues within the life of the denomination. An older but still useful discussion of the church from colonial times through the early twentieth century is provided by Raymond W. Albright, *A History of the Protestant Episcopal Church* (New York: Macmillan, 1964). Although E. Clowes Chorley, *Men and Movements in the American Episcopal Church* (New York: Scribner's, 1950), is historiographically dated, it remains an excellent source of information about party controversies in the nineteenth century. And Robert W. Prichard, *The Bat and the Bishop*

(Harrisburg, Pa.: Morehouse, 1989), contains brief biographies of some important Episcopalians as well as intriguing snippets of information about church history.

Thanks to the editorial efforts of Don Armentrout and Robert Slocum, historians have two major and reliable reference works that offer a comprehensive view of the Episcopal Church. As its name suggests, *Documents of Witness: A History of the Episcopal Church, 1782–1985,* [ed.] Don S. Armentrout and Robert Boak Slocum (New York: Church Hymnal, 1994), provides most of the essential primary sources for the denomination's history. *An Episcopal Dictionary of the Church: A User-Friendly Reference for Episcopalians,* ed. Don S. Armentrout and Robert Boak Slocum (New York: Church Publishing, [1999]), moreover, includes entries on virtually every significant person, place, and event in the history of the Episcopal Church. Shorter than the two preceding books, *Readings from the History of the Episcopal Church,* ed. Robert W. Prichard (Wilton, Conn.: Morehouse-Barlow, 1986), is also a convenient source of primary documents. Comparable in importance to the foregoing works is *Freedom Is a Dream: A Documentary History of Women in the Episcopal Church,* ed. Sheryl A. Kujawa-Holbrook (New York: Church Publishing, 2002). This anthology not only reproduces excerpts from a number of relatively hard-to-find texts but also provides thorough biographical introductions to more than 40 historically significant Episcopal women. Finally, Sandra M. Caldwell and Ronald J. Caldwell, *The History of the Episcopal Church in America, 1607–1991: A Bibliography* (New York: Garland, 1993), is an essential bibliographical guide with references to several thousand primary and secondary books and articles.

ENGLISH ORIGINS

Because the roots of the Episcopal Church lie within the English Reformation, it is essential to understand such events as Henry VIII's break with Rome, the struggle between Protestant and Catholic factions in English society during the mid-sixteenth century, and the emergence of a recognizably "Anglican" tradition under Elizabeth I. A useful place to begin research is *A History of Religion in Britain: Practice and Belief from Pre-Roman Times to the Present,* ed. Sheridan Gilley and W. J. Sheils (Oxford: Blackwell, 1994), which contains essays by scholars on various time periods and regions in Great Britain over the course of two millennia. The classic study of the religious changes that transformed England in the sixteenth century is A. G. Dickens, *The English Reformation,* 2nd ed. (University Park, Pa.: Pennsylvania State University Press, 1989), published originally in 1964. The scholar Diarmaid MacCulloch has produced two outstanding studies of the most significant leaders in the English Reformation: *Thomas Cranmer: A Life* (New Haven: Yale University Press, 1996), a biography of the archbishop of Canterbury and principal architect of the first *Book of Common Prayer;* and *The Boy King: Edward VI and the Protestant Reformation* (New York: Palgrave, 1999), which analyzes the revolution in English Christian belief and practice that occurred during Edward's brief reign. In addition, Diarmaid MacCulloch, *The Later Reformation in England, 1547–1603,* 2nd ed. (New York: Palgrave, 2001), which is the best introduction to the latter part of the English Reformation in print, demonstrates how the pace and depth of church reform differed from region to region.

Of equal significance to the work of Dickens and MacCulloch are scholarly books that look beneath the surface of official policy to explore the religious views of ordinary English men and women during the Reformation. For example, Christopher Haigh, *English Ref-*

ormations: Religion, Politics, and Society under the Tudors (Oxford: Clarendon, 1993), questions the notion that the triumph of Protestantism was inevitable or that the transformation of the church took place instantaneously as the result of statecraft. Another book that illuminates the complexity of the process of religious change in England is J. J. Scarisbrick, *The Reformation of the English People* (Oxford: Blackwell, 1984). The enduring strength of medieval Catholic piety throughout the Tudor period is ably demonstrated, moreover, in Eamon Duffy, *The Stripping of the Altars: Traditional Religion in England, 1400–1580* (New Haven: Yale University Press, 1992). While it is important to understand the emphasis that historians such as Scarisbrick and Duffy place on the continuity between English religion before and after 1534, the work of Patrick Collinson probes another segment of the English church that believed the initial stages of the Reformation were not radical enough. Collinson's book, *The Elizabethan Puritan Movement* (Oxford: Clarendon, 1967), provides the classic account of the rise of Puritanism as a movement of militant reform within the Church of England. As Collinson also stresses in *The Birthpangs of Protestant England: Religious and Cultural Change in the Sixteenth and Seventeenth Centuries* (New York: St. Martin's, 1988), "Protestant" England did not begin with Henry VIII but only emerged 40 years later during the reign of Elizabeth I.

THE COLONIAL ERA

Readers seeking an insightful, well-written, and broad-based introduction to the settlement of Europeans in North America would be wise to begin with Alan Taylor, *American Colonies* (New York: Viking, 2001). Taylor provides an excellent overview of the history of pre-revolutionary America, giving special attention to the international and multicultural implications of colonization. Another important work that focuses on the migration of European cultures to North America is David Hackett Fischer, *Albion's Seed: Four British Folkways in America* (New York: Oxford University Press, 1989). Fischer's book is particularly useful because of the ways in which he weaves religious practices and beliefs into the social history of seventeenth-century Britain and America. Jon Butler, *Awash in a Sea of Faith: Christianizing the American People* (Cambridge: Harvard University Press, 1990), focuses on the movement of European institutions and religious ideas, both informal and formal, to the New World and the tremendous spiritual pluralism that resulted. Butler also gives considerable attention to the often deleterious role of the Church of England and its clergy in colonial America. A recent book that concentrates on the establishment of Anglicanism in England's first permanent American colony is Edward L. Bond, *Damned Souls in a Tobacco Colony: Religion in Seventeenth-Century Virginia* (Macon, Ga.: Mercer University Press, 2000). Analyzing the piety of the colonists as well as the institutional aspects of their faith, Bond demonstrates how Virginia Anglicans were able to create a religious identity distinct from that of their mother country by the end of the seventeenth century.

Although the most comprehensive history of Anglican developments in eighteenth-century America remains John Frederick Woolverton, *Colonial Anglicanism in North America* (Detroit: Wayne State University Press, 1984), there are a number of other works that offer information about particular geographical areas and colonies. John K. Nelson, *A Blessed Company: Parishes, Parsons, and Parishioners in Anglican Virginia, 1690–1776* (Chapel Hill: University of North Carolina Press, 2001), for example, is a masterly study of everyday religious experience in colonial Virginia. Although historians have

338   BIBLIOGRAPHIC ESSAY

tended to dismiss the colonial Anglican establishment as weak and ineffective, Nelson reveals a comparatively vigorous church on the eve of the American Revolution. Readers should also consult S. Charles Bolton, *Southern Anglicanism: The Church of England in Colonial South Carolina* (Westport, Conn.: Greenwood, 1982), to understand the development of the Anglican ethos in another southern colony. In addition, as their titles suggest, the doctoral dissertations of Carol Lee van Voorst, "The Anglican Clergy in Maryland, 1692–1776" (Ph.D. diss., Princeton University, 1978), and Sandra Ryan Dresbeck, "The Episcopalian Clergy in Maryland and Virginia, 1765–1805" (Ph.D. diss., University of California at Los Angeles, 1976), offer chronologically overlapping glimpses into the lives of the ordained leadership in the Chesapeake region throughout the colonial period.

The critical social role performed by the Church of England is one of the subjects of Rhys Isaac's prize-winning book, *The Transformation of Virginia, 1740–1790* (Chapel Hill: University of North Carolina Press, 1982). In Isaac's estimation, "churchgoing in colonial Virginia had more to do with expressing the dominance of the gentry than with inculcating piety" (p. 120). Henry F. May, *The Enlightenment in America* (New York: Oxford University Press, 1976), paints a similar but somewhat more appealing picture of the social virtues that Anglicans held dear: tolerance, moderation, and rationality. "American Anglicanism," May writes, "tried to be at once fervent and comforting, at once missionary and comprehensive" (p. 67). As Rhys Isaac further emphasizes, the rise of evangelical enthusiasm in the mid-eighteenth century not only threatened the religious hegemony of Anglicanism but also coincided with the initial stages of the political revolt of the colonies from Great Britain. Because the emergence of the Methodist movement out of the Anglican establishment is a significant part of this story, readers should also consult books about John Wesley and the origins of American Methodism. Both Dee E. Andrews, *The Methodists and Revolutionary America, 1760–1800: The Shaping of an Evangelical Culture* (Princeton, N.J.: Princeton University Press, 2000), and John H. Wigger, *Taking Heaven by Storm: Methodism and the Rise of Popular Christianity in America* (New York: Oxford University Press, 1998), are excellent studies of early Methodist ideas and leaders. The writings of Devereux Jarratt, an Anglican clergyman who cooperated with the Methodists in the 1770s, provide important insights into the intimate links between colonial Anglicanism and Methodism. A new edition of his widely cited autobiography, *The Life of the Reverend Devereux Jarratt* (Cleveland: Pilgrim, 1995), contains a helpful foreword by David L. Holmes.

The enduring conflict between Anglican and Puritan social thought was one of the major factors in the coming of the American Revolution, adding a religious vocabulary to many of the political debates of the 1760s and 1770s. An excellent introduction to the relationship between religion and politics in the American colonies is Patricia U. Bonomi, *Under the Cope of Heaven: Religion, Society, and Politics in Colonial America* (New York: Oxford University Press, 1986). Two recent books focus closely on Anglican leaders in the revolutionary period. Peter M. Doll, *Revolution, Religion, and National Identity: Imperial Anglicanism in British North America, 1745–1795* (Madison, N.J.: Fairleigh Dickinson University Press, 2000), demonstrates how the aggressive campaign waged by high church Anglicans for an American episcopate heightened dissatisfaction in the colonies with the British government. And Nancy L. Rhoden, *Revolutionary Anglicanism: The Colonial Church of England Clergy during the American Revolution* (New York: New York University Press, 1999), examines the impact of political affairs on Anglican clergy in the colonies. Carl Bridenbaugh, *Mitre and Sceptre: Transatlantic Faiths, Ideas, Personalities, and Politics, 1689–1775* (New York: Oxford University Press, 1962), remains an excellent, detailed account of the Anglican attempt to create an American episcopate and the conflict engendered by that strategy. David L. Holmes, "The Episcopal Church and the American Revolution," *HMPEC* 47 (1978): 261–91, not only ably summarizes the state of Anglicanism before the Revolution but also reviews the reasons why so many Anglicans adopted a loyalist stance when the war broke out.

An important work that delves into the inward experiences and religious ideas of one woman in the Revolutionary era is Joanna Bowen Gillespie, *The Life and Times of Martha Laurens Ramsay, 1759–1811* (Columbia: University of South Carolina Press, 2001). Gillespie examines in great depth the piety of Martha Ramsay, a devout evangelical Anglican who belonged to a prominent South Carolina family. Joan R. Gundersen, "The Non-Institutional Church: The Religious Role of Women in Eighteenth-Century Virginia," *HMPEC* 51 (1982): 347–57, also explores the sometimes neglected subject of women in the colonial churches.

THE EARLY NATIONAL PERIOD

The standard work on the complex events leading to the formation of the Episcopal Church after the American Revolution is Clara O. Loveland, *The Critical Years: The Reconstitution of the Anglican Church in the United States of America, 1780–1789* (Greenwich, Conn.: Seabury, 1956). Frederick V. Mills has also contributed to the historiography of this period with *Bishops by Ballot: An Eighteenth-Century Ecclesiastical Revolution* (New York: Oxford University Press, 1978), which, as its title suggests, concentrates on developments leading to the establishment of the American episcopate; and with "The Protestant Episcopal Church in the United States, 1783–1789: Suspended Animation or Remarkable Recovery?" *HMPEC* 46 (1977): 151–70, which considers the state of the denomination immediately following the Revolution.

As Robert W. Prichard notes in his invaluable book on doctrinal debates among Episcopalians in the early nineteenth century, *The Nature of Salvation: Theological Consensus in the Episcopal Church, 1801–73* (Urbana: University of Illinois Press, 1997), William White almost singlehandedly supplied "the blueprint for . . . adapting a British religious establishment to the conditions of the new American republic" (p. 7). William White, *Memoirs of the Protestant Episcopal Church in the United States of America,* 2nd ed. (New York: Swords, Stanford, 1836), is therefore an indispensable firsthand account of the reorganization of American Anglicanism. John F. Woolverton, "Philadelphia's William White: Episcopalian Distinctiveness and Accommodation in the Post-Revolutionary Period," *HMPEC* 43 (1974): 279–96, and Gregory K. Hotchkiss, "The Revolutionary William White and Democratic Catholicity," *AEH* 70 (2001): 40–74, both do a very effective job of probing White's theology, ecclesiology, and political theory. To these fine studies, moreover, should be added an insightful essay by the historian Jennifer Clark: " 'Church of Our Fathers': The Development of the Protestant Episcopal Church within the Changing Post-Revolutionary Anglo-American Relationship," *Journal of Religious History* 18 (1994): 27–51.

Several specialized studies also add to our knowledge of ideas and events in this period. For example, William H. Swatos, *Into Denominationalism: The Anglican Metamorphosis* ([Storrs, Conn.]: Society for the Scientific Study of Religion, 1979), analyzes the early history of the Episcopal Church using classic sociological terminology derived from the work of Max Weber and Ernst Troeltsch: "church," "sect," and "denomination." Swatos sees clear changes in the understanding of the episcopate in the Episcopal Church as the result of its transformation from a church-type institution into a "denomination." In *Samuel Seabury, 1729–1796: A Study in the High Church Tradition* (Athens: Ohio University Press, 1971), Bruce E. Steiner provides a comprehensive account of the life and thought of the first bishop of Connecticut. Sarah McCulloh Lemmon, "Nathaniel Blount: Last Clergyman of the 'Old Church,' " *North Carolina Historical Review* 50 (1973): 351–64, is a useful sketch of one of the two original Anglican priests who served in North Carolina. Licensed as an SPG missionary in 1773, Blount's career spanned four decades, and his death in 1816 marked the end of the first generation of Episcopal leaders in his state.

Students wishing to know about liturgical practices in the early history of the Episcopal Church should consult the works of Marion J. Hatchett, who served as professor of liturgics and music at the School of Theology of the University of the South. His book, *The Making of the First American Book of Common Prayer, 1776–1789* (New York: Seabury, 1982), is considered to be the standard account of the developments that led to the creation of the 1789 prayer book. Hatchett's article, "Ministry and the *Book of Common Prayer:* Legends, Lies, and Cherished Myths about Prayerbook Revisions," *Sewanee Theological Review* 38 (1995): 267–80, includes an informative discussion of the efforts of Samuel Seabury and others in producing a prayer book for Episcopalians. Byron D. Stuhlman, "Scottish and American Prayer Books: A Different Strand of the Tradition," *Anglican,* October 2000, 5–10, also considers the influence of the liturgy of the Scottish Episcopal Church on the worship of the church in the United States.

THE NINETEENTH CENTURY

For understanding and interpreting the position of the Episcopal Church in American society at the beginning of the nineteenth century, two books are essential. One of these— Robert Bruce Mullin, *Episcopal Vision / American Reality: High Church Theology and Social Thought in Evangelical America* (New Haven: Yale University Press, 1986)—focuses directly on the church itself and examines the ideas of one of its most dynamic leaders, John Henry Hobart. As Mullin convincingly argues, the high church Anglican tradition that Hobart promoted diverged radically from the social, intellectual, and religious culture of the United States in the decades prior to the Civil War. The outlines of that culture are brilliantly sketched in the second book: Nathan O. Hatch, *The Democratization of American Christianity* (New Haven: Yale University Press, 1989), which scrutinizes the popular religious movements that burst upon the American scene between 1780 and 1830. Hatch demonstrates how the spiritual egalitarianism practiced by Methodists, Baptists, and "Christians" quickly swamped the rational orthodoxy and refined liturgical style embraced by established denominations such as the Episcopal Church. Mullin further reflects on this subject—the dissonance between American democratic culture and the religious worldview of the antebellum Episcopal Church—in his article "Denominations as Bilingual Communities," which appears in *Reimagining Denominationalism: Interpretative Essays,* ed. Robert Bruce Mullin and Russell E. Richey (New York: Oxford University Press, 1994), 162–76.

Mullin's scholarly efforts in placing the Episcopal Church against the larger backdrop of American evangelicalism have encouraged the appearance of several important studies that further explore the theological and cultural controversies that troubled nineteenth-century Episcopalians. In contrast both to Hobart's high church tradition and to the dominant rationalism of the colonial Church of England, a number of Episcopal leaders sought to create a new evangelical identity for their denomination during the early years of the American republic. Diana Hochstedt Butler, *Standing against the Whirlwind: Evangelical Episcopalians in Nineteenth-Century America* (New York: Oxford University Press, 1995), analyzes this movement by focusing on Charles Pettit McIlvaine of Ohio. Butler charts the rise and decline of the evangelical party in the Episcopal Church during McIlvaine's lifetime. The fracturing in the ranks of the evangelical party caused by the Reformed Episcopal schism of 1873 is the subject of Allen C. Guelzo, *For the Union of Evangelical Christendom: The Irony of the Reformed Episcopalians* (University Park, Pa.: Pennsylvania State University Press, 1994). Guelzo not only chronicles the early history of the Reformed Episcopal Church but also skillfully illuminates the theological and liturgical ideas of Episcopal evangelicals in the mid-nineteenth century. Another intriguing study of the conflict between high church and evangelical Episcopalians is Richard Rankin, *Ambivalent Churchmen and Evangelical Churchwomen: The Religion of the Episcopal Elite in North Carolina, 1800–1860* (Columbia: University of South Carolina Press, 1993). Rankin argues that the white male elite in North Carolina embraced high church Anglicanism as a defense against those who threatened their social hegemony by espousing the egalitarian spirituality of evangelicalism: middle-class and lower-class whites, enslaved African Americans, and upper-class women.

Although far less scholarly attention in recent years has been devoted to nineteenth-century Episcopal liberalism than to either the evangelical or the high church parties, the principal features of this movement can still be discerned in studies of individual leaders. The open-minded "evangelical catholicism" of William Augustus Muhlenberg and his Memorial movement, for example, are examined both in Alvin W. Skardon, *Church Leader in the Cities: William Augustus Muhlenberg* (Philadelphia: University of Pennsylvania Press, 1971), and in E. R. Hardy Jr., "Evangelical Catholicism: W. A. Muhlenberg and the Memorial Movement," *HMPEC* 13 (1944): 155–92. Certainly the quintessential figure of the broad church movement is Phillips Brooks, whose formative years are the subject of John F. Woolverton's excellent book, *The Education of Phillips Brooks* (Urbana: University of Illinois Press, 1995). An older but still valuable biography of Brooks is Raymond W. Albright, *Focus on Infinity: A Life of Phillips Brooks* (New York: Macmillan, 1961). Biblical scholar and Presbyterian-turned-Episcopalian Charles Augustus Briggs stood at the center of the controversy between theological conservatives and modernists in the late nineteenth century. His ideas and intellectual career are analyzed very perceptively in Mark Stephen Massa, *Charles Augustus Briggs and the Crisis of Historical Criticism* (Minneapolis: Fortress, 1990). William Porcher DuBose, the most original and creative theologian of the Episcopal Church, has gained welcome attention in Robert Boak Slocum, *The Theology of William Porcher DuBose: Life, Movement, and Being* (Columbia: University of South Carolina Press, 2000). And *William Porcher DuBose: Selected Writings,* ed. Jon Alexander (New York: Paulist Press, 1988), not only reproduces significant portions of the theologian's work but also offers a fine introduction to his spiritual and intellectual development.

The Chicago-Lambeth Quadrilateral of 1886–88, a key nineteenth-century document that continues to influence church life more than a hundred years later, has been the subject of scholarly inquiry over the years. See especially *Essays on the Centenary of the Chicago-Lambeth Quadrilateral, 1886/88–1986/88,* ed. J. Robert Wright, published as *ATR,* supplementary series no. 10 (March 1988), and the articles on the Chicago-Lambeth Quadrilateral by John Woolverton, Stephen Neill, John Gibbs, and Jaci C. Maraschin that appear in the June 1984 issue of *HMPEC* (vol. 53). For a thorough analysis of the Quadrilateral and of statements on it by later Lambeth conferences, see Henry Chadwick, *Tradition and Exploration: Collected Papers on Theology and the Church* (Norwich: Canterbury, 1994), in which the discussion about interpretations of the term "historic episcopate" is especially helpful.

One of the most enduring institutional expressions of nineteenth-century Episcopal theological principles was the church boarding school. As David Hein argues in "The High Church Origins of the American Boarding School," *Journal of Ecclesiastical History* 42 (1991): 577–95, such schools were not simply carbon copies of the British public schools but were designed to embody high church sacramental ideas. The prototypical boarding school was meant to be a spiritually nurturing community in which students would gradually grow in grace through the ministrations of the church. David Hein, ed., *A Student's View of the College of St. James on the Eve of the Civil War: The Letters of W. Wilkins Davis* (Lewiston, N.Y.: Mellen, 1988), describes one of the earliest and most influential boarding schools of the Episcopal Church. In addition, David Hein, "The Founding of the Boys' School of St. Paul's Parish, Baltimore," *Maryland Historical Magazine* 81 (1986): 149–59, recounts how one Episcopal charity school, which later became a bastion of privilege, was originally founded to aid the education of Baltimore's poorest children.

Another important study that explores the influence of religious beliefs on the larger culture of the United States in the late nineteenth century is T. J. Jackson Lears, *No Place of Grace: Antimodernism and the Transformation of American Culture, 1880–1920* (New York: Pantheon, 1981). Lears discusses the fascination with medieval Catholicism that arose among the American cultural elite, especially a number of clerical and lay leaders within the Episcopal Church, at the turn of the century. According to Lears, the Anglo-Catholic movement functioned both as a protest against modern society and as a means by which some upper-class Americans comfortably adjusted themselves to modernity.

THE CHURCH AND SOCIAL ISSUES

Readers seeking a general historical overview of Episcopal ideas on social issues should consult Robert E. Hood, *Social Teachings in the Episcopal Church* (Harrisburg, Pa.: Morehouse, 1990). Hood analyses the denomination's social policy statements and resolutions on four major areas: peace and war, race, sexuality, and economic affairs. A recent work that places Anglican teachings within the broader social framework of life in Great Britain, Canada, and the United States is Paul T. Phillips, *A Kingdom on Earth: Anglo-American Social Christianity, 1880–1940* (University Park, Pa.: Pennsylvania State University Press, 1996). Phillips discusses a wide variety of Christian leaders who sought to apply their religious faith to issues of economic and social distress. Similarly helpful is Bernard Kent Markwell, *The Anglican Left: Radical Social Reformers in the Church of England and the Protestant Episcopal Church, 1846–1954* (Brooklyn, N.Y.: Carlson, 1991).

Although, as Harold T. Lewis wryly notes in the introduction to his *Yet with a Steady Beat: The African American Struggle for Recognition in the Episcopal Church* (Valley Forge, Pa.: Trinity Press International, 1996), "the term 'black Episcopalian' approaches the status of oxymoron" (p. 1), his book provides a superb scholarly introduction to all aspects of Afro-Anglican history. Not only is Lewis's narrative highly informative, but his bibliography also lists many other examples of essential reading in this field. J. Carleton Hayden is another significant scholar of the African American presence within the Episcopal Church. Among his journal publications are "Conversion and Control: Dilemma of Episcopalians in Providing for the Religious Instructions of Slaves, Charleston, South Carolina, 1845–1860," *HMPEC* 40 (1971): 143–71, and "After the War: The Mission and Growth of the Episcopal Church among Blacks in the South, 1865–1877," *HMPEC* 42 (1973): 403–27. His doctoral dissertation, "Reading, Religion, and Racism: The Mission of the Episcopal Church to Blacks in Virginia, 1865–1877" (Ph.D. diss., Howard University, 1972), is also an important text, as are his short biographies of several black Episcopal leaders that have been published in *Linkage,* the newsletter of the Office of Black Ministries of the Episcopal Church. Finally, George F. Bragg, *History of the Afro-American Group of the Episcopal Church* (1922; reprint, New York: Johnson Reprint, 1968) is still regarded as the essential primary source of documents and information about black Episcopalians.

There are several fine studies of individual African American leaders in the church. For example, Wilson Jeremiah Moses, *Alexander Crummell: A Study of Civilization and Discontent* (Amherst: University of Massachusetts Press, 1992), and *Civilization and Black Progress: Selected Writings of Alexander Crummell on the South,* ed. J. R. Oldfield (Charlottesville: University Press of Virginia, 1995), both contain excellent biographical material on one of the most significant African American intellectuals of the nineteenth century. Gavin White, "Patriarch McGuire and the Episcopal Church," *HMPEC* 38 (1969): 109–41, describes the career of George Alexander McGuire, chaplain-general of Marcus Garvey's Universal Negro Improvement Association and founder of the African Orthodox Church. Michael J. Beary, *Black Bishop: Edward T. Demby and the Struggle for Racial Equality in the Episcopal Church* (Urbana: University of Illinois Press, 2001), helps close a major gap in the historiography of race relations in the church by examining the life of the first African American to be consecrated an Episcopal bishop.

Two books that provide important insights into the racial and social ideas of white church people in the Progressive Era are Elizabeth Hayes Turner, *Women, Culture, and Community: Religion and Reform in Galveston, 1880–1920* (New York: Oxford University Press, 1997), and Eric Anderson and Alfred A. Moss Jr., *Dangerous Donations: Northern Philanthropy and Southern Black Education, 1902–1930* (Columbia: University of Missouri Press, 1999). In her book, Turner studies the social reform efforts of women's groups in Galveston, Texas, after the 1900 hurricane. In another article related to this subject— "Episcopal Women as Community Leaders: Galveston, 1900–1989," in *Episcopal Women: Gender, Spirituality, and Commitment in an American Mainline Denomination,* ed. Catherine M. Prelinger (New York: Oxford University Press, 1992), 72–110—Turner focuses on women who were members of the Episcopal Church in that southern coastal city. Among the subjects on which Anderson and Moss concentrate in their book is the American Church Institute for Negroes, an Episcopal organization that provided funding for black colleges and educational institutions in the South.

Although far more academic research on American Indians in the Episcopal Church needs to be published, Michael D. McNally, *Ojibwe Singers: Hymns, Grief, and a Native Culture in Motion* (New York: Oxford University Press, 2000), does offer a brief but perceptive glimpse at the denomination's missionary activity among the Ojibwe of Wisconsin and Minnesota. Two books by Owanah Anderson, *Jamestown Commitment: The Episcopal Church and the America Indian* (Cincinnati: Forward Movement, 1988), and *400 Years: Anglican / Episcopal Mission among American Indians* (Cincinnati: Forward Movement, 1997), provide good general overviews of the subject of mission among American Indians. And a number of articles in *Beyond the Horizon: Frontiers for Mission,* ed.

Charles R. Henery (Cincinnati: Forward Movement, 1986), consider the church's domestic missionary efforts in the American West in the late nineteenth century.

Thanks in large measure to the founding of the Episcopal Women's History Project in 1980, the historiography of women in the denomination has been tremendously improved in the past two decades. Certainly some of the most important work in the recovery of women's history has been accomplished by Mary Sudman Donovan. In *A Different Call: Women's Ministries in the Episcopal Church, 1850–1920* (Wilton, Conn.: Morehouse-Barlow, 1986), Donovan tells the stories of women who established and performed crucial social service ministries both in urban areas and in missionary fields after the Civil War. Two of Donovan's published articles—"Women as Foreign Missionaries in the Episcopal Church, 1830–1920," *AEH* 61 (1992): 16–35, and "Paving the Way: Deaconess Susan Trevor Knapp," *AEH* 63 (1994): 491–502—also complement her splendid efforts in *A Different Call.* Other scholars who have produced significant work in the field of Episcopal women's history are Joan R. Gundersen, "The Local Parish as a Female Institution: The Experience of All Saints Episcopal Church in Frontier Minnesota," *CH* 55 (1986): 307–22, and "Parallel Churches? Women and the Episcopal Church, 1850–1980," *Mid-America* 69 (1987): 87–97; Ruth Ann Alexander, "Gentle Evangelists: Women in Dakota Episcopal Missions, 1867–1900," *South Dakota History* 24 (1994): 174–93, and " 'The Perfect Christian Gentleman': Women and Bishop William Hobart Hare in South Dakota Missions," *AEH* 63 (1994): 335–62; Barbara Brandon Schnorrenberg, "Set Apart: Alabama Deaconesses, 1864–1915," *AEH* 63 (1994): 469–90; and Rima Lunin Schultz, "Woman's Work and Woman's Calling in the Episcopal Church: Chicago, 1880–1989," in Prelinger, *Episcopal Women,* 19–71.

Two other scholars promise to bring forth valuable studies of major institutions that have nurtured women's ministries in the Episcopal Church. Joanna Bowen Gillespie, who is working on a history of the Society of the Companions of the Holy Cross, discusses the origins of this organization in "Emily M. Morgan's 'Religious Order': The Society of the Companions of the Holy Cross, 1884," *Journal of the Canadian Church Historical Society* 44 (2002): 83–105. Meanwhile, Fredrica Harris Thompsett is concerned with schools—for instance, Windham House in New York; St. Margaret's House in Berkeley, California; and Bishop Tuttle School in Raleigh, North Carolina—that provided education and training for women workers in the church during the first half of the twentieth century. Thompsett discusses some of her research in this area in "The Genuine Vocations of Windham House Women, 1928–1967: An Overlooked Chapter in Episcopal Women's Leadership," *Journal of the Canadian Church Historical Society* 44 (2002): 139–61.

THE TWENTIETH CENTURY

Although no single work covers the entire history of the Episcopal Church in the twentieth century, several books do offer glimpses into significant periods of the last century. The circumscribed focus of his *Fling Out the Banner! The National Church Ideal and the Foreign Mission of the Episcopal Church* (New York: Church Hymnal, 1996) notwithstanding, Ian T. Douglas gives readers an excellent sense of the national leadership of the denomination throughout much of the twentieth century. David E. Sumner, *The Episcopal Church's History: 1945–1985* (Wilton, Conn.: Morehouse-Barlow, 1987), describes several exciting decades of expansion and controversy in the mid-twentieth century. While John Booty, *The Episcopal Church in Crisis* (Cambridge, Mass.: Cowley, 1988), covers roughly the same tumultuous period as Sumner's *History,* his book offers a more thorough and sympathetic analysis of the challenges that Episcopalians faced. William H. Katerberg, *Modernity and the Dilemma of North American Anglican Identities, 1880–1950* (Montreal: McGill-Queen's University Press, 2001), is particularly helpful, moreover, because of the consideration it gives to Anglicanism in Canada as well as in the United States. Further background on American religiosity during the middle decades of the twentieth century, including reflections on the activities of some notable Episcopalians, is available in two insightful books by Robert S. Ellwood: *The Fifties Spiritual Marketplace: American Religion in a Decade of Conflict* (New Brunswick, N.J.: Rutgers University Press, 1997), and *The Sixties Spiritual Awakening: American Religion Moving from Modern to Postmodern* (New Brunswick, N.J.: Rutgers University Press, 1994). James Hudnut-Beumler, *Looking for God in the Suburbs: The Religion of the American Dream and Its Critics, 1945–1965* (New Brunswick, N.J.: Rutgers University Press, 1994), highlights the thinking of Episcopal theologian Gibson Winter, whose *The Suburban Captivity of the Churches: An Analysis of Protestant Responsibility in the Expanding Metropolis* (Garden City, N.Y.: Doubleday, 1961) remains the classic primary source about church life at midcentury.

One of the most noteworthy events of the twentieth century was the rise and development of the ecumenical movement among Christian denominations both within the United States and worldwide. Standard histories of international ecumenism include *A History of the Ecumenical Movement, 1517–1948,* ed. Ruth Rouse and Stephen Charles Neill (Philadelphia: Westminster, 1954); *A History of the Ecumenical Movement, 1948–1968,* ed. Harold E. Fey (Philadelphia: Westminster, 1970); and Samuel McCrea Cavert, *Church Cooperation and Unity in America: A Historical Review, 1900–1970* (New York: Association Press, 1970). Another excellent and more recent survey is Paul Crow Jr., "The Ecumenical Movement," in *Encyclopedia of the American Religious Experience: Studies of Traditions and Movements,* ed. Charles H. Lippy and Peter W. Williams (New York: Scribner, 1988). Extensive coverage of ecumenism from an Anglican and Episcopal perspective is also provided in George E. DeMille, *The Episcopal Church since 1900: A Brief History* (New York: Morehouse-Gorham, 1955); Charles Duell Kean, *The Road to Reunion* (Greenwich, Conn.: Seabury, 1958); and *A Communion of Communions: One Eucharistic Fellowship,* ed. J. Robert Wright (New York: Seabury, 1979).

In addition to these general works, there are several useful biographical studies of Episcopal bishop Charles Henry Brent, one of the first great leaders of international ecumenism. See, for example, Alexander C. Zabriskie, *Bishop Brent: Crusader for Christian Unity* (Philadelphia: Westminster, 1948), and Leon G. Rosenthal, "Christian Statesmanship in the First Missionary-Ecumenical Generation" (Ph.D. diss., University of Chicago, 1989).

David Hein, "The Episcopal Church and the Ecumenical Movement, 1937–1997: Presbyterians, Lutherans, and the Future," *AEH* 66 (1997): 4–29, is an account of Episcopalians' slowly growing interest in ecumenical dialogue with two major American Protestant denominations. This movement finally reached fruition in the year 2000, when the Episcopal Church ratified the "Called to Common Mission" document, which had earlier been adopted by the Evangelical Lutheran Church in America. The best resources on earlier stages of the Lutheran-Episcopal agreement are *"Toward Full Communion" and "Concordat of Agreement": Lutheran-Episcopal Dialogue, Series III,* ed. William A. Norgren and William G. Rusch (Minneapolis: Augsburg, 1991), and *Inhabiting Unity: Theological Perspectives on the Proposed Lutheran-Episcopal Concordat,* ed. Ephraim Radner and R. R. Reno (Grand Rapids, Mich.: Eerdmans, 1995). Even more up-to-date coverage of the Lutheran-Episcopal agreement is provided by Thomas A. Baima, *The Concordat of Agree-*

ment between the Episcopal Church and the Evangelical Lutheran Church in America: Lessons on the Way toward Full Communion (Lewiston, N.Y.: Mellen, 2003); and *Discovering Common Mission: Lutherans and Episcopalians Together,* ed. Robert Boak Slocum and Don S. Armentrout (New York: Church Publishing, 2003).

Although there is no book-length study of the activities of Episcopalians during World War II, two recent articles suggest one possible area of fruitful investigation. Joanna Bowen Gillespie, "Japanese-American Episcopalians during World War II: The Congregation of St. Mary's, Los Angeles, 1941–1945," *AEH* 69 (2000): 135–69, and Linda Popp Di Biase, "Neither Harmony nor Eden: Margaret Peppers and the Exile of the Japanese Americans," *AEH* 70 (2001): 101–17, both consider the effects on church life of the wartime relocation of American citizens of Japanese descent. Besides these secondary works, Daisuke Kitagawa, *Issei and Nisei: The Internment Years* (New York: Seabury, 1967), provides some firsthand reflections on the reactions of Japanese Americans who were victimized by this shameful episode in American history.

Joanna Bowen Gillespie, the cofounder of the Episcopal Women's History Project, offers an often moving view of contemporary American religion in *Women Speak: Of God, Congregations, and Change* (Valley Forge, Pa.: Trinity Press International, 1995). This book studies the thinking of 60 women of various ages who belong to four Episcopal congregations in different parts of the United States. As Ann Swidler observes in her foreword to *Women Speak,* Gillespie "captures how . . . church members find satisfaction in prayer, feel close to God, respond to the melody of a hymn, or sense the divine in the act of polishing the brass and silver for the altar" (p. vii).

SOCIAL CHANGE AT THE END OF THE MILLENNIUM

The civil rights movement was undoubtedly the most significant event in the domestic life of the United States in the twentieth century. Gardiner H. Shattuck Jr., *Episcopalians and Race: Civil War to Civil Rights* (Lexington: University Press of Kentucky, 2000), discusses both the civil rights activities of Episcopal leaders and the larger impact of the black freedom struggle on the church. Michael B. Friedland, *Lift up Your Voice Like a Trumpet: White Clergy and the Civil Rights and Antiwar Movements, 1954–1973* (Chapel Hill: University of North Carolina Press, 1998), provides an excellent narrative of the involvement of church people in social protests over a 20-year period. Among the figures on whom Friedland concentrates is the activist bishop Paul Moore, who writes about his own experiences in *Presences: A Bishop's Life in the City* (New York: Farrar, Straus, 1997). The life and Christian witness of Jonathan Daniels, the Episcopal seminarian and civil rights worker who was murdered in 1965, is analyzed insightfully in Charles W. Eagles, *Outside Agitator: Jon Daniels and the Civil Rights Movement in Alabama* (Chapel Hill: University of North Carolina Press, 1993). William J. Schneider, [ed.] *American Martyr: The Jon Daniels Story* (1967; reprint, Harrisburg, Pa.: Morehouse, 1992), not only briefly recounts Daniels's story but also publishes a number of his letters and writings about his civil rights involvement. Paul M. Washington, *"Other Sheep I Have": The Autobiography of Father Paul M. Washington,* [ed.] David McI. Gracie (Philadelphia: Temple University Press, 1994), describes the ministry of one of the leading African American priests of the Episcopal Church. Excerpts from the writings of William Stringfellow, the great activist lawyer and theologian, have been published in *A Keeper of the Word: Selected Writings of William Stringfellow,* ed. Bill Wylie Kellermann (Grand Rapids, Mich.: Eerdmans, 1994). Stringfellow's theological and social ideas are also the subject of two collections of essays by his friends and admirers: *Radical Christian and Exemplary Lawyer: Honoring William Stringfellow,* ed. Andrew W. McThenia Jr. (Grand Rapids, Mich.: Eerdmans, 1995), and *Prophet of Justice, Prophet of Life: Essays on William Stringfellow,* ed. Robert Boak Slocum (New York: Church Publishing, 1997).

Several scholarly biographies of bishops who exercised major leadership roles in the church's national affairs during the 1960s have appeared in recent years. Kenneth Kesselus, *John E. Hines: Granite on Fire* (Austin, Tex.: Episcopal Theological Seminary of the Southwest, 1995), describes the life and ministry of the controversial 22nd presiding bishop of the Episcopal Church. John Booty, *An American Apostle: The Life of Stephen Fielding Bayne, Jr.* (Valley Forge, Pa.: Trinity Press International, 1997), probes the public career of the first executive officer of the Anglican Communion. David Hein, *Noble Powell and the Episcopal Establishment in the Twentieth Century* (Urbana: University of Illinois Press, 2001), illuminates the history of the mid-twentieth-century Episcopal Church through the life of a prominent clergyman in Virginia and Maryland. Finally, S. Jonathan Bass, *Blessed Are the Peacemakers: Martin Luther King Jr., Eight White Religious Leaders, and the "Letter from Birmingham Jail"* (Baton Rouge: Louisiana State University Press, 2001), while not strictly a biography, devotes considerable attention to Charles C. J. Carpenter and George Murray, the Episcopal bishops of Alabama during the heyday of the civil rights movement in their state.

Readers wishing to learn about the involvement of Episcopal women in civil rights activities will want to read two classic accounts, now republished with important new material added: Anne Braden, *The Wall Between* (1958; reprint, Knoxville: University of Tennessee Press, 1999), and Sarah Patton Boyle, *The Desegregated Heart: A Virginian's Stand in Time of Transition* (1962; reprint, Charlottesville: University Press of Virginia, 2001). *Pauli Murray: The Autobiography of a Black Activist, Feminist, Lawyer, Priest, and Poet* (1987; reprint, Knoxville: University of Tennessee Press, 1989) describes the remarkable and varied career of the first African American woman ordained to the Episcopal priesthood. Another important woman's narrative, which describes the involvement of white Episcopalians in a pioneering urban ministry effort in the 1950s, is Jenny Moore, *The People of Second Street* (New York: Morrow, 1968).

Women's ordination is, understandably, a topic that has received considerable coverage over the past 25 years. The best overall treatment of this movement is Pamela W. Darling, *New Wine: The Story of Women Transforming Leadership and Power in the Episcopal Church* (Cambridge, Mass.: Cowley, 1994), which begins its historical discussion in the seventeenth century and concludes in the early 1990s. Heather Ann Huyck, "To Celebrate a Whole Priesthood: The History of Women's Ordination in the Episcopal Church" (Ph.D. diss., University of Minnesota, 1981), is especially valuable because of its use of interviews and unpublished manuscript materials. In *A Still Small Voice: Women, Ordination, and the Church* (Syracuse, N.Y.: Syracuse University Press, 1995), Frederick W. Schmidt examines five denominations, including the Episcopal Church, and offers a sociological analysis based on 50 interviews with ordained women. Mary S. Donovan, *Women Priests in the Episcopal Church: The Experience of the First Decade* (Cincinnati: Forward Movement, 1988), and John H. Morgan, *Women Priests: An Emerging Ministry in the Episcopal Church, 1975–1985* (Bristol, Ind.: Wyndham Hall, 1985), are two other useful studies about the first 10 years in which women exercised ordained ministry in their denomination. For a wider perspective on the American situation, readers should also examine two books on the movement for women's ordination in the Church of England: Brian Heeney, *The*

Women's Movement in the Church of England, 1850–1930 (Oxford: Clarendon, 1988), and Sean Gill, *Women and the Church of England: From the Eighteenth Century to the Present* (London: SPCK, 1994).

There are several important autobiographical accounts by Episcopal women clergy of the process that led them to seek and exercise priesthood. Carter Heyward, *A Priest Forever: One Woman's Controversial Ordination in the Episcopal Church* (1976; reprint, Cleveland: Pilgrim, 1999), and Alla Bozarth-Campbell, *Womanpriest: A Personal Odyssey* (New York: Paulist, 1978), both describe the process that led to their ordination as members of the "Philadelphia 11" in July 1974. Another member of that first group of women priests, Suzanne R. Hiatt, discusses the strategy that eventually gained women the right to be ordained in "How We Brought the Good News from Graymoor to Minneapolis: An Episcopal Paradigm," *Journal of Ecumenical Studies* 20 (1983): 576–84. And Sandra Wilson writes about priesthood from her perspective as an African American in " 'Which Me Will Survive All These Liberations . . . ': On Being a Black Woman Episcopal Priest," in *Speaking of Faith: Global Perspectives on Women, Religion, and Social Change,* ed. Diana L. Eck and Devaki Jain (Philadelphia: New Society, 1987), 130–37.

INDEX

Pages in **bold** indicate the location of the main entry.

ABOUT THE AUTHORS

DAVID HEIN teaches in the religion and philosophy department of Hood College. He is the author of *Noble Powell and the Episcopal Establishment in the Twentieth Century* and the coauthor of *Essays on Lincoln's Faith and Politics*.

GARDINER H. SHATTUCK JR. is the author of *Episcopalians and Race: Civil War to Civil Rights* and the coauthor of *Encyclopedia of American Religious History*.